MAKING SPACE

MAKING SPACE

Merging Theory and Practice in Adult Education

EDITED BY Vanessa Sheared
AND Peggy A. Sissel

Foreword by Phyllis M. Cunningham

BERGIN & GARVEY
Westport, Connecticut • London

Library of Congress Cataloging-in-Publication Data

Making space : merging theory and practice in adult education / edited by Vanessa
 Sheared and Peggy A. Sissel ; foreword by Phyllis M. Cunningham.
    p. cm.
   Includes bibliographical references and index.
   ISBN 0–89789–600–9 (alk. paper)—ISBN 0–89789–601–7 (pbk. : alk. paper)
    1. Adult education—Social aspects—United States.   2. Discrimination in
 education—United States.   3. Critical pedagogy—United States.   I. Sheared, Vanessa,
 1956–   II. Sissel, Peggy A.
 LC5225.S64M24   2001
 374'973—dc21   00–057928

British Library Cataloguing in Publication Data is available.

Library of Congress Catalog Card Number: 00–057928
ISBN: 0–89789–600–9 (hc)
      0–89789–601–7 (pb)

First published in 2001

Bergin & Garvey, 88 Post Road West, Westport, CT 06881
An imprint of Greenwood Publishing Group, Inc.
www.greenwood.com

Printed in the United States of America

The paper used in this book complies with the
Permanent Paper Standard issued by the National
Information Standards Organization (Z39.48–1984).

10 9 8 7 6 5 4 3

For the women who made space for us
in their lives: our mothers, Ida and Ethel.
And for our children, Jamil, Patrick, and Erin,
whose voices we celebrate.

Contents

Foreword

In 1986, John Niemi, chair of the Commission of Professors of Adult Education (CPAE), working with Harold Stubblefield, proposed a broad publishing agenda to its parent group, the American Association of Adult and Continuing Education (AAACE). Among the books planned was a twenty-fifth anniversary follow-up of the "black book," *Adult Education: Outlines of an Emerging Field of University Study* (Jensen, Liveright, and Hallenbeck 1964), which was the professors' first attempt to define graduate study in adult education. The anniversary book, *Adult Education: Evolution and Achievement in a Developing Field of Study*, was published in 1991 (Peters, Jarvis et al. 1991). Its goal was "to reflect on the accomplishments of the field of study since the publication of the black book, to characterize the field of study, and to consider its future possibilities."

In May 1992, a strong critique emerged in a general session at the Adult Education Research Conference (AERC), where several of the edited book's authors appeared in a symposium. The issues were clear: the CPAE and its new seminal book were rejected as being Eurocentric, racist, gender insensitive, elitist, and exclusionary. For many, the twenty-fifth anniversary book was a carbon copy of the original black book. True, there were two women authors, but where were the voices of the marginalized groups? Why were there mostly reports on formal adult education sponsored by institutions?

This forum became a watershed within the CPAE and the AERC. Before the weekend was out, Ralph Brockett unilaterally announced that a Jossey-Bass source book would be devoted to race and feminist concerns in adult education. A vote was taken at the AERC business meeting to approve a resolution to bring out an alternative book, and it was also decided that it should be published by the AAACE and its Publication Standing Service Unit. The Saskatoon resolution, approved with one nay vote, proclaimed:

The 1991 Black Book, endorsed by the Commission of Professors of Adult Education, claims to represent the whole field of adult education. However, it is a book that reproduces the status quo and silences the voices that would challenge that perspective. These silenced voices represent the future of the field.

Therefore, the Adult Education Research Conference requests that the Publications Standing Service Unit of the American Association of Adult and Continuing Education in consultation with the leadership of the feminist caucus of the Adult Education Research Conference develop a process for publishing a book to reflect these voices. Further, the Adult Education Research Conference requests that the American Association of Adult and Continuing Education begin negotiation with Jossey-Bass and/or other leading publishers in the field to complete their representation of the field.

Following the confrontation, some professors never returned to the AERC; some said it was nothing but a group of "lefties." Robert Carlson wrote a critique suggesting that the hegemonic exclusion of the right was being replaced by an exclusionary hegemonic left as gatekeepers of the association (Carlson, 1992, 5). The strong feelings that the new black book engendered caused it to be called the "black and blue" book.

In the fall of 1992, in response to the Saskatoon resolution, the CPAE agreed to sponsor a proposal for the book. One year later, in May 1993, at the AERC held at Penn State, a jammed feminist caucus reacted to the CPAE's request for proposal. The content of the new book was discussed and an elaborate plan devised to ensure inclusivity. This proposed book was affectionately called the "pink and purple" book. Yet, one year later, it was reported at the AERC (Knoxville) that no proposals had been received. With some encouragement, in June of that same year two proposals had been submitted; Vanessa Sheared and Peggy Sissel were selected as co-editors.

In November 1995, the AAACE publications committee endorsed the selected editors and approved the publication of the book under the association's auspices. The co-editors were told they would hear from the Association on how to proceed. After several months, the co-editors, having not heard from the Association, contacted the Washington office. They were told by the editorial staff member that there was no interest in the book from the publishers who had been contacted, and it would therefore not be published. Yet, after further investigation, it was discovered that the few publishers who had been approached were ill-targeted and given sketchy, incomplete, and/or erroneous information. In fact, it appeared as if, rather than to promote the book, the intent had been to ensure that the book would not be published.

With this lack of support, the co-editors officially withdrew the book from the AAACE in February 1996; by May they had formed an advisory committee; by October a call for papers was disseminated; by January 1997, 54 chapter proposals had been submitted. By May 1997, the advisory committee had read the chapter proposals, provided their assessments to the editors, and selected the chapter authors. In December 1997, Bergin & Garvey (Greenwood Publishing Group) agreed to publish the book, now called *Making Space.*

That same year, in November of 1997, AAACE members from the Commission of Professors in Adult Education (CPAE) and the Commission of Adult Basic Education (COABE) voted no confidence in the Association's staff leadership. By the fall of 1999, AAACE was struggling to survive. However, *Making Space* was on its way to being published.

What are the lessons that we can learn from these events? One lesson seems clear: gatekeeping as a conscious or unconscious act was not in the best interests of the Association. It would appear that the refusal of the Association to balance the interests, the visions, the commitment of all its members contributed to its demise. The 1999 feminist caucus of the AERC brought up salient concerns; they asked:

• What knowledge is critical for inclusion?
• How do we break the mold of gatekeeping?
• How do we ensure marginal group representation?
• How do we provide for reflection on content?
• How do we get a worldwide view with a range of voices?
• How do we reach out to social movements, grassroots groups, alternative epistomologies?

Clearly, there has been a pattern of struggle within the U.S. national association, beginning with the AAAE that came into existence in 1926 through the assistance of the Carnegie Foundation. In fact, Law (1992), in his critical review of the second black book, suggests that the first black book did not, as Houle wrote, have its origin with the 15 professors meeting in 1955, who wished to express for themselves and others "the nature of adult education as an academic discipline." Rather, he suggests, the important meeting was held in New York City in 1924, when Frederick Keppel, president of Carnegie Foundation, expressed the concern that the expanding practice of adult education had grown up outside our best education traditions and leadership, and so without the guidance and control by which it might have profited. Law suggests that professionalism has backed adult education into an academic cul-de-sac. Law concludes that "To a large extent the making of adult education as an academic subject is the story of the interaction among professionalization, the aspiration of an emerging professorate, and the influence of philanthropic foundations" (p. 157). This story is ignored in the black and blue book.

As we move forward into this new millennium and century, it would appear that the debate has been sharpened within our associations. Are we colleagues within a vocation or professionals within a discipline? To what degree will ideology frame the associations to which we belong? To what degree do we recognize the structure of the dominant society and its pressures to control us? And to what degree will we democratize our practice and challenge the marginalization of others?

As we look at this book, it appears that these editors have managed to create their own organization, share their creation of the book with others, and produce a book that looks much more like the field than its predecessors. This has been done without organizational sponsorship and it has taken almost a decade to accomplish this feat.

Phyllis M. Cunningham
Northern Illinois University

REFERENCES

Carlson, R. (1992). "Open Season on Gatekeepers." *CPAE Newsletter* (Commission of Professors of Adult Education, Northern Illinois University; Phyllis Cunningham, ed.) (Summer), 5.

Jensen, G., Liveright, A., and Hallenbeck, W. (1964). *Adult Education: Outlines of an Emerging Field of University Study*. Washington, DC: Adult Education Association of the U.S.A.

Law, M. (1992). "The New Black Book: What Does It Tell Us about Adult Education?" *Adult Education Quarterly* 42(4), 256–257.

Peters, J. M., Jarvis, P., and Associates (eds.). (1991). *Adult Education: Evolution and Achievement in a Developing Field of Study*. San Francisco: Jossey-Bass.

Acknowledgments

Many individuals and institutions must be thanked for the role they played in the emergence of this book, from its conceptual stage to its completion. First, thanks to Ralph Brockett, under whose leadership the Commission of Professors of Adult Education (CPAE) formed the ad hoc committee whose mission it was to entertain proposals for this book. Next, our gratitude goes to Annie Brooks, who chaired that ad hoc committee, and to committee members Arthur Wilson, Talmadge Guy, Jorge Jeria, and Trudy Kibbe Reed, who commented on the proposed outline of the book and selected us as editors. Special thanks also goes to Carol Kasworm, who, as chair of CPAE, assisted us in ensuring the autonomy and integrity of the book, and our editorial freedom by negotiating its release from AAACE.

A note of appreciation is also extended to our respective universities, San Francisco State University (Vanessa) and the University of Arkansas at Little Rock (Peggy). As a result of several small institutional grants that were made to each of us for the purpose of developing this book, and the support given to us from each of our departments, we were able to undertake the required mailing, faxing, and phone calling that is necessary when both editors and contributors are time zones away.

Not to be overlooked in our thanks are the members of this book's advisory board. The selection of chapters for this book was undertaken through a juried process. Upon acceptance of the prospectus by CPAE, Drs. Sheared and Sissel issued an international call for papers. Proposals were received from around the world, and were reviewed and critiqued by an advisory board of international scholars of adult education. To ensure inclusivity, we convened a group of individuals who we believe represent cross-sectional perspectives, and multiple and intersecting positions and realities. We thank you for your advice, direction, time, efforts, and commitment to the field of adult education, as well as (most importantly) to the development of this book:

Dr. Donna Amstutz, University of Wyoming

Dr. Hal Beder, Rutgers, the State University of New Jersey

Ms. Marie Clinton Bruno, Arkansas Department of Workforce Education

Dr. Scipio A. J. Colin III, National Louis University

Dr. Phyllis Cunningham, Northern Illinois University

Dr. Talmadge Guy, University of Georgia

Dr. Tom Heaney, National Louis University

Dr. David Hemphill, San Francisco State University

Dr. Jorge Jeria, Northern Illinois University

Dr. Carol Kasworm, North Carolina State University

Dr. Athalinda MacIntosh, University of Surrey, Great Britain

Dr. Jacob Perea, Dean, College of Education, San Francisco State University

Dr. Joyce Stalker, University of Waikato, New Zealand

Dr. Harold Stubblefield, Virginia Polytechnic Institute and State University (retired)

Dr. Libby Tisdell, National Louis University

Dr. Loida Velaquez, University of Tennessee at Knoxville

Also, thanks are given to all the contributors in this book. Without their voices, and those of their students, their colleagues, and their communities, it would not have been possible.

As for us, we as editors feel very fortunate to have been given the opportunity to guide this book, despite its trials and tribulations. Since the spring of 1996 we have made space for this book in our own schedules as we pursued our other professional responsibilities and negotiated our personal lives. During that time Peggy gave birth to a daughter and her son entered public school, while Vanessa put her son through high school and sent him off to college. Both of us were given the wonderful opportunity to become Kellogg Fellows through that foundation's Houle Scholars in Adult and Continuing Education program. We both became department chairs at our respective universities. Together we not only grew to know the depth and breadth of our field more deeply, but came to know each other as well, taking comfort in our commonalities and reveling in our differences. In other words, we developed a friendship. It is in this spirit that we offer you this book.

Finally, thanks must be given to Lynn Taylor of Greenwood Publishing Group, whose support and encouragement throughout its production was, and is, greatly appreciated.

Part I

Deconstructing Exclusion and Inclusion in Adult Education

Chapter 1

Opening the Gates: Reflections on Power, Hegemony, Language, and the Status Quo

Peggy A. Sissel and Vanessa Sheared

As Phyllis Cunningham so aptly details in the foreword to this book, in 1992 the Commission of Professors of Adult Education (CPAE) officially cited the exclusion of certain voices and knowledge bases within the adult education literature. The development of this book is a response to that growing awareness. While debate leading up to it was not without contention, ultimately CPAE members both recognized and honored the fact that learners, practitioners, and scholars of adult and continuing education represent both genders and a multiplicity of ethnicities, languages, classes, lifestyles, and cultural experiences. Furthermore, their advocacy not only emphasized the need to incorporate varied perspectives, but also the importance of addressing and analyzing the reasons why the adult education literature had previously excluded the voices of women and "others."[1]

As editors, we have attempted to provide scholars and practitioners representing a wide range of adult education and lifelong learning frameworks (both established and previously unheard voices in the field) a forum to dialogue about adult education as a social phenomenon, a field of practice, and a body of research. Broadly stated, we offer this book as the beginning dialogue and critique of our social, political, economic, and historical forms of hegemony operating in the field. We provided the authors with a forum to explore hegemony, within the contexts of their lived experiences. Throughout this book we have attempted to examine the ways in which hegemony has constrained our thinking about adult education and learning; influenced practice, structured learning environments; and limited the participation of some people because of their language, sexual orientation, race, gender, and class. Relatedly, the book addresses the ways in which hegemony has silenced and made invisible the voices and contributions of those who have historically been marginalized.

So, we begin this edition with a dialogue on hegemony and marginalization as it affects adult educational theory and practice, as well as our role as editors. Simply stated, hegemony refers to the ways in which an individual or a group achieves and maintains power and control over:

- how history is examined, interpreted, and presented;
- how resources are distributed to certain members in society and not others;
- how one language acquires status and legitimization and is appropriated in all areas of the discourse; and
- how some individuals/groups, and not others, gain or have access to positions of authority, whereby they control the historical, political, social, and economic base in any given society.

Those who control these resources—ideology, information, access, and material conditions—and the micro-politics surrounding them (Ball 1987; Sissel 2000) sit at a powerful center. Those who have either been forced out or who have chosen to move outside of the center are considered to be in the margins (Sheared 1998). Aronowitz and Giroux (1985) speak to the politics of this exclusion, yet, they argue that hegemony is more than mere exclusionary practice. Rather, hegemony

represents more than the exercise of coercion: it is a process of continuous creation and includes the constant structuring of consciousness as well as a battle for the control of consciousness. The production of knowledge is linked to the political sphere and becomes a central element in the state's construction of power. (p. 88)

Hegemonic practices and structures normalize and, indeed, reify the experiences of some members of society, while negating the realities of others. These are the marginalized "others" whom this book attempts to address. Sheared (1992) has written that marginalization can be thought of as

the silencing of lived experiences in discourses constructed through legislation and policies created by the dominant culture, which either "commatizes or negates"[2] the political, economic, historical and social realities of those living in the margins of society. (p. 73)

While on the surface it would appear that one either can "be in the margin or in the center," the reality is that individuals operate in multiple and intersecting margins and centers. So, on the one hand, depending upon what people's role in society is, where they are situated in society and how they view themselves will determine whether and in what contexts they are in the margin or the center. Oppressive structures and systems predicated on racism, sexism, classism, homophobism, and other "isms" function to force "others" into the margins. When one is forced into the margins, one becomes marginalized. As hooks (1984) has concluded, "To be in the margin is to be part of the whole but outside the main body" (p. ix). She goes on to say that those who are in the margins develop "an oppositional worldview." In other words, they develop not only a sensitivity to factors like racism, sexism, classism, homophobism, and other "isms," but they also develop an ability to critically reflect on how these things affect not only those in the margins but those in the center as well.

As we reflected on these issues and reviewed each chapter, our roles as editors became clearer. We began to focus on how each of us, as well as the entire academic community, overtly or inadvertently participate in the maintenance or perpetuation of hegemony as knowledge producers and disseminators.

ON MAKING SPACE AND CHALLENGING HEGEMONY

The issues and analyses presented in this book are illustrative of hooks' analogy of the way the body politic of adult education has functioned in the past. As the term "making space" suggests, and as we began to more fully realize, in order to make space for others, we had to challenge our own reasons and goals for doing such a book. We had to acknowledge that, while our end goal was to make space for others, in part, we too were responsible for determining whose voices would be heard. Given that, we struggled with ourselves and with others to ensure that, as we made space for others, we did not marginalize those who we claimed had sustained a hegemonic state within the field.

When we began this endeavor, we did so because we believed many voices had been left out of the discourse and the history of adult education. Our goal then was to not only expand and challenge the way we think about past as well as future practices in adult learning, but to make space for other voices and people whose presence and participation may not have formerly been included in the discourse of adult education and lifelong learning. We initiated a call, therefore, to encourage those who had been left out to come into the fold and tell their stories. We wanted to hear from the margins and we wanted them to tell those of us in the academy what we had left out. *We wanted them to put us in our places.*

To our amazement, those sending in proposals were typically already a part of the academy, or were graduate students who aspired to become a part of it. Yet, this was not surprising, given the weightiness of the rewards or punishments meted out in higher education—the tenure-track faculty appointment, and tenure itself (see Chapter 16 in this volume). The reality of the "publish or perish" world we are a part of in the academy clearly dictated this level of response.[3]

In retrospect, this situation was also not remarkable considering the number of women, the fervor of their voices, and the multiplicity of the responses that were elicited at the women's caucus session, which was held during the Penn State Adult Education Research Conference in 1993. Although the room was filled with present and future academics, the result of this session was the generation of lengthy lists of those who had been left out of the discourse of the field: women, and people of different races, voices, realities, and circumstances.

While we used the notes from this meeting to help us conceptualize our call for chapters for the book, we also overlooked the reasons why these women, and others like them in the academy (including men of emancipatory minds), would be the very ones to submit proposals. In fact, they were speaking not only for those with whom they worked in communities, but for themselves as well—responding from their perspective of both learner and learned, both marginalized and empowered. For although women, African Americans, Latinas, first-generation scholars,[4] and others may now be a part of the academy, they also remain apart from it in many ways (see Chapters 5 and 16 in this volume). In a scholarly world—still often hostile to Women's Studies, African American Studies, Latino Studies—those of us interested in pursuing lines of research in these areas are sometimes told that our work is inherently biased because of our group membership, is dangerous to the health of our careers, or simply is ill-conceived.

So, while our first reaction was to ask each other what we might do in order to get to those voices in the margins, slowly, and then suddenly with a great thud, the source of our dilemma became clear. We as editors then concluded that it is the nature of academic dialogue and who is allowed to participate in it that is at the heart of the problem. Thus, while this book can be one small contribution toward resolving the gaps that exist between the "academy," prac-titioners, and the citizenry, it is only the beginning. The term "making space" has other connotations as well. Resources of space, time, and place are related to the material conditions of our lives, and our efficacy as lifelong learners and our roles as educators. In her work *A Room of One's Own* (1929), Virginia Woolf spoke eloquently of the way in which white middle-class women were marginalized by exclusionary practices within higher education and public as-pects of society. While her pointed reflections connected material resources, access issues, and the politics of control over one's time as resources that either constrain or enhance the intellectual vitality and power of women during the early twentieth century, her analysis is as relevant in this century as in the last.

In a similar way, Ralph Ellison's classic novel, *Invisible Man* (1952), which examined issues of race and identity, still reminds us of the oppressive force of racism and the way in which it negates the daily lived experiences—indeed, the very personhood of African Americans. When one is invisible, one does not take up space in our minds, our hearts, nor our economic, historical, political, or social concerns. Such invisibility is directly connected to material conditions and personal and programmatic resources. For as Sheared (1992, 1998) has noted in her research on African-American women and federal welfare policies and programs, people are silenced as a result of their not having resources appropriated to their needs or concerns. Moreover, resources are not appropri-ated to the individuals or groups in question when they have no meaning or relevance or do not exist as an important entity for those who maintain power in the center. Sissel's (2000) recent work on the silence and invisibility of adult learners (largely female parents) in another federal "helping" program, Project

Head Start, also empirically validates the connection between invisibility, legitimacy, and the lack of appropriation of material resources.

This connection is also apparent in the reported experiences of emerging scholars. As some white females, African Americans, Latinos/Latinas, Gay/Lesbians, and other often marginalized aspiring scholars have shared with us over the years, as graduate students they were often discouraged or given a difficult time when they wanted to conduct research about race, gender, and ethnicity. In fact, at some institutions, faculty committees were frequently less than supportive and sometimes outright rejecting. In responding this way, professors promoted hegemony and accommodated status quo thinking in the field. Such stories make it apparent that "the body" that represented the body politic in the field was often that of a white, middle-class male who clearly did not understand the significance or relevance of these issues (see Chapter 4 in this volume). Collectively, these bodies were typically armed with paternalistic and cautionary admonishments that any research focus on white women and/or "others" might ruin potential careers, be inherently biased, or be considered less scholarly. For instance, Amstutz (1994) recalls:

At a Commission of Professors of Adult Education meeting, two assistant professors proposed a preconference on African American research issues. A member of the executive committee responded immediately, "Oh, but it must have high quality and be researched based." (p. 40)

Recall that these same arguments were often expressed in the 1970s and 1980s in relation to the use of qualitative research methodologies in the field, which were often derided as being soft, overly intuitive, or biased—terms frequently used by chauvinists to describe and put down women. Interestingly, it is through the application of historical, anthropological, philosophical, and action science methodologies that the experiences, perspectives, and voices of white women and "others" were allowed to emerge.

Thus, this work attempts to address and challenge oppressive systems and practices in adult education and lifelong learning while expanding the critique to a more inclusive arena: matters of power and politics in relation to gender, race, class, ethnicity, culture, and sexual orientation. In doing so, we believe the scholars in this book suggest new lines of inquiry while reminding us that hegemonic practices in contemporary society have far-reaching historical roots that are embedded deep within our cultural consciousness and social and institutional structures.

NEGOTIATING HURDLES: GOING AROUND THE GATEKEEPERS

The challenging of perspectives, practices, and power structures is often a daunting undertaking, regardless of the context. As Phyllis Cunningham noted in the foreword, the development of this book has not been without contention. In fact, even with a mandate, the book almost did not happen.

While the CPAE called for the creation of a book of its kind in 1992 at the Saskatoon Adult Education Research Conference, from that time until it was turned over to us to manage independently in 1996, the idea struggled along. Initially, while a CPAE committee had been put in place to accept proposals, as of 1994, no one was willing to step up to the plate to submit one. Thus, that year, because we both saw the need for and importance of such a book, and despite the fact that neither of us was sure that we could "make space" for such an undertaking in our personal and professional lives, we merged forces to submit a proposal. (Regarding this, a special note of thanks must go to Phyllis Cunningham here, for it was she who suggested that we become a team, even though we did not know each other at the time.)

For the next two years we waited as the process of review, approval, and then disapproval took place. We say disapproval because, despite the formal approval of the final proposal by CPAE and AAACE, the ultimate roadblock to its development occurred after this approval process had been completed. Despite being sanctioned by the various oversight committees, when it was turned over to the paid AAACE staff who would oversee its production, they clearly expressed their disapproval of the book, labeling it as unimportant and uninteresting. In fact, they openly derided it for including the voices of gays and lesbians. Needless to say, we were dismayed by this turn of events, and began to have a great deal of concern about our possible lack of full control of the book's content. Subsequent to this, we also discovered apparent attempts by the AAACE staff to block its full consideration by appropriate publishers. Thus, in the spring of 1996, and with the assistance of the CPAE board, we disengaged the project from the auspices of AAACE.

Following this, a flurry of activity took place. Committed to engaging in an open process that would invite a variety of voices, as well as attend to the diversity of issues so aptly expressed at both the Saskatoon and the Penn State Adult Education Research Conferences, we issued a worldwide call for chapters via mail and the Internet. This call yielded 54 chapter proposals from the United States, Canada, South America, Africa, and Australia. We also formed an advisory board (see Acknowledgments) that helped us select—on a blind review basis—chapter proposals for the book. Around this time we also were fortunate to be offered a publishing contract with Greenwood Publishing Group.

BROADENING THE CIRCLE: WHAT WE MEAN BY INCLUSION

The book that you hold in your hands is the result of many efforts to be inclusive of a variety of perspectives and worldviews, cultures, ethnicities, and backgrounds. Yet, while valuing the importance of diversity, inclusivity, and multicultural and global perspectives, this book does have its limitations in terms of inclusion. While our intent was to hear from or provide space to a variety of voices and multiple positionalities, we recognize, for example, that there are no Native Americans represented here. This book does however, include varied perspectives and positionalities that we believe challenge some basic assumptions and ideals which we as educators and participants hold about the role of education in a democratic society.

In addition to promoting cultural inclusion and diversity, as editors we have also endeavored to ensure clarity in the text. Adhering to the position that overly academic language has the potential to limit access and promote exclusivity, we continually challenged our contributors to write in a way that grounded or connected their theoretical positions and practice implications. We also encouraged them to provide illustrations and concrete situations in order to make clear what often is obfuscated because of the use of "academic" language, that is, language that is often abstract and obtuse, which often is intended to be heard and used by those in the center or those who purport to understand it, while clearly excluding those in the margins.

In relation to this, we also asked them to address their own positionality and the context, from which they were writing. We challenged them to approach their topic from a critically reflective perspective that promotes expanded ways of thinking about the concept of marginalization, and the ways in which we as educators (and the programs and practices that we promote) may be complicit in disempowering or oppressing others. In so doing, we ourselves were challenged by the authors. As a result of the ongoing critique, discussion, and questioning that took place in relation to each and every chapter, we believe that it has been a learning experience for all of us.[5]

OVERVIEW OF THE BOOK

Thus, *Making Space* addresses the various hegemonic frameworks that now shape adult education, and critiques the philosophical, sociolinguistic, and historical foundations of the field that have made issues of class, race, ethnicity, gender, and sexual orientation invisible in the current "mainstream" adult education literature. Chapter 2 begins with David F. Hemphill's illuminating discussion of the pitfalls and promises of critical theory, postmodernism, and multiculturalism as frameworks from which to analyze adult education theory and practice. Hemphill takes the position that many theories of adult education reflect claims of twentieth-century Western social sciences that are no longer well supported and which have hegemonic implications for the field. New approaches to adult learning theory are addressed via critical social perspectives, postmodernism, and multiculturalism, and while each of these perspectives are critiqued for their limitations, biases, and internal hegemonic frameworks, their potential for helping to shape adult education in the future also is explored. In doing so, he takes the essentials of these three frameworks and makes them relevant to the field in an understandable way.

In Chapter 3, Daniele D. Flannery and Elisabeth Hayes offer a feminist perspective of adult learning and address the importance of a more inclusive approach, indeed, a feminist approach, to knowledge and learning. Emphasizing the work of Africana, Latina, Euro-American and other postmodern feminists who are developing new ways of understanding human diversity, Flannery and Hayes describe new perspectives on authority in knowledge creation, identity, and individual agency within/against social structures. Furthermore, they address how the feminist perspectives identified above point to more inclusive theories of adult learning in general.

Sue Shore, in Chapter 4, also addresses issues of power and knowledge in adult education theory. Using the concept of "whiteness," Shore exposes mainstream views of adult education as being centered on male, Western perspectives that not only decontextualize adult education practice but marginalize those who are the other. In this chapter Shore focuses on the tensions within some strands of adult education literature that seek to understand and investigate conditions of inequality and their relations with adult education, and yet continue to normalize and render invisible the power of white, Western phallocentric thought. While Shore argues that mainstream adult education theory has a limited capacity to deal with issues of whiteness, masculinity, and privilege, at the same time she notes that dealing with these issues through the lens of difference is a limited approach. Shore draws on three themes in the literature to argue her case:

1. the child/adult binary which promotes the concept of a fully developed and naturally responsible adult;
2. the deferral to a methodology of collaborative and politically neutral facilitation;
3. the tendency to describe and contextualize adult education practice, often in isolation from more recent developments in social theory concerning identity and subjectivity.

Following Shore's discussion of the omnipresence of whiteness as a normative construct within the field, Sherwood E. Smith and Scipio A. J. Colin III, in Chapter 5, make explicit the realities of being nonwhite in higher education. This chapter critiques the social, political, and historical forms of hegemony operating in the field of adult higher education as they impact on African-Ameripean[6] faculty. The information provides an important resource for the improvement of the quality of life experiences of African-Ameripean faculty, and serves to aid in the retention and tenuring of more African-Ameripean faculty (AFF) and better informing non-African-Ameripean faculty. Through the voices of African-Ameripean faculties' own critiques of the qualitative impacts of their rewards, frustrations, and contributions in adult education, the reader comes to understand how African-Ameripean faculty operate within a context of internal and external influences that define their frustrations and rewards.

These insights suggest specific ways faculty and administrators can better support, retain, and tenure African-Ameripean faculty.

Chapter 5 ends this opening dialogue, and then is followed by four subsequent parts, each of which deals with different aspects of adult education practice and ways of thinking about, researching, and theorizing about adult education. These differing perspectives are presented through historical analysis, phenomenological reflection, case study, and other qualitative approaches. While each of these four sections is introduced with our editorial comments, they each are briefly described below.

Part II addresses the function of adult learning within certain important social and historical movements and phenomena. In this part of the book, the work of Cheryl A. Smith, Jane M. Hugo, Bernadine S. Chapman, Fred M. Schied, and Su-fen Liu and Frances Rees reveals insights about adult learning practice and policy in a variety of informal, nonformal, and workplace contexts within the United States. They take us from the antebellum South and its reconstruction to the industrial North and its social parlors, union halls, and postmodern training rooms.

In Part III, Mary Beth Bingman and Connie White, Irene C. Baird, Donna Amstutz, and Ruth Bounous each pose critical questions about the adult basic education context as it is described in four distinct settings: community-based programs, prisons, federally funded programs, and workplace settings. Each of these chapters not only provides readers with grounded descriptions of the way that Adult Basic Education (ABE) programs are structured in those settings, but also offers thoughtful critique and analysis about the learning/teaching endeavor. They examine how fundamental philosophies, frameworks, structures, and strictures within programs intersect with, enhance, or debilitate efforts toward creating community and promoting learning.

Culture and its influence on learning processes, settings, and outcomes is the focus of Part IV. Chapters in this section provide readers with five different cultural perspectives on teaching and learning, including that of five women (African-American, Latina, Middle Eastern, and white) and one gay white man. Identifying themselves as both learners and teachers, Angela Humphrey Brown, Rosita Lopez Marcano, Lynette Harper and "Mira," André P. Grace, and Elizabeth J. Tisdell address concepts of identity, community, and empowerment. They share with us the ways in which these notions have shaped their practice, and the potential that inclusivity can yield for creating emancipatory learning spaces for all.

In Part V, each of the authors (Merilyn Childs, John Garrick and Nicky Solomon, and Jorge Jeria), and we, the editors, in our concluding chapter, challenge those who call themselves adult educators, regardless of venue, to critically examine our aims and agendas. Most significantly, we ask that we begin to look at the institutions we work in as sites of contestation. By juxtaposing the democratic principles and ideals that have been at the roots of the field, with the realities of the twenty-first-century workplace and the market, we present readers with compelling questions about the future of our practice, the implications of marginalization, empowerment, or co-optation, and opportunities and cautions for those engaged in this work.

CONCLUSION

Thus, while this book hopes to challenge readers to think about our own complicity in marginalizing others, it is also about the marginalization of the field of adult education. As early as the mid-1950s, Clark (1958) discussed this issue in terms of how and where the discipline of adult education was situated in institutions of higher education. For many in the academy, this marginalized status within institutions of higher education has caused those engaged in this work to be marginalized as well. Inevitably, this has caused many in the field to struggle for identity, resources, and a voice within these institutions, and raises questions about the culture of higher education, its meaning systems, and ideologies, and the reason that adult education has obtained status as the "other" in colleges of education. Viewed in political terms, if the ethos of the field of adult education is grounded in the accommodation of students, then this cultural norm situates the field as resistant to the status quo and counterculture in the academy (Sissel 2001). Indeed, in the decade of the 1990s we witnessed an ever-increasing marginalization of the field when, as a result of restructuring efforts at campuses across the United States, programs were either disbanded or remodeled into units focusing on workplace training and human resource development. While many embrace this, the authors in this book raise critical questions about what these changes might mean for adult education as a field of practice, for our students, for ourselves as trainers and educators, and for our communities (see in particular Chapters 20–22).

Therefore, we hope that this book will be used by educators, graduate students, policy makers, and practitioners who not only seek to gain a more broad-based, cultural, and critical understanding of the field of adult education, but who hope to be advocates for emancipatory practice. Furthermore, we recognize that the academic field of adult education has isolated itself in an effort to set itself apart as a field of study. While this might have been necessary in the past, we believe that isolationism, as well as other "isms," have constrained opportunities for dialogue, contributed to our marginalization, limited our acquisition of resources, and ironically, have led to our promoting hegemonic rather than emancipatory spaces for both educators and learners.

We also hope that this book helps scholars, practitioners, and learners engage in dialogue around issues of race, gender, class, sexual orientation, age, culture, and geography, and the intersecting realities of history, politics, and economics. This anthology will hopefully provide readers in a myriad of fields with a broader view of adult education in terms of the historical events, philosophical underpinnings, and programmatic discourses.

Given the changes in the global economy, politics, and social structures, we hope that this anthology adds to our understanding of how the field of adult education and the phenomenon of lifelong learning can further our ability to communicate, and resolve some of the pressing issues of contemporary society. To this end, we believe that open dialogue and reflection among academicians and practitioners representative of a range of ethnicities, languages, classes, life-styles, and cultural experiences must take place. This anthology seeks to expand the knowledge base about these factors, as well as provide practical information about how people are addressing the social, political, and economic realities of their lives, and those of learners in their classrooms, workplaces, and communities. Its aim is to honor the perspective, experiences, and knowledge of those who have been marginalized, and to use their learning as our guide, instead of the other way around.

As we open this dialogue, we ask that, as you read these pages, you reflect on the power of dialogue, the importance of creating community, and the value of diversity.

NOTES

1. The term "other" has been used by Africanist, Latino, gay/lesbian, feminist scholars to connote their marginalized status within society. It is a term most often used to suggest the loss of voice or the silencing of a particular group. Shore, in Chapter 4, provides a more in-depth analysis of this term as she discusses "Whiteness" as a race.

2. O'Brien (1984) provided an analysis of the Marxist and neo-Marxist perspectives on women, in which she asserted that women's issues are "commatized" by things that might or might not have anything to do with who they are and what they contribute to their families or societies. She indicated that women's issues in particular were "com-matized" in this manner: women (comma) blacks(comma) children(comma) Greenpeace (comma). The word "comma" demonstrates how women's realities and issues are broken out and compartmentalized in society. Women are seen as broken parts of a whole, rather than as a whole. In the case of welfare and literacy, the realities of those entering adult literacy programs are "commatized" or negated in favor of some larger good.

3. We use this term liberally, for while we began this task viewing the academy as those who are a part of the institution of higher education, we now recognize that the academy must be viewed more broadly. We now recognize that to be a part of the academy, is in itself to be a part of the hegemony that perpetuates the marginalization and exclusion of others from the discourse; and from having power and control over how they are viewed by others, and ultimately, how they view themselves.

4. This term refers to "working-class academics," self-identified scholars who are first in their families to attend college, much less achieve doctoral degrees and academic positions. The prejudices and constraints that they face has been the topic of a new scholarly Working Class Academics conference which is held every two years. In 1999 it was held at the University of Arkansas at Little Rock.

5. In fact, during the editorial process, it was pointed out to us that the act of editing was in itself a traditional academic endeavor that is oppressive and disempowering. It was argued that when editors seek clarification from authors, or when they suggest that authors restructure a piece, insert additional language, or delete passages, the author's

"voice" then becomes negated. While this view was held by only a couple of individuals, and in fact almost all authors expressed their appreciation for our efforts at challenging them, at ensuring coherency and flow, and at seeking clarification when needed, we do think that the views of a few should be valued, and thus, we have raised this issue here as being a possible topic for future debate in the field.

6. Colin uses this term to connote the relationship of people of African ancestry to that of Africa and Europe. For a more thorough analysis, see Chapter 5 of this volume and Colin (1988, 1996).

REFERENCES

Amstutz, D. A. (1994). "Staff Development: Addressing Issues of Race and Gender." In E. B. Hayes and S.A.J. Colin III (eds.), *Confronting Racism and Sexism.* San Francisco: Jossey-Bass.

Aronowitz, S., and Giroux, H. (1985). *Education under Siege: The Conservative, Liberal, and Radical Debate over Schooling.* South Hadley, MA: Bergin & Garvey.

Ball, S. J. (1987). *The Micropolitics of the School: Towards a Theory of School Organization.* London: Methuen.

Clark, B. (1958). *Marginality in Adult Education.* N.p.: The Center for the Study of Liberal Education for Adult Education.

Colin, Scipio A. J. III. (1988). "Voices from beyond the Veil: Marcus Garvey, the Universal Negro Improvement Association, and the Education of Ameripean Adults." Doctoral Dissertation, Department of Educational Leadership and Educational Policy Studies, Northern Illinois University.

Colin, Scipio A. J. III. (1996). "Marcus Garvey: Africentric Adult Education for Selfethnic Reliance." In Elizabeth Peterson (ed.), *Freedom Road: Adult Education of African Americans,* 41–65. Malabar, FL: Kreiger Publishing Co.

hooks, b. (1984). *Feminist Theory: From Margin to Center.* Boston: South End Press.

O'Brien, M. (1984). "The Commatization of Women: Patriarchal Fetishism in the Sociology of Education." *Interchange* 15(2), 43–60.

Sheared, V. (1992). "From Workfare to Edfare, African American Women and the Elusive Quest for Self-Determination: A Critical Analysis of the JOBS Plan." Unpublished Doctoral Dissertation, Northern Illinois University.

Sheared, V. (1994). "Giving Voice: An Inclusive Model of Instruction—A Womanist Perspective." In E. B. Hayes and S.A.J. Colin III (eds.), *Confronting Racism and Sexism.* San Francisco: Jossey-Bass.

Sheared, V. (1998). *Race, Gender, and Welfare Reform.* New York: Garland Publishing Co.

Sheared, V. (1999). "Giving Voice: Inclusion of African American Students' Polyrhythmic Realities in Adult Basic Education." In T. C. Guy (ed.), *Culturally Relevant Adult Education.* San Francisco: Jossey-Bass.

Sissel, Peggy A. (2000). *Staff, Parents, and Politics in Head Start: A Case Study in Unequal Power, Knowledge, and Material Resources.* New York: Falmer Press.

Sissel, P. A. (2001). *When "Accommodation" Is Resistance: Towards a Critical Discourse on the Politics of Adult Education.* Athens: University of Georgia.

Chapter 2

Incorporating Postmodernist Perspectives into Adult Education

David F. Hemphill

The canon of received knowledge regarding theory and practice in the field of adult education implies a sweeping claim of universality. Until recently, the literature of adult education has been dominated by relatively uncritical works that instruct us on topics such as "how adults learn" or "how to motivate adult learners," often implying that all adults may be characterized in general ways when it comes to their learning. This has led to the development of adult teaching and learning theories that rest upon insufficiently examined claims grounded in mid-twentieth-century-Western social science. Many in the field have employed unitary constructs such as "motivation," "the self," "the individual," "the community," "rationality," "competence," or "critical thought" as if there were well-accepted, universal understandings of these ideas by and for people from all cultures, genders, and backgrounds. Recent thinking calls these into question. In fact, if we broaden our intellectual perspectives to accommodate diverse contributions from the perspectives of race, class, gender, culture, and language, there are many more ideas available to us regarding motivation, self, community, or complex adult cognition than those traditionally promoted in the adult education mainstream.

For both practitioners and researchers in adult education, then, it is becoming increasingly clear that unexamined universal generalizations about adults are not well supported. Claiming universality for existing adult education constructs is a problem, for at least two reasons:

1. These universal generalizations operate hegemonically to marginalize learners and practitioners who do not conform to generalized learning or motivational patterns; and

2. The generalizations frustrate adult education practitioners because they often do not

reflect the needs of those who are culturally, socially, economically, and linguistically marginalized. Those who come into adult basic education programs exemplify this reality.

Consequently, as adult educators we must build theories and practices for our field that take us away from perpetuating universal myths. We must devise approaches that help us to better understand and act in concert with the particular realities of diverse adult learners and complex adult learning contexts.

Not only are received constructs of adult education problematic from moral, political, or practical perspectives; they are also relatively outdated in terms of the contemporary intellectual discourse in the humanities and social sciences, disciplines that have traditionally informed applied fields like adult education. For example, investigations of the interactions of language, culture, gender, power, class, race, and economics in the context of postmodernity have become commonplace and well accepted throughout the humanities and social sciences in the past decade. In a related development we have seen the creation of an entirely new interdisciplinary field called "cultural studies," which offers a context for new thought about culture, power, and language.

Unfortunately, the content of these new discourses, until recently, has remained marginalized from the mainstream of adult education thinking. Nevertheless, our colleagues from cultural studies, women's studies, anthropology, linguistics, history, sociology, ethnic studies, literature, and philosophy have much to offer us as we construct new paradigms to understand and enhance adult learning. This chapter weaves some of these contributions together to suggest enhanced perspectives for us as adult educators.

INCLUSION OF A POSTMODERN PERSPECTIVE

The prefix "post" has been grafted with increasing frequency onto many concepts of late-twentieth-century academic discourse in the humanities and social sciences. We see such terms as "postmodern," "poststructuralist," "postcolonialist," and "postfeminist" in increasingly wide use to describe related areas of thought. The language of these discourses is often dense and hard to comprehend, provoking understandable charges of elitism and irrelevance to everyday educational practice. Attempting definitions often confounds authors, and many books on the topic begin with frustrating expositions of "why postmodernism can't be defined."

These frustrations notwithstanding, there are important ideas emerging from these discourses that can assist us as adult educators. We can surely discern from these various "post" discourses a sharpened interest in power and language, with an emphasis on a multiplicity of perspectives that include race, class, gender, and culture. We can also identify in them a sharp critique of the received European intellectual traditions of "modernity" that began with the Enlightenment. At the same time, we may view postmodernist contributions as additions to the already well-advanced critical theories of adult education (Brookfield 1989; Freire 1970; Mezirow 1991). Within the field of educational studies, the subfields of educational theory and curriculum theory display the greatest recent interest in postmodernism, as reflected in the work of authors such as Doll (1993), Giroux (1991), Popkewitz and Brennan (1998), Slattery (1995), and Usher and Edwards (1994).

To simplify our discussion, we will arbitrarily use the term "postmodernism" to include ideas from the various "post" discourses ("postmodernism," "post-structuralism," "postcolonialism," and "postfeminism"). There are distinctions among the "post" discourses, to be sure, but here we will group them together for the purpose of extracting ideas for adult education. In addition, rather than presenting a covering definition of postmodernism, we will offer instead a series of useful concepts emerging from postmodern discourses that have implications for adult education.

A CRITIQUE OF MODERNITY AND ENLIGHTENMENT THOUGHT

One important idea in postmodernist discourses is reflected by the word "modern" embedded in the term "postmodern." Postmodernism is, if nothing else, a critique of key dimensions of modern Western thought. The "modernism" referred to here is the body of Western thought whose origins can be traced to the time of the Enlightenment in seventeenth- and eighteenth-century Europe. As Toulmin argues,

In the seventeenth century, a vision arose which was to captivate the Western imagination for the following three hundred years: the vision of . . . a society as rationally ordered as the Newtonian view of nature. While fueling extraordinary advances in many fields of human endeavor, this vision perpetuated a hidden yet persistent agenda—that human nature and society could be fitted into exact rational categories. (1990, 30)

The Enlightenment was accompanied by a retreat from belief in the supernatural (decried as "metaphysics") and a rapid embrace of "scientific" and "rational" explanations for natural and social phenomena. Characteristic of this emergent thinking was a rigid set of mental structures that placed great weight on following form and rules, and fitting phenomena into categories. Descartes exemplified such a stress on structure through his emphasis on thinking in terms of "either/or" Cartesian dichotomies (Wilson 1969). His famous distinction between mind and body was followed by many other such dichotomies that remain powerful in Western and North American thought. Current examples of such dichotomies might include: science/metaphysics, rational/emotional (or irrational), religious/secular, physical/mental, observable behavior/mental operations, public/private, or individual/group. In adult education discourse the influence of such dichotomous thinking can be seen in the following concepts: competence/incompetence, literacy/illiteracy, motivated/unmotivated, at risk/not at risk, and self-directed/other-directed.

White (1987) makes a similar argument about the rigidity of modernist thought. He suggests that a fixation with form at the expense of content can be discerned in the development of modernist Western thought. In a treatment of the nature of narrative discourse in the writing of Western history, he analyzes "what counts" as valid historical narrative, or "the discourse of the real." He concludes that "following the rules" of the narrative form counts more than the content of the narrative in assessing its ultimate validity. Accordingly, he notes,

the more an account conforms to an expected narrative form, the more weight it is given. Thus an account is deemed to be an account of "the true" or "the real" only to the extent that it conforms to expected historical narrative form. (White 1987, 24)

Similar patterns of emphasis on correct technical form and sequence over intrinsic content of thought can be observed in the operation of Western thought forms such as the scientific method and the British and North American legal systems.

A related idea is reflected in Lyotard's (1984) famous characterization of postmodernism as incredulity toward meta-narratives. Postmodernism in his view is a critique of the tendencies of modernist, Enlightenment thought to seek universal, systematic explanations for all phenomena, whether social or physical. This critique is also applied to late Marxism and critical theory as modernist forms. Postmodernists argue that the class analysis of Marxism, while helpful, cannot be accepted as a "meta-explanation" for all political, social, and economic interactions. Indeed the ideas of Foucault (1972) have emerged forcefully to challenge the hegemony of Marxist theories about issues of power and the politics of social change. But as Popkewitz and Brennan point out,

This challenge to Marxist theories . . . is not to displace them with another hegemony, but to recognize that there are certain changing conditions in the construction of power that are not adequately articulated through Marxist theories and that are obscured in some instances in previous critical traditions. Our interest is with a view of power that is both different from and, and at certain points, complementary to that of the structuralism of Marxist theories. (1998, 4)

A particularly lively debate has involved the critical theorist Habermas (1975, 1984) and postmodernist Lyotard (1984). Habermas' project of understanding communicative action and rational discourse as the universal grounding of a normative social theory is said to fall squarely within the modernist Enlightenment tradition. As Best and Kellner note, "all of his [Habermas'] postmodern critics claim that he uncritically reproduces the heritage of Enlightenment rationalism" (1991, 240).

Modernist thought may have created for adult educators an overreliance on Western logic, rationality, and critical thinking, leading to the presumption that such cognitive forms have universal application and a privileged position of legitimacy. To address this tilt in the direction of Western thought, adult educators need to accommodate—indeed, encourage—the differing forms of language and thought adult learners may bring to the classroom. Adult educators should not make the mistake of expecting all students' learning processes and products to conform to expected dominant cultural patterns (for example, linear problem solving, scientific investigation, or pre-set Western notions of critical thinking strategies). Without careful analysis, adult educators may misunderstand narratives or communicative strategies employed by students from different cultures as being "wrong."

Adult educators need to clarify the different discourse systems and cognitive processes at work in their classrooms to enable themselves to help "translate" among thinking and language systems for their students. We should work to enable adult learners to "code switch" consciously among discourses and cognitive systems. In addition to teaching the dominant cultural forms of knowledge—like English, reading, writing, math, and Western science—adult educators should also teach students to acknowledge other forms of discourse. Adult educators must avoid portraying dominant discourses and privileged cognitive forms such as rationality, Western critical thinking, or science as the "highest orders" of discourse or thought, or as the only solutions for problems. Such approaches can marginalize learners whose backgrounds do not reflect the dominant cultural center.

THE DECENTERED SUBJECT AND MULTIPLE, OVERLAPPING FORMS OF MARGINALIZATION AND IDENTITY

A related and equally important theme found in "post-" discourses (particularly postcolonialism and postfeminism) is a complex analysis of domination, marginalization, and identity from multiple cultural and gender perspectives. An explanation of power relationships emerges that goes beyond the systemic, hierarchical explanations of modernist liberals or Marxists, to add race, culture, language, and sexual orientation. Postmodernists argue that in contemporary life we experience multiple forms of marginalization that for differing reasons push many away from the dominant center of cultural, political, and economic power. Moreover, it is argued that the complexity of contemporary marginalization cannot be explained primarily by a single theory of socioeconomic class, as classical Marxism and critical theory suggest.

Postmodernists start with the image of a dominant center with multiple, overlapping forms of marginalization. Ferguson describes the dominant center in the following way:

The place from which power is exercised is often a hidden place. When we try to pin it down, the center always seems to be somewhere else. Yet we know that this phantom center, elusive as it is, exerts a real, undeniable power over the whole social framework of our culture, and over the ways that we think about it. . . . It defines the tacit standards from which specific others can then be declared to deviate, and while that myth is perpetuated by those whose interests it serves, it can also be internalized by those who are oppressed by it. (1990, 9)

The dominant center is where the "subject" of modernist discourse is said to reside. It is sometimes difficult to grasp the idea of what is meant by "subject," particularly for many educators who are themselves from the dominant cultural center. The basic idea is that the taken-for-granted—or "default"—position of most texts we see in our field is a male, European or European American subject. The implied voice of the narration—the voice of authority—in our educational discourses is frequently that of the dominant cultural center.

Conversely, postmodernists describe voices that do not emanate from the dominant center as being "other," and they devote considerable attention to the project of legitimating discourses which are termed "other." This process is called "decentering" the subject of cultural and political expression, and it means "giving voice" to the other, or "pivoting the center," as Brown (1990) and Sheared (1994) would say. Decentering, then, involves shifting the stated or implied center or voice of discourse away from the previously unquestioned dominant, male, Eurocentric subject. hooks points with optimism to the promise of decentering:

Postmodern culture with its decentered subject can be the space where ties are severed or it can provide the occasion for new and varied forms of bonding. To some extent, ruptures, surfaces, contextuality, and a host of other happenings create gaps that make space for oppositional practices which no longer require intellectuals to be confined by narrow separate spheres with no meaningful connection to the world of everyday. (1990, 31)

Discussions of the "subject" have considerable relevance for adult education. Freire's (1970) work on participatory literacy argues for a pedagogy of literacy education that engages adult learners as knowing subjects—rather than as objects—of adult education. He argues for shifting the subject of the learning away from the teacher, the dominant center of the classroom, to the learner. Sheared (1994) argues in similar fashion that the adult education experience should be a venue for "giving voice" to learners who may otherwise be marginalized from the center of many discourses of power in society. Postmodernist analysis can contribute to adult educators' thinking about and understanding of the multiple forms of marginalization that many adult students experience. Our goal should be to engage them in "pivoting the center" of the discourse of their learning so that they—rather than the unitary Western male subject—are at the center of the learning experience. Postmodern perspectives can thus help us develop adult education practices that respectfully legitimize adult learners' lives, perspectives, discourses, and voices.

The concept of the unspoken dominant cultural center can also be of use to us in our thinking about curriculum—both in content and form. We can help learners think about whose voice is represented in the various texts we employ in our teaching: who is talking and what perspective is being represented? Our goal should be to transmit the idea that there is no neutral value position in any text or curriculum, and that the dominant cultural power position, as Ferguson (1990) tells us, is often hidden, transparent, or taken for granted as a given condition or universal.

THE LEGITIMATION OF POPULAR CULTURE

Another interesting emergent theme of postmodernism is its focus on popular culture. One of postmodernism's goals is to legitimize all forms of cultural expression, including those previously marginalized by concepts of "high" culture such as Eurocentric arts (symphony orchestras, Western art museums, etc.). Postmodernism has contributed to increased interest in popular culture and media on the part of many authors (Baudrillard 1988; Giroux and Simon 1989; Poster 1989). As hooks puts it,

Much postmodern engagement with culture emerges from the yearning to do intellectual work that connects with habits of being, forms of artistic expression, and aesthetics that inform the daily life of writers and scholars as well as a mass population. . . . It's exciting to think, write, talk about, and create art that reflects passionate engagement with popular culture, because this may very well be "the" central future location of resistance struggle, a meeting place where new and radical happenings can occur. (1990, 31)

Postfeminists such as Grewal and Kaplan (1996) also argue for the relevance of postmodernism to feminism for its analysis of popular culture and multiple forms of marginalization, or "scattered hegemonies." As they note,

Postmodernism cannot be dismissed simply as the apolitical celebration of Western popular culture. Rather, it can be read as part of the operations of transnational culture; as the cultural expression of "scattered hegemonies," which are the effects of mobile capital as well as the multiple subjectivities that replace the European unitary subject. (Grewal and Kaplan 1996, 7)

This postmodernist focus on popular culture can contribute to the work of adult education. We can surely benefit from the employment of popular media forms for educational purposes—to include video, music, computers, and multimedia. In addition, however, our work should also include the critique and deconstruction of these popular forms through development of fields such as media literacy. Hemphill, Ianiro, and Raffa (1995) note, for example, that marginalized adult literacy learners can be singularly dependent upon popular electronic media (particularly television) for information about the dominant culture, as they have so few opportunities to interact with members of that culture on a daily basis. However, they are also found to display relatively uncritical acceptance of media images. Postmodernist thought can assist us as we develop media and technological literacy approaches to engage adult learners as critical media and technology users.

LANGUAGE, CONSTRUCTIONS, AND FLOATING SIGNIFIERS

For postmodernists, language is neither a deep-structured genetic code nor a transparent medium for transmitting ideas. Some think that meaning in language is constructed through an endless play of differences between signifiers, governed by shifting relations of difference and power. Meaning is constituted in ideologically organized, socially influenced signifying practices. Language has heavy power in a hegemonic sense, rejecting the notion of the free, independent subject, a tenet of Enlightenment modernism (Giroux 1991). Postmodernists view language, then, as not just a tool for expression, but also as a structure that defines the limits of communication and shapes the subjects who speak (Poster 1989).

Postmodernists view all meaning expressed through signs or language as constructions. Whether theories of science, parts of speech, rap tunes, or ad jingles—all are cultural constructions that were made by someone, and all are reflective of particular cultural positions or historical contexts, reflecting someone's interest. As Miyoshi (1991, 42) notes, "There is no innocent or neutral reading." Derrida (1978, 1981) argues that we must view books, too, as arbitrary constructions. He stresses the indeterminate meaning of texts, noting that their meanings are open to endless interpretation and reinterpretation. Bakhtin expands this sense of indeterminacy to all language. He argues that all utterances are transitional and dialogical in nature:

The most important feature of the utterance . . . is its *dialogism*, that is, its intertextual dimension. . . . All discourse is in dialogue with prior discourses on the same subject, as well as with discourses yet to come, whose reactions it foresees and anticipates. (Todorov 1984, x)

Thus, for postmodernists, all linguistic phenomena are part of an infinitely continuous web of communications whose meanings are not solely determined by the individual but are always open to redetermination by others. As Best and Kellner put it, postmodernists,

gave primacy to the signifier over the signified, and thereby signaled the dynamic productivity of language, the instability of meaning, and a break with conventional representational schemes of meaning. . . . The signified is only a moment in a never-ending process of signification where meaning is produced not in a stable, referential relation between subject and object, but only within the infinite, intertextual play of signifiers. (Best and Kellner 1991, 21)

This emphasis on arbitrariness and indeterminacy, then, flavors postmodern views of virtually all cultural constructions, be they films, scientific theories, musical compositions, or school curricula.

If we keep in mind the postmodernist emphasis on viewing all human expressions of meaning as constructions, it is a bit easier to understand the commonly heard term "deconstruction." To deconstruct a meaning or an idea is to understand it as a construction and to uncover its evolution, unpacking the interests it serves and marginalizes. There are similarities between the postmodernist notion of deconstruction and the Marxist notion of critique. However, one major point of difference between the two has to do with their ultimate grounding. Marxist critique is ultimately grounded in Western rationality, while postmodernist deconstruction is not. Marxist critique of social, educational, political, or economic questions makes ultimate reference to the canons of Western logic and rationality in assessing validity claims and in resolving conflicting claims.

In contrast, however, the deconstruction of postmodernists has no such ultimate point of reference. This is because postmodernists view Western Enlightenment rationality itself as a massive, problematic construction, indeed as a major target for deconstruction. Therefore, deconstruction proceeds without ultimate reference to any single system of codified meaning.

Baudrillard (1988) argues that the media-saturated postmodern era has also seen the evolution of a linguistic mutation he calls "floating signifiers." He suggests that in the past, pre-industrial societies maintained a communication structure in which signs were attached to referents (identifiable objects or phenomena) and were expressed in a relatively stable context that offered a consistent interpretive framework. Thus, if a sign or its meaning were to be called into question, there was a basis for judging its validity. However, in late-twentieth-century and early twenty-first-century postindustrial culture, which is saturated by mass electronic media, signs are often separated from their referents (the objects or phenomena that gave them their original meaning). This results in signs being extracted from meaningful social contexts and redeployed in the media as "floating signifiers."

Thus, we have forms of thinking and communicating that now use these floating signifiers—to sell products, candidates, or schooling policies—with little reference to modernist reason or the Western logic of argumentation. Images are used to incite desire and to convey complex messages quickly. Electronic mass media especially—but not exclusively—employ this new language form which transmits floating signifiers to the population. An example of this can be seen in the history of the song "I Heard It Through the Grapevine." Originally a soul tune popularized by Gladys Knight and then Marvin Gaye, more recently the song has been appropriated for television commercials promoting California raisins and subsequently other commodities such as cosmetics. The song's initial meaning has been appropriated for a purpose that has no connection to the original context of its creation. It has thus become a "floating signifier."

The complex postmodernist view of language recounted above has significant applications to adult education. There are two important parallels to the post-modernist view of the primacy of language in Freire's (1970) work. The first has to do with Freire's idea of the "power of naming," as a primary conceptual underpinning of his literacy pedagogy. Freire clearly recognizes the world-constitutive power of language when he argues the following:

To exist, humanly, is to *name* the world, to change it. Once named, the world in its turn reappears to the namers as a problem and requires of them a new naming. . . . Saying that word is not the privilege of some few men, but the right of every man. (Freire 1970, 76)

Thus, Freire's participatory literacy pedagogy, through use of nonverbal codi-fications, engages learners in generating the names for the themes that will be the focus of their literacy instruction.

Freire also adopts a notion of dialogue that is not far from Bakhtin's, although Freire clearly stays within a modernist paradigm by implying that there is some ultimate moral and rational grounding for truth in dialogue:

Dialogue is the encounter between men, mediated by the world, in order to name the world. . . . If it is in speaking their word that men, by naming the world, transform it, dialogue imposes itself as the way by which men achieve significance as men. Dialogue is thus an existential necessity. (Freire 1970, 76–77)

Following Bakhtin (Todorov 1984), we can expand Freire's understanding of dialogue to conceive of all language use as a kind of "meta-dialogue." The idea that all utterances are in dialogue with prior and subsequent discourses on related topics, as if in a continuous web, should influence our thinking and teaching about language.

We can also apply to literacy education the postmodernist idea that all forms of expressed meaning are constructions. In textual literacy or media literacy instruction we can engage learners in developing understandings of the arbi-trariness of the authorship and editing functions in making print or media texts. We can present the argument that all texts, videos, films, or songs are construc-tions that were made by someone, and they all reflect a point of view. Probably the best way to drive home this message is through engaging learners in making their own texts (whether print, electronic media, or some other form), and then reflecting on the arbitrariness and indeterminacy of the process (Hemphill, Ia-niro, Raffa 1995).

In other areas of language teaching (adult ESL [English as a second Language] or adult literacy), too, we can certainly convey to adult learners the power of language, not just as a transmitter of ideas, but as a powerful process that shapes us as we use it. When teaching reading—particularly at higher levels of comprehension and interpretation—we can also emphasize the postmodernist view of openness and indeterminacy in textual meaning. We can recount the view of reading as a dialogue between the reader and the text, noting that the meaning differs with each reading, depending upon the interpretive context and the reader.

Finally, Baudrillard's (1988) idea of floating signifiers can help us to understand the nature of the cognitive processes of many young people coming to adult education who have grown up in a media-saturated culture. Floating signifiers may help to explain a learner mind-set that is intensely familiar with—and most comfortable with—quick, high-quality audiovisual images that are not subject to rational analysis. The idea of floating signifiers can also be presented to learners as a part of a media literacy curriculum.

FOUCAULT ON KNOWLEDGE, POWER, AND THE ORGANIZATION OF KNOWLEDGE

Michel Foucault (1972, 1973, 1980) has been particularly influential in re-shaping postmodern ideas about knowledge and power and notions of order in bodies of knowledge. He closely connects the ideas of power and knowledge by arguing that there is tremendous power in development, naming, and operation of knowledge. In employing the term "power/knowledge," in fact, he claims that this power (mental force) may not differ much from physical force or might. For Foucault, knowledge is not a cognitive abstraction, but rather social practice that generates action and participation. Foucault further argues that power/knowledge is exerted by a powerful minority who are able to impose their ideas of truth on the majority. In the area of the human sciences, the construction of truth is said to involve deciding matters that define humanity (Fillingham 1993; Popkewitz and Brennan 1998).

Foucault, echoing other postmodernists discussed earlier, suggests that power/ knowledge works primarily through language. When children learn to speak, they pick up the basic knowledge and rules of their culture at the same time. Therefore, all the human sciences are claimed to define human beings at the same time as they describe them, and work together with such institutions as mental hospitals, prisons, factories, schools, and courts to have specific and serious effects on people. Foucault focused throughout his work on a central mechanism of the social sciences—the categorization of people into "normal" and "abnormal." Indeed, he argued that this categorization scheme was one of the major ways that power relations are established in society (Fillingham 1993).

Another important contribution is Foucault's emphasis upon discontinuity and difference in history and his interest in exploring complex correlations in place of simple causality (Harvey 1989). He argues that stability in systems of thought and discourse can exist for relatively long periods, and then quite suddenly shift. He also admonishes us to be wary of clean-cut, well-organized categories of knowledge, thought, or action that are presented as "givens":

We must question those ready-made syntheses, those groupings that we normally accept before any examination, those links whose validity is recognized from the outset; we must oust those forms and obscure forces by which we usually link the discourse of one man with another . . . we must accept . . . that they concern only a population of dispersed events . . . As soon as one questions that unity, it loses its self-evidence; it indicates itself, constructs itself, only on the basis of a complex field of discourse. (Foucault 1972, 22–23)

He further suggests that we must deconstruct the ways in which we organize and transmit knowledge through formal schooling:

We must also question those divisions or groupings with which we have become so familiar. Can one accept, as such, the distinction between the major types of discourse, or that between such forms or genres as science, literature, philosophy, religion, history, etc. and which tend to create certain great historical individualities? We are not even sure of ourselves when we use these distinctions in our own world of discourse, let alone when we are analyzing groups of statements which, when first formulated, were distributed, divided, and characterized in quite a different way: after all, "literature" and "politics" are recent categories, which can be applied to medieval culture . . . only by a retrospective hypothesis. (Foucault 1972, 22)

Foucault urges us, then, to recognize the contingency and historicity in the formulation of all categories of knowledge. His thinking on power, knowledge, language, and structures of knowledge can inform our work as adult educators. If knowledge and language are indeed the deep and powerful forces Foucault describes, then the work of adult education takes on even greater significance than we might have previously thought. This heightened understanding may enable us to enhance the motivation for adult learners if we can help them understand that control of knowledge may well have as much power as physical force, and that control of knowledge structures by others controls their lives.

Foucault's work can also help us understand how adult educators are susceptible to participating in the marginalization and stereotyping of our students as "illiterate" adults, "welfare recipients," or other negative images. Foucault can help us to see how schooling is a part of institutionalizing and deciding what is "normal" and "abnormal." It is part of a categorization scheme that establishes and enforces power relations in society. Foucault can help adult educators to come to grips with a basic contradiction of education—that it can be either empowering or disempowering—or sometimes simultaneously both. He can also help us to clarify what our role is. Since adult education is often the education of last resort after the failure of other forms of schooling, Foucault can enhance our conception of the importance of what we do.

Furthermore, Foucault encourages us to be critical of how knowledge is organized—whether in terms of broad disciplines or specific course curricula. All forms of organizing knowledge, he tells us, are contingent, occurring due to existing organizations and constellations of power in a given moment—and not given in some cosmic hierarchy. This has important implications for curriculum development. As we saw before, Freire's emphasis on focusing on learner-generated and learner-constructed knowledge is important and offers us a pedagogy consonant with Foucault's thinking.

CONCLUSION

The complexities of postmodern discourses are both challenging and frustrating. They are incomplete, unapologetically fragmented, lacking an overarching paradigm, and constantly shifting—much like our lives. It is clear that complex cultural and technological changes that are now under way will unavoidably have major effects on how we conceive of knowledge—its construction, conceptualization, storage, transmission, and social functioning. Adult educators must begin to insert themselves into the issues being raised by postmodern discourses. These discourses offer a path—albeit a frustrating and convoluted one—to understanding present and future phenomena that are no longer well suited to modernist, rational explanations. Adult education is too important an enterprise to be left to ossify in a decaying paradigm.

REFERENCES

Baudrillard, Jean. (1988). *Selected Writings*. Stanford, CA: Stanford University Press.

Best, Steven, and Kellner, Douglas. (1991). *Postmodern Theory: Critical Interrogations*. New York: Guilford Press.

Brookfield, S. (1989). *Developing Adult Critical Thinkers*. San Francisco: Jossey-Bass.

Brown, Elsa B. (1990). "African-American Women's Quilting: A Framework for Conceptualizing and Teaching African-American Women's History." In Micheline Malson et al. (eds.), *Black Women in America: Social Science Perspectives*. Chicago: University of Chicago Press.

Derrida, Jacques. (1978). *Writing and Difference*. Chicago: University of Chicago Press.

Derrida, Jacques. (1981). *Positions*. Chicago: University of Chicago Press.

Doll, William E., Jr. (1993). *A Post-Modern Perspective on Curriculum*. New York: Teachers College Press.

Ferguson, Richard et al. (eds.). (1990). *Out There: Marginalization and Contemporary Cultures*. New York: Museum of Contemporary Art and MIT Press.

Fillingham, Lydia. (1993). *Foucault for Beginners*. New York: Writers and Readers Publishing.

Foucault, Michel. (1972). *The Archaeology of Knowledge*. New York: Pantheon Books.

Foucault, Michel. (1973). *The Order of Things: An Archaelology of the Human Sciences*. New York: Vintage.

Foucault, Michel. (1980). *Power/Knowledge: Selected Interviews and Other Writings by Michel Foucault, 1972–1977* (C. Gordon, ed. and trans.). New York: Pantheon Books.

Freire, P. (1970). *Pedagogy of the Oppressed*. New York: Continuum.

Giroux, Henry (ed.). (1991). *Postmodernism, Feminism, and Cultural Politics: Redrawing Educational Boundaries*. Albany: State University of New York Press.

Giroux, Henry, and Simon, Roger (eds.). (1989). *Popular Culture, Schooling, and Everyday Life*. New York: Bergin & Garvey.

Grewal, Inderpal, and Kaplan, Caren. (1996). *Scattered Hegemonies: Feminism in Postmodernist, Transnational Perspective*. Minneapolis: University of Minnesota Press.

Habermas, Jürgen. (1975). *Legitimation Crisis*. Boston: Beacon Press.

Habermas, Jürgen. (1984). *The Theory of Communicative Action, Volume One: Reason and the Rationalization of Society*. Boston: Beacon Press.

Habermas, Jürgen. (1990). *The Philosophical Discourse of Modernity*. Cambridge, MA: MIT Press.

Harvey, David. (1989). *The Condition of Postmodernity: An Enquiry into the Origins of Cultural Change*. Cambridge, MA: Basil Blackwell.

Hemphill, David, Ianiro, Sally, and Raffa, Damien. (1995). "Media, Technology, and Literacy in Immigrant and Multicultural Contexts." *School of Education Review* (San Francisco State University) (Spring), 27–32.

hooks, bell. (1990). *Yearning: Race, Gender, and Cultural Politics*. Boston: South End Press.

Lyotard, Jean-François. (1984). *The Postmodern Condition: A Report on Knowledge*. Minneapolis: University of Minnesota Press.

Mezirow, J. (1991). *Transformative Dimensions of Adult Learning*. San Francisco: Jossey-Bass.

Miyoshi, Masao. (1991). *Off Center: Power and Culture Relations between Japan and the United States*. Cambridge, MA: Harvard University Press.

Popkewitz, Thomas, and Brennan, Marie (eds.). (1998). *Foucault's Challenge: Discourse, Knowledge, and Power in Education*. New York: Teachers College Press, Columbia University.

Poster, Mark. (1989). *Critical Theory & Poststructuralism: In Search of a Context*. Ithaca, NY: Cornell University Press.

Sheared, Vanessa. (1994). "Giving Voice: An Inclusive Model of Instruction—A Womanist Perspective." In E. Hayes and S.A.J. Colin III (eds.), *Confronting Racism and Sexism*, 27–32. San Francisco: Jossey-Bass.

Slattery, Patrick. (1995). *Curriculum Development in the Postmodern Era*. New York: Garland Publishing Co.

Todorov, Tzvetan. (1984). *Mikhail Bakhtin: The Dialogical Principle*. Minneapolis: University of Minnesota Press.

Toulmin, Stephen. (1990). *Cosmopolis: The Hidden Agenda of Modernity*. Chicago: University of Chicago Press.

Usher, Robert, and Edwards, Richard. (1994). *Postmodernism and Education*. New York: Routledge.

White, Hayden. (1987). *The Content of the Form: Narrative Discourse and Historical Representation*. Baltimore, MD: Johns Hopkins University Press.

Wilson, Margaret (ed.). (1969). *The Essential Descartes*. New York: Mentor.

Chapter 3

Challenging Adult Learning:
A Feminist Perspective

Daniele D. Flannery and Elisabeth Hayes

> If the imagination is to transcend and transform experience it has to question, to challenge, to conceive of alternatives, perhaps to the very life you are living at the moment. You have to be free to play around with the notion that day might be night, love might be hate, nothing can be too sacred for the imagination . . . to call experience by another name. For writing is re-naming.
>
> —Adrienne Rich (1979), 43

INTRODUCTION

In this chapter, we critique the hegemony of adult learning through the perspective of feminism. In particular, we focus on the social construction of gender for women and the challenges to adult learning which a focus on gender offers. This chapter comes from our reflections and feelings on our own varied learning experiences. It is a beginning. We offer it to you in the hope that through your pondering of your own life experiences, you will offer further alternatives.

PERSONAL EXPERIENCES OF LEARNING

Daniele

In my (Daniele) life I've always had a learning style which was different from the kind of learning promoted in most formal learning settings. I learn through feelings, experiences, and information incubating within me for a while. It's an affective and kinesthetic thing! When it finally "feels right," "I know," "I've got it." To people who make sense of things the way I do, I don't have to use many words, complete thoughts, or logical sentences to share what I have learned. With others who learn like me, everything clicks; we understand each other. We judge the authenticity of the knowing and what is known, that is, the learning, from what "feels" right. I communicate my learning differently from dominant standards, by drawing, or with poetry or music, or in an experiential workshop. Because of what learning is like for me, I've challenged the universality of adult learning theory in my classes and in articles I've written (Flannery 1995). Then, falling back on academic rationality, I logically extended my personal experiences to others. I argued that adult learning theory must include cultural, class, and gendered learning styles.

Despite this perspective, however, I had little "feeling" for what this was about until recently. My ongoing participation in a women's spirituality group has helped me to understand how profoundly issues of gender have influenced me and my learning. For example, in our group we have reflected on our own personal stories of religion and spirituality. As a result, I became more aware of, and in fact was amazed at the strength of male influences on my images of God, on my ways of thinking about spirituality, and on the lived practices which I still tend to measure myself against. I realized that as a child my religion held up a pervading image of being a Soldier of Christ ready to die for my religion. (I still remember the constant reminders in school in California in the 1950s that the communists might invade from China and we, even though children, could well be tortured for our religion.) What I was left with was a spirituality based on endurance and the importance of being strong and suffering. If, as a woman, you couldn't live up to the soldier image, then you were limited to being mothers, caretakers, and responsible for hospitality.

Today, after such reflection, I am unlearning and relearning my own spirituality along with my sisters in the group. I learn naturally by "feeling" who I am as a spiritual person and knowing from deep inside how I have to live that spirituality for today.

Betty

In contrast to Daniele, I (Betty) have a style of learning that fits quite well with the kind of learning that is valued in many academic settings. I rely on logic and rationality in most of my learning, and I approach most new situations by trying to make "sense" of them intellectually. I love to analyze ideas and concepts! However, when it comes to something that requires "embodied" knowing, I have a hard time. Learning to dance posed more of a challenge to me than much of my graduate course work—I just couldn't "figure out" how to do it. As an adult literacy teacher I first began to question the value placed on "my" kind of learning. My students came from very diverse cultural, racial, and economic backgrounds. While they often struggled with academic learning, I saw that they were very adept learners in other situations. For example, one student was a skilled landscaper with a wonderful talent for visualizing gardens and working with plants. Another, a leader in her church and community, was skilled at motivating and inspiring other people. Reading feminist scholarship deepened my understanding of different ways of knowing as just as valid as the dominant mode. My own learning approach certainly fits more with the dominant mode, the stereotypical "male" learner, but to paraphrase Sojourner Truth, "ain't I a woman too?" Too, because of my own experience I am suspicious of any attempt to generalize about the learning of women or any other group of learners. Working with Daniele has had a big influence on my appreciation of other approaches to learning and knowing. We are so different! She decides when something she's written is complete when she reads through it and it "feels" right. In contrast, I am satisfied when I read my draft and the ideas seem to be logical and well-ordered!

Most recently, I began a meditation practice that has heightened my awareness of the limitations of "rational" learning. In a class specifically designed for women, the teacher helps us become aware of how cultural norms prompt us to "disconnect" from our bodies and emotions, to distrust them and suppress them. Meditation has engaged me in a type of transformative learning that, rather than relying on rational thought, seeks to go beyond thoughts altogether. Because of such strong experiences of gender and learning in our own lives, we offer one piece of our efforts that helped us in re-naming our own learning.

AN INTRODUCTION TO ADULT LEARNING

Adult learning as an area of study attempts to understand how adults learn. In so doing, all kinds of learning may be studied, including, but not limited to, cognition, brain-based learning, behavioral modification, and social learning.

Within the field of adult education considerable attention has been given to those aspects of learning deemed more relevant to adults. These include adult development and its connection to adult learning (Merriam and Clark 1991); adults' ability to reflect on their own experiences (Schon 1987), to learn from their many life experiences (Lee and Caffarella 1994), to be self-directed (Candy 1991), and to be transformed by their experiences (Mezirow 1991). These aspects of adult learning are put forth generically as what adults do. Often, systematic steps of how to engage in the particular perspective, say, engage in reflective learning, are detailed. Facilitators are urged to promote these practices in their classrooms.

Key Feminist Ideas

We present here the primary philosophical assumptions of feminism which provide the basis for our challenges to current adult learning. We acknowledge there are many different feminisms, but we present broad feminist principles as the basis for our considerations. Feminism places women at the center of consideration. It asks, what is it to be women? What are women's experiences? Feminism recognizes that to be women is to be gendered, that is, to be products of social and cultural belief systems and practices about being women, not simply biological factors. As gendered we learn who we are as women; how to act, how to interact with others, how we are valued because of our gender, what place in the society we have because of our gender. Gender relations differ in diverse historical, cultural, ethnic, and class milieus. Thus, gender cannot be separated from race and class. Postmodern feminists challenge the universal ways reality is portrayed, suggesting, instead, multiple realities. Gendered relations are about power and position, among women and between men and women. Aida Hurtado (1996) writes that "socially constructed markers," such as gender, race, class, and ethnicity, determine placement and relative power. They are interlocking aspects of experience which entitle certain persons and deny status and power to others. As a result, there are similarities and differences among women. Thus, feminists hold that women differ in resources and limitations, in power and powerlessness and in positionality. We can't assume that sexism affects white women and women of color in the same way (Reid 1993). Feminists of color challenge white women to consider the privilege and positions they have because they are white.

For feminists there are gendered ways of knowing and learning (Harding 1996). Because women and men are exposed to different elements of societal regularities, women and men often interact with different parts of nature. Even when interacting with the same part of nature, men and women, because of gendered differences, may have different interests and have different socially produced ways of organizing knowledge and of engaging in discourse. For example, Sandra Harding notes that in one study women research scientists conceptualized experimental science in whole units, and stressed the connection between thinking and feeling for judging results. Men research scientists conceptualized experimental science in small discrete parts. They stressed the primacy of objective thinking for judging results.

As with gender relations, these gendered knowledge systems may differ by society, culture, ethnic group, locality, and so on, thus again potentially resulting in differing knowledge systems among women as well as between women and men. For example, Nell Noddings (1995) notes that "women have access to privileged knowledge with respect to issues of gender, the poor with respect to poverty, blacks and other ethnic minorities with respect to race, and perhaps students with respect to schooling" (p. 17). Nancy Goldberger (1996) demonstrates women's ways of knowing as enabled or restricted depending on race, class, culture, experiences, and so forth. In summary, these key feminist ideas challenge the unidimensional, static, and universal characteristics of adult learning (also see Chapter 4 in this volume). They point to women's lives (and men's), as multidimensional, as fluid in different settings, different positionalities, with different resources and limitations, and clearly as diverse.

FEMINIST PERSPECTIVES: NEW WAYS OF SEEING ADULT LEARNING

With these initial feminist ideas as a foundation, we proceed to challenge adult learning. Three areas are central to our feminist challenge of adult learning: identity, authority in knowledge creation, and agency within social structures. Key perspectives related to each area are provided along with concrete examples to illustrate how these perspectives illuminate a previously marginalized or invisible aspect of adult learning. Each perspective is then used to challenge some specific aspects of adult learning. Finally, we demonstrate how the feminist perspectives point to alternative and more inclusive perspectives on adult learning.

Identity

Feminist perspectives offer new ways of understanding human identity, taking into account the intersection between race, class, gender, and other social identities. First, women are not all alike. They differ because of race, class, sexual preference, and so forth. For example, generalizations are frequently made about women's self-esteem as being low. However, some African-American women frequently express greater feelings of competence and self-confidence than white women, perhaps because their upbringing is more likely to promote competence and decisiveness. On the other hand, many Asian women appear to experience lower self-esteem due to cultural factors: "Since the image of the passive, demure Asian woman is pervasive, the struggle for a positive self-identity is difficult" (Walsh 1987, 146). Lesbian women with positive homosexual identity have higher self-esteem than do those with a less positive homosexual identity. With regard to race and ethnicity, lesbians and gays who are African-American and Native American are often regarded as betraying their ethnic communities because of the belief that reproductive sexuality contributes to the survival of the group.

Second, feminist perspectives challenge the concept of single, unitary identities, and instead point to the significance of multiple identities shaping a woman's self-concept. People have family identities, social identities, Chicano-women identities, and working-class identities all at the same time. As Vanessa Sheared (1994) and other black feminists have pointed out, African-American women are not either African-American or women; they are "both/and." Sadly, the concept of multiplicity has been treated as pathological, often leading people to deny or repress different identities. Cherri Moraga (1981) writes, "I think: what is my responsibility to my roots?—both white and brown, Spanish-speaking and English? I am a woman with a foot in both worlds; and I refuse the split" (p. 34). Another woman, Cecilia, talks about the stigmatization of certain social identities and the conflicts that they can create. Cecilia learned early that it was bad to be Mexican, speak Spanish, and have brown skin. In high school, feeling so embarrassed about her body being brown, she wouldn't shower at gym time. She left home as a young adult, denied her origins, and tried to adopt mainstream American behavior. She found she didn't fit there either. In time, she stopped oppressing herself; she accepted who she was. She was Mexican and American, and brown, and a woman in both cultures, each with their own expectations of women.

Third, feminist perspectives reflect that women may be powerful and powerless at the same time. For example, many Latina women experience powerlessness in their own cultures with expectations that they act submissive and subservient to males in order to be seen as "good women" (Espin 1984). At the same time, in their work, they often experience power and position, say, as providers of health care and of mental health services such as counseling. Negotiating this duality can be challenging, however, both personally and professionally (see Chapter 16, this volume).

Based on these feminist perspectives, we challenge the lack of diversity within the adult learning literature, wherein one-dimensional and static generalizations about adult learners are pervasive. For example, low self-esteem is frequently cited in the literature as an attribute of adult women learners. This generalization takes into account neither diversity among women nor the potentially different meanings of self-esteem for different women. This generalization oversimplifies the multiple experiences of women. Yes, self-doubt was found to be a primary theme in studies on women's learning in higher education environments (Hayes and Flannery 1995). However, in other studies women express a high degree of self-esteem (Roundtree and Lambert 1994). Too, some studies noted that self-doubt within learning environments was related to gendered devaluation of women's abilities, and were responses to men's dominance of a classroom situation (Kelly 1991). Johnson-Bailey and Cervero (1996) presented a group of African-American women as using silence in the classroom to deal with racism and sexism.

Generalizations assume stasis, rather than change. Yet, there is literature with accounts of social and individual change. Latinos, for example, hold traditional attitudes toward women's roles, but with acculturation, education, and work outside the home, these views become less restrictive (Walsh 1987). Thus, we must move beyond these limited conceptualizations to understand the complex intersections of gender, race, class, and other factors in the social and individual experiences and identities of adult learners. Recognizing this, we challenge the field to accept that adult learning perspectives cannot be put forth as universal for all people. We need to look at women as having similarities and differences from each other; each woman as having multiple identities; and women's power and position as varying, depending on the situations they are in. Because development is about learning, unlearning, and relearning, we must challenge the universality of adult developmental theory that presumes a linear, hierarchical process of change experienced by a unitary self, often based on white male, middle-class samples. We must reexamine and challenge adult developmental theories that assume middle-class whiteness as a standard for studying and explaining development, and therefore learning. To do so, we must conduct or engage in developmental research with people of various classes, races, and ethnicities. Too, we can listen to each other's stories of development. We must also seek to understand human lives and learning, as reflective of a dynamic interplay of identities, shaped both by individual choice and social context, and founded on interrelationships among mind, body, and spirit. For example, instead of categorizing people as different types of knowers, as in *Women's Ways of Knowing* (Belenky, Clinchy, Goldberger, and Tarule 1986), we can give more attention to how individuals move back and forth among different ways of knowing, and under what circumstances. We need to also seek to understand how transformative learning, rather than being a move toward a certain kind of "ideal" perspective, might instead consist of a more complex shifting in and among co-existing perspectives, as adults engage in a continual process of negotiating multiple identities.

Rather than striving for generalizations, we must seek better ways of understanding the uniqueness of individual learners, considering historical, social, economic, and political influences on gender, race, and class. One way we do this in our classes is, without mentioning political, economic, historical aspects, we have people read an autobiography of someone from a different race, class, culture, sexual preference, and so forth. We then talk about the works from the lens of what we can learn about adult development and adult learning from that person's life. We find that the places of spirituality, sexuality, politics, power, and other forces come up naturally in the book discussions, and that people reverence rather than judge the life stories they read. Through the writings of others, we can work with students to understand the many ways of knowing such as emotional, sensing, intuition, and so forth. Requiring their own autobiographical writing about their movement among different ways of knowing, or on transformative learning times in their own lives, would be helpful exercises to deal with these aspects.

Authority in Knowledge Creation: The Challenge

Feminists challenge traditional criteria concerning who creates knowledge and how to judge knowledge claims in theory building as well as in everyday life. The traditional way of viewing "authority" emphasizes a mode of rational argument and excludes other, more diverse ways of knowing. In her discussion of Black feminist thought, Collins (1991) proposes an alternative basis for knowledge claims that includes concrete experience as a criterion of knowing. While Collins offers us a particular way of assessing knowledge and wisdom for African-American women, she also provides us with a paradigm that we can use to shift the way we traditionally view knowledge and learning. The main question becomes, "How do YOU know?" That is to say, what is your personal experience? From your story, is your life believable to us? Dialogue among hearers is used to assess knowledge claims and is judged by the passion of expression and the commitment of the speaker, not solely by its internal logic. There is an important ethic of caring for people's wisdom from the past and an ethic of personal responsibility for one's own knowledge claims. Value is placed on various kinds of knowing based in experience, intuition, connection, and embodiment. As Collins concludes, the wisdom then of African-American women based on both their everyday lived experience and on the wisdom collected through generations is acknowledged and valued by themselves as well as others. It is our acceptance of this alternative way of viewing learning that helps us begin to rethink and reframe how knowledge and learning can be viewed for women as well as men. Another challenge to what is knowledge is voiced by working-class women who have made a distinction between the varying forms of knowledge by juxtaposing "local truth" and "common sense" with "school knowledge" (Lutrell 1984; Baird 1994). Common sense or local truth refers to learning in the course of the everyday. School knowledge refers to book learning, to college, to credentials. School knowledge was often deemed to be unattainable by working-class women. The learning story of a woman auto mechanic exemplifies this. The woman held up a manual for car repair, saying it was her guide. When the interviewer commented that she thought the woman had said she couldn't read, the woman said she couldn't. Reading was school knowledge done through *school books*. That she couldn't do. What she could do was "common sense" learning, which she did with her work.

Based on these feminist perspectives, we can begin to challenge adult learning to broaden its understanding about who are the respected knowledge makers and what is the *actual knowledge* that is considered to have or give authority. Within the university we urge greater inclusiveness, noting that Collins (1991) charged that African-American women have long held outsider status with respect to the generation of knowledge within academic settings. We add that many other women are also considered as outsiders in knowledge making. Too, we urge the incorporation of those voices that are outside of the academy into the discourse in order to give greater depth to our understandings of adult learning.

We challenge the presentation and representation of *knowledge* as being exclusive to one group as opposed to being inclusive of all learners. For example, Johnson-Bailey and Cervero (1996) and Scott (1991) contend that the knowledge and perspectives of African-American women are both similar and different from other women and from other African-American women. Such knowledge results from African-American women's position of oppression, and unique economic and political status. We challenge adult education to examine the ways in which knowledge is produced, presented, and made available to all learners. The continued use of our current academic parlance and conceptualizations will only result in the continued dichotomization of learning and in the different valuing of learning. Peoples' referring to "school learning" and "common sense learning" is one example of this split. They point out that there is a perceived lack of application between school learning and an individual's lived experiences. Notions of deficiency in learners and privileging of specific learning such as "critical thinking" as a primary goal for education are other examples of similar dichotomizations occurring in the academy. Additionally, we are challenging the dominant criteria of logical rational critiques that locate, judge, and communicate knowledge about adult learning. We further challenge the notion of theory building as it is currently defined, for it has relied *only* on logical/ analytical modes of thought, "empirical" data, and the values and assumptions of white, middle-class male scholars. For example, Mezirow's (1991) work on perspective transformation rationally argues for a theory in abstracted, linear form, using sequenced isolated elements. In teaching this concept to adults, the process and steps required are also enumerated in the same form. However, for some, the theory will not make sense in this form, but rather will be understood only when, for example, a story is told about one's own personal transformation. Theories of transformative learning must therefore extend beyond "rational discourses" and intellectual "perspective" transformation to include, and value, the transformative nature of learning which we each experience—one that may be somewhat dependent on the cognitive, but that also includes spiritual, emotional, intuitive, and other embodied dimensions.

Finally, we must challenge the ways in which adult learning perspectives, as well as teachers and facilitators, include or do not include multidimensional and diverse aspects of adult learning. In doing so, we challenge the ways in which we gather and represent what is known as generalizations, "models," and abstractions in adult learning theory. We must ask ourselves: what can we learn about how one acquires knowledge and learning from doing either an autobiography or oral history, or reading fiction, or observations of popular culture? We must also ask ourselves about the ways in which our teachings and traditions derived from non-Western cultures influence the discourse, and how this representation might prevent us from understanding this knowledge in the same way it was shared with us.

We urge adult educators to place value on the kind of knowing that is based in experience, intuition, connection, and embodiment. For example, Johnson-Bailey and Cervero (1996) reaffirmed Collins' (1991) findings that some African-American women learn through an experiential knowledge that is transmitted through generations of lived experiences and oral histories. This is often viewed as being done for the good of the community as a whole and is done in the spirit of taking personal responsibility for one's own learning process. This means that assessments which consider multiple knowledges and multiple ways of making and presenting knowledge must be developed and used.

We challenge those in adult education and adult learning theory who emphasize the need for teachers to teach adults how to engage in experiential learning as if the adults didn't already learn from their experience. In fact, much adult learning *is* from experience. It is an insult to people to act as if that is not the case. If the real issue is that formal education has de-skilled people from using experiential learning in education settings, then educators must acknowledge this and re-teach people how to bring their experiences into formal classrooms that have disallowed this practice.

Too, we challenge the narrow range of experiences used in learning settings. Pertinent experiences in people's lives have been neglected in favor of convenient experiences that have taken place in classrooms. In women's learning, it is women's experiences such as learning, unlearning, relearning one's identity as a woman, motherhood, learning to be lesbian, widows learning how to make decisions at 60 years old which once were the domain of their husbands, that are among the contests in which women have expertise to speak about learning. Finally, we critique the sole emphasis on critical thinking as essential for learning from experience. Critical thinking, we suggest, violates many people's experiences by dissecting them into meaningless parts. For a number of people, experiences speak for themselves; they do not have to be artificially directed through cognitive, linear, verbal processes.

Agency within/against Social Structures

Feminists offer new perspectives on how individuals both conform to and resist oppressive social relations and belief systems that are reproduced in settings like school, family, and work. First, feminists have indicated the importance of understanding the intersections of different contexts in shaping people's experiences and responses to oppressive forces. Anyon (1984) writes that people experience differing sets of power relations at home, work, and in educational settings. Therefore, in order to understand learning in any context, we must understand how individuals move among these settings and negotiate the often conflicting relationships that occur between and among these situations. For example:

Mary was sexually abused by her mother and the men in her mother's life while she was growing up. She feared any exchange between people. She was particularly frightened of women. When she participated in formal learning settings, she had to slip in and out unnoticed and be in class with as much anonymity as possible. She selected lecture formats because this assured limited contact with her male teachers, and objective exams protected her from having to engage in any self disclosure.

Second, feminists have shown how concepts of accommodation to and resistance of oppressive forces must be interpreted in diverse ways that take into account people's experience of multiple oppressions. For instance, Mary's choices of learning settings above are her purposeful and active choices to resist potentially oppressive forces having any new influence in her life. A second example is the way nonparticipation in formal learning settings has typically been viewed as a deficit on the part of a person. More recently, it has been suggested that such nonparticipation may be an act of resistance associated with a rejection of mainstream educational achievement. In Shoemaker's dissertation (1993), a group of African-American women, despite participating in an odious and hostile environment, deliberately chose educational achievement as a way to economic status and power, a way to resist oppression in society as a whole. For them, participation was both rejection of mainstream educational settings and a chosen means to attain a societal power. In the area of adult learning, examples of portraying people as deficit are abundant. Adult learners who do not speak in the learning setting are seen as deficit. Yet, Juanita Johnson-Bailey's (1994) research found that African-American women's silence in the classroom, previously thought to reflect passive acceptance of their subordinate role, may be a deliberate way of maintaining safety in a racist and sexist environment.

We challenge the idealizing of certain worldviews and values in the teaching/ learning exchange. These result in treating those with other worldviews and values as deficient, as passive, as alien, invisible, and unworthy. Second, we challenge all aspects of adult learning and participation theory that treats women learners in particular as passive victims of social forces (Hayes and Smith 1994). Learners are not passive objects of oppressive social forces, nor are they free from the influence of these forces. Accommodation and resistance to social structures are choices people make all the time for their own reasons. We must also see and appreciate resistance as a form of agency, whether learners choose not to participate or to use educational credentials as a means of resisting other forms of oppression. We must retell more sophisticated accounts of how adult learning involves accommodation and resistance to social structures. We must also challenge a narrow focus on single learning settings in describing learning, and more toward more inclusive understanding of how individuals negotiate the intersections of different contexts for learning, especially neglected contexts such as the home. In addition, we must challenge dichotomous interpretations of learner behavior as either passive or resistant. For example, we can question the devaluation of silence in epistemological theory such as *Women's Ways of Knowing* (Belenky et al. 1986). Silence, rather than reflecting a lack of voice and passive stance toward knowledge creation, may for some learners be a deliberate act of concealing their knowledge, knowledge that might be threatening to the status quo.

CONCLUSIONS

In conclusion, we challenge each of you to join with us in reexamining and transforming our own theories of adult learning. We urge far more genuine dialogue on how to portray adult learning as it really is, multidimensional, fluid, and diverse. Finally, we urge the exploration of images and metaphors as ways to help us conceptualize adult learning as dynamic. For a beginning, we recall Margaret Mead's (1957) image of a lattice, where learning is horizontal, vertical, cross-ways and interconnected, and her daughter Mary Catherine Bateson's (1990) metaphor of learning as improvisation, an art where we "combine familiar and unfamiliar components in response to new situations, following an underlying grammar and an evolving aesthetic." We close with a wish for you and for ourselves from the writings of bell hooks (1989):

> There is always a conscious attempt on my part to challenge. I mean there is not a day of my life that I am not critiquing myself and looking at myself to see if my politics are borne out in the way that I live and the way that I talk and present myself. . . . I always ask people to shift their paradigms. (p. 169)

REFERENCES

Anyon, J. (1984). "Intersections of Gender and Class: Accommodation and Resistance by Working Class and Affluent Females to Contradictory Sex Role Ideologies." *Journal of Education* 166(1), 25–48.

Baird, I. C. (1994). "Learning to Earn 'the Right Way': Single Welfare Mothers in Mandated Education Programs." Unpublished Doctoral Dissertation, Pennsylvania State University.

Bateson, M. C. (1990). *Composing a Life*. New York: Plume.

Belenky, M. F., Clinchy, B. M., Goldberger, N. R., and Tarule, J. M. (1986). *Women's Ways of Knowing: The Development of Self, Voice and Mind*. New York: Basic Books.

Candy, P. C. (1991). *Self-direction for Lifelong Learning*. San Francisco: Jossey-Bass.

Collins, P. H. (1991). *Black Feminist Thought: Knowledge, Consciousness, and the Politics of Empowerment*. Boston: Unwin Hyman.

Espin, O. M. (1984). "Cultural and Historical Influences on Sexuality in Hispanic/Latina Women." In C. Vance (ed.), *Pleasure and Danger*, 149–164. Boston: Routledge & Kegan Paul.

Flannery, D. D. (1995). "Adult Education and the Politics of the Theoretical Text." In B. Kanpol and P. McLaren (eds.), *Critical Multiculturalism: Uncommon Voices in a Common Struggle*, 149–163. Westport, CT: Bergin & Garvey.

Goldberger, N. R. (1996). "Cultural Imperatives and Diversity in Ways of Knowing." In N. Goldberger, J. Tarule, B. Clinchy, and M. Belenky (eds.), *Knowledge, Difference, and Power*, 335–371. New York: Basic Books.

Harding, S. (1996). "Gendered Ways of Knowing and the 'Epistemological Crisis' of the West." In N. Goldberger, J. Tarule, B. Clinchy, and M. Belenky (eds.), *Knowledge, Difference, and Power*. New York: Basic Books.

Hayes, E., and Flannery, D. D. (1995). "Adult Women's Learning in Higher Education: A Critical Review of the Scholarship." *Initiatives* 57(1), 29–40.

Hayes, E., and Smith, L. (1994). "Women in Adult Education: An Analysis of Perspectives in Major Journals." *Adult Education Quarterly* 44, 201–221.

hooks, b. (1989). *Talking Back: Thinking Feminist, Thinking Black*. Boston: South End Press.

Hurtado, A. (1996). "Strategic Suspensions: Feminists of Color Theorize the Production of Knowledge." In N. Goldberger, J. Tarule, B. Clinchy, and M. Belenky (eds.), *Knowledge, Difference, and Power*, 372–392. New York: Basic Books.

Johnson-Bailey, J. (1994). "Making a Way Out of No Way: An Analysis of the Educational Narratives of Re-entry Black Women with Emphasis on Issues of Race, Gender, Class, and Color." Unpublished Doctoral Dissertation, University of Georgia.

Johnson-Bailey, J., and Cervero, R. (1996). "An Analysis of Educational Narratives of Reentry Black Women." *Adult Education Quarterly* 46(3), 142–157.

Kelly, J. (1991). "A Study of Gender Differential Linguistic Interaction in the Adult Education Classroom." *Gender and Education* 3(2), 137–143.

Lee, P., and Caffarella, R. S. (1994). "Methods and Techniques for Engaging Learners in Experiential Learning Activities." In L. Jackson and R. S. Caffarella (eds.), *Experiential Learning: A New Approach*, 43–54. San Francisco: Jossey-Bass.

Lutrell, W. L. (1984). "The Getting of Knowledge: A Study of Working-Class Women and Education." Unpublished Doctoral Dissertation, University of California–Santa Cruz.

Mead, M. (1957). Keynote Speech, National Meeting of the National Education Association.

Merriam, S. B., and Clark, M. C. (1991). *Lifelines: Patterns of Work, Love and Learning in Adulthood*. San Francisco: Jossey-Bass.

Mezirow, J. (1991). *Transformative Dimensions of Adult Learning*. San Francisco: Jossey-Bass.

Moraga, C. (1981). "La Guera." In C. Moraga and G. Anzaldua (eds.), *This Bridge Called My Back: Writings by Radical Women of Color*, 27–34. New York: Kitchen Table Press.

Noddings, N. (1995). *Philosophy of Education*. Boulder, CO: Westview Press.

Reid, P. T. (1993). "Women of Color Have No 'Place.' " *Focus: Newsletter of the Psychological Study of Ethnic Minority Issues, Division 45 of the American Psychological Association* 7, 1–2.

Rich, A. (1979). *On Lies, Secrets and Silence*. New York: W. W. Norton.

Roundtree, J., and Lambert, J. (1994). "Participation in Higher Education among Adult Women." *Community/Junior College Quarterly of Research and Practice* 16(1), 85–94.

Schon, D. D. (1987). *Educating the Reflective Practitioner*. San Francisco: Jossey-Bass.

Scott, K. Y. (1991). *The Habit of Surviving: Black Women's Strategies for Life*. New Brunswick, NJ: Rutgers University Press.

Sheared, V. (1994). "Giving Voice: An Inclusive Model of Instruction—A Womanist Perspective." In E. Hayes and S.A.J. Colin III (eds.), *Confronting Racism and Sexism*. San Francisco: Jossey-Bass.

Shoemaker, H. J. (1993). "A Psychological-Phenomenological Study of African American Women's Decisions to Enter Higher Education at Midlife." Unpublished Doctoral Dissertation, Saybrook Institute.

Walsh, M. R. (1987). *Women, Men and Gender: Ongoing Debates*. New Haven, CT: Yale University Press.

Chapter 4

Talking about Whiteness: "Adult Learning Principles" and the Invisible Norm

Sue Shore

> I am waiting for them to stop talking about the Other, to stop even describing how important it is to be able to speak about difference. . . . Often their speech about the Other is a mask, an oppressive talk hiding gaps, absences, that space where our words would be if we were speaking. Often this speech about the Other annihilates, erases: No need to hear your voice when we can talk about you better than you can speak about yourself. Only tell me about your pain. I want to know your story. And then I will tell it back to you in a new way. Tell it back to you in such a way that it has become mine, my own. Re-writing you, I write myself anew. I am still author, authority, I am still the coloniser, the speaking subject, and you are now at the centre of my talk, Stop.
>
> —bell hooks (1990), 151–152

INTRODUCTION

It is well-known that adult education programs operate in the teeth of a system for whom racism and sexism are primary, established, necessary props of profit (Audre Lorde, cited in Thompson 1983, 133).[1] In this chapter, rather than explicate the effects of this system on the *Other*, I examine how the notion of Whiteness[2] is central to, and embedded in, the discursive and material practices of this system. Yet talking *about* Whiteness is risky business, theoretically, politically, and practically. It runs the risk of reifying and privileging the (White) self at the very same time when social theorizing promotes understandings of identity as complex, historical, contingent, and located. It also runs the risk of maintaining a hold on that public space where other stories could be (hooks, 1990). However, I think explicit discussions of Whiteness are necessary to foreground the paradoxes of Whiteness described as everything and nothing, literally overwhelmingly present and yet apparently absent (Dyer 1997, 39; see also Morrison 1992). Moreover, these paradoxes are themselves situated and contingent; and who is named or names themselves White, for example is open to change over time.

Furthermore, the terms "Blackness" and "Whiteness," as used in Australia, are associated with histories and constructions somewhat different from those in other countries. Black in this context most often refers to a range of indigenous subject positions associated with Aboriginal and Torres Strait Islanders, and White to a range of White settler subjectivities (Meaghan Morris, cited in Ang 1995, 69), although some would prefer to call these White colonizer subjectivities. My use of the term "Whiteness," for example, is influenced by past experiences as a (White) educator in Aboriginal adult education in Australia, and my understandings of this subject position are profoundly shaped by the binaries set up within this particular context.[3] I maintain use of the terms "Black" and "White" here to foreground my concerns about the resounding silences around discussion of White racial formation (Omi and Winant 1994) in adult education literature in general.

In this chapter I show how recent writing within the fields of feminism and cultural studies detail the discursive strategies that enable Whiteness to be positioned unquestioningly as the invisible norm, a norm that *appears* to have no tangible effects on pedagogy. I maintain that these strategies are assisted by dominant discourses of liberal (adult) education and are central to the notion of adult learning principles. To demonstrate this, I explore three conceptual frames commonly deployed in adult education literature: debates about andragogy and pedagogy; the abstraction of the neutral facilitator; and the notion of target groups. The latter is a common policy and provision technology (Butler 1999) used in Australia to address the funding and pedagogic needs of disadvantaged groups, while generally remaining silent on the ongoing needs of those *advantaged* by skin color (but also by gender, sexual preference, physical mobility, geography, and financial security).

SELECTING A POINT OF "ARBITRARY CLOSURE"

> The category human has no meaning when spoken in White.
> Hinami Bannerji, cited in Smith (1987), 222

Over the last 15–20 years, theoretical developments in social theory have challenged the status of the sovereign subject, formed at birth and engaged in a process of maturation that culminates in the development of a rational, free-willed, agentic subject: the adult. Many of these developments attempt to destabilize the White (male) Western canon, which feminists and scholars of color (both problematic terms, I admit) have also critiqued for decades. Yet somewhat different questions and challenges have emerged from the literature of new social theory. Much of the writing from women of color, cultural studies, and postcolonial critics argues that, in the process of decentering the Western canon, imperialism, colonialism, and racism continue to be influential in distributing resources to the mythical norm (Lorde 1984, 116). Theory that attempts to destabilize the canon offers new possibilities for rethinking the subject in ways that move beyond the less elastic frames conjured up by conventional sociological analyses of identity. Yet, like many adult educators and other cultural critics with backgrounds steeped in concerns for social change, I am ambivalent about these conceptual and linguistic shifts. I recognize the capacity of new theoretical developments to bring complexity and richness to theorizing identity. On the other hand, many researchers and practitioners in adult education are unaware of the extent to which everyday practices are both saturated and situated by humanistic discourse (Usher 1993b, 17), or the degree to which notions of Whiteness are imbricated with/in humanistic discourses of adult learning principles.

In a contradictory move, I want to bring some arbitrary closure (Hall 1987) to the language of new social theory by talking explicitly about the effects of Whiteness on educational practice. Like Hall, I use this strategy to signal that while discourse is endless, "I need to say something, something just now." It is not forever, not totally universally true (Hall 1987, 45). But I need to talk, critically I hope, about this notion of Whiteness that seems so ever-present yet intangible in the dominant literature of adult education. Investigating Whiteness has helped me to see its effects on policy and pedagogy; effects that are difficult to see, precisely because of my location within White discourse(s).

WHITENESS: AN (ADULT) EDUCATION AGENDA

Despite the emergence of a significant body of literature interrogating identity, the study of Whiteness as an (adult) education agenda is minimal. It is more often framed in terms of dominance or the mainstream. There is very little work which balances the tensions between a macro perspective on white/Western hegemony [as] the systemic consequences of global historical development over the last 500 years (Ang 1995, 65) and the everyday pedagogic practices which emerge in adult education settings.

In the evolving field of studies of Whiteness there are concerns about this new intellectual fetish (Fine et al. 1997, xii), which may be yet another way to appropriate space for White interests. Nevertheless, current discourses of education are of little help to educators who want to disrupt what appear to be determining structural systems, yet fail to recognize the complicitous ways in which both liberal and oppositional discourses might reinscribe the White subject. With Frankenberg, I maintain that a more useful strategy in adult education is to assign *everyone* a place in the relations of racism (Frankenberg 1993, 6; emphasis in original).

However, there are also risks in a call to consider White people a race, just as the term "race" is problematic for people of color. Notions of race call forth discourses of biological essentialism; discourses that are not only unhelpful in theorizing pedagogy, but also downright dangerous in terms of their deployment around difference. Rather than be drawn into this risky territory, I have found Omi and Winant's use of the term "racial project" to be helpful in understanding racial formation as the sociohistorical process by which racial categories are created, inhabited, transformed, and destroyed (1994, 55). This process involves historically situated *projects* in which human bodies and social structures are represented and organized (p. 56; emphasis in original). Thus [a] *racial project is simultaneously an interpretation, representation, or explanation of racial dynamics and an effort to reorganise and redistribute resources along particular racial lines* (p. 56; emphasis in original). My task in this chapter is to understand the effects of White racial formation and the subsequent ways in which these effects are written *out* of adult education theorizing through a process of discursive deracialization (Rattansi 1992, 14); the systematic removal of detail about racial formation in explaining social phenomena.

LOOKING AT WHITENESS

Many researchers have begun to explore the concept of Whiteness as a lived social construction. Ruth Frankenberg (1993, 1) describes it as

a location of structural advantage, of race privilege, a standpoint, a place from which white people look at ourselves, at others, and at society, a set of cultural practices that are usually unmarked and unnamed.

For David Roediger (1994), examining Whiteness is one way of shifting the understanding that it is unmarked. An exploration of the terms and conditions of Whiteness foregrounds the reliance of the category White on a corresponding category Black, yet at the same time exposes the illusion of both as natural categories (Roediger 1994). Studying Whiteness foregrounds the questions of when, why, and with what results so-called White people have come to identify themselves as White (Roediger 1994, 75), or not, as well as revealing the material and moral conditions which have accompanied such positionings.

While many non-White people see and feel the effects of Whiteness as systematic and monolithic, there is an emerging body of work which suggests otherwise. Whiteness may be framed in a multitude of ways:

- as an individual characteristic, personalized and therefore not in need of examination at all;
- as evoking individual guilt and thus needing to be denied, confessed, and/or reconciled (Friedman 1995);
- as an unstable category in danger of imminent collapse (Dyer 1997);
- as a form of extreme behavior which in its most violent or unusual forms can be disavowed by ordinary White folk (Dyer 1997);

• as a terror (hooks 1990) or something to be feared; and

• as victimized, a view which reflects the resentment many middle- and working-class Whites feel in response to the changing economic and cultural circumstances evolving from greater perceived diversification of public life; hence Whiteness is seen as in need of *equal* treatment (Gallagher 1995).

This brief summary does not cover all of the literature falling under the guise of studies of Whiteness, nor is it aimed at formulating a grid on which to map a new shifting White identity. It is also not intended to diminish the monolithic effects of Whiteness foregrounded by some non-White scholars. Rather, it is aimed at providing a means by which White adult educators might refocus explorations of pedagogy in order to develop a language that enables critical engagement with understandings of Whiteness, rather than re-doubl[ing] its hegemony by naturalizing it (Fusco, cited in Gallagher 1995, 173).

In the preceding paragraphs on looking at Whiteness, many of the writers I have quoted are academics, and it could be argued, adult educators. Yet little of their work seems to find its way into the body of work cited by researchers and practitioners in adult education. Furthermore, the problem with many local strategies for responding to Whiteness within educational settings is precisely that they are located within social institutions of *education*. Educational strategies, therefore, are often incorporated into what Basil Bernstein calls pedagogic discourse: a discourse that places many constraints on everyday practice (Bernstein 1996).[4] For example, Bernstein suggests that

pedagogic discourse [is] a rule which embeds two discourses; a discourse of skills of various kinds and their relations to each other, and a discourse of social order. . . . Often people in schools and in classrooms make a distinction between what they call the transmission of skills and the transmission of values. These are always kept apart as if there were a conspiracy to disguise the fact that there is only one discourse. In my opinion there is only one discourse, not two, because the secret voice of this device is to disguise the fact that there is only one. (1996, 46)

In drawing on Bernstein's work here, I intend to show how practices within education settings are implicated in the process of discursive deracialization by generally refusing to foreground how constructions of Whiteness guide adult education provision.

Bernstein's work resonates with writers who are critical of liberal discourse. MacCannell (1992), for instance, proposes that liberal humanistic discourse provides a scaffold for the ideas and beliefs we are able to speak into existence. In relation to the interests of this chapter, such a discourse frames White engagement with the Other in quite specific terms, through grammar and rhetoric as well as in social and economic relations (MacCannell 1992, 122). This is illustrated by my contention that adult education theory has a number of strategies for naming the Other, but few apart from reference to the mainstream to deal with White practices. The power of this rhetoric presents challenges for thinking through[5] (Frankenberg 1993) the implications of Whiteness as a racial formation (Omi and Winant 1994, 55–56) and the effects of that formation on pedagogy.

I contend that what are claimed to be the intangible qualities of Whiteness within texts, and the elusive recontextualizing principles (Bernstein 1996, 47) of pedagogic discourse (which work in concert to render the interrogation of Whiteness problematic), are not unmanageable tasks for adult educators.

So, how do adult learning principles establish a conceptual terrain within pedagogic discourse to elide the influences of Whiteness on practice?

THREE CONCEPTUAL FRAMES WITHIN ADULT EDUCATION LITERATURE

In the preceding sections of this chapter, I provide a framework for rereading the literature in adult education and, at the same time, draw attention to practices of discursive deracialization (Rattansi 1992, 14), practices which normalize Whiteness and particularize Otherness. Specifically, these practices include debates about andragogy and pedagogy, the notion of the neutral facilitator, and the deployment of target groups as a means of securing deserved funding and appropriate pedagogic practice for minority groups (Chapters 13 and 14 in this book).

I want to spend some time on all three of these frames, looking at how the wider research literature on Whiteness might help to destabilize some of the canonic elements of adult learning principles.

DEBATES ABOUT ANDRAGOGY AND PEDAGOGY

In adult education much has been made of the distinctions between andragogy and pedagogy. Modern andragogical approaches are drawn predominantly from the work of Malcolm Knowles, and his work is frequently referred to where debate is framed around the adult/child binary. Rather than focusing on the adult/child debate, though, I draw attention here to the assumptions of liberal individualism built into the literature on *adult* learning principles and the degree to which this work continues to promote generic (White) understandings of the adult learner. For example, in the recent Australian Review of National Policy—Adult and Community Education (ACE), the principles used to guide that review were as follows:

- Adults learn most effectively when they are actively involved in decisions about management, content, style, and delivery of their learning.
- Adult learning is fostered through a curriculum and methodology which involves collaboration between teacher and learner.
- Adults are capable of learning throughout life.

• The individual learner is the focus of the learning process in ACE.

• Adult learning acknowledges the skills, knowledge, and experience adults bring to the learning setting. (Kelly Associates 1997, 20)

A similar set of adult learning principles appears in the *Teaching and Learning Facilitator's Guide* (TAFE NSDC 1992, sec. 2.1) a staff development package for novice adult and vocational educators.

An astute reader may well ask why I would begin with these populist frameworks when work of this kind has been challenged and found wanting by many good researchers.[6] I contend that these challenges seem to have had little effect on the way in which adult learning principles have been established as a taken-for-granted fact. In fact, they so resemble common sense that one would seem a malcontent to challenge them. The principles operate as a regime of truth, a connection between *power* and *knowledge* which is produced by, and produces, a specific *art of government* (Gore 1993, 55; emphasis in original). This results in claims for a universal form of adult education practice as well as the development of technologies to prescribe conduct in learning settings (Foucault 1988). Examples of these technologies include self-directed learning, neutral facilitation, negotiated curriculum, the importance of *relevant* content, and so on (also see Chapter 21 in this volume).

In elaborating on Knowles' work on self-directed learning, for example, Burstow 1994, 6–7) indicates the clear preferences embedded in the model:

independence over both dependence and interdependence; isolation over relation; the individual over society; the explicit over the implicit; the straight forward and highly directional over the tentative, the groping toward, and the divergent; the cognitive over the emotional; the objective over the subjective or intersubjective; and the logical, scientific, and highly measurable over the artistic and non-numeric.

To quote Donna Haraway (1991), there are no "subjugated standpoints" here. The "god-trick promising vision from everywhere and nowhere equally and fully" (p. 191) is breathtakingly apparent in this model of "adult learning," yet nowhere is this vision explicitly informed by the notion that knowledge is always partial, never finalized. Contrary to the central tenets of dominant adult learning literature, the application of experiential learning techniques along with the exhortation to walk in the Other's shoes[7] will not result in pure, unmediated access to the knowledge and experience of the racialized (gendered, sexualized) body. There may in the end be some things we will never know.[8] What particularizes the White body, yet is ignored in analyses of adult learning principles, is what Dyer (1997, 23) calls spirit: get-up-and-go, aspiration, awareness of the highest reaches of intellectual comprehension and aesthetic refinement. The ethos of an adult education for all means that the specificity of the White body within andragogy, the body who can know, is obscured, and the prospect of *not knowing* is rendered immaterial.

EQUAL PARTNERS IN LEARNING: THE MYTH OF NEUTRAL FACILITATION

A second frame, which elides the power of Whiteness in shaping pedagogy, is the deferral to a methodology of neutral facilitation. Whether based on Knowles' early claims for andragogy or revisited through more recent versions of adult learning principles, neutral facilitation valorizes the individual learner's experiences and assumes that stories of experience will reveal the truth about learners' lives. (See Usher 1993a for a more problematic reading of experience.)

Furthermore, many educators have talked about the challenge of connecting individual experience with wider issues of systemic power and privilege, yet many also recognize the limits of these practices when the mechanism by which they are facilitated is within a liberal discourse. A key element of feminist and radical adult education practice is the sharing of stories, yet this sharing process is problematic when differences are negotiated through the maze of practices which make up pedagogic discourse in learning settings. Often (White) educators look to the Other to be educated about the experience of being disadvantaged. Yet many writers (see, for example, Razack 1993; Camper 1994; Friedman 1995) have suggested that these stories are not heard. Underlying themes of the Other's oppression and struggle are lost in White needs to reframe narratives of colonialism as stories of helping, followed by personal confusion when confronted with a past we were not taught. These writers suggest that telling stories of difference results in limited changes to individual or systemic practice.

The confessional and self-regulating nature of these storytelling activities (Foucault 1978), in the context of a group which may not share Omi and Winant's historical and more expansionary views of racial formation, is papered over by the assumption of common educational goals. Such learning settings assume it is possible to leave the effects of racial formation in the corridor, beyond the classroom walls. Thus, we can forget for a moment that we are White while never forgetting that Others are not.

So, facilitation only feels neutral for those who can comfortably comply with the rules of small group and more formal learning settings espoused by adult learning principles. These rules include the requirement to confess to total strangers and to engage in critical thinking while at the same time suppressing emotion, contradictions, and moments of incommensurability. In such settings the power of Whiteness to shape issues such as authority, expertise, competence, power-knowledge, and what counts as real experience are central to the myth of neutral facilitation.

TARGET GROUPS

A third frame within the literature and practice of adult education, especially in Australia, is that of target groups traditionally conceived as minorities, or individuals, disenfranchised by historical and systemic conditions of oppression and exclusion. More often than not this exclusion is framed in terms of individual differences and deficits on the part of the Other, rather than the version I forward here, which suggests there is much complicity from within educational systems.

Nevertheless, the concept of target groups is a core tenet of Australian educational policy. It rests on the assumption of a stable center and a struggling margin that aspires to the lifestyle and values of that center. The current Australian Adult Community Education (ACE) policy identifies the following categories of adults who are underrepresented in employment and training and in need of more adequate and responsive provision to meet their needs as:

- people from geographically isolated communities;
- people from culturally and linguistically diverse backgrounds;
- Aboriginal and Torres Strait Islander people;
- people with a disability;
- older people;
- unemployed and people with low incomes;
- women and men with low levels of schooling;
- people with low literacy levels;
- young people. (MCEETYA 1997, 15)

The discourse of special needs that existed in an earlier version of the *National Policy* (MCEETYA 1993; see also Shore 1997 for a critique of this policy) has been reframed in this more recent document to reflect a more responsive approach to learners. However, the implicit message within this new policy still operates to represent ACE as a home for those people excluded from Lorde's mythical norm (1984, 116). Those people represented by the target groups are invited to participate in ACE programs precisely because of their difference from the norm, their Other status.

These categorizations reflect Australian educational concerns for equity and inclusivity, yet there are two problems with this. First, as Joan Scott (1992) notes, categorizations still leave in place a unified concept of identity (pp. 13–14), a stable unified subject, beneath the categorization Aboriginal, woman, and so on. This inevitably limits the ways in which complex theorizations of identity might evolve from such frames. Second, it blurs the specificity of the center that defines these categorizations *and* at the same time relies on them for its existence.

The offer to participate, particularly in forms of community education, is tied up with tolerance and differential treatment accorded to the Other. The move to include the Other is simultaneously a move to include and dissolve their difference; it ignores its assimilationist effects, elides Whiteness, and at the same time seeks harmony in the move. It is this desire for harmony that at times confounds strategies to think through issues of difference, and represses the possibilities for pedagogy that might emerge when we conceptualize Whiteness as a racial formation. People such as Russell Ferguson (1990) have been working through these tensions for many years. He claims that men cannot dissociate themselves from women's issues, straight people cannot ignore the struggles of gay and lesbian people, and White people cannot declare themselves indifferent to racial politics. It is too easy for sympathetic self-effacement to become just another trick for quiet dominance (p. 13).

I believe that examples of sympathetic self-effacement in adult education often go unnoticed for two reasons. First, as Usher (1993b, 21) notes, adult education has for too long been oppressed itself to be overly concerned about the possibility of oppressing others.

ACE work in Australia is often undervalued and underpaid. Many educators in this field have had to fight to claim a legitimate space for their work as well as adequate funding for the learning groups they facilitate. One effect of this is that educators themselves may pay less attention to the ways in which adult education practices constitute oppressive regimes for participants.

Second, much of the dominant literature in adult education operates from a stance which desires to make the Other visible. Yet this often involves legitimating from the center a space in which the Other can speak, where the Other gets to operate or be visible, only because of the largesse of the center. Listen to Mary Ann Bin-Sallik, who experiences this often:

We are getting weary of being asked to give our opinions and participating in decision making processes only to find that our opinions and participations have been what Freire regards as false generosity. I find it harrowing when educators seek my time and ask my opinions and then find all the excuses as to why my suggestions won't work, or that the bureaucracy makes it difficult to implement change. I feel that I have been used to either help these people: a) to become neurotic teachers; or b) to feel comfortable with their neurosis; and even worse, I have been colluding with them. So I shall have to stop. (Bin-Sallik 1992, 14)

One challenge facing White educators is how to move our thinking beyond these positions because so much educational provision promotes the use of target groups and, wittingly or otherwise, consigns the responsibility for pedagogy, advocacy and social action to these Other streams. The Other, as learner, has the option to take up classes within these streams. White educators within the mainstream may have no requirement to engage with pedagogies which confront our own racial formation because, to use Rattansi's words there is no problem (i.e., blacks) here (Rattansi 1992, 12).

Thus, the concept of target groups is fraught with conceptual dangers (Butler 1999) and pedagogical problems. I am not suggesting ACE policy should deny support for target groups or withdraw equity measures underpinned by understandings of target groups. Nevertheless, White educators may need to be cognizant of how this streaming displaces a responsibility to think through our own racial formation.

(RE)INTRODUCTION: MAKING CHOICES

I want to suggest that (White) racial formation of the kind elaborated by Omi and Winant (1994) needs to be foregrounded in adult education because it matters as much to the mainstream as it does to educators working in targeted streams. Much of the literature investigating Whiteness acknowledges the hegemonic conflation of being White/Whiteness with oppressive practices. It seeks to acknowledge this hegemony and at the same time move beyond reified categories of identity. Yet this particular quality, the oppressiveness of Whiteness, must not be ignored in the potential rush to render Whiteness more tangible. Like McIntosh (1988, 4), I have found that my schooling gave me no training in seeing myself as an oppressor. I was taught to see myself as an individual whose moral state depended on her individual moral will. I suggest that those of us who might make a connection with the term "White adult educator" need to become answerable for what our schooling has taught us to see (Haraway 1991), or not see.

For White educators this involves an explicit choice, and Aileen Moreton-Robinson, an Indigenous Australian woman, believes we should not ignore this. She posits,

For Indigenous people, whiteness is visible and imbued with power; it confers dominance and privilege. White race privilege means white people have more lifestyle choices available to them because they are the mainstream. Belonging to the mainstream means white people can choose whether or not they wish to bother themselves with the opinions or concerns of Indigenous people. (1998, 39–40)

I am not convinced that all White people have access to the better lifestyle implicitly suggested by Moreton-Robinson. Nevertheless, it is time for many of us to make this choice, to bother ourselves with the opinions and concerns of the Other in ways that do change our practice. If we take Bin-Sallik, hooks, Moreton-Robinson, and Razack seriously, then we have to do the hard work to understand what a productive exploration of Whiteness might be for ourselves as much as for Others.

I recognize that some White adult educators, particularly feminists, do work with the tensions inherent in the challenges posed by Razack (1993), while others work at listening to the voices of Others. It is not my intention to render this work invisible. I also acknowledge that this work often constitutes a difficult, at times painful process of self-reflexivity. What I have also found, though, is that this (White) pain often erases the effects of the stories of Others. I don't subscribe to the notion of hierarchies of pain. I do think, though, that adult education theorizing would be more productive if it paid some explicit attention to how Whiteness is theorized within.

This work may in fact be done in collaboration with our colleagues and friends of color, but seeking approval for our learning is problematic. Furthermore, we cannot rely on them to smooth the passage and absorb the discomfort emerging from this process. Historically, the Other has been doing this for centuries, and despite the best of intentions, I believe many of the practices of adult education are designed to ensure that this dependency relationship continues.

NOTES

1. Adult education here refers to the adult and community education activities that occur in many neighborhood centers and TAFE colleges in Australia. These activities generally come under the umbrella of lifelong learning programs that are "learner centred, responsive to community needs, accessible and inclusive, diverse, varied and flexible" (MCEETYA 1997). They are often distinguished from programs offering a vocational or tertiary curriculum to adult learners. Although I believe the framework I offer here has relevance across all of these learning settings, I am referencing my work specifically to the adult community education field, which makes explicit claims for empowerment of its learners.

2. Despite the problematic nature of the strategy, I capitalize Whiteness (except where I have drawn on quotations) as a means of drawing attention to the socially constructed nature of the term.

3. Australia is also a highly industrialized country, albeit with pockets of "third" and "fourth" world conditions of existence. Located in the South, it nevertheless exhibits characteristics of the North and is further evidence of the paradoxes and limitations involved in the use of such terms.

4. Bernstein's use of codes and pedagogic/regulative/instructional discourse may be read as somewhat deterministic. However, I believe his work provides a framework for understanding cultural work *within* educational institutions, and this point is at the heart of my concerns as to how the new scholarship on Whiteness (particularly that emanating from literary theory and film studies) might be deployed by adult educators.

5. Ruth Frankenberg identifies three aspects of "thinking through race" in her work on White women's understandings of their racial locations: "first and most literally, it suggests a conscious process; second, it occurs within an always already-formed field of understandings of race, and third, it accepts that all bodies are "racially positioned in society" (1993, 142). My thanks to Vicki Crowley for reminding me that Frankenberg did not intend to reinforce old binaries between thought and feeling in drawing on the term "thinking" through race.

6. See, for example, Hall (1993); Rockhill (1996); Tisdell (1995); Stalker (1996); Lee, Scheeres, and Shore (1996).

7. This is a favorite metaphor used in adult education training programs to promote understanding of the issues and dilemmas confronting Others.

8. Aileen Moreton-Robinson guided my thinking here, prompting me to connect discourses of Western science, assumptions about the capacity to "know" embedded in adult education pedagogies, and alternative approaches to knowing.

REFERENCES

Ang, I. (1995). "I'm a Feminist but . . . : 'Other' Women and Postnational Feminism." In B. Caine and R. Pringle (eds.), *Transitions: New Australian Feminisms*, 57–73. St. Leonard's, Australia: Allen & Unwin.

Bernstein, B. (1996). *Pedagogy, Symbolic Control and Identity: Theory, Research, Critique*. London: Taylor & Francis.

Bin-Sallik, M. (1992). "Liberating the Curriculum: A Dialogue with Plato." In J. Perry, S. Burley, and J. Mulraney (eds.), *Liberating the Curriculum: A Report of the Australian Curriculum Studies Association Curriculum 91 Conference*, Adelaide, July 1991. Belconnen: Australian Curriculum Studies Association.

Burstow, B. (1994). "Problematizing Adult Education: A Feminist Perspective." *Canadian Journal for the Study of Adult Education* 8(1), 1–14.

Butler, E. (1999). "Technologising Equity: The Politics and Practices of Workplace Learning." In D. Boud and J. Garrick (eds.), *Understanding Learning at Work*, 132–150. London: Routledge.

Camper, C. (1994). "To White Feminists." *Canadian Women's Studies* 14(2), 40.

Dyer, R. (1997). *White*. London and New York: Routledge.

Ferguson, R. (1990). "Introduction: Invisible Center." In R. Ferguson et al. (eds.), *Out There: Marginalisation and Contemporary Culture*, 9–14. Cambridge, MA: MIT Press.

Fine, M. et al. (1997). *Off White: Readings on Race, Power and Society*. London and New York: Routledge.

Foucault, M. (1978). *The History of Sexuality: Volume 1. An Introduction* (R. Hurley, trans.). Harmondsworth: Penguin Books.

Foucault, M. (1988). *Technologies of the Self: A Seminar with Michel Foucault* (L. H. Martin, H. Gutman, and P. H. Hutton, eds.). Amherst: University of Massachusetts Press.

Frankenberg, R. (1993). *The Social Construction of Whiteness: White Women, Race Matters*. London and New York: Routledge.

Friedman, S. S. (1995). "Beyond White and Other: Relationality and Narratives of Race in Feminist Discourse." *Signs: Journal of Women in Culture and Society* 21(1) 1–49.

Gallagher, C. A. (1995). "White Reconstruction in the University." *Socialist Review* 24 (1/2), 165–187.

Gore, J. (1993). *The Struggle for Pedagogies*. London and New York: Routledge.

Hall, B. (1993). "Re: Centering Adult Education Research: Whose World Is First?" *Studies in Continuing Education* 15(2), 149–161.

Hall, S. (1987). "Minimal Selves." In L. Appignanesi (ed.), *Identity Documents 6*, 44–46. London, Institute of Contemporary Arts.

Haraway, D. (1991). *Simians, Cyborgs and Women: The Reinvention of Nature*. London: Free Association Books.

hooks, b. (1990). *Yearning. Race, Gender, and Cultural Politics*. Boston: South End Press.

Kelly Associates. (1997). *ACE 2000: Towards a Learning Society*. Melbourne, Australia: Strategic Solutions.

Lee, A., Scheeres, H., and Shore, S. (eds.). (1996). Special Issue: "Feminist Perspectives on Continuing Education." *Studies in Continuing Education* 18, 2.

Lorde, A. (1984). *Sister Outsider*. Trumansburg, NY: The Crossing Press.

MacCannell, D. (1992). *Empty Meeting Grounds: The Tourist Papers*. London and New York: Routledge.

McIntosh, P. (1988). "White Privilege and Male Privilege: A Personal Account of Coming to See Correspondences through Work in Women's Studies." Working Paper No. 189. Wellesley, MA: Wellesley College Centre for Research on Women.

Ministerial Council for Employment Education Training and Youth Affairs (MCEETYA). (1993). *National Policy. Adult Community Education*. Carlton, Victoria: MCEETYA.

Ministerial Council for Employment Education Training and Youth Affairs (MCEETYA). (1997). *National Policy. Adult Community Education*. New South Wales, Australia: NSW Department of Training and Education Coordination.

Moreton-Robinson, A. (1998). "White Race Privilege: Nullifying Native Title." In *Bringing Australia Together: The Structure and Experience of Racism in Australia*, 39–44. Woolloongabba, Australia: Foundation for Aboriginal and Islander Research Action.

Morrison, T. (1992). *Playing in the Dark: Whiteness and the Literary Imagination*. Cambridge, MA: Harvard University Press.

Omi, M., and Winant, H. (1994). *Racial Formation in the United States: From the 1960s to the 1990s*, 2nd ed. New York: Routledge.

Rattansi, A. (1992). "Changing the Subject? Racism, Culture and Education." In J. Donald and A. Rattansi (eds.), *"Race," Culture and Difference*, 11–48. London: Sage.

Razack, S. (1993). "Story-telling for Social Change." *Gender and Education* 5(1), 55–70.

Rockhill, K. (1996). "Challenging the Exclusionary Effects of the Inclusive Mask of Adult Education." *Studies in Continuing Education* 18(2), 182–194.

Roediger, D. R. (1994). *Towards the Abolition of Whiteness. Essays on Race, Politics, and Working Class History*. London and New York: Verso.

Scott, J. W. (1992). "Multiculturalism and the Politics of Identity." *October* 61 (Summer), 12–19.

Shore, S. (1997). "Women in Australian Community Education: Challenges to Policy and Questions for Academic Practice." *Convergence* 30(1), 24–33.

Smith, D. (1987). *The Everyday World as Problematic: A Feminist Sociology*. Boston: Northeastern University Press.

Stalker, J. (1996). "Women and Adult Education: Rethinking Androcentric Research." *Adult Education Quarterly* 46(2) (Winter), 98–113.

TAFE National Staff Development Committee (NSDC). (1992). *Teaching and Learning. Facilitator's Guide*. Canberra, Australia: Department of Employment Education and Training.

Thompson, J. (1983). *Learning Liberation: Women's Responses to Men's Education*. London: Croom Helm.

Tisdell, E. (1995). *Creating Inclusive Adult Learning Environments: Insights from Multicultural Education and Feminist Pedagogy*. Columbus, OH: ERIC Clearinghouse on Adult, Career, and Vocational Education.

Usher, R. (1993a). "Experiential Learning or Learning from Experience: Does It Make a Difference?" In D. Boud, R. Cohen, and D. Walker (eds.), *Using Experience for Learning*, 170–180. Buckingham, SHRE: Open University Press.

Usher, R. (1993b). "Re-examining the Place of the Disciplines in Adult Education." *Studies in Continuing Education* 15(1), 15–25.

Chapter 5

An Invisible Presence, Silenced Voices: African Americans in the Adult Education Professoriate

Sherwood E. Smith and Scipio A. J. Colin III

The purpose of this chapter is to "give voice" to eight African-American/ African-Ameripean[1] members of the Adult Education Professoriate who shared their experiences regarding the impact of racism on their professional lives (Smith 1996). We believe that in giving voice to their experiences we can begin to create a dialogue, a discourse about the ways in which African-American/ African-Ameripean lives are interwined and interconnected, as well as share how these voices have influenced the field of education. Moreover, we hope that through this discourse we can begin to change the ways in which we operate in higher education as well as society. Their stories, like those discussed by Brown (Chapter 15), highlight the ways in which African-American/African-Ameripean educators have had to operate in order to create space and change, not only in education, but in American society.

It is important to note that we view racism as an ideology of racial superiority and inferiority, based on pigmentation, that was created by Euro-Americans and is perpetuated by them for their sociocultural benefit: social, educational, political and economic (Colin and Preciphs 1991; Fiquero 1991; Hacker 1992; Welsing-Cress, 1972). As such, we believe that every aspect of the lives of African Americans/African Ameripeans has and continues to be impacted by racist attitudes, ideology, and practices.

The following will not be a discussion regarding the existence of racism, for, based upon our experiences, previous research, and the experiences of the research participants, the question of its existence is a moot point. Therefore, we have decided not to become entangled in the senseless debate that is often reflected in Euro-American responses of: "Prove it," "Aren't you just over-reacting?" and "We are tired of hearing about it." As Barbara Smith (1982) has stated: "for those of you who are tired of hearing about racism, imagine how much more tired we are of constantly experiencing it, second by literal second, how much more exhausted we are to see it constantly in your eyes. . . . I want to say right here that this is not a 'guilt trip.' It's a fact trip. The assessment of what's actually going on." (p. 48)

The fact is that African Americans/African Ameripeans are constantly confronted by an ideology of racial superiority and inferiority. Furthermore, the lived reality of these individuals is that racism influences the entire context of their lives. Heretofore, previous research has often portrayed these individuals as "helpless" victims of the higher education structure, rather than as members of a racial group who—though victimized by racism and confronted with attitudes and behaviors that continuously challenge their knowledge and skills—have been able to survive and function as a result of using their culturally grounded coping mechanisms[2] (Colin 1999). Hopefully, the sharing of these educators' voices will better inform the field as to what some of the salient issues are regarding racism and its impact on education and society. As Hayes and Colin (1994) suggest, "adult educators may first need to recognize the biases in their own practice. . . . Many adult educators remain unaware of the racism (and sexism) reflected in their individual actions, educational curricula, and teaching strategies as well as in the practices of their organizations" (p. 15). While this chapter hopes to highlight these issues, it does not purport that others are not sensitive to these issues, for some are. It does, however, hope to suggest that the presence of African-American/African-Ameripean educators, their stories, and their histories in the literature as well as in higher education are needed if we want to make visible the invisible, and give voice to the silenced.

CULTURALLY GROUNDED COPING MECHANISMS

Through the lives of the eight African-American/African-Ameripean educators highlighted here, we hope to illustrate the mechanisms in their professional and personal lives that helped them cope with racism—coping mechanisms that are grounded in an Africentric belief and value system. ("Africentric" is a term used to articulate the centrality of those individuals whose ancestors come from Africa, and whose experiences are uniquely contextualized by their culture and history.) Their comments reflect an Africentric perspective which combines "finding strength in the spirit" and relying on a network of family, which was articulated as "by blood or by bond," and friends outside their academic communities. Colin (1999) refers to these strategies as "Culturally Grounded Coping Mechanisms." She uses this term to describe the ways in which African-American values, spiritual and philosophical beliefs, are employed to help them understand their sociocultural history and positions within American society.

Being true to one's self and one's God was a common theme among these educators. This connection between culture, history, and spirituality—this Africentric way of knowing was and is a source of both empowerment and frustration. To be an educator without this is to lose sight of one's self in relationship to one's community. In other words, an education devoid of this understanding will lead to the perpetuation of the status quo in the classroom as well as in society. The question one must ask then is: how can we make space in the classroom or in society for all, if any one of us, teachers included—is left out? One educator spoke about the importance of being true to one's "self," and what it means to be "Black" in relation to the academy and the community:

Excuse me but if I lose sight of my roots, then I lose sight of who I am as a Black person. Then kick me in my butt. Because higher education is not worth it if that's what is going to happen to me. Make me go home, because I've lost all my senses. So you've got to make sure you keep that sense of yourself. Because it's all too easy to get caught up and wrapped-up into this world, which is just a sort of a mirage to some extent. . . . And they would just as soon see you fall on your face in some instances than see you succeed. So you have got to maintain that balance with who you are, especially, I think as African Americans, you have to make sure you're grounded. Every class I teach we're talking about race, class and gender issues. And there are [students] looking at me strange, asking why do we have to talk about it here? Because I'M BLACK."

These comments reflect the culturally grounded values and beliefs of these educators regarding the importance of maintaining connectedness to their families and communities. They also tell the story about how they made sense of the "self" (Collins 1991; hooks 1994) and maintained that sense of "self"— their African-ness in a Euro-American-dominated academy and society. Most significantly, these individuals expressed the difficulties they encountered in maintaining their racial identity. For some, it was indeed their Africentric values, their sense of community, and their ability to negotiate that enabled them to participate within both the academy and their communities. An understanding of their dual roles was necessary to their survival, both in the academy and in their communities. As one educator voiced, "Interactions that I have with colleagues that are across the country are real important . . . [There are other] interactions I maintain with my family for sanity. And they help me stay grounded, and understand what the real deal is."

For some, the ability to remain a part of their community is seen as being in conflict with those of the general academic culture. They are often confronted with the reality that their knowledge, their history, and their culture are often ignored or negated in both the classroom and society. Moreover, the articulation of Africentric ideas and concepts is interpreted by some of their Euro-American counterparts as a personal attack. One faculty member articulated it thus: "it was as if I had talked about their Mamas." In reference to this, another educator recounted this story:

I asked the question in one of my Sociology classes why we're not studying the words of Du Bois . . . and the professors took that personally. But you see, that exclusion was a confrontation to my reality! I was trained and conditioned not to just look at what was there, but what was not there. So I had a sense of what should have been there.

THE INVISIBLE: AFFECTIVE AND COGNITIVE ISOLATION

The voices of these African-American/African-Ameripean educators also reflected the ways in which they were confronted by personal and institutional forms of racism. This led to what we refer to as a two-dimensional nature of isolation. Colin (1999) goes on to say that this is a form of what she considers "affective isolation and cognitive isolation" (p. 1). Affective isolation speaks in part to the impact of "being the only one" or "being the first," whereas cognitive isolation is expressed as being isolated from "like-minded people." This occurs most frequently when one engages in research that focuses on Africentric or race-specific issues. Some of these educators expressed this as isolation from others with whom they shared cultural values, spiritual beliefs, and had similar philosophical grounding. One, for instance, stated:

I've got this very broad group of people I am forced to interact with, because of the nature of my profession, who may hate me and disrespect me because of my race or group membership. And then the other group with all its element, that is more positive. So it's the former group that's the least important. Any group or individual that attempts to diminish me, . . . my family [or] my race is least important to me.

Being the only one was also characterized by one of these educators as being the "token bottleneck," whereby one's presence resulted in a departmental and institutional attitude of closure regarding the further recruitment of African-American/African-Ameripean faculty. It was further stated that "if you fill one (position) with another Black person then people will wonder, 'What's going on with this race stuff?' "

These attitudes raise an important issue in that there is no equivalent limitation regarding Euro-American faculty. Rarely, and for significantly different reasons, is it stated that "we have all the white faculty we need." These faculty members are often confronted with the realization that their presence is supposed to resolve the issue of "diversity" and that their departments or institutions have met the minimum hiring requirement of African Americans/African Ameripeans. Thus, they can now avoid being labeled a racist institution. As this educator mused:

I think part of that has to do with the fact of being the only Black. I think that's probably the case around the country. . . . People do count the number of faces that are of color on different committees. Well I'll give you a case right now: We have for the first time ever a minority person as dean. . . . One of the first appointments was a Black to head a program. Now they are advertising for a position for Associate Dean for continuing education outreach. Say, for example, if I wanted to go for that position, I would feel like you have two people in very powerful positions in the office already . . . I feel hindered that way. I think people count the numbers of African-Americans when they're looking at diversity.

As these African-American/African-Ameripean faculty discovered, their presence and the color of their skin can often determine their roles in the academy, as well as in society. For example, their willingness or nonwillingness to serve on certain committees can often negatively impact their promotion and tenure within the academy. To reject a committee assignment can be potentially damaging. When one is the "in-house colored authority," it can be both overly time-consuming and equally injurious to one's career. One educator described the problem thus:

Committees were an abuse of my time and my presence. On the other hand, I recognized what the value is behind having diversity representation. It was always kind of a conflict. Do I say "no," if I know that the only reason I'm there is my race? But it was an abuse of my personal time. On the other hand, if there are no African American faculty on the committee, I'm going to be as likely as anyone else to respond that no one made an effort to include representation from diverse groups on this committee. So I sit on the committee because I feel that somebody needs to do it. I go because I am supposed to be a representative.

More times than not, when a faculty member gives voice concerning "minority" issues, specifically those concerns regarding racism, departmental colleagues tend to become uncomfortable. Moses (1989) and Harvey (1993) have both concluded that Euro-American administrators tend to be irritated when we African-American/African-Ameripean faculty point out racist policies or practices. Harvey (1998) states:

On this subject, it matters not whether the discussion is general or specific, not if the academicians involved are presidents, deans, faculty members or students, the reaction is the same, and the automatic response to the stimulus of the claim is denial. When examples of racism are cited to document the charge, occasionally a smidgen or two of the reality may get through, but for the most part many faculty display a "herd mentality" that is widely discussed in the organizational and psychological literature.

RESEARCH AND COGNITIVE ISOLATION

There exists a conceptual void in the knowledge base about the field regarding the inclusion of the sociocultural and intellectual histories of African Americans/ African Ameripeans and the validity of the Africentric Paradigm as both an analytical frame and research methodology. Only recently have the voices of African-American/African-Ameripean researchers been "heard." The edited works of Neufeldt and McGee (1990) and Peterson (1996), the contributions of Colin (1988, 1994, 1994b, 1996, 1999), Easter (1995, 1996), Guy (1993, 1996),

Guy and Colin (1998), Sheared (1992, 1994), Johnson-Bailey (1994, 1999), and Johnson-Bailey and Cervero (1996) are examples of the significant contributions African-American/African-Ameripean researchers have made to the historical and theoretical literature in the adult education field.

The recent scholarship that has emerged out of the Africentric Paradigm clearly challenges the universality of Eurocentric research designs and concepts regarding the construction of knowledge and the purposes of research. The Colin-Guy Interpretive Model of Africentric Curriculum Orientations (1998) is designed to facilitate the de-centering of Eurocentric curricula by providing "a historically-grounded normative basis for refocusing curriculum from an Africentric perspective . . . this model (is) a means of selecting, discussing, and critiquing African Ameripean/African American content" (Colin and Guy 1998, 50–51). And Sheared's (1994) research reconceptualizes the interconnectedness of race and gender within the Africentric Paradigm, providing an alternative, culturally grounded, womanist perspective regarding learning needs and styles.

In various ways, the agendas of all these researchers focused on African-American/African-Ameripean issues and concerns as they centered around race, gender, class, and multicultural issues. It may be true that the voices of these researchers have been "heard," but given their experiences of the interviewees, it appears that the field is not "listening."

Most of these faculty members continue to express a sense of cognitive isolation in terms of getting support for their research agendas. As one faculty member stated: "my research area is particularly focusing on Blacks. White faculty know it and yet there is very little interest in what I am doing." This researcher went on to describe the risks one takes and how it affects one's position in the academy as well as one's discipline:

When I say risk, I mean anytime you're dealing with race, class, and gender, the whole multicultural debate, and there's a generation of older faculty and administrators who occupy positions of influence and authority who resist that critique that says what's been happening in their discipline has been arbitrarily exclusionary of people of color, of women and so forth. And because they are in positions of power, they can make decisions that can affect the people—junior faculty in particular—who are making those kinds of critiques. Any of us who are involved in the university and say that within our own field, class, race or gender, or any of the other issues related to cultural diversity—any of us who make those kinds of critiques and develop research programs based upon a view that those kinds of differences make a difference in the field—can be subject to recrimination, or can be adversely impacted by decisions, by those faculty who are in place to say *"we don't agree with you."*

As a result, many African-American/African-Ameripean researchers do not have as many outlets to discuss their research interests or paradigms. Discussions that would lead to one being able to sharpen one's skills or stimulate one's thoughts are very limited. The lack of interest by Euro-American colleagues and the inability to explore their thoughts with other African-American/African-

Ameripean scholars is further exacerbated when their work is not included in journals or publications. Some critiques have labeled this work as limiting and lacking focus because of its emphasis on the African diasporic experience. Reflecting on the general disinterest by Euro-American colleagues, one researcher said:

Well, let's say for example coming into a place and being new: it's almost taken for granted that you already know what to do. . . . You're left out on a limb with no one to really guide you or help you get your things published where they need to be published. And usually their comment is, "Well, you're going to have to change your focus if you want to get your work done," rather than encourage you to do what you need to do.

Despite the risk of further exclusion and the lack of support for the research being conducted by these researchers, they still persist in conducting research about their lived experiences. They continue to seek out ways to conduct their research studies within an Africentric perspective. In spite of the risk they take, there is an intrinsic reward as they apply this paradigm to their problems and issues affecting the African diaspora. The ability to draw upon one's culturally grounded coping mechanisms has given them a sense of purpose which reinforces their resolve to do their research in spite of the inherent risks. One faculty member stated it this way:

The rewards I guess for me would be that I stick to what I believe in my research areas. I'm not going to sell myself short to do something I am not really interested in. And if my work can be accepted at that point then that is a very strong piece for me. I know, sometimes we have to do some compromising, but I think if you look at what's out there. . . . That we Black faculty in adult education may have to take a chance and just go out on the limb and stick to what we believe.

However, the frustration resulting from cognitive isolation for faculty members can be overwhelming. When asked about the hindrances they faced in the university, one faculty member emphatically stated: "I would not ask someone else to join me at my present institution, HELL." It was clear that for some, even though they would like to have other African-Ameripean scholars join them, they did not want anyone else to experience the same racist attitudes that they have. For others, they saw themselves as looking out for those who would come after them, so they saw themselves as making space for others. It was their duty.

INCLUSION: CHANGING PEDAGOGY AND PARADIGM

Quite often the faculty and students assume that when African-American/African-Ameripean faculty members choose to position themselves within an Africentric Paradigm, they neither know nor understand the Eurocentric body of knowledge that undergirds their discipline. They, then, are seen as being intellectually limited. This myopic view ignores the fact that these scholars, not unlike their Euro-American colleagues, are required to "know, understand, and articulate" Eurocentric concepts, philosophies, and theories in order to obtain their doctorates, long before they are ever encouraged to espouse Africentric concepts, philosophies, or theories.

Several of these faculty members talked about their experiences with their students, as well as colleagues, who directly challenged their knowledge and skills and questioned the validity of their membership in the professoriate. One faculty member said: "It's this interesting kind of interplay that you find yourself in as an African-American/African Ameripean walking into a classroom that is predominantly White. And you know, they're not expecting you, or it's interesting if you're sitting in an office and the person turns to you and thinks you're the secretary."

Colin (1999) describes this as an "Academic Catch 22"; a paradox grounded in racism that results in some students thinking that African-American/African-Ameripean faculty members are only knowledgeable about "race issues." The result of this view is that some students have consciously or unconsciously come to believe that only analyses and interpretations of Euro-American faculty members are acceptable. Confronted with such beliefs, African-American/African-Ameripean faculty members have concluded that their Euro-American colleagues knowingly or unknowingly promote racist perceptions and beliefs to students. These perceptions and beliefs then perpetuate the myth that their African-American/African-Ameripean "colleagues" are intellectually limited and that Euro-Americans probably know "more about you and yours than you can know about yourself." Thus, the disacknowledgment or debasement of an Africentric Paradigm serves as a form of "public invalidation" which is rooted in an ideology of racial superiority and inferiority by both students and colleagues.

Colin (1999) suggests that even though African Ameripeans are perceived by their colleagues and students as being "monoparadigm," they are not. In fact, she concludes that, as a result of African Ameripeans having to know and interpret what is perceived as being the universal knowledge as well as that which has been labeled as other ways of knowing, they are in fact "biparadigm."

In spite of these challenges, perceptions, and frustrations, teaching and student interactions are still viewed by these African-American/African-Ameripean educators as being one of the most rewarding aspects of their jobs. These individuals see themselves as being mentors and facilitators of learning both in and outside of the classroom. They continue to give time and energy to all their students. They attempt to gain a connection to and with their students—building bridges between the visible and the invisible, the voiceless and those with voice. The following comments illustrate not only how they viewed themselves, but how they viewed their relationship with their students:

I've always had to prioritize. And my first priority has always been my students, whether they've been in my class or my advisees.

Interacting with students was very important to me. Not just the teacher kind of inter-action, but that whole kind of communication between faculty and student. I don't mean a friendship kind of level, but in a personal interactive way. Beyond just the teacher oriented facilitator level, but feeling connected.

This is what fascinates me, that interaction, that dialogue, that support I feel I receive from adult learners. And I think that is very key for me. . . . That is where I feel that my support really is. That is my support base, the adult learners within the program.

I guess one other interaction is important, student interaction. Because there are days I do not want to go into the classroom and I certainly do not want to teach. But just being in the classroom, I interact with the students and all of a sudden there is something that happens. And it seems to work.

One of the things that was always most rewarding was really the work in graduate advising as embodied in supervising dissertations. I mean, some don't go as well as you hoped, but the kind of rewards that come from seeing someone complete the project. . . . And maybe take somebody that others don't have faith in initially. . . . And people are pleased that they have been able to carry out a research project that makes a contribution to the field.

The aforementioned sentiments are consistent with these faculty members' ex-pressed cultural values about their professional and personal commitment and responsibility to their communities and the academy. They represent an under-standing of the reality that often their rewards occur not "because of . . ." but "in spite of . . .".

CONCLUSIONS: MAKING THE INVISIBLE VISIBLE

We will end this chapter as we began it. In order for understanding to occur and change to take place, we must give voice to the voiceless and make visible the invisible. The stories of these eight faculty members attempt to help us understand that in order for us to end racist practices we must understand its impact on us all. If we fail to engage in intellectual discourses about this, it will continue to resurface again and again—ultimately calling into question what those in the field of adult education mean by inclusiveness. Our inability to grapple with these issues through a dialectical discourse only serves to highlight the racism that prevails in the academy and in society (Colin 1994a; Colin and Guy 1998; Ross-Gordon 1991). This is especially true for those of us who espouse the use of a critically reflective paradigm in our practices.

As the stories of these eight African-American/African-Ameripean faculty members have suggested, we must expend time and energy interpreting and dealing with the multiple forms of racial oppression that exist daily in both our professional and our personal lives if change is to occur. Through their struggles and through their research agendas they see themselves as not only challenging the assumed universal truths, but they see themselves as being responsible for creating space for the multiple voices; ways of knowing and paradigms that can be used to aid in a better understanding of themselves as well as others. (Caplan 1993; Cose 1993; Hayes and Colin 1994; Moses 1989; Sheared 1994; Smith 1996; Washington 1991)

While African-American/African-Ameripean scholars have consistently spoken out against the norms and defaults used to marginalize them, they have also argued that it is the inclusion, not exclusion, of their lived experiences that will result in a true critically reflective practice (Colin 1994a; Ellsworth 1989; hooks 1994). Clague (1992), Gregory (1995), and hooks (1994) have all concluded that although encounters with racist attitudes and behaviors are frustrating and challenging, its impact can only be repositioned when support is provided by institutions on an interpersonal level.

If the field of adult education is to fulfill its commitment to the goals of "social change" and "social justice," then first and foremost, those of us in the professoriate who espouse such notions must confront, acknowledge, and eradicate racist attitudes and behaviors at the personal, as well as organizational level. We must change the way we view and interpret other ways of knowing. Furthermore, as Helms (1992) suggests, "to make a decision to abandon racism means one must be willing to acknowledge the ways in which one has been a racist. To observe the ways in which racism is maintained requires that one not only be aware that racism exists on some abstract level, but in specific, observable, concrete ways" (p. 140).

Additionally, we must all assume responsibility for restructuring the academic environment. Hopefully, this will result in a more inclusive conceptualization of "knowledge" as well as an understanding about those who are deemed to be "knowledgeable" (Asante 1980, 1992, 1998; Banks 1995; Boyer 1990; Collins 1991; hooks 1994; Ross-Gordon 1990; Sheared 1994).

NOTES

1. The term "African-American/African-Ameripean" is used because of Colin's belief that such terms as colored, black, Afro-American and African American are culturally inappropriate and historically incorrect. She feels that any term that identifies a race of people also identifies a land of origin and should be genetically, socioculturally, and historically correct. African-Ameripean describes any person of African descent born in the United States. The use of *African* denotes primary genetic roots and land of origin (there is no "Afrocan" continent). *Ameri*-reflects the voluntary assimilation with various Native American societies (particularly the Cherokee and Seminole), and *-pean* reflects the forced assimilation with various European ethnic groups, particularly the British,

French, and Irish, during slavery in the United States. This term was originally used by Colin (1988).

2. Culturally Grounded Coping Mechanisms are those values, spiritual and philosophical beliefs, and so on that are rooted in and reflective of the sociocultural history and life experiences that are indigenous to this racial group (Colin 1999).

REFERENCES

Asante, Molefi Kete. (1980). *Afrocentricity: The Theory of Social Change*. Buffalo, NY: Amulefi Publishing Co.

Asante, Molefi Kete. (1992). *Afrocentricity and Knowledge*. Trenton, NJ: Africa World Press.

Asante, Molefi Kete. (1998). *The Afrocentric Idea*. Philadelphia: Temple University Press.

Banks, J. (1995). "The Historical Reconstruction of Knowledge about Race." *Educational Researcher* 24(2), 15–22.

Boyer, E. (1990). *Scholarship Reconsidered: Priorities of the Professoriate*. Princeton, NJ: Princeton University Press.

Caplan, P. (1993). *Lifting a Ton of Feathers*. Toronto: University of Toronto Press.

Clague, M. (1992). "Hiring, Promoting and Retaining African-American Faculty: A Case Study of an Aspiring Multi-cultural Research University." Paper presented at the annual meeting of the Association for the Study of Higher Education, Minneapolis, October 28–November 1.

Colin, Scipio A. J. III. (1988). "Voices from Beyond the Veil: Marcus Garvey, the Universal Negro Improvement Association, and the Education of Ameripean Adults." Doctoral Dissertation, Department of Educational Leadership and Educational Policy Studies, Northern Illinois University.

Colin, Scipio A. J. III. (1992). "Culturally Grounded Community Based Programs." Unpublished manuscript, North Carolina State University, Raleigh, NC.

Colin, Scipio A. J. III. (1994a). "Adult and Continuing Education Graduate Programs: Prescription for the Future." In Elisabeth Hayes and Scipio A. J. Colin III (eds.), *Confronting Racism and Sexism*, 53–62. San Fransisco: Jossey-Bass.

Colin, Scipio A. J. III. (1994b). "African Ameripean Adult Education: An Historical Overview of Selected Activities." *PAACE Journal of Lifelong Learning* 3, 50–61.

Colin, Scipio A. J. III. (1996). "Marcus Garvey: Africentric Adult Education for Selfethnic Reliance." In Elizabeth Peterson (ed.), *Freedom Road: Adult Education of African Americans*, 41–65. Malabar, FL: Krieger Publishing Co.

Colin, Scipio A. J. III. (1999). "The Pillaging of a Paradigm: Africentric Scholars and Scholarship under Siege." Unpublished manuscript, National-Louis University.

Colin, Scipio A. J. III, and Guy, Talmadge C. (1998). "An Africentric Interpretive Model of Curriculum Orientations for Course Development in Graduate Programs in Adult Education." *PAACE Journal of Lifelong Learning* 7, 43–55.

Colin, Scipio A. J. III, and Preciphs, Trudie K. (1991). "Perceptual Patterns and the Learning Environment: Confronting White Racism." In Roger Hiemstra (ed.), *Creating Environments for Effective Adult Learning*, 61–70. San Fransisco: Jossey-Bass.

Collins, P. (1991). *Black Feminist Thought*. New York: Routledge.

Cose, E. (1993). *Rage of the Privileged Class*. New York: HarperCollins.

Easter, Opal. (1995). *Nannie Helen Burroughs and Her Contributions to the Adult Education of African Americans*. New York: Garland Publishing Co.

Easter, Opal. (1996). "Septima Poinsette Clark: Unsung Heroine of the Civil Rights Movement." In Elizabeth Peterson (ed.), *Freedom Road: Adult Education of African Americans*, 109–122. Malabar, FL: Krieger Publishing Co.

Ellsworth, E. (1989). "Why Doesn't This Feel Empowering? Working Through the Repressive Myths of Critical Pedagogy." *Harvard Educational Review* 59(3), 297–324.

Fiquero, P. (1991). *Education and the Social Construction of "Race."* New York: Routledge, Chapman and Hall.

Gregory, S. (1995). *Black Women in the Academy: The Secrets to Success and Achievement*. Lanham, MD: University Press of America.

Guy, Talmadge C. (1993). "Prophecy from the Periphery: Alain Locke's Philosophy of Cultural Pluralism and Adult Education." Unpublished Doctoral Dissertation, Department of Educational Leadership and Policy Studies, Northern Illinois University.

Guy, Talmadge C. (1996). "The American Association of Adult Education and the Experiments in African American Adult Education." In Elizabeth Peterson (ed.), *Freedom Road: Adult Education of African Americans*, 89–108. Malabar, FL: Krieger Publishing Co.

Guy, Talmadge C., and Colin, Scipio A. J. III. (1998). "Selected Bibliographic Resources for African American Adult Education." *PAACE Journal of Lifelong Learning* 7, 85–91.

Hacker, Andrew. (1992). *Two Nations*. New York: Charles Scribner's Sons.

Harvey, William. (1998). "Fight the Power: The Impact of Leadership Upon the Advancement of African American Faculty in Predominantly White Colleges and Universities." In Paula Young (ed.), *The Color of Leadership: The Research Findings of African American Scholars*. Dubuque, IA: Kendall/Hunt.

Hayes, Elisabeth, and Colin, Scipio A. J. III. (1994). "Racism and Sexism in the United States: Fundamental Issues." In Elisabeth Hayes and Scipio A. J. Colin III (eds.), *Confronting Racism and Sexism*, 5–16. San Fransisco: Jossey-Bass.

Helms, Janet E. (1992). *A Race Is a Nice Thing to Have: A Guide to Being a White Person or Understanding the White Persons in Your Life*. Topeka, KS: Content Communications.

hooks, bell. (1994). *Teaching to Transgress: Education as the Practice of Freedom*. New York: Routledge.

Johnson-Bailey, Juanita. (1994). "Making a Way Out of No Way: An Analysis of the Educational Narrative of Reentry Black Women with an Emphasis on Issues of Race, Gender, Class and Color." Unpublished Doctoral Dissertation, University of Georgia.

Johnson-Bailey, Juanita. (1999). "Participation and Retention Concerns of Black Women Adult Learners." In Daphane Nitri (ed.), *Pedagogy for Adult Learners: Methods and Strategies. Volume 2: Models for Adult and Lifelong Learning*. Detroit, MI: Wayne State University Press.

Johnson-Bailey, Juanita, and Cervero, Ronald M. (1996). "An Analysis of the Educational Narrative of Reentry Black Women." *Adult Education Quarterly* 46(3), 142–157.

Moses, Yolanda T. (1989). "Black Women in Academe: Issues and Strategies." Project on the Status and Education of Women. Washington, DC: Association of American Colleges. Published report ref-ED311817.

Neufeldt, H. G., and McGee, L. (eds.). (1990). *Education of the African American Adult: An Historical Overview.* Westport, CT: Greenwood Press.

Peterson, E. A. (ed.). (1996). *Freedom Road: Adult Education of African Americans.* Malabar, FL: Kreiger Publishing Co.

Ross-Gordon, J. M. (1990). "Serving Culturally Diverse Populations: A Social Imperative for Adult Education." *New Directions for Adult and Continuing Education* 48, 5–15.

Ross-Gordon, J. M. (1991). "Needed: A Multicultural Perspective for Adult Education Research." *Adult Education Quarterly* 42(1), 1–2.

Sheared, Vanessa. (1992). "From Workfare to Edfare: African American Women and the Elusive Quest for Self-Determination." Unpublished Doctoral Dissertation, Department of Educational Leadership and Policy Studies, Northern Illinois University.

Sheared, Vanessa. (1994). "Giving Voice: An Inclusive Model of Instruction—A Womanist Perspective." In Elisabeth Hayes and Scipio A. J. Colin III (eds.), *Confronting Racism and Sexism,* 27–37. San Fransisco: Jossey-Bass.

Smith, Barbara. (1982). "Racism and Women's Studies." In Gloria T. Hull, Patricia Bell Scott, and Barbara Smith (eds.). *All the Women Are White, All the Blacks Are Men, But Some of Us Are Brave.* Old Westbury, NY: The Feminist Press.

Smith, Sherwood Eugene. (1996). "The Experience of African-American Faculty in Adult Education Graduate." Unpublished Doctoral Dissertation, Department of Educational Leadership and Policy Studies, Ball State University.

Tisdell, E. (1993). "Interlocking Systems of Power, Privilege, and Oppression in Adult Higher Education Classes." *Adult Education Quarterly* 43(4), 203–226.

Washington, V., and Newman, J. (1991). "Exploring the Meaning of Gender Disparities among Blacks in Higher Education." *Journal of Negro Education* 60(1), 19–33.

Welsing-Cress, Frances L. (1972). *The Cress Theory of Color-Confrontation and Racism (White Supremacy).* Washington, DC: Frances L. Welsing-Cress.

Part II

History Revisited and Claimed

Part II of *Making Space* addresses adult learning within certain important social and historical movements and phenomena. In Chapter 6, Smith explores the learning and entrepreneurship of African-American women in the 1800s and their involvement in capitalist ventures and use of commercial enterprise as a way of engendering their own freedom and that of others during slavery and Reconstruction. Smith's reclamation of the historical roots of this marginalized group of adult learners and leaders, whose roots and traditions reach back to ancient Africa, is an inspiring description of the way in which historical role models can help contemporary learners find validation, and voice.

In Chapter 7, Hugo addresses the way in which gender, race, and class intersect with the construction of knowledge and the epistemological development of women, and exposes the way in which the social perceptions of what women can and cannot do in society shapes the education that is offered to them. Her chapter emphasizes the importance of forming connections and relationships among women within the learning venue. Through a historical case study of a 110-year-old women's study club in New York State, Hugo presents a compelling description and analysis of how the politics of knowledge and the negotiation of difference and dissent get played out among a group of middle-class white women.

Following on this theme of the politics of knowledge, Chapman's work in Chapter 8 takes the reader back to the rural South to expose the role that corporate American philanthropy played in the support of racism in the South at the turn of the century. This chapter presents a historical analysis of the influence that northern philanthropists had in relation to southern whites and southern educators. Through a critical analysis of the way in which churches, benevolent societies, and philanthropists promoted and financed education for newly freed Blacks, and then subsequently promoted the founding of Black colleges, the role of northern money in endorsing the social, political, and economic safeguards of the southern White hegemony is presented.

In Chapter 9, Schied focuses a critical eye on the corporate world, revealing the historical antecedents to workplace learning. Schied examines the emergence of Human Resource Development (HRD) and the concomitant struggle over knowledge in the workplace. By tracing the origins of workers' education, specifically the emergence of resistance and alternative forms of learning and knowledge created within the context of the labor movement, and juxtaposing that history with the role of the military and business in creating the field of HRD, Schied presents a compelling argument for why critically reflective dialogue about who controls workers' knowledge must be a part of the contemporary discourse in HRD.

In Chapter 10, Liu and Rees examine the role of adult education in workplace ageism and challenge adult educators to explore their own role in promoting ageism in training settings. Addressing ageism in the workplace in relation to gender, ethnicity, and class, Liu and Rees present a thorough historical overview of legislation that made discrimination based on age illegal while pointing out that despite this, older workers are still often not the beneficiaries of training. Through a critical analysis of adult education and the literature in gerontology and critical gerontology, these fields are examined for possible roles in perpetuating ageism in the workplace.

At the heart of each of these chapters is the issue of the politics of knowledge, and the way in which the epistemological struggles for knowledge and for ownership among the marginalized cannot be understood without examining how their lived experiences intersect with racist, classist, and patriarchal hegemonic structures and institutions. In reclaiming these voices, the contributors offer us a reminder that learning from the past is essential to reframing the future.

Chapter 6

The African-American Market Woman: Her Past, Our Future

Cheryl A. Smith

Black women are a prism through which the searing rays of race, class and sex are first focused and, then refracted. The creative among us transform these rays into a spectrum of brilliant color, a rainbow which illuminates the experience of all mankind.
—Margaret B. Wilkerson in Hine (1998)

INTRODUCTION

As an entrepreneur and adult/entrepreneurship educator, I am continuously impressed with Black women entrepreneurs' strength and resiliency. I have seen that in spite of the double yoke of racism and sexism, they have made significant contributions to the American economy. Yet, in spite of their contributions, very little is known in adult education literature about their entrepreneurial involvements, due to the fact that we live in not only a racist, but also a sexist society. It is through the lens of racism, sexism, power, and control that the story of the African-American market woman is told.

The term "market woman" often evokes images of women selling produce in outdoor markets. A different interpretation can serve to illuminate the marketing and business skills of Black women entrepreneurs that are rooted in the long-standing entrepreneurial traditions of the powerful market women of ancient Africa. The reality is that women of African descent have a long history of entrepreneurial activities, skills, and successes, beginning with those traditions (Herskovits 1941; Walker 1993). I believe that it is this heritage that has helped African Americans survive; and more importantly, it helped African-American women endure during the Colonial and Antebellum eras of American history—a period of time when most Africans arrived in America and when chattel slavery, an extraordinarily brutal system of oppression, was practiced.

Thus, this chapter offers an analysis of Antebellum African-American market women entrepreneurs. In it, I hope to give voice to a group who have been heretofore marginalized in both adult education and entrepreneurship history, and I suggest that it provides a way for adult educators and others to engage in a dialogue about history, race, gender, and class in America.

AFRICAN-AMERICAN WOMEN'S INVISIBILITY: THEIR CONTRIBUTIONS TO FAMILY AND SOCIETY

The contributions of women, and African-American women in particular, have been undervalued and often invisible in the marketplace, primarily because historically they have been left out of the discourse on race or gender or economics. Swantz, a participatory researcher and anthropologist with over 40 years' experience researching women's businesses in Africa and developing countries, notes that the concepts used in standard macro-economics as well as the methods used to gather statistics, depreciate the economic activities of women (1994, 3). Swantz and others attribute this nonvaluation of women's work to traditional macro-economics, which sets different values for work done by women and men, and which in fact deems women's informal $11 trillion-dollar contribution of labor in the global economy as virtually worthless (Burbridge 1997). Furthermore, women's micro-enterprises, which typically are staffed with less than 10 employees (Women's World Banking 1995), while adding to the Gross National Product (GNP) are not a topic of study because their contributions are viewed as individual in nature and not contributing to the global marketplace (Swantz 1995).

Yet, women often choose to keep their businesses small. They do so for lifestyle reasons; they manage naturally by team rather than by hierarchy and are more often concerned with ethical, environmental, and personal issues involved in business operations (Birley 1989; Brush 1992; Godfrey 1992; Swantz 1994, 1995).

Burbridge (1997), an African-American economist, notes that as women contribute more to the labor market it often goes unnoticed, and Black women, she concluded, are often more disadvantaged with respect to either White women or Black males than is reflected in data which only focuses on incomes (p. 117). She concluded that the dominant paradigm which guides research in economics does not adequately address the relevant issues of Black women's economic conditions, past or present; and furthermore, any discussion of this will require the incorporation of many variables: family and market; wealth and resources and income; macro- and micro-economic variables (pp. 103–104). Thus, a holistic and womanist approach that takes into account the historical experiences and present-day contexts of Black women's realities is more likely to produce a balanced and accurate view of the economic status of Black women.

THE BLACK FEMINIST CRITIQUE

The Afrocentric feminist position provides the most appropriate place for us to start in an examination of the market woman. I believe it is through the lens of Black women scholars that we can begin to understand the way Black women view themselves and how they have been viewed in society and ultimately within the marketplace. Black feminist scholars such as Collins (1990), Zinn and Dill (1994) and Mullins (1994), have embraced a multiracial feminist position, for it connects race, gender, and class, and does not offer a singular or unified feminism but a body of knowledge situating women and men in *multiple* systems of domination (Zinn and Dill 1994, 11). They further state that there is a distinct difference between women of color and White women. Carby, in discussing British feminism, states that both feminist theory and practice have to recognize that White women stand in a power relation as oppressors of Black women. This then, as she sees it, compromises any feminist theory and practice founded on the notion of simple equality (Carby 1993, 25).

Also, since domination and power are intrinsically linked and White males continue to dominate most systems and structures in the global marketplace, racism ensures that Black men do not have the same relations to patriarchal/ capitalistic hierarchies as White men. (Carby 1993, 25) This is not to say that there are no intraracial issues of power imbalances or sexual politics between Black men and women; but they are often different from those between White women and men because of African cultural traditions and the need of African Americans to survive in the new world. There is a complementarity of roles between Black men and women that is necessitated by the historical and social contexts, resulting in an egalitarianism within Black families that was and is critical to the survival of the family as a whole. Thus, the multiracial feminist perspective supports a womanist position as described by Sheared, in that this position challenges us to think critically about such issues as racism, sexism, language, religious orientation and sexual orientation (1994, 29) as they are played out in the marketplace. And yet, while women's roles and economic contributions have been essential to the survival of Black families and communities, the paucity of information about Black women is striking. Most of the well-known accounts of slavery in America consistently fail to discuss the status, conditions, contributions, or interior lives of women, either slave or free, in the Colonial or Antebellum eras in the United States (Sterling 1984; Lerner 1972; Bennett 1996; Vaz 1997). A notable exception is a work by Deborah Gray White (1985), *Ain't I a Woman? Female Slaves in the Plantation South*, in which she contends that the difficulty in finding source material about the female slave was and is directly related to the double oppression of sex and race distinctive to the African-American woman:

A consequence of the double jeopardy and powerlessness is the black woman's invisibility. Much of what is important to Black Americans is not visible to whites and much of what is important to women is not visible to men. Whites wrote most of antebellum America's records and African-American males wrote just about all of antebellum records left by blacks. To both groups the female slave's world was peripheral. (p. 23)

A standout exception is Ophelia Settle Egypt's interviews with ex-slave women, published in 1945 as *Unwritten History of Slavery*. Egypt and her research team were the only African-American women to collect these remembrances, thereby obtaining narratives inclusive of stories [that White men] interviewers would probably have been reluctant to hear (Goodson 1997, 15).

As a result of these women's stories, and as Amott and Mattei (1991) suggest in their multicultural economic history of women, we can all find inspiration and direction in the strength, resiliency, and bravery of African-American women (p. 191). Thus, by researching the historical perspective in entrepreneurship it provides us with the means to rediscover the positive role models that have been so deeply buried in the African-American culture. Furthermore, by showing an appreciation for their economic efforts we can begin to provide excellent role models for the entire business landscape (Butler 1991, 324).

ENTREPRENEURSHIP: FROM AFRICA TO THE AMERICAS

Many of the entrepreneurial skills, strategies, and values used by African Americans in the new world were in part brought from Africa. They were retained and/or adapted in the community in such a way as to enable them to survive, and in some cases prosper under unimaginably oppressive conditions (Herskovits 1941; Williams 1974; Walker 1993). According to Williams (1974), entrepreneurship in West Africa began prior to the three Great Empires of the Western Sudan, which had operated from the seventh century to the sixteenth century A.D.: The Kingdoms of Ghana, Mali, and the Songhay Empire. Williams, an African-American historian who conducted a massive study of Black civilization, concluded that there is a uniformity between the basic social structural outlines throughout the African diaspora. These included an economic system based on communal ownership of land, a value system based on the right of individuals to obtain an education and earn a living, and a social system in which kinship groups were paramount. The educational system was structured around age-set roles and gender-specific education, in which apprenticeship provided both intellectual and operational skills learning (Williams 1974, 173–187).

Williams, Herskovits, and Meier and Rudwick (1968) all describe the West African economic system as being sophisticated, tightly structured, successful, and far-reaching. This recognition is important in light of the need to correct the record of Black economic history, for in reference to Blacks, Euro-Americans tended to view most things African as primitive, unsophisticated, and dysfunctional.

In *The Myth of the Negro Past*, Herskovits (1941) discussed African women as being, for the most part, sellers in the market who retained their gains and became independently wealthy as a result of creating disciplined organizations to protect their interests in the market (p. 62). In addition, they maintained craft guilds and kinship-based mutual aid societies, which served as the predecessors of both formal and informal support networks that have always existed in the Black community.

AFRICAN-AMERICAN WOMEN IN THE MARKETPLACE

According to Walker (1993), after being transplanted to the new world, African women participated in the economy of colonial America in three major domains: in household areas, in food and clothing production, and as market brokers and traders. African women also provided services in specialized skill areas that were clearly related to the economic activities in their homeland. These included child care, midwifery, textiles, weaving, dyeing, quilt-making, basketry, pottery-making, and pharmacopeia. They also used their farming skills as the basis of their participation in the economic activities, which enabled them to dominate this sector of the economy in the South (Walker 1993, 395).

The prevailing social and political conditions of the times—chattel slavery and systemic racial and sexual discrimination and oppression—were also powerful motivators for African-American women in business during this era. Ironically, as a result of their abilities to hire people, they themselves became slave-owners. Their motivation for this practice, however, both male and female, was to obtain freedom for themselves and their families. Manumission was especially important for enslaved women, who wanted to purchase their children, or others, in order to protect them and prevent them from being sold away.

Women as Entrepreneurs: From Slavery to Freedom

Individuals with specialized skills, whether on the plantations or in the towns, and whether slave or free, engaged in entrepreneurial activities in order to make money and to improve their day-to-day lives. Both free and enslaved Blacks, whether in the North or the South, were motivated by freedom for others and independence from the poverty resulting from racism (Berlin 1974). According to Sterling (1984), this was especially true in urban areas.

As male employment opportunities narrowed, women's wages became increasingly important to their families' survival. In urban areas, as many as eight out of ten women were day workers, most of them laundresses . . . perhaps 15 percent of the female work force were dressmakers and hairdressers, another 5 percent operated lodging houses or small shops. (pp. 215–216)

In keeping with African traditional gender-specific skill areas, the businesses African-American women established were primarily in the service sector. A few of the most desperate women turned to illegal activities such as prostitution, establishing houses of ill repute, and making and selling illegal liquor (Walker 1993, 396). In spite of this, they remained true to their ultimate goal, which was to liberate themselves and their families from slavery under the White regime.

Harriet Jacobs, a slave woman for 27 years, escaped to the North, became an abolitionist and activist, and wrote and published her own story. In her autobiography, she gives an account of her maternal grandmother's (Molly Horniblow) entrepreneurial activities during slavery.

[She was] much praised for her cooking and her nice crackers became famous in the neighborhood.... After working hard all day for her mistress, she began her baking, assisted by her two oldest children. The business proved profitable; and each year she laid by a little, which was saved for a fund to purchase her children. (Jacobs 1861, 6)

Urban slaves were often able to live out and hire out their time to earn their own money. Some specialized occupations included seamstress or mantua maker, cook, midwife, healer/folk doctor, market seller, which were especially amenable to entrepreneurship and, in fact, were the basis for the domination of many sectors of the economy in the South by Blacks, including Black women. Sterling (1984) cites Lucy Tucker, who had sent a letter to her mother informing her that "[I] Have a good husband & give the white people 25 [cents] a day [the fee for hiring her own time] . . . I follow washing, ironing dishes &cc [etc.]" (p. 49).

Another female slave, Janet Minor (in Walker 1993), established a home health care service before she was manumitted in 1825. She used her nursing skills and knowledge of pharmacopoeia of folk medicine, used the profits to free 16 women and children from slavery, apprenticed one of those she freed who became a cupper and leecher specialist, and kept her books and accounts. Alethia Browning Tanner (in Smith 1996), is yet another example. Described as a gardener, she hired herself out as a slave in order to buy her freedom in 1810 (p. 325). She then opened a vegetable market at Lafayette Square, and her customers included Thomas Jefferson. She then went on to purchase 17 other family members and friends, including her sister for $800 and her 5 nieces and nephews for an average of $500 per child. After 1836, when all her family was purchased, she began freeing her neighbors. According to *Alexander's Magazine*, a local Washington, DC publication, she then extended her purchasing power elsewhere. They reported that: "Having apparently smashed the slave market, she turned her attention to buying churches" (p. 329). One of the churches she purchased was the First Bethel Church on Capital Hill.

Although most enterprises were in towns and urban settings, there were Black women who owned and managed plantations or commercial farms all over the South. The women who were able to manage such farms relied upon their skills and knowledge obtained from their foreparents as well as former slave masters. One example of a former slave becoming an entrepreneur is Marie Therez

(1747–1816), who was a slave until the age of 46 in Louisiana. She was able to establish a 12,000-acre cotton plantation with 200 slaves *she* had purchased, using her business profits to buy both her children and grandchildren out of slavery (Mills, in Walker 1993, 395).

Thus, in spite of slavery and racial oppression, some African-American women became so successful that they achieved local and regional, and in very rare cases, national recognition. Several, in fact, made fortunes in the health and beauty supply business, wholesale distribution, commodities brokering, catering, and dressmaking. Only the commercial activities of Elizabeth Keckley (1818–1907) have gained wide historic recognition, however, due to her work as a dressmaker and confidante to Mary Todd Lincoln. In an interview with a friend, she said: "I dressed Mrs. Lincoln for every levee. I made every stitch of clothing she wore. I dressed her hair" (Sterling 1984, 248–249). The success she enjoyed due to her expertise as a designer enabled her to buy her own freedom and maintain an independent business in which she employed 20 seamstresses (Walker 1993, 397).

The Use of Profits

The ways in which African-American women used their business profits distinguished them from others, for they used their profits to organize mutual benefit societies. These societies had their roots in the African mutual aid societies, and were operated by middle-class Black women (Hine 1993) who recognized that the African traditions of family and kinship were all the more urgent in the new world (p. 829). These societies helped establish an institutionalized gender role and identity for African-American women in the way they related to religion, sickness, death, education, household economies, social welfare, family, and kinship.

Successful women business owners also used their profits in the Abolitionist and anti-slavery movements. The very successful Redmond family of Salem, Massachusetts, a two-generation family of entrepreneurs, were active in the anti-slavery movement as was the Cuffee family of New Bedford. San Francisco's Mammy (Mary Ellen) Pleasant, a famous madam, used her wealth to help finance John Browns raid on Harper's Ferry (Walker 1993, 397). In Philadelphia, prominent Black women established the Colored Female Free Produce Society, in 1831, to promote the boycotting of goods produced by slaves. An alliance was developed between White and Black women that encouraged individuals to sacrifice by depriving themselves of molasses, sugar, rice, cotton, and tobacco in order to break the stranglehold of the country's slavery-based economics (Taylor 1993, 267).

Cooperative Economics

Like these women, many African women had positions of leadership in their communities, were economically self-sufficient, formed and controlled guilds and kinship-based mutual aid societies, and were the linchpins that held their families together. "Characterized by ingenuity, creativity and innovativeness . . . [they] participated in business while having to contend with slavery, racism and sexism . . . they no doubt had developed a formidable business acumen" (Walker 1993, 397).

Because of the horrific conditions for African-American women during the Colonial and Antebellum periods of U.S. history, working women whether slave or free, had to have help if they were to survive as breadwinners and mothers. As a result of this duality they learned how to practice cooperative economics. One such effort was the Female Trading Association, in which 100 women in New York City formed a cooperative grocery store. Although short-lived, it provided a training ground for large numbers of women to learn the ways of business through the sale of:

dry groceries of every description, at 157 Orange st., (near Grand st.) where they dispose of articles, cheap for cash . . . Flour, Indian meal, grits, hominy, rice, beans, peas, coffee, cocoa, teas, chocolate, hams, pork, beef, fish, shoulders, butter, lard, soap, starch, candles, cheese, oil, raisins, citron, spices of all descriptions, sugars, white and brown, brooms and brushes. (Sterling 1984, 218)

In addition to learning how to market themselves and their wares, they also had to learn how to cooperate with one another, so that they all achieved. According to White (1985), the self-reliance and self-sufficiency of slave women must not only be viewed in the context of what the individual slave woman did for herself, but what slave women as a group were able to do for one another (pp. 119–120). Cooperative work with childrearing was especially necessary because of illness, or with pregnancy and childbirth, and because husbands could be and were sold. Thus, other forms of nonmonetary exchange took place in which social capital accounts were built.

This informal support system remains an important source of social capital in the Black community today. While frequently unrecognized by mainstream economists and often maligned by social scientists and politicians, critics of Black family life such as Daniel Patrick Moynihan and E. Franklin Frazier have condemned Black women's struggles to keep their families together. Calling these arrangements a dysfunctional matriarchal system, traced to slavery times, they concluded that this led to the domination of Black men by Black women. This they believe then, led to the destruction of the Black family (Stack 1974; White, 1985). Even though this position has been promulgated in society and history, it is contrary to what really occurred. In fact, slave women did what pioneer American women did on the frontier: they mustered their reserves, persevered, and helped others survive (White 1985, 159–160). They did what women have done since time immemorial—made themselves a bulwark against the destruction of their families.

Maya Angelou (in Harris 1996) wrote: "Each day we must rid ourselves of the lies we've been told about ourselves" (p. 15). This is especially true for African-American women, given that many of their stories remain untold. Some of these activities, such as learning how to read and write, were dangerous, therefore they were virtually unknown outside their immediate families or within the African-American community.

Although sexually exploited by White men and to some extent by Black men, they were also economically exploited and oppressed by White women; yet, they survived. As Yvonne Scott concluded, habits of survival, as well as business skills and strategies were also retained informally as "we teach these habits to each other, often by example" (Scott 1991, 9). Thus, the African-American woman found ways to not only market herself and her skills or trades; she also found ways to bring her community along with her. Whether it was through the hiring or purchasing of family members or friends, the African-American market woman of the Antebellum period created situations in which others could achieve as well.

This legacy of entrepreneurial excellence continued in the post–Civil War and Reconstruction eras. During this period, women like Maggie Lena Walker (1867–1934) and Madame C. J. Walker (aka Sarah Breedlove, 1867–1919) embodied the entrepreneurial spirit. M. L. Walker established the first bank owned by a woman in America in 1920, and called it the St. Luke's Penny Savings Bank (Weare, in Hine 1993, 831). Madame C. J. Walker invented the Walker method for hair straightening, and became the first Black self-made woman millionaire in the United States (Sterling 1984, 437).

Even today, the heritage of mutual aid societies and cooperative networks continues through such organizations as the Black Women Enterprises of New York State, the Coalition of 100 Black Women, the National Negro Business and Professional Women's Organizations, and the Madame C. J. Walker Foundation. Black female sororities also offer similar emotional, physical, and financial support to their members via education and networking opportunities.

THE CONTEMPORARY LANDSCAPE: HAS ANYTHING CHANGED?

Demographic and statistical evidence points to the fact that women and minorities are expected to account for the largest segment of new business owners in the coming decade. Statistical summaries indicate that, as of 1998, there were 9.1 million women-owned businesses, accounting for 38 percent of all small businesses, and generating $3.6 trillion in annual sales (NFWBO Report 1998). Additionally, it has been found that while the number of minority female business owners, including Hispanic, Asian, and African-American women, has increased from 392,000 in 1987 to 1.1 million, African-American women still own the largest number of businesses 405,200 (*National Foundation of Women Business Owners Report* 1996). Thus, minority women–owned businesses are making a significant impact on the growth and health of the U.S. economy.

In spite of these impressive gains, African-American women still only account for 3 percent of the population of small business owners. They have the least amount of export activity and, in New York State, post the lowest average sales/ firm of all groups, including men of the same group and other minority women (Kerka 1993). Women of color have trouble succeeding by any criteria when they cannot access capital and markets, many of which are still closed by the elite oligarchy, the old boys' network, and their policies (see Chapters 4 and 16 in this volume). Clearly, gender alone does not account for universal business concerns, outcomes, and issues among women business owners.

Public Policy, Entrepreneurship, and African-American Women

Some federal and state programs have been initiated which aim to move others—minorities, women, the disabled, immigrants, and low-income people— to economic self-sufficiency through small business ownership. These initiatives include the establishment of Individual Development Accounts (IDAs) through which low-income individuals can accumulate assets to be used for education, entrepreneurship, or homeownership without jeopardizing their public assistance. The Assets for Independence Act S. 1106 introduced by Senator Dan Coats (R-IN) in 1997 and the Entrepreneurship Development Act introduced by Senator Ted Kennedy (D-MA) in 1998 provide funding for entrepreneurship development, training, and asset augmentation (AEO Exchange 1997). Aida Alvarez, the head of the U.S. Small Business Administration (SBA) has made a firm commitment to increasing the number of SBA loans to minority women. This combination of increased access to capital and training, which includes business skills, life skills, economic literacy, and network support, represents an emerging approach to entrepreneurship development that is especially helpful to members of communities who have been left behind in the so-called economic recovery.

While the links between adult education and entrepreneurship education seem obvious, very few scholars and practitioners in either field make the mutually beneficial connection. This connection is critical in the present political and economic context, since both entrepreneurship and adult education are expected to benefit from the present economic climate, which necessitates job creation and the acquisition and upgrading of skills for occupational advancement and financial survival. Because small business has been the primary source of job creation and economic expansion in America for the past decade, education and training programs that are effective in maximizing the success of these enterprises are pivotal in promoting all-encompassing economic growth (Levinson 1997; Rivkin 1995; Butler 1991). Additionally, since many publicly funded entrepreneurship and training programs are increasingly aimed at low-income, historically marginalized individuals—women, people of color, residents of rural communities, and the disabled—the retraining of educators, trainers, adminis-

trators, and lenders to recognize and respect the myriad perspectives and experiences is often needed. An understanding of this diverse group of learners
and business owners will enable them to be more effective in achieving their
goals.

IMPLICATIONS FOR ADULT EDUCATION: THEORY AND PRACTICE

It is my contention that by examining the strategies and practices that historically guided African-American women entrepreneurs, teaching practices can be
enhanced and curriculum materials developed that benefit both adult and entrepreneurship education working with marginalized groups. By operating in concert we can begin to promote an emancipatory and inclusionary process by
which those in the margins begin to actively participate in the economic gains
being made by those in our society who are in the center. This can occur only
when we in adult and entrepreneurship education begin to develop programs
that:

1. enable individuals to become more critically aware of the social, historical, and political contexts that shape their realities;
2. value their voices and worldviews; and
3. give them the tools to act as change agents for the benefit of themselves, their families,
   and their communities.

So, what can we do to create this environment? We can:

- Assign readings that reflect and celebrate the cultural heritages and histories of a variety
  of learners.
- Promote opportunities for critical reflection of our own roles as educators.
- Critically analyze the content of the curriculum we use in terms of whether it positions
  learners as subjects to be domesticated or active agents to be empowered.
- Use learning activities that recognize and value cross-cultural perspectives.
- Provide opportunities for students to examine their histories and myths and tell their
  own stories, and give voice to them by helping them disseminate their accomplish-
  ments.

Some of these approaches have been effective in teaching new entrepreneurs,
who report feeling empowered and inspired after hearing stories about past and
present entrepreneurs. Learning activities that tap into cultural preferences in
terms of processes and the development of curriculum materials that meet the
needs of different populations are increasingly being used in micro-enterprise
training programs across the country. They are being used especially in those
programs that are community-based and have diverse populations. One example

is the Business Neighborhood Organization of Women in Atlanta. This organization's mission is Business and Sisterhood, which is fulfilled in part by developing and using training materials geared to the cultural preferences of their group of African-American women. Another example, the Phenomenal Women of Baltimore, provides low-income women with entrepreneurial training in a learning circle model. Finally, the Women's Venture Fund in New York City provides loans to women business owners using a peer lending model where borrowers are placed in lending circles in order to provide support and mentoring as they grow their businesses. While role modeling, mentorship, apprenticeship, and use of networks, informal learning, and cooperative business strategies have deep roots in the African-American community, all are not necessary nor necessarily used by every Black woman entrepreneur. However, they have been identified as factors that can have an impact on success in this and other small business communities.

Adult education efforts that are concerned with building human capital can benefit from some of the new initiatives occurring in the field of entrepreneurship and micro-enterprise development and training. One area is economic literacy training, defined as the ability to control and make conscious choices about the kind of work you do, how much you earn, and what kinds of goods and services you can buy in your neighborhood (AEO Institute 1998, 13). Used in conjunction with adult basic education programming and career exploration and development, economic self-determination through entrepreneurship can be a vehicle for individual human resource development, community revitalization, and community economic development.

CONCLUSION: MARKET WOMEN OF THE FUTURE

I believe that the recognition and use of the histories of marginalized entrepreneurs can challenge traditional economic theories and contribute to new and expanded frameworks. These new ways of thinking about economic activity can be used to examine larger issues of economic imbalance, empowerment, and the relationship of gender, race/ethnicity, and class to money and power in U.S. society. New paradigms can also be used to encourage an increasingly multidisciplinary and multicultural approach to both adult and entrepreneurship education. The employment of these strategies has the potential to enable adult educators to better harvest and use what Daloz et al. call gifts from the margin— greater self-knowledge, greater awareness of others, and a kind of comfort from life at the edge (1996, 76).

By revisiting and reclaiming history we can begin to create a new vision that enables us to construct our own knowledge, to rename ourselves, and to redefine our practices and positions within society. In attempting to take back our power we must examine the language we use, redefine it, and create a paradigm that includes all voices. Terms like *entrepreneurship, wealth, success*, and *power* must be explored in their historical context. One way for adult educators to do this is to practice the African principle of *Sankofa—The wisdom of learning from the past*. The inclusion and implementation of the strategies learned from one group of invisible, marginalized individuals—African-American women entrepreneurs—is just the beginning. It is a beginning toward understanding and reclaiming one's history through the voices and experiences that have shaped and continue to shape our realities.

As Malson et al. (1988) and other African-American women scholars have contended, I believe that the collection and interpretation of information about African-American women, and by extension, other traditionally marginalized groups, offer a way toward understanding our pasts, as well as in creating our futures. We must engage in work that frees our imaginations and allows us to conceive new theories, new languages, and new questions (Malson et al. 1988, 3). We need to discover how we can function in an oppressive culture, change it, and live beyond mere survival. The African-American market woman is just one example of how we can gain control over our lives if we have control over our economic institutions and our place in the marketplace. As Sterling so aptly states:

The strengths and skills that black women were forced to develop had been transmitted to their descendants . . . thrown on their own resources . . . they learned the art of survival, of acquiring a vitality that made them unique. They were full of sturdiness and singing. (1984, xv)

REFERENCES

Amott, T., and Mattei, J. (1991). *Race, Gender and Work: A Multicultural Economic History of Women in the US*. Boston: South End Press

Association for Enterprise Opportunity (AEO). Economic Literacy and Asset Development Institute. (1998). *Economic Literacy and Asset Development*. Washington, DC: AEO.

Bates, T. (1989). "Entrepreneurship, Human Capital Endowments and Minority Business Viability." *Journal of Human Resources* 20, 540–554.

Bennett, L. (1962). *Before the Mayflower: A History of the Negro in America 1619–1962*. Chicago: Johnson Publishing Co.

Bennett, L. (1996). "Black and Green: The Untold Story of the African-American Entrepreneur." *Ebony* (February).

Berlin, I. (1974). *Slaves Without Masters: The Free Negro in the Antebellum South*. New York: Pantheon Books.

Birley, S. (1989). "Female Entrepreneurs: Are They Really Different?" *Journal of Small Business Management* 27 (1) (January), 107–117.

Brimmer, A. (1997). "Preamble: Blacks in the American Economy: Summary of Selected Research." In T. Boston (ed.), *A Different Vision: African-American Economic Thought, Vols. 1 and 2*. New York and London: Routledge.

Brookfield, S. (1994). "Adult Learning: An Overview." In T. Husen and N. Postwhite (eds.), *International Encyclopedia of Education*. Oxford: Pergamon Press.

Brown, A. (1997). "The Myth of the Universal Adult Educator: A Literature Review."

Proceedings of the 38th Annual Adult Education Research Conference, Oklahoma State University, May, 43–48.

Brown, K. D. (1993). "Womanist Theology." In D. C. Hine (ed.), *Black Women in America: An Historical Encyclopedia*. New York: Carlson Publications.

Brush, C. (1992). "Researching Women Business Owners: Past Trends, a New Perspective and Future Directions." *Entrepreneurship Theory and Practice* 16(4), 5–20.

Burbridge, L. (1997). "Black Women in the History of African-American Economic Thought: A Critical Essay." In T. Boston (ed.), *A Different Vision: African-American Economic Thought, Vols. 1 and 2*. London and New York: Routledge.

Butler, J. S. (1991). *Entrepreneurship and Self-Help in the Black Community: A Reconsideration of Race and Economics*. Albany: State University of New York Press.

Carby, H. (1993). "White Women Listen!" In S. Jackson (ed.), *Women's Studies: Essential Readings*. New York: New York University Press.

Cassara, B. (ed.). (1990). *Adult Education in a Multicultural Society*. New York: Routledge.

Clarke, J. H. (1972). "The Meaning of Black History." In R. V. Haynes (ed.), *Blacks in White America Before 1865: Issues and Interpretations*. New York: David McKay Co.

Collins, P. H. (1990). *Black Feminist Thought*. New York: Routledge.

Crossette, B. (1995). "The Second Sex in the Third World." *New York Times*, September 10.

Curry, L. P. (1981). *The Free Black in Urban America, 1800–1850: The Shadow of the Dream*. Chicago and London: University of Chicago Press.

Daloz, L. et al. (1996). *Common Fire: Lives of Commitment in a Complex World*. Boston: Beacon Press.

Fratoe, F. (1988). "Social Capital of Black Business Owners." *Journal of Black Political Economy* (Spring), 33–50.

Godfrey, J. (1992). *Our Wildest Dreams: Women Entrepreneurs Making Money, Having Fun, Doing Good*. New York: HarperCollins.

Gunderson, G. (1989). *The Wealth Creators: An Entrepreneurial History of the United States*. New York: Truman Talle.

Gutman, H. (1977). *The Black Family in Slavery and Freedom, 1725–1925*. New York: Vintage Press.

Harris, F. (1996). *About My Sister's Business: The Black Woman's Road Map to Successful Entrepreneurship*. New York: Simon & Schuster.

Herskovits, M. J. (1941). *The Myth of the Negro Past*. Boston: Beacon Press.

Hine, D. C. (ed.). (1993). *Black Women in America: An Historical Encyclopedia, Vols. 1 and 2*. New York: Carlson Publications.

Hine, D. C., and Thompson, K. (1998). *A Shining Thread of Hope: The History of Black Women in America*. New York: Broadway Books.

Humber-Faison, J. (1988). "No Flowers Please: The Black Female Educator and the Education of Adult Freemen." Unpublished Doctoral Dissertation, Teachers College, Columbia University.

Ihle, E. L. (1990). "Education of Free Blacks Before the Civil War." In H. Neufeldt and L. McGee (eds.), *Education of the African-American Adult: An Historical Overview*. Westport, CT: Greenwood Press.

Jackson, S. (ed.). (1993). *Introduction to Women's Studies: Essential Readings*. New York: New York University Press.

Jacobs, H. A. (1861). *Incidents in the Life of a Slave Girl: Written by Herself* (Originally edited by L. Maria Child). Boston: Published for the Author. (1987). Edited and with an Introduction by J. F. Yellin. Cambridge, MA: Harvard University Press.

Jones, Y. (1985). "Afro-American Urban Life: New Directions for Research!" Paper presented to Central States Anthropological Society, April.

Kerka, S. (1993). "Women and Entrepreneurship." ERIC Digest (Report No. EDO-CE-93-143). Washington, DC: Office of Educational Research and Improvement (EDD00036) (ERIC No. ED363 799).

Lerner, G. (ed.). (1972). *Black Women in White America*. New York: Vintage Books.

Levinson, J. C. (1997). *The Way of the Guerilla: Achieving Success and Balance as an Entrepreneur in the 21st Century*. Boston and New York: Houghton Mifflin Co.

Lind, M. (1995). "To Have and Have Not: Notes on the Progress of the American Class War." *Harper's Magazine* (June).

Livesay, H. (1982). "Entrepreneurial History." In C. A. Kent et al. (eds.), *Encyclopedia of Entrepreneurship*. Englewood Cliffs, NJ: Prentice-Hall.

Malson, M. et al. (1988). *Black Women in America: A Social Science Perspective*. Chicago and London: University of Chicago Press.

Meier, A., and Rudwick, E. (1968). *From Plantation to Ghetto*. New York: Hill & Wang.

Mullins, L. (1994). "Images, Ideology and Women of Color." In M. Zinn and B. Dill (eds.), *Women of Color in US Society*. Philadelphia: Temple University Press.

National Foundation of Women Business Owners Report. (1996).

Nespor, V. (1994). "Learning Processes That Contribute to the Effective Decision Making Processes of Small Business Owners." Unpublished Doctoral Dissertation, Teachers College, Columbia University.

NFWBO Report. (1998). In Clarke, R. (1999). "Sisters Inc.: Successful Black Women: Making It Happen." *Black Enterprise* (August), 59–63.

Peterson, E. (1992). *African-American Women: A Study of Will and Success*. Jefferson, NC: MacFarland & Co.

Plaschka, G., and Welsch, H. (1990). "Emerging Structures in Entrepreneurship Education: Curricular Designs and Strategies." *Entrepreneurship Theory and Practice* (Spring), 55–71.

Rivkin, J. (1995). *The End of Work: The Decline of the Global Labor Force and the Dawn of the Post-Market Era*. New York: G. P. Putnam and Sons.

Ross-Gordon, J. M. (1991). "Needed: A Multicultural Perspective for Adult Education Research." *Adult Education Quarterly* 42(2), 1–16.

Scott, K. Y. (1991). *The Habit of Surviving*. New Brunswick, NJ, and London: Rutgers University Press.

Sheared, V. (1994). "Giving Voice: An Inclusive Model of Instruction—A Womanist Perspective." In E. Hayes and S.A.J. Colin III (eds.), *Confronting Racism and Sexism*. San Francisco: Jossey-Bass.

Smith, J. C. (ed.). (1996). *Powerful Black Women*. Detroit and New York: Visible Ink Press.

Stack, C. (1974). *All Our Kin: Strategies for Survival in Black Communities*. New York: Harper and Row.

Sterling, D. (ed.). (1984). *We Are Your Sisters: Black Women in the Nineteenth Century*. New York: W. W. Norton.

Stubblefield, H. W., and Keane, P. (1994). *Adult Education in the American Experience: From the Colonial Period to the Present*. San Francisco: Jossey-Bass.

Swantz, M. L. (1995). "Women's Economics: Do Women Need Another Economic Theory?" Keynote Address presented at the Third International Conference on Development and Future Studies.

Swantz, M. M. (1994). "Women Entrepreneurs in Tanzania: A Path to Sustainable Livelihood." Paper presented at a public seminar, UNU/WIDER (World Institute for Development Economics Research), Helsinki, September 22.

Taylor, S. A. (1993). "Colored Females Free Produce Society." In D. C. Hine (ed.), *Black Women in America: An Historical Encyclopedia.* New York: Carlson Publications.

U.S. Census Bureau Report. (1992).

Vaz, K. M. (ed.). (1997). *Oral Narrative Research with Black Women.* Thousand Oaks, CA: Sage Publications.

Walker, J. K. (1993). "Entrepreneurs in Antebellum America." In D. C Hine (ed.), *Black Women in America: An Historical Encyclopedia.* New York: Carlson Publications.

Weare, W. (1993). "Mutual Benefit Societies." In D. C. Hine (ed.), *Black Women in America: An Historical Encyclopedia.* New York: Carlson Publications.

Whitaker, L. H. (1990). "Black Adult Education Before 1860." In H. Neufeldt and L. McGee (eds.), *Education of the African American Adult: An Historical Overview.* Westport, CT: Greenwood Press.

White, D. G. (1985). *Ain't I a Woman? Female Slaves in the Plantation South.* New York: W. W. Norton.

Williams, C. (1974). *The Destruction of Black Civilization: Great Issues of Race from 4500 B.C. to 2000 A.D.* Chicago: Third World Press.

Women's World Banking. (1995). "Innovative Banking for Microbusinesses."

Zinn, M., and Dill, B. (eds.). (1994). *Women of Color in US Society.* Philadelphia: Temple University Press.

Chapter 7

Creating an Intellectual Basis for Friendship: Practice and Politics in a White Women's Study Group

Jane M. Hugo

Twelve years ago, as I began to explore adult education history, I found the nearly invisible or certainly "forgotten" history of women's formal and nonformal adult learning perplexing. With my scholarship focusing on women's learning, I found that published adult education histories were typically of little help in illuminating women's learning spaces or leadership. Furthermore, once I began to undertake historical analysis of this aspect of women's lives, I realized that the power and the potential for investigating women's adult learning was great (Hugo 1990).

Thus, the focus of this chapter is on the phenomenon of women's learning. In particular, it is an analysis of how one group of women undertook nonformal learning together, through the creation and nurturing of a women's study club in one community. By necessity, such an undertaking requires an investigation of both the learning and teaching methods, as well as an analysis of the factors that may influence community-building, namely, the intersection of race, class, and gender, both within institutions and between diverse populations. It also means that I need to focus on the ways in which language and culture organize our lives and experiences across the life span (see, for example, Burstyn 1990; Cremin 1976; Eisenmann 1997; Gere 1997; Scott 1984; Weiler 1997).

For example, it is recognized that there is a relationship between social perceptions of what women can and cannot do in society and the education they choose for themselves or the education society offers them (see, for example, Cott 1977; Solomon 1985; Rothman 1978; Kerber 1993). In addition to this, it is recognized that limitations on women's broader participation in society worked to foster women's single-sex or homosocial networks—networks that have been found to create strong relationships among women. These same factors contributed to the creation of a distinct women's culture and influenced women's participation in education (see, for example, Smith-Rosenberg 1985; Wollons 1990; Freedman 1979; Rosaldo 1974).

While adult educators must question generalizations made about any one group's experience, interests, and constructions (for example, extrapolating the experience of White, middle-class women to all women), we must also critically analyze existing research about women's learning spaces. I believe that this is vital to our being able to understand the political, pedagogical, or personal relationships that shape women's learning and through which they make sense of their lives. Clearly, all is far from understood about the oppositional aspects and the reproductive processes that are at work when women create their own educational spaces.

This chapter seeks to explore these oppositional and reproductive elements and to enrich our understanding about the way communities of learners mediate diverse external influences and use them to both maintain social stability and promote social change (Cremin 1976). As Belenky, Clinchy, Goldberger, and Tarule (1986) have suggested, women have a particular way of learning and knowing that is grounded in making connections with one another. These connections subsequently help them make sense of the world. I examine these issues through an exploration of the role and function of the value of female association or sorority in one particular study club called the "Coterie."

OVERVIEW

Over a 100-year period from 1885 to 1985, the associational life of the Coterie was a key element in the politics of knowledge that organized its learning space. Through an analysis of this group's associational life and the way the women operationalized their values about learning, knowledge, and the importance of congeniality, we come to understand the choices the members in this club made throughout the years of its development. In doing so, we can link their experience to the politics of knowledge which influenced and was created within that system. In Kathleen Weiler's (1997) words, we come to understand that "people are not simply defined by an ideological construct of what should be, but negotiate conflicting discourses in the context of their own life activities and desires" (p. 652). It is through this conflicting discourse then, that the Coterie's history unfolds.

I begin this chapter with a brief overview of the nineteenth-century stimulus for the development of women's study clubs across America, and then introduce the Coterie. A discussion concerning the importance of sorority (or fellowship) in the club is explored. I also examine the ways in which the club's politics of knowledge—as exemplified by the interplay between accommodation and resistance to societal norms, and the attendant privilege and marginalization—shapes these women's learning space. Finally, I will suggest some ways in which the experiences the women had in the Coterie might help adult educators begin to understand the complexities of women's lives and their experiences within varying organizational contexts.

THE CLUB MOVEMENT: A PLACE FOR POWER

An explosion of women's associations began in the middle of the nineteenth century and continued into the first quarter of the twentieth century. Continuing education provided an intellectual basis for friendship and was a socially acceptable focus for association (Blair 1980). Sorosis, a New York City women's club founded in 1868 and the New England Women's Club, founded in Boston the same year, were the progenitors of thousands of such clubs that sprang up across the country between the 1870s and 1890s. Some examples include the Association for the Advancement of Women (AAW, founded by Sorosis in 1873), the Women's Educational and Industrial Union (WEIU, founded in 1877 in Boston), the General Federation of Women's Clubs (GFWC, founded in 1890), and the National Association of Colored Women's Clubs (NACW, founded in 1896). These national networks established systems for communicating policies, plans, agendas, curricula, and strategies of influence, which began to challenge the boundaries of the female "private sphere" of the home and the male "public sphere" of government, business, science, and higher education. The study of culture and cultural uplift were common goals.

As women's clubs evolved, social action, civics, and social welfare issues came to the forefront. According to Ely and Chappel (1938), "Education not for self, but for service" (p. 128) became the motto of the General Federation of Women's Clubs. Cultural studies persisted through support of the fine arts, music, literature, and drama departments, but the quality of public education, the establishment of public libraries and playgrounds, public health issues, and pure food were also areas of concern for the Federation through the turn of the nineteenth century.

Despite two million participants in the early part of the twentieth century, the club movement began to decline in the 1920s. In her study of literacy and cultural work in women's clubs, Anne Ruggles Gere (1997) has suggested that the following factors contributed to this:

1. The development of the National League of Women Voters and the National Association for the Advancement of Colored People (which did the work previously done by women's clubs);
2. The changing social realities that resulted in a decrease in immigrants (which undermined the focus of some clubs), and increases in women in the workforce (which negatively affected club membership);
3. A lack of political consensus once suffrage was gained;
4. The Depression; and

5. The conflict in relationships between mothers and daughters because of the changes
   in opportunities that had occurred in the workforce for the daughters (253–255).

Furthermore, the distortions and reductive images assigned to these clubwomen
by critics hostile to their social and educational missions further exacerbated
these issues. Scorned for promoting feminized men and weaker families and
homes, and accused of creating women who are unattractive, selfish, well-
intentioned but incompetent, and self-righteous (Gere 1997, 256–264), women's
clubs were the butt of jokes and cartoons in the *New Yorker* (Martin 1987).

Contemporary historians of the club movement have acknowledged that racial
and class divisions existed (see, for example, Davis 1981; Gere 1997; Giddings
1984; Scott 1991). Even though women's issues intersect across race, class, and
gender, race and class were factors that divided women because power and
privilege were afforded to some and not to others, based on skin color. Gere
(1997) writes, "White middle-class club-women, for whom race was a prominent
feature of self-identification—just as it was for women from other social backgrounds—devoted considerable energy to constructing and affirming their positions of privilege and power by using exclusionary tactics, both literally and
figuratively" (p. 5). She further notes that White, working-class clubwomen often excluded African-American women as members, just as White, middle-class
Protestant groups barred Jewish women.

According to Gere, the women in each of these different social locations
created clubs that were shaped around their own interests. "Black women and
white women followed parallel but quite separate tracks," writes Anne Firor
Scott (1991). "Despite many similarities in their interests and methods of work,
the two seldom intersected" (p. 180). For instance, African-American women
championed the need for race-oriented groups that aided racial uplift. Jewish
and Morman women linked self-education and community action with their
respective religious traditions; and working-class clubwomen sought, among
other things, to change the representation of working women as lacking refinement while at the same time building pride in the labor roots they shared (Gere
1997, 5).

The cultural and civic self-education designed by the Coterie members from
1885 to 1985 responded to the particular concerns relevant to their privileged
positions as White, middle-class women, and also reflected their roles as wives,
mothers, workers, citizens, or friends at the same time. As is suggested in the
following section, this sororal space produced education that supported personal
relationships, valued women's experiences in American society, and sought to
promote mutual improvement by disseminating knowledge relevant to their multiple roles.

THE COTERIE IN CONTEXT

The Coterie was established in 1885 in Fayetteville, New York, eight miles
from Syracuse, the largest metropolitan area in central New York State. Like

many other women's study clubs that started between the Civil War and the beginning of the twentieth century, the Coterie dedicated itself to the self-improvement of its members through education. It grew out of a Shakespeare study group composed of couples who read and discussed Shakespeare's works. When the couples' club "season" ended in the spring of 1885, the story goes, Harriet Wilkin, Mary Collin, and eight other women from the Shakespeare group decided to continue meeting over the summer months "for the purpose of pursuing a prescribed course of reading. . . . Upon a vote being taken, it was unanimously decided that such a society be formed." The following fall, the Shakespeare group reconvened, and the summer's women-only group, calling itself the Social Art Class, continued as well. Several months later, the women's group took the name "Coterie," which means a small group of like-minded people. Its objective was "mutual improvement and a united effort toward a higher social and intellectual life" (Coterie Minutes [CM] April 28, 1885).[1]

"In America, literature and the elegant arts must grow side by side with the coarser plants of daily necessity" (Washington Irving), became the motto of the Coterie. Taking education as their principal objective, the Coterie members read together, presented original papers to each other, brought in outside speakers, and occasionally took action together. One of the club's founders wrote this about the group's early days: "It was a time of intellectual activity among women all over the land. . . . Not one of us a college woman, we were all well acquainted with 'the coarser plants of daily necessity'—[the club] readings stimulated our minds and gave us an outlook upon a wider world" (Wilkin 1935).

The Coterie had much in common with other small women's study clubs that began during the mid-nineteenth century to the 1920s. Because it was a culture club and not a service club, its main orientation was toward individual self-improvement through the acquisition of culture rather than toward community improvement or social reform. Similar to other study groups that grew out of missionary efforts and benevolent societies in the early part of the nineteenth century, the Coterie had a constitutional organization and elected officers. Membership was by invitation only. Eligibility for membership was, in part, tied to living in the Fayetteville and Manlius areas, and membership in this organization was capped between 30 and 40 women, expanding or contracting as conditions changed over time in the club. Since women joined the club in their late thirties or early forties, it was not uncommon for women to remain active members for 20 years or more. The club often granted honorary membership to women who were members of long standing. This then meant that they could continue to enjoy the benefits of the group without having to pay dues or do the work required of active members.

The club met two afternoons a month in members' homes between September and June, the club's "season." Annual dues were minimal, ranging in the period studied from fifty cents to three dollars per year. As in most other women's study clubs, leadership rotated and all members shared in the work of the club, be it serving as a hostess in one's home, doing a presentation, or serving on occasional committees. Active members alternately gave a presentation or helped host the club each year.

The Coterie was a study club, and therefore its meetings included members giving presentations that focused on a specific topic. Each year's program was developed by two members that had been elected to serve as directors for that season. The directors generally polled the membership for topic suggestions prior to setting up the program for the following season. At times during the club's history, the club chose a theme for the entire season and the directors assigned members topics related to the theme or arranged for an outside speaker. For example, the club spent three years studying aspects of Italy and Italian culture, and seven years investigating facets of American history. Reading aloud from print material was the most common presentation format in the early part of the club's history. As early as 1925, individual members frequently selected and prepared their own presentations, synthesizing information from a variety of sources. Materials for study were garnered through members' access to personal and public libraries, through personal contacts with people working in a variety of educational and social institutions, and from life experiences of the members, their families, and their friends. Meetings always included some opportunity for socializing. For many years, this break in the program was called a "recess."

Programmatic changes often occurred in response to the sociopolitical events of the times. For instance, during the 1917–1918 season, the period of American involvement in World War I, the Coterie curtailed its meeting schedule to accommodate the increased volunteer efforts of members. The topics discussed at this time included the work of hospitals in France, the Red Cross, and women's accomplishments in relief work.

The Coterie has continued to meet without interruption since its founding in 1885. In all, four generations of members have renewed this learning circle. Currently, its twelve meetings fall between October and May. Membership continues to be drawn from an area defined by the Fayetteville-Manlius town line, although the club makes individual exceptions. While there were no women of color members during the first 100 years (1885–1985) of its existence, the club has become more diverse. There are women represented from various religious backgrounds, work experiences, and marital situations. In addition, the average age of women joining the club has gradually increased.

As in days past, the club's programs include member-prepared papers or presentations on topics chosen by each member, and meetings are still held in members' homes. The topics chosen range from presentations given on solid-waste disposal, issues of aging, horticulture, or the history of a local park. The meeting's order of business also remains much the same as it was at the turn of the nineteenth century. Silver tea and coffee services—whether borrowed from the public library or belonging to individual members—still grace the tables, along with china cups and delicate sweets. The Coterie remains a vehicle for approximately 30 White, middle-class women's self-improvement and social interaction.

SORORITY AS A DISCOURSE STRUCTURE

In defining the type of learning group it wanted to be, the Coterie made sorority—"the heightened understanding and loyalty to women" (Ranlett 1974)—a core value in its club culture. A woman who was a Coterie member from 1917 to 1988 told me in 1985, "as you work through this and get some more information, you'll realize the value of people, and that's all I'll say it is— it's the value of each other. We got interested in each other" (CI [member interviews] 12, October 2, 1985). In the annual report for 1950–1951, the club secretary noted, "Perhaps it is the person first and subject matter second that makes our Coterie program such a rich experience for all of us. Surely no annual report should omit the fellowship that is the background for all our endeavors in Coterie" (CM May 8, 1951). This emphasis on the value of female association, of building an intellectual basis for friendship, had two consequences. First, it gave the women the chance to appropriate and use "favored" ways of speaking and acting and to share the forms of knowledge valued by their social and economic group (O'Connor 1989, 57–60). Second, it led to the establishment of discourse rules that enabled the members to negotiate the private and public, the personal and political, the emotional and intellectual dimensions of their lives within the club context. An examination of the nature and role of sorority within the Coterie should enable us to understand the social discourse that directed the members' educational enterprise.

LAYING A FOUNDATION FOR MUTUALITY AND COHESIVENESS

The Coterie has been a "diversity of interests [and] community of interests" for over 100 years (CS [survey responses] 17, 1989). The club's foundation for female association had several building blocks. A good part of the Coterie's sense of community stemmed from its homogeneity in terms of race and class, as well as friendships established between the members. "Knowing" in this case was based on familial ties, neighbor-relations, race, religious affiliation, and class, each of which will be briefly discussed below.

Familial networks provided an early cornerstone for sorority in the Coterie. Mothers and daughters, sisters, in-laws, and cousins were part of the pool from which candidates were drawn. In addition, a club survey showed that family experience with study clubs seemed to be part of what attracted several nonrelated women to the Coterie in the 1980s.

Friends and neighbors made up the larger pool of likely candidates. In this way, new members always knew one or two other women in the club. In the beginning, the boundaries of Fayetteville were the geographical limits of membership. "Long ago, when all members lived close together in Fayetteville," recalled one member, "the hostess of the day could look out of her window at ten minutes of two and see all the ladies walking toward her house from all directions" (CS 21, 1989). Eventually, the club redefined its boundaries to match the newly consolidated Fayetteville-Manlius school district lines. In addition to proximity, interest in the village and its locale created a sense of belonging, especially for women who moved to Fayetteville. "For someone not a native Syracusan," reported an honorary member, "it has meant becoming a part of an old established community through the older women who were much a part of the history of the area" (CS 17, 1989). Another said, "It made me feel more at home in Fayetteville" (CS 2, 1989).

Whiteness was an assumed and mostly invisible point of cohesion for the majority of Coterie members between 1885 and 1985. The racial homogeneity of the group mirrored the culturally and politically dominant group in society and the village across the club's history. People of color or ethnic minorities and their cultures or contributions to the American culture were objects of study, but they were generally viewed as the "other."

Religious affiliation was another common denominator, among the first generation of Coterie members, at least. Many were affiliated with the Presbyterian church and served together in women's church-related organizations. While this was not as common by the 1980s, several members still shared church affiliation (CI 3, July 7, 1989). The women's Anglo-Saxon, Christian heritage—with its primary emphasis on European culture and values—provided Coterie members with a common cultural language and set of rituals.

Closely aligned to the familial, friendship, or religious factors, they built sorority upon their shared class status. They were wives and family of businessmen, manufacturers, merchants, clergy, and professionals. However, beginning with the 1950s, many began to be full-time wage-earners as teachers, librarians, physicians, nurses, psychotherapists, secretaries, financial planners, social workers, and professors. They lived and met in homes that could accommodate 30 or more women for an afternoon meeting. Many were active as volunteers in a variety of community organizations because, in part, the demands and privileges of their class created a type of leisure time that "required" useful outlets. The social and volunteer networks maintained by several members gave them access to university administrators and faculty, community officials, a variety of social organizations, and leading citizens. By 1989, with few exceptions, the members had all completed some form of higher education, and many had pursued graduate education (CS 1989).

Finally, the women who joined the Coterie were able to build relationships with fellow members based on the intersection of their privileged roles; in other words, their experiences as White, middle-class American women. Their volunteer community work often clustered around sex-segregated efforts in community health, recreation, the environment, education, or village improvement issues. Their academic training was in areas such as education, music, art, home economics, library science, nursing, languages, the fine arts, English, journalism, or social work; and because of their shared class and racial positions, Coterie women could count on being able to understand each other's life stories, situated as they were around events such as marriage, childbirth, schooling, sickness, children leaving home, career moves, combining paid work with family life, financial (in)security, retirement, care of aging relatives, and death. The sororal commitment to mutual improvement and support prompted the members to integrate selected experiences into their educational work rather than view them as disconnected from their intellectual efforts.

At the same time sorority gained support from the intersection of these roles, it also gained momentum from women's desire to be more than the roles allowed. Letters, club records, and interviews indicate that the women felt the social dissonance between women's intellectual aspirations and their socially assigned relational responsibilities. For example, the Coterie's cofounder, Miriam, wrote,

Mary was shocked when I told her how old I was [42 yrs.] the other day, and I am convinced that I am past the marrying days and must confine myself to literature, science, and religion. Men do not flourish around much in these parts, and John and Hubbard are still delinquents and I am so absorbed that I say "so be it." (Collin 1891)

A hundred years later, interviews with several members, most of whom had been married, echoed a similar split between women's roles and intellectual development. They expressed a need to "use their minds," to act on a conviction that they were not going to stagnate as they took on roles as wives, homemakers, and mothers.

SORORITY MANIFESTED IN THE COTERIE'S CLUB LIFE AND CULTURE

The Coterie's educational efforts were shaped by values similar to those historian Ellen Lagemann (1979) found operating in the educational biographies of the five Progressive Era women she studied: personal affiliation, interpersonal orientation, common interest, mutual support, trust of other women, congeniality, and both individual and community development. The club's incorporation of these sororal values into its culture established the group's rules of discourse and was a linchpin in its politics of knowledge, its educational practice.

Terrence O'Connor's (1989) discussion of the cultural politics of school-based discourses has noted the connection between group affiliation and the type of discourse carried on in and by a group. Members of groups establish a "cultural voice" for the group, and this voice becomes a shared system of signs and symbolic language, including language, ideas, behaviors, dress, and ritual. This cultural voice is based on "the particular social structure, value choices, and range of ideas that are maintained and legitimated" by group interactions (p. 63).

Carroll Smith-Rosenberg (1985) echoed this approach to understanding the meanings of women's lives, in particular social-structural locations. She said that language, meaning verbal and nonverbal communication, "subtly mirrors the social location and relative power of its speakers. . . . [it is] rooted in, and expressive of, social relationships and social experiences" (p. 43).

The sororal nature of this study group hinged on sustaining a cohesive, supportive community of members. The club accomplished this by institutionalizing sororal values through its membership process, club governance and structure, meeting format, club etiquette, language, and pedagogy (Hugo 1996). For the purposes of this chapter, I will briefly address three: etiquette, language, and pedagogy. These three sites of sororal values and voice underscore the paradoxical relationship that co-existed in the Coterie—the valuing of the person and personal alongside the management of dissonance and debate.

CLUB ETIQUETTE—GREASING THE WHEELS AND
AVOIDING CONFLICT

The development of the Coterie as an intellectual basis for friendship made congeniality a central virtue; and by following the club etiquette one could show and produce congeniality and avoid or manage conflict. Codified as well as uncodified standards of etiquette "grease the wheels" of the Coterie. As one member said, "Maybe it's an unwritten law, or maybe it's just instinctive that in a group like that [Coterie] you don't create dissension of any kind. Well, there's nothing like a good rousing fight; on the other hand, it's not conducive to pleasant relationships and this is supposed to be, after all, very ladylike, on the whole" (CI 10, August 10, 1989).

When I observed that following rules seemed important to the Coterie, a member replied, "They're manners. Manners are what make the world go round. Why? That's the reason for all the protocol. If you know exactly how you're supposed to conform, you do and everything goes very smoothly. It's only when somebody throws a monkey wrench that things get into a turmoil" (CI 10, August 10, 1989).

Coterie etiquette applied to topic choices, presentation and discussion manners, decision making, and interpersonal relations. For instance, one member told me, "You don't want to elicit big arguments . . . if you feel strongly about something that you think there might be strong diversity of opinion, you don't talk about it or you try to present varying points of view" (CI 7, July 13, 1989). Finally, club etiquette made certain that club decisions took members' physical and emotional needs into consideration. For instance, the selection of a home for the meetings held during the winter months was influenced by whether one's driveways, walkways, and streets were accessible or could be navigated by older members.

CLUB LANGUAGE: MAKING SPACE

The strength of sorority within the Coterie's club culture was evident in the language members used to describe the club, themselves as learners, and the club's intellectual work. In many ways the language revealed the women's recognition that their educational work required them to accept the opposites in their lives, that is, to live with and to work within the social contradictions of being women who wanted a life of the mind.

The metaphors used by the Coterie members between 1885 and 1985 were images taken from their experiences of the world. For them, the club was a hearthstone, a circle, a community chain, the child of their affections, a 96-year-old lady exhibiting all the signs of vigorous old age. Within the dominant gender ideology, the social function and psychic identity of many members were to be ladies, homemakers, nurturers, community supporters, and mothers. Yet, another set of metaphors suggested that the club also kept open a space that was somehow "other than" those the members regularly occupied; the club was a safe harbor from a busy world, a crossroads, an oasis, an old-girl network.

The members of the Coterie identified themselves as learners, ladies, students, and "earnest seekers of knowledge" who, as travelers, took "intellectual journeys." Programs "transported" members to other countries and other cultures. Even while there was a language of traveling away from the known, there was also language that described their meetings as "happy gatherings in pursuit of friendship and knowledge" (CM 1977 Annual Report).

Traditionally, women have been the ones responsible for feeding and nourishing their families and guests. In the Coterie, the women literally and figuratively nourished one another. Learning was often equated with eating food or having a meal. As one club secretary noted in 1890,

No mere apologies for food were offered—whipped syllabubs nor dainty trifles popularly supposed to suffice for the ordinary feminine intellectual palate: but food in the truest sense—fresh, wholesome, invigorating, stimulating, seasoned sufficiently with delicate wit and humor, garnished and set forth with the jewels of polished rhetoric and pleasing elocution. (CM April 22, 1890)

Meetings were often called "banquets," "a feast of reason" that fed the members' spirits. Learning was also often called "entertainment," a word associated with the pleasure and hospitality of being a guest. But the club minutes across all four generations also spoke about the "work" required to maintain the study club. The sororal values woven into the Coterie enabled the women to share equally in both the pleasure and the labor of "the child of their affections."

SORORAL PEDAGOGY

The club's method of work, or its pedagogy, was constructed so as to be congruent with this sororal context for learning. From one generation of Coterie women to the next, they emphasized the value of the person and the personal, and focused pedagogically on helping women make connections between one another. One member told me, "I think a personal point of view adds a great deal to a subject—plus books, the interpretation of [books]" (CI 9, August 10, 1989).

I noted four strategies that club members were socialized to use in order to connect learning to their lives. Personalization of topics, reminiscing, collaborations on presentations, and group discussions were the means through which the women connected to one another and to their subject matter. The club minutes are replete with illustrations, like:

1. Letter-writing and sharing firsthand impressions of major events like World War I and II were used to add a personal dimension to a subject.

2. Retelling stories about how and why the founding members decided to study together and form the Coterie is an example of how they used reminiscing.

3. Designing a program together, like a musical or play, was a way for them to collaborate on presentations.

4. Eliciting anecdotes on a subject after a presentation was a way to corroborate one another's experiences or insights, and as one member pointed out, to keep the discussion "light and lively" and make "human contact" through which a member says, "Oh, this has happened to me, has it happened to you?" (CI 5, July 7, 1989)

Thus, the Coterie's sororal context set a tone for the pedagogy used by the club members. Equally important, however, were the ways in which the Coterie women conceptualized knowledge and the ways they used it in this setting. While the club covered a spectrum of cultural and civic topics, the ways in which the members dealt with these topics, fostered exchange, and disseminated information were prescribed by parameters of behavior and social norms designed to minimize potential conflicts.

While the club's emphasis was on establishing an intellectual basis for friendship, there were discernible limits within this learning space. The sororal relations that the club fostered depended on a high degree of homogeneity, and, as a result, the Coterie excluded various kinds of women. For example, they didn't invite women of color, women of limited means, and women of means whose personalities were judged to be too overbearing. In doing so, the club filtered out those differences that might prove to be counterproductive to the life of the group. At the same time however, it sought to maintain a sufficient range of experiences among the women in order to keep the group interesting.

Although homogeneous in many broad ways (namely, in terms of their class, race, and social roles), the Coterie women were not uniform in their beliefs and personal actions inside or outside the club's circle. In fact, the historical research, interviews, and observations I undertook revealed that cross-currents existed below the unanimous statements of camaraderie in the club. As I reviewed club documents and examined the members' anecdotal recollections, I came to understand that in accepting an invitation to join the Coterie, each woman agreed implicitly to use the discourse structures that served to support the fellowship established in the circle. Established members modeled acceptable discourse behavior for new members. For some this meant discovering a new voice, and for others it meant fostering the voice they already had. For still others, it meant suppressing some aspects of their voice in order to use others.

So, sorority—with its values and accompanying race, class, and gender dynamics—was not only an impetus for these women to come together to learn, but it was also an organizing feature of the Coterie's educational work throughout the club's history. The club's language, rules, expectations, conventions, and rituals gave form to the group's educational discourse, creating a "voice" that took its cadence, intonation, and inflection from White, middle-class values and power relationships. But what can the Coterie tell us about what women believed was worth knowing? The remainder of this chapter sheds some light on the answer to this question.

THE COTERIE'S POLITICS OF KNOWLEDGE

For over 100 years, the Coterie circle has remained unbroken, and its intellectual work has remained meaningful to its members. To create an intellectual basis for friendship, each club generation had to construct its own set of power relationships that would guide what knowledge would be primary to the members. In effect, the women constructed a politics of knowledge out of the dominant power relationships in which the club and its members were embedded. The end result was a politics of knowledge that supported and protected the club's people-first-and-subject-matter-second orientation.

When I say the Coterie members "constructed" a politics of knowledge, I mean that they "understood" that certain power relations existed in their broader society, and they were, in fact, selectively appropriating those relationships into the Coterie's educational agenda. For example, these women fashioned their educational work to complement the relational values they believed were necessary to their growth and to the maintenance of the Coterie. I would argue that the relational context and the club's politics of knowledge became reciprocal constructs—each reinforcing the other. In other words, the pursuit of the intellect and friendship were intertwined and interwoven.

The club's politics of knowledge, therefore, served several important functions in the creation and maintenance of a sororal learning space. First, it provided members with an understanding of the "knowledge boundaries" that were to guide their work, given the race, class, and gender arrangements in place for each generation. These knowledge boundaries placed certain knowledge, practices, and outcomes at the center of the club's work and others at the periphery (see, for example, Ingraham 1994; Lagemann 1987). Next, the club's politics of knowledge moderated the hierarchical relationships established by the dominant understandings of "expert" and "nonexpert." Lastly, it was this politics of knowledge that validated the methods and strategies the members used to man-

age their organization and disseminate knowledge in ways that fostered harmony
and minimized dissent.

CLASS, RACE, AND GENDER DISCOURSES IN THE DEFINITION OF DOMINANT AND SUBORDINATE KNOWLEDGE BOUNDARIES

An analysis of the Coterie's civic and cultural curricula established that the
members adopted many of the dominant discourses of privilege and race (Hugo
1996). As a result, their curricular choices set them a part from racial and economic minorities, supported individualism, promoted high culture, and alternately celebrated American "progress" at home and abroad or heralded the
dangers of social trends that threatened White middle-class life. In addition, their
selection of subject matter simultaneoulsy constructed women of their social
location as guardians of Western culture and the public sphere, and as consumers
of information intended to help them "understand" and "adjust" to (i.e., accept)
social changes beyond their control.

The Coterie women also used discourses of femininity to construct their politics of knowledge. Biklen (1995) defines "femininity" as a "cultural construct
about gender that yokes together a particular set of perspectives and characteristics that may relate to nurture, help, certain kinds of bodily presentation, and
a specific relationship to men" (p. 177). While these discourses privileged men
and women's expertise in different areas, it constructed men's leadership in
knowledge-making.

It's not that the women ever sat down and decided to focus on what was
important to men. But they appeared to have had an internalized understanding
that certain kinds of knowledge were considered more valuable than others, and
they acted on that understanding to a large degree. The club's politics of knowledge favored disciplines like the liberal arts and social sciences, which had been
socially constructed as supporting feminine virtues and sensibilities, but were
controlled by men. Within these disciplines, history, geography, sociology (after
1906), literature, art, music, political science, and psychology were common
subject areas in which men were the principal creators of the knowledge. The
clubwomen acknowledged these subjects as the dominant areas of inquiry on
which they could draw.

The topic analysis mentioned earlier also revealed that the members persisted
in linking their intellectual development and civic involvement with their maternal roles. For instance, the "people first" orientation was an expression of a
gender ideology that assigned women to be the caregivers and nurturers. The
clubwomen repeatedly used biographical narratives, personal experiences, or assessments of the impact of events and ideas on people as their point of entry
into discussions about cultural and civic topics. In a society that suspected education could "de-sex" women, the Coterie women from each generation
wrapped their learning in feminine symbols like the home, children, the parlor,
polite conversation, the tea table, "lady" clothes, and food.

Each generation of Coterie women brought their knowledge and interests as women to the table. This knowledge may have come from the "minor" areas of the humanities and social sciences, such as when the club devoted meetings to women writers, the wives of political leaders, women's customs in another country, home economics, or the decorative arts; or it may have come from the women's own experiences or experiences of women like them. For example, during my review of the club's curricula, I found that the First and Second World Wars, the Progressive Era, the New Deal Era, and the two women's rights movements became occasions for the Coterie women to call attention to women's involvement and concerns in society.

The Coterie women recognized what, in the eyes of the dominant knowledge purveyors (e.g., publishers and academics), was subordinate knowledge. It was often the knowledge relegated to or produced by women. The Coterie resisted the dominant–subordinate male and female arrangements and respectfully focused on women's topics and experiences. By doing so, they moderated the distinction between experts and nonexperts.

HANDLING THE EXPERT VERSUS NONEXPERT HIERARCHY

The Coterie's politics of knowledge gave the members a way to manage the hierarchical dynamics of "expert" and "nonexpert" within their learning space. Up until at least the mid-1970s, the women routinely perceived that the dominant knowledge they sought was either too distant, beyond them, too complex, or was outside of their experience. In effect, the Coterie women internalized the cultural authority claims made by academic discourses and specialists that emerged in tandem with the women's club movement. So, in their role as receivers of knowledge, they experienced the power imbalance between themselves and those who created or had mastered the knowledge they studied.

However, while these clubwomen valued academic expertise, the club's politics of knowledge also placed value on nonacademic expertise that became visible in the choices the women made in their hobbies and homemaking skills. Consequently, unlike in formal school settings, the club members did not permanently place one another in "expert" and "nonexpert" categories. As a result, the powerful position of expert and the less powerful position of nonexpert were constantly shared and rotated as the women moved between their roles as teachers, hosts, and learners. Thus, the politics of knowledge helped to minimize the effects of intellectual or experiential differences among the members.

MANAGING HARMONY THROUGH THE ORGANIZATION AND DISSEMINATION OF KNOWLEDGE

The congeniality so central to club etiquette discussed earlier was supported by the club's knowledge work. The Coterie's politics of knowledge required that its members present information without reference to their particular biases or perspectives. That is, they had to discuss it in a "nonpartisan" or "objective" manner. Members had to take in the information publicly and integrate it or contest it privately. Overt challenges to members' ideas and a close critical analysis of "received" knowledge were antithetical to the Coterie's politics of knowledge. Members could use many different strategies to organize and carry out their intellectual work. These included description, synthesis, comparison and contrast, debate, recitation, lecture, demonstration, parody, panels, and general discussion. But, because the purpose of the knowledge was to help maintain a set of relationships, the women across all four generations created and maintained an analytical threshold. In the club circle, confrontation was viewed by the members as being unladylike and counterproductive to the group's relational values—especially congeniality. Long's (1986) and Daniels' (1988) research on other middle-class women's contexts supports this finding.

In spite of this culture of congeniality, the evidence I found in the Coterie's records suggests that its members didn't shy away from all controversial subjects, for the world often intruded. So, the club used its politics of knowledge to manage potentially divisive topics. The controversial topics the club addressed included suffrage, birth control, abortion, youth counterculture, feminism, the peace movement prior to and following the First World War, racism, and environmental degradation. However, as members explained and as the minutes illustrated, the presentations on these topics explained situations rather than interrogated or analyzed them.[2] The total silencing of a topic, as was the case with the Vietnam War, is an example of the club's ability to protect itself against a socially divisive issue that could have had a negative impact upon the group. If the directors felt that a presenter could not find a way to safely "explain the situation," or if they believed a topic touched another member too personally, then they would not suggest the topic for a program. The issue then went unaddressed and was silenced by the total membership.

CONCLUSION

The Coterie was based on values embedded in relationships, and the members constructed an internal politics of knowledge that supported and protected those relationships. I asked one member how the club has held its members together. She told me that it was able to hold its members together because the club represents "a value of long standing [that] they want to keep going . . . this thing that's been going on now for over a hundred years presents something that women do together . . . they're using their minds" (CI 10, August 10, 1989). If we as adult educators and researchers dismiss forms of self-determined education like the Coterie, we overlook the opportunity to study a "configuration of learning" (Cremin 1976) where we can see the interplay of the personal, pedagogical, and sociopolitical realities of women as learners.

The experiences of the Coterie can provide scholars and practitioners with a view of the inner workings of one women's nonformal learning space. The

Coterie, I think, lets us see a messy middle ground where paradoxes and contradictions exist in a world signified by gender, class, and race.

The White, middle-class women who joined the Coterie wanted both intellectual stimulation and social interaction. To achieve this, they accepted the costs of maintaining their group: valuing the person and suppressing dissonance and debate. The sororal values they followed allowed the members to create a woman-centered learning space, one that stood in contrast to their experience of formal schooling and in contrast to the social construction of "woman" as being nonintellectual. They created, re-created, and maintained this space over a 100-year period even though, in doing so, the women also reproduced many of the status quo social arrangements that organized their own gender constraints.

By linking education, work, and relationship together the Coterie was able to reconcile the "divorce of reason from feeling and emotion and of self from other" that educational philosopher Jane Roland Martin (1985, 191) observed in liberal and vocational education. Based on Martin's distinctions between productive and reproductive processes in education, I believe that the Coterie constructed an educational realm that included not only those productive processes related to culture, politics, and economics (historically associated with men), but also the reproductive processes related to nurturing and what Martin calls the "transmission of skills, beliefs, feelings, emotions, values, and even world views" (p. 178). The club provided one response to the dissonance that many liberally educated women felt between the ideals of education and the domestic roles society had constructed for them as wives and mothers. The reciprocal nature of the club's politics of knowledge and its sororal values demonstrate how women in their social and historical situation could create intellectual value from the productive and reproductive aspects of their lives.

Higher education has prided itself on scientific rationality that, in effect, separates reason and emotion. This discourse of learning has resulted in what Jane Roland Martin (1985) calls "the journey from intimacy to isolation" (p. 189). The Coterie's history suggests that some women who had gone through higher education chose to reverse that journey and to create a learning environment that led, if not to intimacy, at least to fellowship. As Belenky et al. (1986) argue, confirmation and community are not the consequences of women's intellectual and emotional development, they are the prerequisites (pp. 193–194). The practice and politics of learning in the Coterie call us to examine more carefully the interconnected realities that create the world in which we live and learn.

NOTES

1. This chapter makes reference to three different types of data provided by the Coterie or its members. The first type is club minutes (hereafter noted in the text as CM followed by the date). The Coterie minute books are available for 1885 to the present. Minutes are missing for the following periods: 1898–1904, 1922–1924, and 1934–1939. The

minutes are kept at the Fayetteville Free Library, Fayetteville, New York. The second type is member interviews (hereafter cited in the text as CI followed by the interview code number and the date of the interview). Interviews, lasting anywhere from an hour to three hours, were audiotaped by the author with 13 members of long standing. All the women interviewed lived in Fayetteville, New York, at the time of the interviews. Members were told that their names would be kept confidential. The author retains the audiotapes and complete transcripts of the interviews. The third type is survey responses (hereafter cited in the text as CS followed by the number of the respondent and the year). Between April and June 1989, I gave all Coterie members, active and honorary, a questionnaire that asked for personal information (e.g., marital status, children, educational background, work experience, hobbies, and other associational affiliation) as well as for their impressions of the club (e.g., favorite anecdotes, what they valued most highly about the club, what they liked about being a hostess or a presenter for meetings, what made a "good" Coterie presentation, and how the club was different from school). Twenty-nine women responded.

2. Long's "Women, Reading, and Cultural Authority" (1986) discusses the reactions of women in reading groups she studied to the "facts" presented in books they read. She noted that the women read and discussed books differently from professionals. The women, because their club situation emphasized "sharing rather than competition and personal connection to the book rather than rational argumentation *from* it, groups usually truncated the process of making a case for any given interpretation of a book" (p. 603). Not having to build an argument or defend an interpretation encouraged the women, in Long's view, to "remain at the easiest or most 'natural' level of response" (p. 604). Long argues that the women in the reading groups held on to an innocence of meaning. By this she meant that they behaved as if words were neutral, "a transparent veil over objective reality." In addition, she perceived the female readers as operating out of the assumption that books represent or imitate reality and so they needn't question the "crafted nature of the text."

REFERENCES

Belenky, M. F., Clinchy, B. M., Goldberger, N. R., and Tarule, J. M. (1986). *Women's Ways of Knowing: The Development of Self, Voice, and Mind.* New York: Basic Books.

Biklen, Sari Knopp. (1995). *School Work: Gender and the Cultural Construction of Teaching.* New York: Teachers College Press.

Blair, Karen J. (1980). *The Clubwoman as Feminist: True Womanhood Redefined, 1868–1914.* New York: Holmes & Meier.

Burstyn, Joan N. (1990). "Review of *The Sound of Our Own Voices* by Theodora Penny Martin." *Journal of Higher Education* 61 (September/October), 594–596.

Collin/Park/Knapp Collection. Diaries and letters. Syracuse, NY: Onondaga Historical Association.

Coterie. Minutes, programs, and papers. Fayetteville, NY: Fayetteville Free Library.

Cott, Nancy F. (1977). *The Bonds of Womanhood: "Woman's Sphere" in New England, 1780–1835.* New Haven, CT: Yale University Press.

Cremin, Lawrence A. (1976). *Public Education.* The John Dewey Society Lecture, no. 15. New York: Basic Books.

Daniels, Arlene Kaplan. (1988). *Invisible Careers: Women Civic Leaders from the Volunteer World*. Chicago: University of Chicago Press.

Davis, Angela Y. (1981). *Women, Race, and Class*. New York: Random House.

Eisenmann, Linda. (1997). "Reconsidering a Classic: Assessing the History of Women's Higher Education a Dozen Years after Barbara Solomon." *Harvard Educational Review* 67 (Winter), 689–717.

Ely, Mary L., and Chappell, Eve. (1938). *Women in Two Worlds*. New York: American Association for Adult Education.

Freedman, Estelle. (1979). "Separatism as Strategy: Female Institution Building and American Feminism, 1870–1930." *Feminist Studies* 5 (Fall), 512–529.

Gere, Anne R. (1997). *Intimate Practices: Literacy and Cultural Work in U.S. Women's Clubs, 1880–1920*. Urbana: University of Illinois Press.

Giddings, Paula. (1984). *When and Where I Entered: The Impact of Black Women on Race and Sex in America*. New York: William Morrow.

Hugo, Jane M. (1990). "Adult Education History and the Issue of Gender: Toward a Different History of Adult Education in America." *Adult Education Quarterly* 41, 1–16.

Hugo, Jane M. (1996). " 'Perhaps It Is the Person First and Subject Matter Second': Social Relationships and the Construction of Cultural and Civic Curricula in a Women's Study Club 1885–1985." Unpublished Doctoral Dissertation, Syracuse University.

Ingraham, Chrys. (1994). "The Heterosexual Imaginary: Feminist Sociology and Theories of Gender." *Sociological Theory* 12 (July); 203–219.

Kerber, Linda K. (1993). " 'Why Should Girls Be Learn'd and Wise?' The Unfinished Work of Alice Mary Baldwin." In Nancy A. Hewitt and Suzanne Lebsock (eds.), *Visible Women: New Essays on American Activism*, 349–380. Urbana: University of Illinois Press.

Lagemann, Ellen Condliffe. (1979). *A Generation of Women: Education in the Lives of Progressive Reformers*. Cambridge, MA: Harvard University Press.

Lagemann, Ellen Condliffe. (1987). "The Politics of Knowledge: The Carnegie Corporation and Formulation of Public Policy." *History of Education Quarterly* 27(2), 205–220.

Long, Elizabeth. (1986). "Women, Reading, and Cultural Authority: Some Implications of the Audience Perspective in Cultural Studies." *American Quarterly* 38 (Fall), 591–612.

Martin, Jane Roland. (1985). *Reclaiming a Conversation: The Ideal of the Educated Woman*. New Haven, CT: Yale University Press.

Martin, Theodora Penny. (1987). *The Sound of Our Own Voices: Women's Study Clubs 1860–1910*. Boston: Beacon Press.

O'Connor, Terence. (1989). "Cultural Voice and Strategies for Multicultural Education." *Journal of Education* 171, 57–74.

Ranlett, Judith Becker. (1974). "Sorority and Community: Women's Answer to a Changing Massachusetts, 1865–1895." Unpublished Doctoral Dissertation, Brandeis University.

Rosaldo, Michelle Zimbalist. (1974). "Woman, Culture and Society: A Theoretical Overview." In M. Z. Rosaldo and L. Lamphere (eds.), *Woman, Culture and Society*. Stanford, CA: Stanford University Press.

Rothman, Sheila M. (1978). *Woman's Proper Place: A History of Changing Ideals and Practices, 1870 to the Present.* New York: Basic Books.

Scott, Anne Firor. (1984). "On Seeing and Not Seeing: A Case of Historical Invisibility." *The Journal of American History* 71 (June), 7–21.

Scott, Anne Firor. (1991). *Natural Allies: Women's Associations in American History.* Urbana: University of Illinois Press.

Smith-Rosenberg, Carroll. (1985). *Disorderly Conduct: Visions of Gender in Victorian America.* New York: Oxford University Press.

Solomon, Barbara Miller. (1985). *In the Company of Educated Women: A History of Women and Higher Education in America.* New Haven, CT: Yale University Press.

Weiler, Kathleen. (1999). "Reflections on Writing a History of Women Teachers." *Harvard Education Review* 67 (Winter), 635–657.

Wilkin, Harriet D. "Early Days of Coterie." Manuscript written in 1935 and used as part of the fiftieth anniversary program. Coterie Papers. Fayetteville, NY: Fayetteville Free Library.

Wollons, Roberta. (1990). "Women Educating Women: The Child Study Associations as Women's Culture." In Joyce Antler and Sari Knopp Biklen (eds.), *Changing Education: Women as Radicals and Conservators*, 51–67. Albany: State University of New York Press.

Chapter 8

Northern Philanthropy's Ideological Influence on African-American Adult Education in the Rural South

Bernadine S. Chapman

Wealthy White philanthropists have historically participated in the African-American experience in America. From wealthy, White abolitionists who saved the lives of runaway slaves, to wealthy patrons who financially supported many writers of the Harlem Renaissance, to the various foundations that exist today—philanthropic efforts have been motivated by a desire to assist this group of "others." This desire to assist the "other" has often been used as a means to maintain control or to perpetuate the ideology of philanthropic organizations.

The focus of this chapter is to address and explicate the roles and functions of northern philanthropic organizations in relation to the control they maintained over African Americans in the rural South. In it, I will argue that through the mechanism of funding educational initiatives focusing on "Black industrial education" (Spivey 1978, 16–17), key philanthropic institutions were not only complicit in supporting racist beliefs, practices, and inequities against these peoples, they assisted in the maintenance of racist cultural practices. While Spivey and others have noted that the main concern of the South was to maintain hegemonic control in an economic and cultural sense, the educational institutions funded by them in fact promoted racism and inequity. Heretofore, this issue has been overlooked within the field of adult education.

In the words of Gramsci (in Graubard 1987), it is through these institutions that "the dominant class in a society [invariably uses] its power to articulate views and propagate opinions that keep subordinate classes in line: the genius of such class is that it creates institutions, like foundations, to achieve these ends" (Graubard 1987, vi). It is because of the key role that philanthropic organizations and other public and private funding streams have played, and continue to play, in program development for marginalized groups that an examination of this phenomenon is needed. In doing so, I hope to provide adult educators with a discourse that critically reflects upon past practices, which will ultimately liberate and create equitable programs for marginalized groups of people in the future.

HISTORICAL OVERVIEW

The education of African-American adults has largely been overlooked or discounted by historians. However, over the last 10 years there have been studies and books published by African-American adult educators (McGee and Neufeldt 1985; Peterson 1995) as well as by some Euro-American adult educators, like Stubblefield and Keane (1994), that are including the participation of African-American adults in adult education history. As these scholars suggest, in order to understand the true complexity of one's field as well as the contributions that many ethnic groups have made to it, any historical analysis must include all these voices. Therefore, I believe that in examining the history of adult education, we must examine the role of philanthropy in the development of institutions that have affected so many of our lives. Moreover, I believe that it is through this examination that we can understand the political, economic, and social control philanthropists have had. Given that programs and institutions designed to educate African Americans have relied to a great extent on philanthropic giving and government aid for their existence, it is therefore extremely important that we take the time out to examine how this form of giving has ultimately served to control and shape their lives.

A historical antecedent to African Americans' invisibility in educational pursuits relates to the reality that, during the antebellum and Civil War periods, it was illegal, according to public policy in most southern states, for African-Americans to be educated. In spite of this, African-American adults persisted and courageously worked to obtain an education under the most difficult circumstances. This meant that those who wanted to learn or acquire literacy during this time had to endure hardships as well as use clandestine means to achieve their goals (Bond 1966, 175).

In fact, the risks that African Americans took to obtain an education (my interpretation) demonstrates how committed they were to altering their oppression, even if meant that they would be severely penalized. Thus, the commitment of African-American adults to education runs deep, and nowhere is this more evident than during the Civil War and Reconstruction Eras. For example, Anderson (1973) stated that even before President Lincoln issued the Emancipation Proclamation, and Congress' creation of the Bureau of Refugees, Freedmen, and Abandoned Lands (commonly known as the Freedmen's Bureau), African Americans began making plans to systematically instruct the vast numbers of their people who could not read. Others, such as those in the missionary movement, were also readying to provide assistance.

THE MISSIONARIES

Prior to the Civil War, numerous religious groups and organizations had become active in the abolitionist movement. After the war, the South was inundated with religious-based charitable organizations which had started channeling northern dollars toward the newly liberated African Americans. Proclaimed as the "educational philanthropists" of that era (Peeps 1981, 253) these organizations worked directly and indirectly toward meeting the multiple needs of African Americans during that time.

The American Missionary Association (AMA) was one of the first agencies to respond to early appeals made by Union army officers who had reported that the African Americans left behind on plantations and in army camps and settlements needed food, clothing, and teachers. Soon after, other societies organized to provide service. These included the American Baptist Home Mission Society, the Congregationalists, the National Freedmen's Relief Association of New York, the Port Royal Relief Committee of Philadelphia, the Society of Friends of New York and Philadelphia, among many others (Peeps 1981, 255).

Among the major ecclesiastical groups supporting African-American relief efforts were the Methodist, Presbyterian, Baptist, and Congregational churches. It is important to note that while the Congregationalists in the AMA were egalitarian activists who strongly promoted equality among the races and the development of African Americans as free autonomous citizens, they in fact were promoting a paternalistic ideology. This ideology portrayed the newly emancipated African American as inferior by heredity.

CREATION OF THE FREEDMEN'S BUREAU

It was during this early postwar period that more than four dozen northern missionary organizations (some of which were highlighted above) began focusing their efforts on the South. The leaders of these societies quickly began to realize that the work was enormous, and too large an undertaking for any one association, or for even an amalgamation of well-intentioned individuals. So they developed a centralized or organized unit to focus on the maintenance and coordination of educational programs and activities, as well as protect the legal rights of African Americans. Their lobbying resulted in the creation of the Freedmen's Bureau by Congress. This Bureau became the official agency responsible for the coordination of services aimed at protecting the rights of those who had recently been emancipated from slavery.

The protections offered to African Americans by the Freedmen's Bureau during the period immediately following the war were vital given the reality of the "black codes" that had been instituted in the South after the war. These laws provided White Southerners with the means to accept the abolishment of slavery, but also gave them an opportunity to establish new forms of dominance (which they had patterned after northern class relationships) over their former African-American slaves' job potential off the plantation. Whites were often unwilling to enter into work contracts with the Freedmen because of their prevailing southern feelings and opinions about issues of equality. Therefore, while there was a significant need to secure funds for supplies to educate African Americans, the primary focus of the Freedmen's Bureau had to be the civil and political rights of those African Americans who had been recently liberated through the war efforts. Thus, the Freedmen Bureau's efforts to safeguard these rights are the greatest example of what the establishment of this organization meant to African Americans.

The irony in this, as Donald Spivey (1978) notes, was that "as the dominant authority over black destinies at the end of the Civil War, the Bureau clearly indicated with its actions that the newly found freedom was to be severely circumscribed" (Spivey 1978, 3). In other words, in reality, the Bureau served as a "conservative bulwark," as he saw it, that ultimately neglected African Americans' efforts in their pursuit of freedom and equality, instead privileging the preservation of White Southerners' control. Spivey also agrees with W.E.B. Du Bois' assessment, during the early 1900s, that the purpose of the Freedmen's Bureau was to develop a system of labor that benefited the White landowner. In preserving sharecropping, tenant farming, and debt peonage—recognized as free labor—the economic reenslavement of African Americans was assured. The education and total freedom of African Americans were ultimately reduced to an afterthought and became invisible in the federal government's agenda for serving this group of people.

THE DEBATE: EDUCATION OR COMMON RIGHTS

The meaning of education for former slaves, now emancipated adults, was a topic of debate during this time. Some African Americans envisioned a broad view of freedom in which education was seen as a necessary but not the most important, nor a sufficient means for achieving their goals. For example, Martin R. Delaney (Butchart 1980, 177) spoke militantly about the need for land, for cooperative effort, and for an armed African-American militia. Fredrick Douglass also spoke out for a more comprehensive approach toward supporting equality, liberty, and justice. He also strongly supported focusing on schools and education. In general, this was a common sentiment expressed throughout the southern states by both educated and illiterate African Americans, especially at the Black conventions held in the late 1860s. The core feeling among most African Americans was that education was subordinate to their demands for economic, political, and equal treatment before the law, both in the work and social environments (Butchart 1980).

Thus, Robert Purves, a free Black and member of the American Anti-Slavery Society, and others took sharp exception with leaders of the American Freedmen's Union Commission, a northern White benevolent aid society, that "education was important or more important than the ballot for Negroes" (But-chart 1980, 177). While the White-run Freedmen's Bureau supported the contention that education itself was the major tool to freedom, the nature and content of this education was at issue. In fact, the various groups and organizations providing education to African Americans had vastly different philosophies and purposes.

For instance, the church-led organizations were typically in agreement with the Freedmen's Bureau about the purpose of education for Blacks: each group emphasized education's ability to bind and neutralize. Attendant to this belief, they conceived of education for African-Americans as a means to manipulate the African-American community, to limit its aspirations and power, and to maintain a dependent status on the dominant class. Therefore, the hidden curriculum of African-American education included an emphasis on usefulness, virtue, Christianity, and obedience. The materials supplied by the Freedmen's Bureau were evidence of this ideology and emphasized "docility, obsequiousness, and morality, and hardly mentioned the need or desire for political equality" (Butchart 1980, 146). African Americans resisted an industrial education that promoted subordination rather than liberation. They desired the traditional liberal or classical curriculum. Justice, protection, the acquisition of land and power were equally important also (Butchart 1980, 65). Thus, almost from the beginning, a chasm based on such ideological differences developed between Caucasians and African Americans regarding the scope and meaning of education and the priority it should be given.

REGIONAL DIFFERENCES: THE RACIAL DIVIDE

Complicating these existing racial divisions was the fact that while White northern aid societies promoted a narrow, pacifying vision of education for African Americans, southern Whites opposed it entirely and displayed resistance in ways ranging from cool indifference to violent assaults on northern teachers and their school properties. Such deep antipathy is what Butchart (1980) interprets as being a reaction to the "continuation of a peculiarly Southern way of dealing with problems, frustrations, or fears . . . prompted by racism, rebellion, and political consideration" (p. 181). This was related to the perspective that education in any form should not be provided to those considered to be inferior.

Such violent reactions to the education of African Americans functioned to reassert the existing southern hegemony in every facet of life. Indeed, southern Whites were fearful, even terrified, about losing their social control. This included control over African Americans as a source of labor, but also control over the privileged lifestyle, culture, and customs that Whites enjoyed in the South. The idea of mass education for African Americans was an additional undesirable ingredient that promised to threaten the coveted southern socioeconomic and political views which had become essential to the southern way of doing things. To them, a rising tide of educated African Americans would widen the slippery fissures that already existed between African Americans and Whites on issues of freedom, equality, liberty, and justice.

It was because of these divisive race relations, differences among the various organizational ideologies concerning services to African Americans, and the reality of a war-ravaged South in need of major repair to its infrastructure, that the northern philanthropists were called upon to make substantial contributions.

THE EMERGING ROLE OF PHILANTHROPIC FOUNDATIONS

In response to the concerted call for support from missionary societies, as well as from African-American and White leaders, the northern philanthropists began to organize for the effort. They developed goals and objectives for giving, and set up processes to determine who was to receive what funds for which purpose and when. The George Peabody Fund was the first major philanthropic body to provide aid to the educational development of southern states after the Civil War.

In 1867, Peabody requested that this fund be used for "the promotion and encouragement of intellectual, moral, or industrial education among the young of the more destitute portions of the Southern and Southwestern states of our Union." (Leavell 1970, 61). Most of the money from the Peabody Fund supported White primary, normal schools, even though Peabody, an international merchant and financier, had earmarked funds for "improving education among the poorer classes of the South without regard to race" (Curtis and Nash 1965, 172). According to Leavell, once established, the fund emphasized four areas of charitable giving: the promotion of common schools; scholarships for teacher training and the establishment of normal schools; establishment of a permanent public school system in the South; and the promotion of science education and industrial pursuits.

A small number of these grants were allocated to African-American teachers' colleges. According to Peeps (1981), the fact that the Peabody Fund gave money to African-American private colleges is significant for two reasons. On the one hand, it established a trend-setting philosophy, which advocated for the education of African Americans. On the other hand, the Peabody Fund took the position that it would cooperate with southern opinion. Curtis and Nash (1965) concluded that "This meant that segregation was maintained, vocational training was promoted, . . . and control of the institutions was kept out of Negro hands" (p. 175).

As the years passed and leadership of the Peabody Fund changed into the hands of the next generation, the views that Blacks were infantile with low mental abilities (Enck 1970) remained. As an influential philanthropy, the ideology of the Peabody Fund leaders spilled over to other philanthropic groups, such as the Slater Fund.

The Slater Fund was more specific in its giving than the Peabody Fund. John

F. Slater, a Rhode Islander who obtained his wealth from textile manufacturing, established the fund particularly for African Americans. Slater was convinced that education for African Americans was needed after he heard a very powerful sermon exhorting the faithful to use their wealth to advance the opportunities of others. Committing a million dollars for the education of African Americans, in 1882 Slater appointed a board of ten White males to administer the fund and gave them complete autonomy to appropriate the fund for "uplifting the lately emancipated population of the southern states" (Leavell 1970, 63).

Programs funded by the Slater Fund had to emphasize morality and citizenship. To accomplish this, Slater believed that African Americans should receive a combination of the common branches of secular learning and religious training. Additionally, he stressed that his money be distributed "in no partisan, sectional, or sectarian spirit" (Fisher 1986, 3). The money had to be used to promote and not discourage African Americans in the South from helping themselves. In 1890, the Slater Fund and the Peabody Fund merged. Eventually, the Peabody Fund was completely dissolved, and in 1914 it became a part of the existing Slater Fund (Fisher 1986, xii, 108; Curtis and Nash 1965, 172). The county training school then evolved out of George Peabody's desire to establish a school system. The fund emphasized community-centered programs aimed directly at helping rural African-American adults improve their living conditions.

In 1903, the General Education Board (GEB) was incorporated to fund projects for rural adult education for African Americans. The GEB earned special recognition because of its extensive influence and financial contributions to education in the South. Curtis, in his observation of the GEB, states, "No other agency, public or private, exerted a comparable force in shaping Negro Higher Education (1965, 173). The GEB began with a one-million-dollar bequest from John D. Rockefeller, and by 1921, the Board's endowment had risen to $129 million. "The Board" had significant influence and power which it used in a broad educational mandate. The GEB acquired and exercised "virtual monopolistic" control of educational philanthropy for the North and South (Harlan 1969, 87). Eventually, it gained operational control of the previously mentioned funds, and the agents from the other philanthropies that worked for or with the GEB.

The trustees of both the Slater Fund and the GEB were vocal and adamant supporters of "White superiority," and noted that Southerners had won them over to their way of thinking. Critics of this group characterized philanthropists and their supporters as thoroughly "Southernized" (Enck 1970, 91–92). Thus, although they established policy for southern rural education and were major spokesmen for funds, which primarily provided for the education of African Americans, they *still* took the position that African Americans were racially inferior.

William H. Baldwin, Jr., the first president of GEB, articulated this general attitude toward African Americans for the Board. He became interested in the African-American situation during his years with the J. P. Morgan Southern

Railroad. He viewed African Americans as "invaluable laborers who were properly suited for the South" (Fosdick 1962, 11). Baldwin also believed that African Americans could not be educated much beyond the three "Rs." In fact, the view that the African American should not be educated out of his/her environment was the dominant refrain. So, Baldwin, as did many others, believed industrial work was the key. "He must work . . . at trade and on the land. . . . Except in the rarest of instances, I am bitterly opposed to the so-called higher education of Negroes" (Fosdick 1962, 11).

Wallace Buttrick, long-time chairman of the board at the GEB, also insisted on excluding African Americans from the administrative positions in the foundation. Buttrick was afraid of alienating White Southerners; therefore, he did not support any bold innovations for African Americans. As a result, funds were allocated to agricultural and vocational training rather than to liberal arts and professional instruction, in keeping with the southern White's opinion of what was needed to keep the African American in his/her place.

PHILANTHROPIC DILEMMA: "BLACK INDUSTRIAL EDUCATION" OR CLASSICAL EDUCATION

The debate that ultimately ensued between W.E.B. Du Bois and Booker T. Washington is a classic example of how African Americans were affected by this ideology, philanthropy's influence, and ultimately, the funding their schools received. This debate centered around whether Blacks should be given a classical education or an education that focused on trades and skills—more aptly referred to as "Black industrial education." This debate did not begin with them, but was escalated by them, as they sought to determine the type of education African Americans should receive in order to obtain control over their own lives.

The debate between these two, as well as others, is one that gives us insights into how philanthropic giving shaped and controlled the lives of African Americans. Even while advocating for the power and support of the Freedmen's Bureau, missionary and church groups continued providing basic education, and in some cases more advanced levels of education, to African-American adults. For example, the Congregationalists believed in developing the broader intellectual capabilities of African Americans. Supported by the AMA, this denomination is recognized as having had the greatest single impact on southern Black education (Butchart 1980), as a result of its efforts in establishing numerous prominent colleges and universities for African Americans.

These included Fisk (1866) in Nashville, Tennessee; Atlanta University (1867) in Atlanta, Georgia; Howard University (1867) in Washington, D.C.; and Talladega College (1867) in Talladega, Alabama. The educational philosophy of these schools reflected "classical" training, but emphasized the provision of "the rudiments of learning" (Holmes 1934, 172). Since most African Americans began their educational process with little or no education, these colleges and universities had to begin teaching them at the elementary and secondary levels.

This, therefore, provided a strong rationale for establishing schools that focused on classical training. The curriculum focused on the liberal arts, which included literature and the arts as a way to develop the entire person into a citizen. Moreover, it was seen as a way to "uplift" the African-American community.

As noted previously, however, because the northern philanthropists accepted and aligned themselves with the Southerners' way of thinking, the notion of racial uplift and the promotion of the life of the mind was antithetical to their idea of merely training African Americans as a useful source of labor. The result was that philanthropic support was freely given to those institutions and individuals that promoted this ideology and taught "Black industrial education. Thus, "Black industrial education" was important to White Southerners for reasons which were grounded in both racism and capitalism.

The idea of "Black industrial education" was initiated in 1868 and promoted by General Samuel Chapman Armstrong, formerly of the Union Army. This term evolved during the same time that conventional industrial education was being developed to meet the needs of the industrial revolution. The focus of conventional industrial education was on the use of machinery and the creation of vocational skills for factory and industrial jobs, as well as work related to new, emerging agricultural technology. This was also a time in which the industrial structure and the education needed to participate within it were characterized by growth and change in society. Black industrial education, on the other hand, involved training for menial jobs including low-level agricultural work, blacksmith work, and some carpentry for men, as well as crafts and domestic labor services for women. It also involved "attitudinal training" that stressed docility, obedience, a love for hard work, and the acceptance of a demeaning and subservient social role within the existing social order. This concept was consistent with the social and political reality that White Southerners had about African Americans' place and role in society. Furthermore, Jim Crow had a stranglehold on the country as legal segregation and discrimination defined the lives of Black and White Americans.

Through the generous support of Northerners, General Armstrong was able to promote his ideology through the founding of the Hampton Institute. Interestingly, even though its members were not keen advocates of Armstrong's "Black industrial education," the AMA also provided some support to Hampton. The AMA generally accepted the teaching of skilled trades such as printing, carpentry, and blacksmithing for student work programs, as well as character development. However, these courses were viewed as insignificant for intellectual and leadership training. The proponents of the Hampton model never accepted this interpretation of industrial education and later resistance emerged from AMA leaders at the close of the nineteenth century (Anderson 1988, 67). In 1881, Dr. Booker T. Washington, a Hampton graduate and protégé of Armstrong's, founded the Tuskegee Institute, which ultimately became highly instrumental in promoting the ideology of Black industrial education. This was done with significant support from northern philanthropists.

The Washington camp worked diligently to please White society and to make African Americans "the best labor in the world" (Spivey 1978, 96). According to Donald Spivey, Washington was considered the "great Moses" of the South by the northern industrial barons. In siding with northern philanthropists and southern educators, and thereby promoting an education of skills and trades, Booker T. Washington ultimately clashed with those who believed that African Americans should be given an education in the classics.

To help promote the goals and initiatives of the Hampton Institute and Tuskegee, an endowment of one million dollars was presented to these institutions by Anna Thomas Jeanes, in 1907. The purpose of this money was to create the Negro Rural School Fund. It later became known as the Jeanes Fund. As a result of the Jeanes' contribution, and the collaboration that was forged in 1911 with the GEB and the John F. Slater Fund, the system of "Black industrial education" became even more entrenched in the southern way of life (Anderson 1988; Lester 1938). A three-pronged approach was used to facilitate the work of this group's collaboration. This team included a White male state supervisor, a county training school, and a Black female serving as the Jeanes Industrial Teacher Supervisor, who traveled among the rural schools introducing and supervising women in simple forms of industrial work. So, the Jeanes' School Movement was started in 1908 (NASC Interim History Writing Committee 1979).

Emerging in opposition to this movement, however, were those who promoted "classical" education for Blacks. As noted previously, Du Bois and Washington did not see eye to eye on what type of education Blacks ought to receive. The debate became particularly divisive between the proponents of "classical" training (Du Bois) and those who promoted "Black industrial education." In fact, Du Bois and Washington engaged in many heated debates over these issues. A forceful advocate for "classical" instruction, Du Bois found much support for his position in the Black community; and as would be expected, lines were drawn and loyalties strengthened between those who were in the "classical" institution camp and those that were in the Black industrial education camp.

For example, one outcome of the Du Bois camp's efforts was the emergence of the Niagara Movement, which fought for civil liberties as well as equal educational opportunities. In 1910 this movement produced the National Association for the Advancement of Colored People (NAACP). Ironically, even though many northern philanthropists supported the Black industrial education movement, in supporting the newly emerged NAACP they were lending credence and support to classical education for African Americans. In fact, Black universities and vocational schools that were started during this time and that remain in existence today are further evidence of this point. Much of the funding for these organizations continues to be from White philanthropists. However, they now also rely on federal and state aid to continue their growth and stability within the community.

EDUCATORS' RESISTANCE TO BLACK INDUSTRIAL EDUCATION

While there were many leaders within the African-American community who supported the Jeanes' Movement and its prevailing ideology concerning the role that education should play in African Americans' lives, there were many that did not. In fact, ironically many of those who had been trained in private mission schools or African-American schools that followed the classics or liberal arts curriculum resisted the Jeanes' model. Likewise, former students of those programs, those who were teachers, or even Jeanes supervisors also resisted it. Thus, it is important to note that not all rural teachers were willing functionaries who taught "Black industrial education." For example, in 1913, Leo Favrot, a Jeanes State Supervisor for Arkansas, reported indifference to industrial education among Black teachers. Furthermore, other state supervisors reported that those Black colleges that had been specifically commissioned to promote industrial education were not doing so (Anderson 1988a, 142). This discovery, along with widening resistance among teachers in rural areas, triggered a special conference that brought together all GEB state supervisors within the Black southern school system. The conference participants produced recommendations suggesting some modifications to the "Negro County Training Schools" curriculum. The result was that liberal arts subjects began to be interspersed with industrial education courses in the school curriculum.

In sum, some African Americans did not readily accept the Black industrial education concept presented to them by General Armstrong, the southern educators and the northern philanthropists. They perceived it as another method of restricting their social, economic, and political rise and of deeply burying them into a system that was unjust and unequal; and, there were definitely those who preferred "classical" and liberal arts training, a training which sought to cultivate the intellect and prepare African Americans to participate on any level in American society. One approach could thrive and flourish under segregation, while the other demanded the death of segregation.

PHILANTHROPY: BENEVOLENCE OR RACIST REACTIONISM?

Many motives have been assigned to the philanthropic work of Northerners in terms of African Americans and southern rural education. African-American liberal scholars and historians like Horace Mann Bond, John Hope Franklin, and Henry Bullock have contended that White philanthropists were motivated entirely by benevolence, even though they appeared paternalistic. In spite of this, their giving served the interests and needs of the early emancipated slaves. In fact, in their view, the philanthropists' zeal to uplift the Black race and to establish schools for them was considered to be of the highest form of benevolence or "noblesse oblige." In addition, voices such as Bond, and others, saw the schools as institutions that promoted and offered needed social, economic, and moral elevation to this group (Finkenbine 1982, 45). (All of this is from one citation.)

On the other hand, a more critical perspective of northern philanthropy, as represented by James D. Anderson, Ronald Butchart, and Donald Spivey, has squarely focused on the racist character and hegemonic interests of the philanthropic elite, especially those who wanted to develop institutions that would mold individuals to accept a particular form of economic order and White rule in the postwar South. The work of these scholars promotes the idea that Black schools were institutions created primarily out of concern for industrial conquest and White dominance in the United States. Their specific motive appeared to be the development and maintenance of a White industrialist hegemony in the New South (Finkenbine 1982, 45).

Indeed, one could argue that the North was keenly aware of the South's economic, political, and social status, and the fact that masses of African-American adults needed jobs, education, and permanent housing. Furthermore, due to the lack of these basic necessities and the existing oppression, many African Americans did not want to remain in the South, so they began their migration to the North. The philanthropic elite living in the North really did not want African Americans to move northward; they wanted the African-American problem to remain a southern one. So their philanthropic giving was not out of caring for African Americans, but was done in order to keep African Americans in their place—in the South.

CONCLUSION

While the early history of philanthropy toward African Americans in this country appears to have worked to keep them inferior and unable to fully assimilate into American society, it nonetheless enabled them to receive training and education. In fact, vocational and domestic education became the springboard for many to reach newer intellectual and economic heights. With education comes empowerment, and soon African Americans were able to fully assimilate into this country. From this perspective, early philanthropic efforts built the bridge that African Americans would ultimately cross as they continued their quest to achieve educational, social, and political equality in the United States. White philanthropists or Southerners in the nineteenth and early twentieth centuries could never have assessed the hunger African Americans had for education; for if they had, they might not have contributed their monies to those programs that ultimately gave African Americans a chance to participate more fully in American society.

Even though "Black industrial education" was strongly resisted by many members within the African-American community, the Jeanes program, in particular, significantly influenced southern rural education, and developed many functional adult programs. The programs initiated under the Jeanes Movement are now being carried out by the Cooperative Extension Service of the U.S. Department of Agriculture's county and home demonstration agents.

There are other parallels. For instance, 90 years ago, the Jeanes supervisors were required to link schools and communities. Today, rural school reform is "starting with the assumption that rural schools need to be tightly linked to their communities. This is consistent with Jacqueline Spears' analysis of what is currently occurring in schools. According to her, "we have looked especially carefully at broad issues and mandates, such as the requirement that schools develop missions that reflect multicultural ideals, in an effort to understand how schools translate those broad mandates into language and goals more appropriate to the needs of the local community" (Spears 1991, 3). Today's practitioners, like their Jeanes counterparts, are also looking more carefully at adult learning that takes place as more community members become involved in educational reform issues.

Clearly, African Americans continue to participate in adult education programs and activities throughout the United States. Programs are offered in both urban and rural communities through Cooperative Extension Services, community colleges, community organizations, churches, and places of employment. Modern-day philanthropic organizations, like the MacArthur, Ford, Kellogg, and Annenberg/CPB foundations, continue to support both urban and rural, and classical and vocational educational initiatives for adults and children. While educational, economic, and social opportunities have advanced for African Americans, many programs designed to serve this population continue to receive funding from White philanthropists. Undoubtedly, given that funding of such programs is needed in order to survive, it is inevitable that the same questions concerning who controls what will continue to be asked.

It is, therefore, important that we in adult education continue to engage in a discourse about these matters, as many of our programs that serve the disenfranchised are receiving such funding. Likewise, the urban adult educator needs a broader understanding of these issues. As Jon Van Til (1990), another contemporary scholar and critic of philanthropy, has suggested: "philanthropy can be misguided, ineffective, and deceptive in its application. . . . Where the advance of a society is concerned, no invisible hand guides the philanthropists. This form of activity, like so many others, may produce clarity or deception, hope or despair, progress or the persistence of injustice" (1990, 27). As adult educators often bound by funding mandates and program directives, we must continually reflect on our role in promoting hegemony, or resisting it.

REFERENCES

Anderson, James D. (1973). "Education for Servitude: The Social Purpose of Schooling in the Black South, 1870–1930" Doctoral Dissertation, University of Illinois at Urbana–Champaign.

Anderson, James D. (1978). "Hampton Model of Normal School Industrial Education,

1868–1900." In V. P. Franklin and J. D. Anderson (eds.), *New Perspectives on Black Educational History*, 61–96. Boston: G. K. Hall.

Anderson, James D. (1988a). *Education of Blacks in the South, 1860–1935*. Chapel Hill: University of North Carolina Press.

Anderson, James D. (1988b). "Northern Foundations and the Shaping of Southern Black Rural Education, 1902–1935." In B. E. McClellan and W. J. Reese (eds.), *The Special History of American Education*, 287–312. Chicago: University of Illinois Press.

Barksdale, Richard, and Kinnamon, Kenneth. (1972). *Black Writers of America: A Comprehensive Anthology*. Englewood Cliffs, NJ: Prentice-Hall.

Bond, Horace Mann. (1966). *The Education of the Negro in the American Social Order*. New York: Octagon Books.

Bullock, Henry Allen. (1967). *A History of Negro History Education in the South: From 1619 to the Present*. Cambridge, MA: Harvard University Press.

Butchart, Ronald. (1980). *Northern Schools, Southern Blacks, and Reconstruction Freedmen's Education, 1862–1875*. Westport, CT: Greenwood Press.

Chapman, Bernadine S. (1990). "Northern Philanthropy and African American Adult Education in the Rural South: Hegemony and Resistance in the Jeanes Movement." Doctoral Dissertation, Northern Illinois University.

Curtis, Merle, and Nash, Roderick. (1965). *Philanthropy in the Shaping of American Higher Education*. New Brunswick, NJ: Rutgers University Press.

Daniel, Walter G., and Holden, John B. (1966). *Ambrose Caliver: Adult Educator and Civil Servant*. Washington, DC: Adult Education Association.

Dillard, James Hardy. "Jeanes Fund Report." Accession No. 9498, Box 15, Folder 1908–1910. Charlottesville: Jeanes Foundation, James Hardy Dillard Papers, University of Virginia Library.

Dillard, James Hardy. Report, "Report to Mr. Chairman and Gentlemen of the Board," 9 December 1908. Accession No. 9498, Box 15, Folder 1908–1934. Charlottesville: Jeanes Foundation, James Hardy Dillard Papers, University of Virginia Library.

Enck, Henry S. (1970). "The Burden Borne: Northern White Philanthropy and Southern Black Industrial Education, 1900–1915." Doctoral Dissertation, University of Cincinnatti.

Finkenbine, Roy E. (1982). "A Little Circle: White Philanthropists and Black Industrial Education in the Post-bellum South." Doctoral Dissertation, Bowling Green State University.

Fisher, Donald. (1983). "The Role of Philanthropic Foundations in the Reproduction and Production of Hegemony: Rockefeller Foundation and the Social Sciences." *Journal of British Sociological Association* 17(2) (May), 206–233.

Fisher, John E. (1986). *The John F. Slater Fund: A Nineteenth Century Affirmative Action for Negro Education*. Lanham, MD: University Press of America.

Fosdick, Raymond B. (1962). *Adventure in Giving: The Story of the General Education Board*. New York: Harper and Row.

Graubard, Stephen R. (1987). Preface to the Issue, "Philanthropy, Patronage, Politics." *Daedalus*, v–xx.

Gross, Ronald. (1977). *The Lifelong Learner*. New York: Simon and Schuster.

Harlan, Louis. (1969). *Separate and Unequal: Public School Campaigns and Racism in the Southern Seaboard States, 1901–1915*. New York: Atheneum.

Holmes, Dwight O. W. (1934). "The Beginning of the Negro College." *Journal of Negro Education* 3(2) (April), 168–93.

Kellogg, W. K. Foundation. "Programming Guidelines." http://www.wkkf.org/base system/sec/wkkf/filecomponent/187_prog_gen_gdln.html_, 1–1.

Leavell, Ullin Whitney. (1970). *Philanthropy in Negro Education.* Westport, CT: Negro University Press.

Lester, Robert M. (1938). *The Corporation and the Jeanes Teacher.* New York: Carnegie Corporation of New York.

McGee, Leo, and Neufeldt, Harvey. (1985). *Education of the Black Adult in the United States.* Westport, CT: Greenwood Press.

Merriam, Sharan B., and Brockett, Ralph G. (1997). *The Profession and Practice of Adult Education.* San Francisco: Jossey-Bass.

Miller, Bruce A. (1995). "The Role of Rural Schools in Rural Community Development." *ERIC Digest* (August), ED No. 384 479, 1–5.

NASC Interim History Writing Committee. (1979). *The Jeanes Story: A Chapter in the History of American Education, 1908–1968.* Jackson, MS: Southern Education Foundation.

National Negro School News. February 1911, Accession No. 9498, Box 15, Folder 1921–1935. Charlottesville: James Hardy Dillard Papers, University of Virginia Library.

Peabody, Francis Greenwood. (1920). *Education for Life: The Story of Hampton Institute.* New York: Doubleday.

Peeps, J. M. Stephen. (1981). "Northern Philanthropy and the Emergency of Black Higher Education-Do-Gooders, Compromisers, or Co-Conspirators?" *Journal of Negro Education* 50, 251–269.

Peterson, E. A. (ed.). (1996). *Freedom Road: Adult Education of African Americans.* Malabar, FL: Kreiger Publishing Co.

Reid, Ira De A. (1936). *Adult Education Among Negroes.* Washington, DC: The Association of Negro Folk Education.

Rice, Jessie Pearl. (1949). *J.L.M. Curry, Southerner, Statesman and Educator.* New York: King's Crown Press.

"Rich Learn How to Give Money Away." (1998). *News & Record,* May 3, A12.

Spears, Jacqueline. (1998). "Lessons Learned from Our Work in Rural Adult Education." Speech given at the 1991 National Conference on Rural Adult Education Initiatives (March). http://www/personal.ksu.edu/~rcled/raed/lessons.html, 1–3.

Spivey, Donald. (1978). *Schooling for the New Slavery: Black Industrial Education, 1868–1915.* Westport, CT: Greenwood Press.

Stubblefield, H. W., and Keane, P. (1994). *Adult Education in the American Experience from the Colonial Period to the Present.* San Francisco: Jossey-Bass.

Van Til, Jon. (1990). "Defining Philanthropy." In Jon Van Til and Associates (eds.), *Critical Issues in American Philanthropy,* 19–38. San Francisco: Jossey-Bass.

Wuthnow, Robert. (1990). "Religion and the Voluntary Spirit in the United States: Mapping the Terrain." In Robert Wuthnow and Associates (eds.), *Faith and Philanthropy in America,* 3–21. San Francisco: Jossey-Bass.

Chapter 9

Struggling to Learn, Learning to Struggle: Workers, Workplace Learning, and the Emergence of Human Resource Development

Fred M. Schied

INTRODUCTION

Human Resource Development (HRD), a concept barely known until about 25 years ago, has become the dominant model for workplace education. Indeed, HRD has become the fastest growing segment of adult education (Dirkx 1996). While definitions of HRD vary somewhat, the fundamental objective of HRD is on maximizing organizational effectiveness in order to support organizational goals. Thus education, whether formal, nonformal, or informal is designed to meet these organizational goals. Watkins (1989) expands this concept in a way that reflects the total development of individuals within an organizational context. She asserts, "Human resource development is the field of study and practice responsible for the fostering of a long-term, work-related learning capacity at the individual, group and organizational level" (p. 427). Watkins further argues that the centrality of learning requires the active involvement of employees, and that retraining and the outsourcing of the workforce are two of HRD's biggest challenges.

Carter (2000) argues that missing from this conceptualization is the central function of HRD as an all-inclusive process that links training and development in order to shape and control employees. As Rothwell and Sredl (1992) conclude, HRD professionals are instruments of control. The following statement highlights this:

HRD professionals are frequently responsible for facilitating the socialization of individuals into work settings. . . . As individuals are socialized, they conform to a body of articulated or inarticulated ethical standards and norms of behavior. . . . HRD professionals are also asked frequently by their employers to train others on . . . corporate codes of conduct and implement change that will bring employee behavior into compliance with legal, regulatory, and other mandated requirements. (p. 190)

It is ironic, then, that proponents of HRD make some of their elaborate, unsubstantiated claims. One recent article even went so far as to suggest that HRD, when framed within adult education, is a process that leads to a democratic workplace (Dirkx 1996).

Despite the vast amount of uncritical literature, the intellectual basis of HRD has been criticized by some progressive adult educators. Baptiste (1994) and Rubenson (1992), among others, have pointed out that the economic rationale for HRD, human capital theory, is much more problematic than its advocates suggest. They challenge human capital theory's basic tenant that long-term benefits or rate of return from investment in education leads directly to increased productivity and economic growth. Foley (1994) has strongly critiqued the notion of a supposedly massive shift to post-Fordist forms of production, arguing instead that workplace reorganization is a technical rather than a historical process. Hart (1992) has cogently argued that the economic foundation of work rests on the unpaid work of women. Nevertheless, despite this growing body of literature, the context and reasons for HRD's emergence have not yet been adequately addressed. Understanding the historical context in which HRD emerged is central to understanding current issues swirling around "who controls learning" and "who controls knowledge production" in the workplace.

Much of the historical work that does exist has uncritically viewed HRD as the latest and most humanistic phase of an ongoing educational process where an organization facilitates the learning of its employees so that they can become more productive and "empowered." Traditional histories have taken an anecdotal and evolutionary approach to the emergence of HRD. Thus, virtually anything remotely resembling education is seen as a precursor to present-day HRD activities.

This has led to some almost bizarre claims as to the historical origins of training and development and its latest manifestation, HRD. These include but are not limited to tracing the origins of HRD back, either to the creation of a "mature" factory system in the 1880s, or to the apprenticeship system. It can even be traced back to 1630, when efficient "management of the factors of production" created the circumstances in which the workforce was educated. In fact, *The Handbook for Training and Development* begins its discussion of the history of training by highlighting the training involved in building a Summarian Palace in 3500 B.C. (Frank 1988; Jacobson 1991; Mech 1984; Miller 1987)!

In contrast to these descriptive, simplistic, and uncritical historical examinations, this chapter argues that HRD has emerged from a specific historical, economic, and social situation that occurred in the United States before and after World War II. Rather than a chronological history, this chapter examines three themes that have led to the creation of the present form of worker discipline, of which HRD is a part. This chapter will begin by addressing Taylorism and the emergence of corporate training that began shortly before and during World War II and led to the creation of the American Society of Training and Development (ASTD). Then, I will discuss the strength of the labor movement after World War II. Finally, I will explore the emergence of human capital theory and its influence on HRD as a field of practice. Embedded in this discussion is the ongoing struggle about who controls workers' knowledge.

TAYLORISM, THE HAWTHORNE STUDIES, AND THE PRODUCTION OF CONTROL

The most influential method used to organize work in the United States has been through the use of scientific management. Based on the works of Frederick Taylor, scientific management (or Taylorism) applied "science" to organizing work. Traditional worker skills were replaced by scientific analysis. Jobs were broken down into their smallest parts, job tasks were strictly defined, and hierarchical structures were developed to provide a logical, rational means to control behavior. All problems, it was argued, would give way to technical solutions. Efficiency and rationality became the gods of industry. Central to this notion was control. According to Taylor (1911), "It is only through enforced standardization of methods, enforced adoption of the best implements and working conditions, and enforced cooperation that this faster work can be assured. And the duty of enforcing the adoption of standards and enforcing this cooperation rests with the management alone" (p. 83). Thus, Taylorism was more than just a narrow efficiency model for production, it opened the door for the scientific study of human behavior.

The first to apply science to the study of human behavior in industry were Elton Mayo and his associates at the Western Electric plant in Cicero, Illinois. The famous Hawthorne studies, as they came to be known, were conducted between 1924 and 1933. Through these studies Elton Mayo and his associates "discovered" that psychological factors were important to increasing the production at the plant. Workers were now seen not as just economic entities but as individuals with both psychological and social needs and interests. Rather than being a reaction against Taylorism, the Hawthorne studies and the entire human relations movement in industry can be seen as bringing science, in the form of psychology, to the shop floor. The human factor in production became subject to scientific investigation through the new discipline of industrial psychology.

The Hawthorne studies, the foundational building block of the entire human relations movement, have come under frequent and consistent attack for both their managerial bias and their methodological problems. Because of their importance, Bramel and Friend (1981) describe these studies as being the genesis of the field of HRD—which is in fact one of the creation myths promoted by industrial psychologists and sociologists. Bramel and Friend also point out that Mayo's advocacy of human relations was rationalized in such a way that the problem began to be seen as how workers could be manipulated into becoming a supportive group—as defined by management.

Rose (1985) and Clegg and Dunkerly (1980) have criticized Mayo for not understanding the historical and social context of the workers within the workplace, thus portraying workers as illogical and irrational. Gillespie (1991), in the most thorough review of the Hawthorne studies, makes the point that Mayo and his colleagues approached their research with some very strong managerial assumptions. Gillespie notes that Mayo and his colleagues assumed, but did not demonstrate, that happier workers work harder. They also equated worker satisfaction with higher levels of production, assumed that workers were not able to organize collectively and deliberately to reshape their work practices in positive ways, and they took for granted complete managerial control of the workplace. As Gillespie notes: "Human relations told managers that no matter how much they might be forced to bargain with unions over wages and conditions, workers' basic understanding of the workplace was flawed by their specific psychological needs and their personal situation. . . . Human relations confirmed managerial assumptions that only management was able to assess what was best for both the company and its workforce" (p. 238).

This has implications for managerial ideology, as Rose (1985) succinctly points out. "What, after all, could be more appealing than to be told that one's subordinates are non-logical; that their uncooperativeness is a frustrated urge to collaborate; that their demands for cash mask a need for approval, and that you [the manager] have a historic destiny as a broker of social harmony?" (p. 124).

Taylorism and the Hawthorne studies provided the intellectual scaffolding for human relations, but it was developments within the corporate sector that provided the structure for human relations training to be applied to workers.

THE AMERICAN SOCIETY OF TRAINING DIRECTORS (ASTD) AND THE EMERGENCE OF CORPORATE TRAINING

Industrial training was provided through corporation schools as early as 1872. These schools varied in structure and content, provided training in everything from technical skills to English as a second language to salesmanship. Increasingly influenced by the Frederick Taylor's management theories, corporation schools were a means to acclimate the workforce to a rationalized industrialization process; efficiency was always of utmost concern. In a revealing statement, a General Electric executive said that a corporation school "is an elementary school conducted by a corporation to Americanize alien railway labor, for instance; or a commercial school with university class rooms, and sometimes university lectures and credit; or a technical school with a course extending, as in one corporation, through four years of work of company worktime" (Steinmetz, quoted in Baker 1983, 57).

Following this trend, in 1913, 35 large corporations banded together to organize the National Association of Corporation Schools (NACS). Largely supported by the New York Edison Company, the NACS became a primary means to educate the workforce without outside control. In fact, while the NACS sought to establish reciprocal relationships with universities for management retraining, the association vehemently opposed any public scrutiny of its activities. The U.S. entrance into World War I in 1917 provided the NACS with the opportunity to offer its services to the Council on National Defense for Industrial Training for the War Emergency. A similar organization, the National Association of Employment Managers (later the Industrial Relations Association of America), also brought corporate educators together. Both organizations were enamored with the scientific management theories of Taylor and both organizations saw their importance rise with World War I mobilization (Eurich 1985; Moore 1980).

Thus, the World War I era brought about the beginning of a national network of corporate control of formal education. With World War II, the template of employer workplace education was formed. A major task during World War II was to train the large numbers of workers who began entering the workforce, many of whom were women. The National Defense Advisory Commission established a massive Training With Industry (TWI) program to assist in training this new workforce.

TWI had several different components. One of those components was a job relations program based on human relations principles. Out of these experiences the War Manpower Commission, a federal government agency, created the basic ideas, still in practice, of on-the job training. The men who provided leadership for this Commission represented the cream of corporate power and prestige and included: C. R. Dooley, personnel relations manager of Socony-Vacuum; Michael Kane of AT&T; Glenn Bardiner of Forstman Woolen Mills, William Conner of U.S. Steel, and Walter Dietz, personnel relations manager of Western Electric.

It is significant that Dietz designed large-scale job relations programs for supervisors during World War II. Familiar with the Hawthorne experiments that had been done at his company (Dietz even hired some of the original Hawthorne researchers to work on this project), the job relations program provided human relations training to almost 500,000 supervisors (Dooley 1945). In 1945, Dooley and Dietz won the human relations award from the American Management Association (Kirkpatrick 1945).

Dietz and the others were important inspirations for the creation of the American Society of Training Directors (ASTD) (later Training and Development). Founded in 1942 at the meeting of the American Petroleum Institute, the ASTD Training Directors began publishing its journal *Industrial Training News* in 1945, and by the end of the 1940s training was an important component of many of the newly created personnel departments (Mech 1984; Steinmentz 1967).

Corporate interest in training and the subsequent founding of the ASTD and the rise of personnel departments during and after World War II was not coincidental. Rather, it was in response to the challenges posed by a newly powerful and confident labor movement eager to become involved in fundamental issues of workplace control, including training and other personnel matters.

WORKERS' KNOWLEDGE AND SHOP FLOOR CONTROL

In his work on the lives of coal miners, John Brophy, a United Mineworkers leader, reflected back on his days of learning to be a coal miner by working with his father. Brophy remarked that: "It was a great satisfaction to me that my father was a skilled, clean workman with everything kept in shape. The skill with which you undercut the vein, the judgment in drilling the coal after it had been undercut and placing the exact amount of explosive so that it would do an effective job of breaking the coal from the solid . . . indicated the quality of his work" (Brophy 1964, 64). Brophy was quite aware that all knowledge didn't start with his generation, that miners had lived and worked and struggled and had passed their working knowledge on to their children and they in turn passed this knowledge on to their children.

Scientific management and Taylorism subsequently threatened this way of life, and the sense of control that one had over one's work. It also set the stage for the struggle over who controlled working knowledge. In mining, for example, once the process became mechanized, work could become subdivided. This subdivided work could come under close supervision by the foreman. As one miner put it: "Anyone with a weak head and a strong back can load machine coal, but a man has to think and study every day like you was studying a book if he is going to get the best of the coal when he uses only a pick" (Morris 1934, 18).

This de-skilling process, with its relentless drive for efficiency, occurred in many industries and at a varying rate. As a result, in the 1930s, a new category of "semi-skilled" workers was invented by the U.S. Census Bureau. Harvey Braverman (1974) has described how anyone working with machinery was considered semiskilled, rather than unskilled. Thus, machine operators from that point on were defined as having more skills than someone who, for example, had spent a lifetime working on a farm. Braverman further describes how this struggle, which began before World War I and reached its peak by World War II, was codified as a legitimate way to control workers' knowledge and skills.

As an outgrowth of this manipulation and control of labor, the union movement grew to unprecedented ranks. By the end of World War II, American organized labor had reached a point where J.B.S. Hardman, educational director for the Amalgamated Clothing Workers, noted the "amazingly rapid growth of unionism and of its power potential [had gone] beyond anything ever known" (Hardman 1951, 53). Indeed, labor union membership had grown fivefold since 1933. In many of the major manufacturing industries (coal, steel, auto, rubber, etc.) union coverage was almost complete. Moreover, an attempt to break the

coal miners' union during World War II had failed and a string of strikes during
the first years after the war resulted in a series of labor triumphs.

"Labor unions," Hardman went on to say, "have become a social power in
the nation and are conscious of their new importance." An extension of labor's
power was the attempt to establish a labor extension service, which was modeled
after the cooperative extension service. Indeed, during the late 1940s, the labor
movement was poised to reassert itself in ways that both threatened management
and harkened back to the early days of John Brophy: the days of worker control
of the shop floor and worker control of knowledge (p. 53).

To labor, everything was open to negotiation, including the right to manage.
The depression and then the war had previously confined the unions' ability to
move beyond "bread and butter" issues such as wages, hours, vacations, and the
rudiments of grievance and seniority systems. Now, however, the Congress for
Industrial Organizations (CIO) advocated a policy that would make unions co-
equal with management with the government acting as an arbitrator. The new-
ness of these demands provoked uneasiness within corporate managers.

Unions demanded (and succeeded, in some industries) the right to become
involved in discipline, bonus charges, job assignments, and involvement in training and education programs. They wanted involvement in financial policy, wage
determination policies, and other production issues as well. In short, labor sought
to co-manage the enterprise (Brody 1980, 1993; Jacoby 1985; Montgomery
1987).

The shop floor had become the site of struggle. The labor movement had
swept through the ranks of foremen, the front line managers. In 1946, one
management official was quoted as saying "We recognize that in some of our
shops the union committeeman exercises greater authority than the foreman."
Similarly, an automobile executive stated: "If any manager in this industry tells
you he has control of his plant he is a damn liar" (quoted in Brody 1980, 181).
As labor historian David Brody (1980) noted, American industry felt itself
embattled on every level; unions felt that they had a right to bargain regarding
all management functions, including training. In some industries, it was shop
stewards who decided how pay rates were to be set and who was to receive
training.

FROM PERSONNEL DEPARTMENTS TO HUMAN
RESOURCE MANAGEMENT

The co-management of enterprises did not occur, however. While the reasons
for this are complex, large corporations refused to surrender their control over
management functions. Unions, for their part, accepted dramatic increases in
wages, strong pension plans, and health and vacation plans in exchange for
giving up their demands around co-management and personnel functions. Thus,
all personnel functions, including training, were now totally under the control
of management.

The modern training function grew out of this context. Training had become a personnel function; it became something that the company largely organized and operated for its own purpose.

The psychological foundations of human relations management fit well with this newly emerged personnel function. Since unions were now removed from personnel decisions, organizations were faced with the task of managing, controlling, and training the workforce. Motivating workers and shaping their behavior became an effective way to control workers. Teaching work skills was a secondary concern. As Loren Baritz stated in *Servants of Power* (1960): "Through motivation studies, through counseling, through selection devices calculated to hire only certain types of people, through attitudinal surveys, communication, role playing, and all the rest in the bag of schemes, social scientists slowly moved towards a science of behavior. A new slick approach to the problem of control. Authority gave way to manipulation, and workers could no longer be sure if they were being exploited" (p. 209).

In fact, management turned to developing ways in which workers could be shaped and controlled. Drawing upon the methods used by the military during World War II, management formed the concept of the ideal worker. This ideology undergirds our expectations of the type of workers required in the present-day information society. This notion is embodied in the statement the Applied Psychological Panel of the National Defense Research Committee used: "Man-machine is the fighting unit, not man alone, not machine alone" (Bray 1948, v). In fact, it was the Air Force that shaped the concept of a weapon system that incorporated the very new idea of a new species: the man-machine system. Operators, viewed as components within these vast weapon systems, came to be viewed as decision makers, problem solvers, and information processors. They were, in other words, human technologies embedded in a vast technological information system interest (Baritz 1960; Levidow and Robins 1989; Smith 1985; Tirman 1984).

During the 1950s, training began to take on a new face. Rather than focusing on just technical training, corporate trainers began focusing on interpersonal skills training. This "human relations training" fit quite well with the newly emerged personnel function. Technical/rational skills were no longer the primary focus. Interpersonal relationship skills replaced this as a priority among management. How to motivate workers became the dominant issue. Human relations training reached its height with the emergence of human capital theory.

IMPLICATIONS OF HUMAN CAPITAL THEORY FOR HRD

That human capital theory should ultimately come to serve as the reigning ideology for corporate education is not a surprise. Generally accepted as having been popularized by (although the ideas have been around much longer) Schultz at the 1960 meeting of the American Economic Association, human capital theory has had a curious history over the last 30 years. (Since the 1970s the theory has been under severe and almost constant attack.) While Carnevale, Gainer, and Meltzer (1988) point out that earnings for workers in jobs involving high technology double for those who complete high school and double again for those who complete college, there is little evidence that increased education *directly* leads to increased productivity and economic growth. For example, the educational demands of the labor market do not match the demands for actually getting the job done. Moreover, minorities and women with equivalent education and jobs earn less and experience higher rates of unemployment than their White male counterparts. Furthermore, as Liu and Rees (Chapter 10, this volume) conclude, older workers are less likely to be included in this discourse at all. Thus, while education is a factor in economic growth, it cannot be argued that it is the only or even the most important variable. If the economic rationale for human capital theory does not hold up under close scrutiny, then the entire intellectual rationale for HRD as an educative process that benefits workers becomes problematic (Baptiste 1994; Berg 1971; Rubenson 1992).

REENGINEERING WORKERS: HRD, ADULT EDUCATION, AND THE "NEW WORK ORDER"

If, as suggested, the economic rationale for HRD is suspect, then the question needs to be asked: what purpose does HRD serve? Increasingly, critics have begun to view HRD as a way of facilitating employee responsibility, commitment, and involvement in such a way that education, labor, and management interests all coincide (Butler 1997; Gee, Hull, and Lankshear 1996; Parker and Slaughter 1994). Couched in a language of worker participation, empowerment, and participatory management, HRD actually masks the new way of controlling workers (see Garrick and Solomon, Chapter 21, this volume). More than a decade ago, Zuboff (1988) highlighted the importance of learning in this new world of work:

Learning is no longer a separate activity that occurs either before one enters the workplace or in remote classroom settings. Nor is it an activity preserved for a managerial group. The behaviors that define learning and the behaviors that define being productive are one and the same. Learning is not something that requires time out from being engaged in productive activity, learning is the heart of productive activity. To put it simply, learning is the new form of labor. (p. 395)

If learning becomes labor, and behaviors that define learning and productivity are one and the same, then what is required are new and different types of workers (see Chapter 20 in this volume). What is required are workers who are responsible, adaptable, enterprising problem solvers with appropriate communication and thinking skills, and who have the capacity for lifelong learning. They also, however, must accept the ideology that the "team" and the quality of one's work are inextricably linked. Gee, Hull, and Lankshear (1996), quoting

James Champy (a leading figure in the reengineering movement, which is one of the many types of management processes that incorporate elements of HRD), paint a chilling picture of what this new worker looks like. According to Champy, "Today, it is not only what you know that counts, it's what kind of person you are. What kind of person you are means, essentially, whether you'll be able to live up to, or at least aspire to the 'values' both social and work related" (Champy, in Gee et al., 1996, 17).

These values are congruent with organizational values. New contemporary and sophisticated management theories and processes, such as total quality management (TQM) and ISO 9000, focus on changing worker participation as a means to control and restructure large segments of the American workforce (Howell 1998; Schied, Carter, and Howell 1998; Schied, Carter, Preston, and Howell 1997; Weiss 1987). The new worker is asked to develop new attitudes on the job, masked in the language of skills. The language itself is framed within psychological notions of control (Gee et al. 1996). Workers need to cooperate and part with rules that constrain the range of work individuals do. Workers must exhibit a willingness to accept increased responsibility, including decision making, customer satisfaction; and increase their communication skills, all while being a team player.

These so-called skills, Noble (1990, 1997) has argued, are largely an assault on worker protection to ensure worker adaptability to corporate decisions concerning products, markets, production processes, and technologies in a global economy. Grenier (1988) has called this form of control "de-bureaucratized control." He states that "the trick is to make workers feel that their ideas count, and their originality is valued while disguising the expansion of managerial prerogatives in to the manipulative area of pop psychology" (p. 131).

Along with the creation of the "new worker," this "new work world" calls for a change toward flatter, supposedly less hierarchical organizational structures. Yet this flattening of the organization results in a centralization of power in that layers of bureaucracy are now stripped away, leaving top managers more in control of information. Worker empowerment is limited to decision making within norms established by the organization. Work teams are allowed to organize their work but only within preexisting norms and values. HRD, with its emphasis on psychological as opposed to more direct and more authoritarian Taylorist forms of control, seeks to restrain both informal relationships in the workplace and the pursuit of alternative actions.

If both workers and management are "in this together" then issues of power, issues of who controls whom are hidden under the cloak of unitary goals. Workplace control, in this form, becomes the province of teams. Thus, the team now disciplines those workers who fail to produce, be it with regard to quality, productivity, absenteeism, or poor attitude. Thus, vertical control has been replaced by a horizontal control in which peer pressure operates through the team as members seek to sanction and correct those who jeopardize or criticize established values within the organization. The result, as this chapter has argued, is a new and powerful form of psychological control masked in the humanistic language of HRD.

One way that adult educators can respond to this new form of control is to engage in critical reflection about the ways in which HRD functions and serves to control our lives in the workplace. Cunningham (1993) has criticized how workplace adult educators speak of "human resources, not people—certainly not workers" (p. 13). She has pointed out that instead of locating themselves in adult education history and acknowledging how the nature of work is socially constructed, HRD practitioners ignore the roots of adult education, which has been "historically aligned with the political and social movements that challenge the assumptions of the present" (p. 13). These HRD professionals "unabashedly side with management to develop human capital and make workers responsible for production from which the managerial class profits first and foremost" (p. 24). If adult education is to be concerned with the democratic possibilities within the workplace, then a first step needs to be an unmasking of the psychological forms of control within the humanistic language of HRD.

CONCLUSION

Increasingly, the boundaries of workplace adult education have been defined by an ideology in HRD that has its roots in global notions of capital formation (see Chapter 22 in this volume.) This chapter has presented an emergent analysis of the origins of HRD as it relates to the production of control and the shifting historical boundaries among production, psychology, and workplace education.

Through this historical analysis, we can begin to unravel the contradictions of adult education practice in the workplace. The control issues in HRD have moved beyond straightforward physical coercion to more subtle forms involving psychological manipulation. This shift calls into question the claim that HRD empowers workers, since in reality, disagreements with management goals and values are seen to be manifestations of character flaws within the individual worker—a position far less than empowering.

REFERENCES

Baker, Jeanette S. (1983). "An Analysis of Degree Programs Offered by Selected Industrial Corporations." Doctoral Dissertation, University of Arizona.

Baptiste, Ian. (1994). "Educating Politically: In Pursuit of Social Equality." Doctoral Dissertation, Northern Illinois University.

Baritz, Loren. (1960). *Servants of Power*. Middletown, CT: Wesleyan.

Berg, Ivar E. (1971). *Education and Jobs: The Great Training Robbery*. New York: Praeger.

Bramel, Dana, and Friend, Ronald. (1981). "Hawthorne, the Myth of the Docile Worker and Class Bias in Psychology." *American Psychologist* 36, 867–878.

Braverman, Harvey. (1974). *Labor and Monopoly Capital*. New York: Monthly Review Press.

Bray, Charles W. (1948). *Psychology and Military Proficiency: A History of the Applied Psychology Panel of the NDRC*. Princeton, NJ: Princeton University Press.

Brody, David. (1980). *Workers in Twentieth Century America*. New York: Oxford University Press.

Brody, David. (1993). *In Labor's Cause*. New York: Oxford University Press.

Brophy, John (ed.). (1964). *A Miner's Life*. Madison, WI: J.O.P. Hall.

Butler, Elaine. (1997). "Persuasive Discourses: Learning and the Production of Working Subjects in a Post-Industrial Era." In John Holford, Colin Griffin, and Peter Jarvis (eds.), *Lifelong Learning: Reality, Rhetoric, and Public Policy Conference Proceedings*. Guilford, UK: University of Surrey.

Carnevale, Anthony P., Gainer, Leila J., and Meltzer, Ann S. (1988). *Workplace Basics: The Skills Employers Want*. Alexandria, VA: American Society for Training and Development.

Carter, Vicki K. (2000). "Learning from Work: Thinking Aversively about Dilbert." Doctoral Dissertation, The Pennsylvania State University.

Clegg, Stewart, and Dunkerly, David. (1980). *Organization, Class and Control*. London: Routledge & Kegan Paul.

Cunningham, Phyllis M. (1993). "The Politics of Workers' Education." *Adult Learning* 5, 13–14, 24.

Dirkx, John M. (1996). "Human Resource Development as Adult Education: Fostering the Educative Workplace." *New Directions for Adult and Continuing Education* 72 (Winter), 41–47.

Dooley, C. R. (1945). *The Training with Industry Report (1940–1945): A Record of the Development of Management Techniques for Improvement of Supervision—Their Use and Results*. Washington, DC: War Manpower Commission, Bureau of Training, Training with Industry.

Eurich, Nell P. (1985). *Corporate Classrooms: The Learning Business*. New York: Carnegie Foundation.

Foley, Griff. (1994) "Adult Education and Capitalist Reorganization." *Studies in the Education of Adults* 26, 121–143.

Frank, Eric. (1988). "An Attempt at a Definition of HRD." *Journal of European Industrial Training* 12, 4–5.

Gee, James Paul, Hull, Glynda, and Lankshear, Collin. (1996). *The New Work Order: Behind the Language of the New Capitalism*. Boulder, CO: Westview Press.

Gillespie, Richard. (1991). *Manufacturing Knowledge: A History of the Hawthorne Experiment*. New York: Cambridge University Press.

Grenier, Guillermo J. (1988). *Inhuman Relations*. Philadelphia: Temple University Press.

Hardman, J.B.S. (1992). "The State of the Movement." In J.B.S. Hardman and M. F. Neufeld (eds.), *The House of Labor*. New York: Prentice-Hall.

Hart, Mechthild. (1992). *Working and Educating for Life: Feminist and International Perspectives on Adult Education*. London: Routledge.

Howell, Sharon L. (1998). "Work Teams, Knowledge Production and Learning: A Critical Case Study of a Workplace Team." Doctoral Dissertation proposal, The Pennsylvania State University.

Jacobson, Shirley. (1991). "Early Human Resource Development Work: Its Impact on

Present-Day Practitioners." In *Proceedings of the 32nd Annual Adult Education Research Conference.* Norman: University of Oklahoma.

Jacoby, Sanford. (1985). *Employing Bureaucracy: Managers, Workers, and the Transformation of Work in American Industry, 1900–1945.* New York: Columbia University Press.

Kirkpatrick, Frank. (1945). "What TWI Has Learned about Developing Training Programs." *Personnel* 6, 114–120.

Levidow, Les, and Robins, Kevin (eds.). (1989). *Cyborg Worlds: The Military Information Society.* New York: Free Association Books.

Mech, Vicki Ann. (1984). "Human Resource Development in the United States from 1630–1980." Doctoral Dissertation, Indiana University.

Miller, Vincent A. (1989). "The History of Training." In Robert L. Craig (ed.), *The Training and Development Handbook.* New York: McGraw-Hill.

Montgomery, David. (1987). *The Fall of the House of Labor.* New York: Cambridge University Press.

Moore, Colleen A. (1980). *Corporation Schools; 1900–1930.* ERIC Document ED 226138. Microfiche.

Morris, Homer L. (1934). *The Plight of the Bituminous Coal Miner.* Philadelphia: University of Pennsylvania Press.

Noble, Douglas D. (1990). "High-Tech Skills: The Latest Corporate Assault on Workers." In Steven H. London, Elvira R. Tar, and Joseph F. Wilson (eds.), *The Reeducation of the American Working Class.* Westport, CT: Greenwood Press.

Noble, Douglas D. (1997). "Let Them Eat Skills." In Henry A. Giroux (ed.), with Patrick Shannon, *Education and Cultural Studies.* New York and London: Routledge.

Parker, Mike, and Slaughter, Jane. (1994). *Working Smart: A Union Guide to Participation Programs and Reengineering.* Detroit: Labor Notes.

Rose, Michael. (1985). *Industrial Behaviour: Theoretical Development Since Taylor.* New York: Penguin.

Rothwell, William, and Sredl, Henry J. (1992). *The ASTD Reference Guide to Professional Human Resource Development Roles and Competencies.* Vol. 1, 2nd ed. Amherst, MA: HRD Press.

Rubenson, Kjell. (1992). "Human Resource Development: A Historical Perspective." In Lynn Elen Burton (ed.), *Developing Resourceful Humans.* London and New York: Routledge.

Schied, Fred M., Carter, Vicki K., and Howell, Sharon L. (1998). "Complicity and Control in the Workplace: A Critical Case Study of TQM, Learning, and the Management of Knowledge." *International Journal of Lifelong Education* 17, 157–172.

Schied, Fred M., Carter, Vicki K., Preston, Judith, and Howell, Sharon L. (1997). "Knowledge as Quality Non-conformance: A Critical Case Study of ISO 9000 and Adult Education in the Workplace." In *Proceedings of the 37th Annual Adult Education Research Conference.* Stillwater: Oklahoma State University.

Smith, M. R. (ed.). (1985). *Military Enterprise and Technological Change.* Cambridge, MA: MIT Press.

Steinmentz, Cloyd S. (1967). "The Evolution of Training." In Robert L. Craig (ed.), *Training and Development Handbook.* New York: McGraw-Hill.

Taylor, Frederick. (1967). *The Principle of Scientific Management* (1911). Reprint, New York: Norton.

Tirman, John (ed.). (1984). *The Militarization of High Technology*. Cambridge, MA: Ballinger.

Watkins, Karen E. (1989). "Business and Industry." In Sharan B. Merriam and Phyllis M. Cunningham (eds.), *Handbook of Adult and Continuing Education*. San Francisco: Jossey-Bass.

Weiss, Donald M. (1987). *Empty Promises*. New York: Monthly Review Press.

Zuboff, Shoshana. (1988). *In the Age of the Smart Machine*. New York: Basic Books.

Chapter 10

The Role of Adult Education in Workplace Ageism

Su-fen Liu and Frances Rees

Issues of diversity regarding race, gender, and class are increasingly emerging as important topics of discussion in the adult education literature. Age, however, is the forgotten diversity issue, according to advocates for older workers (Loftus, in Capowski 1994, 11). One reason for this lack of focus is that, unlike its counterparts racism and sexism, ageism is a much more subtle bias and, therefore, often goes unrecognized (Capowski 1994, 11). Yet, given the current makeup of the population and workforce in the United States, we argue that age should not be neglected in the discourse regarding multiculturalism, diversity, and marginalized learners, workers, and citizens.

This chapter will examine ageism in the workplace from the perspective of adult education. To set a basis for discussion, the changing demographics of the American population and the context of the current and future workforce will be presented first. This will be followed by a discussion on ageism in the workplace and the role adult educators and human resource developers might play in enhancing or reducing workplace ageism. Throughout, concepts of critical educational gerontology and the interrelationship between ageism and other social factors will be highlighted, along with suggested implications for adult education theory and practice.

CHANGING DEMOGRAPHICS AND EMPLOYERS' REACTIONS

In their book *Workforce 2000*, Johnston and Packer (1987) point out that as a result of the aging of baby boomers, the median age of the American population will be 36 by 2000. The number of people between the ages of 20 and 29 will have shrunk from 41 million in 1980 to 34 million in 2000, dropping from 18 to 13 percent of the total population. Relatedly, with this aging of the population, the workforce of the United States is getting older. The most dramatic changes in this area will affect the 45-to-54-year-old group, which, in 1988, represented only 16 percent of the workforce, but is estimated to represent 22 percent of the civilian workforce in the year 2000 (Nuventures Consultants, 1990). These dramatic changes will push the median age of the workforce from 35 in 1984 to 39 in 2000 (Johnston and Packer 1987).

The impact of the aging phenomenon on the workplace has caught the attention of some employers. Recognizing that there would be a shortage of young workers in the fast-food industry, McDonald's took a proactive approach to this phenomenon. In 1986, the McMasters program was established to recruit and train older workers. Although the program is no longer officially in place, by 1994 there were more than 40,000 seniors working in McDonald's restaurants around the world (Capowski 1994).

Days Inns is another highly publicized example of the use of senior citizens as low-wage employees who have the capacity to provide high value to corporations in terms of quality service and cost containment. According to Barth, McNaught, and Rizzi (1993), Days Inns had a difficult time finding enough workers with adequate computer skills to staff its Atlanta reservation center in 1986. Attempts to recruit and hire younger workers would have meant an increase in the starting wages. Instead, Days Inns chose to focus on retired workers—a labor pool which demanded less pay, but who typically learned as rapidly as younger workers when appropriate teaching methods were applied. The result was that older workers proved to be as good as younger workers in terms of productivity (Barth et al. 1993).

These, and other examples of the utilization of the retirement age workforce[1] exemplify how formal corporate policies which value and encourage older workers can not only potentially benefit workers (even with the reality of low wages), but can enhance the productivity and public relations of the company as well. Unfortunately, these success stories do not overshadow the fact that most companies have not put this futuristic strategy in place.

The International Foundation of Employee Benefit Plans (in Capowski 1994) reports that while almost 86 percent of Fortune 2000 companies consider older workers to be a valuable resource, only 23 percent actually have corporate policies in place that encourage the hiring of older employees. An analysis of 50 case studies of U.S. employers reveals that although executives thought that older workers had many desirable characteristics, they were concerned that the elderly might fear the technological aspects of many jobs (Quinn and Burkhauser 1993). In short, while employers regarded older workers as loyal, dependable, experienced, and good with customers, they also perceived them as less flexible, adaptable, and comfortable with new technology (Rix 1998).

The fact is that even though a majority of the employers surveyed believed older workers were a valuable resource, only a few of those companies have policies designed for this age group. This is further indication that many employers have doubts about the ability of older workers to contribute to their companies. This kind of doubt may well be rooted in a social and cultural bias against older people. For, as Capowski (1994) points out, the United States is a youth-oriented, and even a youth-obsessed, culture, and corporate America tends to simply reflect these values.

AGEISM IN THE WORKPLACE

Reinforcing this youth-oriented culture are the pervasive and negative attitudes held in society toward older people. Robert Butler coined the term "ageism" in 1969 in an effort to define this cultural bias. Describing it as the prejudice by one age group toward other age groups (p. 243), the concept of ageism makes explicit a pattern of attitudes and behavior that devalue and negatively stereotype the aging process and old people (Conner 1992, 35). In addressing the age bias factor, Laws (1995) states, "ageism, like racism and sexism, is a form of prejudice, a form of oppression that not only limits people who are the object of that oppression but which also shapes perceptions of people, both young and old, who hold ageist attitudes" (p. 113). She concludes that ageism is manifested and contested in the following five places: (1) the waged labor market, (2) the household, (3) the popular culture, (4) the state, and (5) the built environment. However, the most impact that ageism has had is probably in the workplace, because participation in the waged labor market is a crucial element of citizenship, in the definition of social worthiness, and in the development of a subject's self-esteem (p. 115). For this reason, our discussion is focused on age-related discrimination in the workplace.

The Age Discrimination in Employment Act (ADEA) was passed in 1967 and became effective in 1969. Its mission was to promote employment of older persons based on their ability rather than age; to prohibit arbitrary age discrimination in employment; to help employers and workers find ways of meeting problems arising from the impact of age on employment (The Bureau of National Affairs 1987, 205). Initially, when this federal law was enacted it prohibited age discrimination between the ages of 40 and 65, but was later raised to 70 in 1978. In a 1986 amendment to the ADEA, the age 70 cap was removed (The Bureau of National Affairs 1987).

According to Rix (1990), such legislation was, and continues to be essential, for older workers are undoubtedly often victims of age discrimination. This is evidenced by the fact that after the ADEA was passed, age discrimination charges filed with the federal government rose from about 1,000 in fiscal year 1969 to more than 17,000 in fiscal year 1986 (Rix 1990). In comparison to all charges filed with the Equal Employment Opportunity Commission (EEOC), age bias charges constituted about 18 percent of all charges during the fourth quarter of the 1986 fiscal year (The Bureau of National Affairs 1987). Since that time, formal age discrimination complaints have risen at a rate even faster than complaints about sex and race discrimination (Sterns and Sterns 1997), and according to Rhine (1984), both the number of persons awarded damages and the size of the awards have risen dramatically since 1969.

WORKPLACE AGEISM AND TRAINING

Under the ADEA, it is illegal to use age-related stereotypes or assumptions to judge a person's abilities, physical status, or performance. More specifically, it is illegal to prohibit anyone from participating in employment-related training programs based on their age. All too often, however, older employees are over-looked when it comes to training and career development, and hence become disillusioned and, as a result, unmotivated (Capowski 1994, 12). In fact, according to the American Association of Retired Persons (AARP) (in Capowski 1994, 12), there are many cases wherein older people were passed over for training because it was assumed that they couldn't learn.

Given that in 1985, only 421 of the 24,830 age bias charges filed with the EEOC involved claims of bias in training (The Bureau of National Affairs 1987), it would appear that, based on these official numbers, age discrimination in training programs is not a significant problem. However, since the common attitude expressed among employers was that older workers may not be able to be as flexible and hence, learn as well as younger workers (Rix 1998), this data may appear to be misleading.

Furthermore, the recent data from the National Center for Education Statistics (Darkenwald, Kim, and Stowe 1998) regarding participation rates of older people in work-related education indicates that workers over the age of 56 are significantly less likely to participate in training opportunities (only 8 percent) than workers aged 26 to 55.

Thus, it is possible that the low level of cases being filed for age-related training bias may be related to their not wanting to pursue a legal case, despite the fact that they may have been unequally treated. Because of this reality, we argue that age discrimination as it relates to training is particularly relevant to the fields of adult education and human resource development (HRD), and worth further exploration.

Our standpoint regarding the connection between adult education (AE) and human resource development is that because they share the goal of learning among adults, the two are related. Therefore, our use of the term "adult education in the workplace" can be used interchangeably with HRD and training. While some view this standpoint as being arguable (Barrie and Pace 1998), we accept this connection, in part, due to the fact that participation patterns among adults in both AE and HRD are the same.

Studies of participation indicate that organized adult education in the United States is essentially the social domain of White, middle-class American men and women who are relatively well educated and young (Courtney 1992, 4). Mirroring this participation pattern in adult education, past research by Carnevale, Gainer, and Villet (1990) documents that in general, formal employer-based training is also attended disproportionately more by Whites than by Blacks and Hispanics. In terms of gender, according to Carnevale et al. (1990), both sexes were fairly equal, yet, as Parnes (1984) and now Darkenwald, Kim, and Stowe (1998) point out, class issues are also significant. These studies indicate that training is mainly targeted at managerial and other white-collar workers, with manual workers receiving a disproportionately smaller share.

Younger workers participate more in training than older workers. Carnevale et al. (1990) and U.S. Bureau of the Census (1987) revealed that workers age 25–44, while comprising 52 percent of the workforce, receive 68 percent of the formal training offered, whereas workers age 45–64, who comprise 25 percent of the workforce, receive 22 percent of formal training. Plett and Lester (1991) also confirm that younger workers are the focus of in-service education and training in companies while middle-aged and older workers are not provided adequate training opportunities.

In their work promoting learning organizations, Watkins and Marsick (1993) emphasized the importance of long-term, work-related learning in individuals, teams, and organizations. Others in the field of HRD have also argued that such organizational learning has the conceptual potency to bring about organizational effectiveness in the same way that education is valuable because it leads to personal and social growth (Barrie and Pace 1998, 49). Even though their research does not specifically address issues of diversity in terms of the need for system-wide training and development of employees, it does underscore the importance of having all workers participate in and benefit from workplace training; for it is only through this kind of far-reaching effort that employers will create the desired results that they are seeking in their companies.

Despite the field of HRD's standpoint on the importance of everyone being involved as a learner, interestingly, we find that the literature in the field has not taken a critical position in investigating the phenomena of training discrepancies among different age groups. Therefore, we suggest that the field must begin to ask critical questions about why some workers are participating and others are not. In particular, what are the structural factors that influence the participation of older workers in training programs? Who determines what should be included in training programs? Do current training practices contribute to the prevalence of ageism in the workplace? These three questions can be addressed in three ways: (1) by determining who has access to training; (2) by reviewing the content of training programs; and (3) by looking at the training strategies in delivering programs.

AGEISM IN THE CONTEXT OF ACCESS ISSUES

According to Cervero and Wilson (1994), the audience that receives services in adult education and training programs is determined during the planning stage of program development. Thus, because in the corporate setting it is management who typically, and almost solely, sits at the planning table (see Chapter 9 in this volume), it is therefore managers and not the workers who usually have the ultimate authority in determining who gets offered training (Rothstein and Ratte 1990). During these planning discussions, the concerns and priorities of program sponsors surface, and factors relative to training, particularly regarding target groups and outcomes, are clarified. When productivity and performance are key issues in a training context, decisions are based on economic concerns, a concept relevant to human capital theory when used in HRD (Watkins 1989).

Underlying human capital theory is the assumption that workers' skills and knowledge are capital resources that have been acquired at some cost and that they can command a price in the labor market because they are useful in the productive process (Parnes 1984, 32). According to Watkins (1989), workers' skills and knowledge influence the organization's productivity and opportunities for greater promotion, higher pay, and better job security. In human capital theory, education or training is a major tool used to acquire the needed knowledge and skills; thus, expenditures for improving human capabilities can be thought of as an investment. This investment generates future income or output that are used to justify the monies that have been spent. Whether the investment is profitable or not depends on the returns after costs and benefits are weighed. If benefits are high enough to compensate or even outweigh costs, then the expenditure is considered economically sound.

If managers believe that older workers lack the ability to learn and contribute to the company, they tend to view older workers as a poor investment, and therefore will curtail training opportunities for this age group. When older workers do not receive additional education and training, they are, obviously, not going to be equipped to do their jobs effectively for very long, especially in this era of high technology. As a result, during downsizing or corporate financial crises, older workers are most likely to be asked to retire to reduce corporate costs. Thus, ageism is reinforced when adult educators and trainers embrace human capital theory without acknowledging the value and potential of older adults in the workforce. As Cervero and Wilson (1994) have stated, after all the information is collected about what might be taught in an educational program, the values of those who are responsible for the program determine what is actually taught (p. 163).

AGEISM IN THE CONTEXT OF CONTENT AND DELIVERY ISSUES

In practice then, managers and training personnel not only decide to whom training should be offered, but what should be offered and how it should be offered. Planners and trainers who do not have the awareness nor sensitivity to what content and methods are optimum for older workers will not have the capacity to voice issues during the planning stages of training as it relates to equity and advocacy issues for older workers. Also, if training content does not fit older workers' needs, they may not be sufficiently motivated to learn since they encode information based on its immediate usefulness in the workplace (Carter and Honeywell 1991). For example, in the area of technology, older workers may want to, and in fact, need to begin learning basic computer skills while younger workers may already be at a level that allows them to readily learn advanced computer techniques, like those related to Internet applications.

According to Barth et al. (1993), it is not sufficient to merely provide more training if age-appropriate instructional methods and materials are not included. So, it is important to tailor teaching methods to the learning styles of older workers, since research has shown that older workers do not learn less well; they just learn differently (p. 180). It must be understood then, that older workers have different learning needs.

Mintz (1986) found, for instance, that the learning style of older executives differs from that of younger ones and concluded that, to be effective, our training methodologies must be different from those used with younger workers. Furthermore, Mintz found that some older trainees who were entering the training room for the first time in many years had a sense of unease about the experience—unease that could affect their learning. And, given that the current research concerning cognition suggests that older adults do better in recognition than recall, and place information into memory more consciously and less spontaneously than younger adults (Carter and Honeywell 1991), teaching supports which differ from those provided to younger adults should be strongly considered (Okun 1977). In addition, since changes in visual ability are associated with those over 40, presentation materials should be printed in a larger font size.

To plan an effective training program for older workers, Sterns and Dover-spike (1988) suggest that five factors be considered: motivation, structure, familiarity, organization, and time. Yet it is clear that in spite of this growing body of research and information concerning the older adults, change is slow. For instance, in a study of 12 training and retraining programs across the country, Coberly and Paul (1984) found that not even one of the 12 featured training methods based their curriculum on the age of participants. Such a lack of appropriate teaching methods tends to contribute to diminishing the older worker's self-efficacy and reinforcing feelings of inferiority; and all too often, older workers then tend to internalize the acceptance of noncritical assumptions about their ability to learn (Rocco and West 1998) and become even more passive about attending any training opportunities.

Thus, the lack of consideration about age-related needs may dilute participants' interest and commitment to training. In addition, when one considers the interlocking effect of racism, sexism, and classism that may act in combination to marginalize older workers, it is even more likely that they may be ignored by program planners and left out of the training scene.

AGEISM IN THE WORKPLACE WITH RESPECT TO OTHER SOCIAL FACTORS

Clearly, as Glendenning and Battersby (1990) argue, the conventional tendency to regard older people as a homogeneous group is inaccurate and potentially harmful. Withnall and Percy (1994) also support this argument and suggest that social class, gender, and probably ethnicity provide distinct dimensions to old age. So, given this, they conclude that there are inherent dangers in talking about older people as a homogeneous group whose needs, abilities, and behaviors are amenable to sweeping generalizations as if they had a common way of life (pp. 13–14). In fact, gender, class, and race tend to compound the socially created disadvantages faced by older people.

"Double jeopardy" is a term created to describe the view that those who have a disadvantaged ascribed status throughout life face greater losses in later years than their age-mates in the dominant group (Salmon 1994, 7). So in terms of race, older African Americans are four to five times more likely to be labeled functionally illiterate than older Whites and four times as likely as Whites to have problems in the labor market (Brown 1989). Perrault and Raiford (1983) attribute the high unemployment rate for older African Americans to the social system that consigned them to restrictive employment opportunities throughout their younger years. There is little literature on other racial groups in this regard.

Social system biases also affect women in general as a group. Laws (1995) comments that along with class and ethnicity, differences in gender can influence one's position in the labor force, and hence, one's retirement well-being. Women and men do not experience retirement in the same way. One reason is the disparity in their incomes. It is reported that the average monthly Social Security payment for retired female workers in July 1991 was $520 compared to $682 for retired male workers (AARP 1991). This statistic can be explained partially by the fact that mid-life and older women are represented disproportionately among contingent workers who usually receive less pay and have lower positions. The contingent workforce includes part-time, temporary, and leased workers, and independent contractors (AARP 1991). While many women value the flexibility that contingent work offers because of childbearing and care-giving responsibilities, others take contingent work because they cannot find full-time, yearround jobs.

As for the training and education of older female workers, Pursell and Torrence (1980) report that in some employment service offices, job counseling and training options were less frequently offered to women aged 45 and over than to younger women. In addition, contingent workers, most of whom are women, are rarely offered opportunities for skill training by their employers (Lillard and Tan 1986). They are also unlikely to use their relatively low incomes to invest in their own training (AARP 1991). When ageism is compounded by belief in the stereotype that men grow old gracefully but women age, an investment in training and educating older female workers may not be considered worthwhile, with the consequence that these women are likely candidates for termination when layoffs, mergers, and acquisitions occur (Hale 1990).

Looking at the changing face of the American workplace, analysts realize that there is an increasing proportion of workers who are older female minorities or immigrants. Yet, research on the interlocking relationship among age, gender, race, and class is rare. Needless to say, ageism in the workplace is only complicated by its intersection with other social factors. What is most disturbing, though, is that older female, minority, disabled, lower-class workers are facing serious barriers. Clearly, the extent of ageism relevant to race, gender, and class is rarely documented, even in the gerontology literature—a field which focuses on the social, physiological, and educational needs of older persons. It then is no wonder that very little has been done to change the education and training landscape for this group of individuals.

INFORMING OUR WORK USING CRITICAL EDUCATIONAL GERONTOLOGY

The field of gerontology has traditionally focused on aging as pathological; a disease process which then leads to physical and mental dependency and fragility. As a result of this perspective, older people are viewed as being weak, senile, unable to function, and in need of social services. Consequently, older adults have not and are not viewed as an asset to society, nor do older adults see themselves as assets within American society. According to Moody (1993), the field of gerontology has medicalized old age and has led to replacing the positive images of old age in favor of disease models and biological reductionism (p. xvii). Lending credence to this approach, Battersby (1985) points out that many of the common myths and stereotypes about the intellectual capacity and learning ability of the elderly have been reinforced by poorly conceptualized psychological studies (p. 75).

Educational gerontology as a field of practice is also beginning to be criticized, and as more and more older adults stay healthy and energetic, traditional attitudes are being challenged and changed. According to Glendenning (1992), the conventional paradigms of educational gerontology often lead, in practice, to a domestication of older people rather than to their empowerment and self-fulfillment.

To promote productive aging, Moody (1976, 1993) began to advocate a concept called critical gerontology. He emphasizes the importance of consciousness-raising in order to challenge the current belief system in the field of gerontology. Along with Moody, Glendenning and Battersby (1990) also began to advocate a paradigm shift in education for senior citizens, moving from educational gerontology to critical educational gerontology. Such a change represents moving away from a functionalist approach, where older people are viewed as a social problem, to an approach where the assumptions and implications for educating older adults are challenged. Critical educational gerontology stresses self-empowerment, autonomy, and control over one's life. Withnall and Percy (1994) assert, moreover, that critical educational gerontology involves listening to the experiences of others and developing a capacity for self-criticism.

Yet, it is not only those learners who must take on this perspective; we as trainers and educators must also develop this perspective. For, in addition to embracing more equitable, inclusive, and learner-focused teaching techniques, higher expectations about the value and potential of older learners must be fostered and developed to support the educational endeavors of the older adult learner. While Moody (1976) strongly advocates consciousness-raising for the older adult, it is clear that those of us engaged in training and educating adults must become critically aware of our own ageist beliefs and perspectives. If we want the older adult to participate in the whole learning environment, we must seek out alternative means to address their concerns and needs.

Thus, when critical educational gerontology is applied to the training context, trainers should consider that they too must go through a perspective transformation if they are going to contribute to changes being made in the workplace for the older adult population. As Moody (1976) suggests, educators are in a position to help older adults shed the self-hatred raised by stereotypes and prevailing social attitudes about them. This concept of self-criticism and reflection is, in fact, not unfamiliar in the field of training. In HRD, similar strategies are suggested to help workers free themselves from self-imposed restraints (Watkins 1989). So, by critically assessing their practices adult educators may be prompted to adopt alternative and more critical effective strategies in workplace training programs that are targeted for older adults.

IMPLICATIONS FOR ADULT EDUCATION AND HRD

American trainers and human resource professionals are often unaware of innovations pertaining to older workers that have worked well in other companies (Rothstein and Ratte 1990). As a result, strong retirement incentives persist. According to Quinn and Burkhauser (1993), about half of all American men leave the labor force by age 62. Only one in six continues to work beyond age 65.

To prepare for the future facing older people and the nation, the American government and industries need to cooperate to help older workers stay in the workforce. As Capowski (1994) has advocated, managers need to be made aware that losing an older and experienced workforce often ends up being more expensive. Furthermore, most older workers do want to continue working—even beyond the traditional retirement age, so we ought to capitalize on their desire and their abilities (Capowski 1994). Moreover, according to Sheppard and Rix (1989), about 48 percent of U.S. workers aged 55–64 were somewhat or very interested in learning new skills and participating in job training programs so they could take on a different job. These factors combined means that about 17 percent of U.S. workers aged 50–62 said they were much more likely to delay early retirement if they could receive job training (Sheppard and Rix 1989).

American managers and trainers also need to address, up front, the biased corporate attitudes toward older workers, and work to change corporate policy in this regard. As with any form of prejudice, ageism is manifested in ways that are almost invisible, until the hegemonic aspects of its bias are revealed. Capowski (1994) argues that this often unintentional, very subtle kind of discrimination must be addressed fully and explicitly, and a range of methods must be used to explicate it. In addition to policy changes, as a way to combat this bias, adult educators and trainers need to become aware of, develop skills in, and incorporate strategies which have proved useful in empowerment and emancipation education. According to Inglis (1997), empowerment involves people developing capacities to act successfully within the existing system and structures of power, while emancipation concerns critically analyzing, resisting, and challenging structures of power (p. 4).

CONSCIOUSNESS-RAISING: A FORM OF EMPOWERMENT

Empowerment education is one step that could be used by trainers to help older workers update their skills so they can obtain those rewards that should be available to them within the existing power structure. We offer this caveat, however, that if empowerment is used by management to legitimize changes to increase production and profit which are often above and beyond the interests of employees (Inglis 1997, 6), then this is not empowerment, but a means to maintain the status quo. So, if trainers have not critically questioned and reflected on their own biases against older people, then the training practices they employ will only continue the perpetuation of ageism, since we are, after all, socialized to meet the prevailing societal expectations. Capowski (1994) suggests that just as corporations have asserted that they are blind to race and gender, organizations need to focus now on first becoming age blind, and then on becoming age conscious. When ageism becomes a visible issue, paradoxically, managers and trainers may assert the value of being age blind.

Older workers must also change their thinking and take responsibility for their own careers, including training and career planning. Older adults must therefore be introduced to, if they aren't already aware of, the fact that no matter what their life stage, they are not only eligible, but they should seek out employment, training, and development. Asserting that job opportunities should be open to everyone regardless of age, Sterns and Sterns (1997) advocate having affirmative action for older workers. They believe that, like women and racial minorities, older workers are equally deserving of affirmative action programs that formalize an equal playing field for all prospective job candidates (p. 37).

So it is imperative for older workers to not only critically examine and analyze assumptions about their capabilities, but educators and trainers must also examine their own biases about this age group. It is in the interests of both dominant and marginalized members of society to examine privilege and learn how to create equitable systems and structures (Rocco and West 1998, 172). To promote productive and successful aging, Moody (1976) believes that older people must be led beyond passivity and given the option of second careers and new opportunities for genuine participation, regardless of age.

CONCLUSION

Unlike racism and sexism, ageism is a bias all people will experience if they live long enough (Laws 1995). Helen Dennis (in Capowski 1994) agrees that ageism strikes a chord of fear in people of all ages, so they all have a vested interest in changing their way of thinking (p. 11) about it. In addition, it is predicted that age discrimination will be the civil rights issue of the next decade, mostly because an increasing number of the people who fought for civil rights in the 1960s are now middle aged (Capowski 1994, 11).

Since the age of eligibility for full Social Security benefits is predicted to rise to 67 in 2022 (Rosow 1990), more and more older workers may choose to stay on the job longer. It is time to seriously look at the issue of training an aging workforce. So, as older workers acquire new knowledge and develop their skills and competence at work, they will be better equipped to use their learning experiences and transfer their educational achievements to a post-work stage of life. In other words, they will be better able in later life to meet the challenge of a rapidly changing society and to exercise critical judgment when faced with a wide variety of situations (Withnall and Percy 1994). People are living longer, healthier, and more energetic lives while also participating more in higher education. It is time to reinvent old age and overcome demeaning stereotypes. As Moody (1993) points out, the war against ageism will take its place alongside the struggle against racism and sexism. Developing a sensibility for workplace biases will increase the urgency with which all are confronted.

NOTE

1. Wal-Mart "greeters," senior citizens hired to welcome shoppers at the entrance to the store, are another good example of the use of senior citizens as low-wage employees who provide high value to corporations in terms of service, reliability, cost containment, and good public relations. Ironically, given the reality of their value in this regard, one could argue that this group of workers should be paid more, not less.

REFERENCES

American Association of Retired Persons (AARP). (1991). *The Contingent Workforce: Implications for Midlife and Older Women*. Washington, DC: AARP.
Barrie, J., and Pace, R. W. (1998). "Learning for Organizational Effectiveness: Philoso-

phy of Education and Human Resource Development." *Human Resource Development Quarterly* 9(1), 39–54.

Barth, M. C., McNaught, W., and Rizzi, P. (1993). "Corporations and the Aging Workforce." In P. H. Mirvis (ed.), *Building the Competitive Workforce: Investing in Human Capital for Corporate Success*, 156–200. New York: John Wiley & Sons.

Battersby, D. (1985). "Education in Later Life: What Does It Mean?" *Convergence* 18(1–2), 75–81.

Brown, H. W. (1989). *Literacy Training and Older Americans*. East Lansing, MI: National Center for Research on Teacher Learning. ERIC Document Reproduction Service No. ED 317 795.

The Bureau of National Affairs. (1987). *Older Americans in the Workforce: Challenges and Solutions*. Washington, DC: The Bureau of National Affairs.

Butler, R. N. (1969). "Age-ism: Another Form of Bigotry." *The Gerontologist* 9, 243–246.

Capowski, G. (1994). "Ageism: The New Diversity Issue." *Management Review* 83(10), 10–15.

Carnevale, A. P., Gainer, L. J., and Villet, J. (1990). *Training in America*. San Francisco: Jossey-Bass.

Carter, J. H., and Honeywell, R. (1991). "Training Older Adults to Use Computers." *Performance and Instruction* 30(2), 9–15.

Cervero, R. M., and Wilson, A. L. (1994). *Planning Responsibly for Adult Education*. San Francisco: Jossey-Bass.

Coberly, S., and Paul, C. E. (1984). *Retraining the Older Worker for Changing Technology: Programs and Practices*. East Lansing, MI: National Center for Research on Teacher Learning. ERIC Document Reproduction Service No. ED 255 723.

Conner, K. A. (1992). *Aging America: Issues Facing an Aging Society*. Englewood Cliffs, NJ: Prentice-Hall.

Courtney, S. (1992). *Why Adults Learn: Towards a Theory of Participation in Adult Education*. New York: Routledge.

Darkenwald, G. G., Kim, K., and Stowe, P. (1998). *Adult Participation in Work-Related Courses: 1994–1995*. Washington, DC: National Center for Education Statistics.

Glendenning, F. (1992). "Educational Gerontology and Gerogogy: A Critical Perspective." In E. Berdes, A. A. Zych, and G. D. Dawson (eds.), *Geragogics: European Research in Gerontological Education and Educational Gerontology*. New York: The Haworth Press.

Glendenning, F., and Battersby, D. (1990). "Educational Gerontology and Education for Older Adults: A Statement of First Principles." *Australian Journal of Adult and Community Education* 30(1), 38–44.

Hale, N. (1990). *The Older Worker*. San Francisco: Jossey-Bass.

Inglis, T. (1997). "Empowerment and Emancipation." *Adult Education Quarterly* 48(1), 3–17.

Johnston, W. B., and Packer, A. H. (1987). *Workforce 2000: Work and Workers for the Twenty-first Century*. Indianapolis, IN: Hudson Institute.

Laws, G. (1995). "Understanding Ageism: Lessons from Feminism and Postmodernism." *The Gerontologist* 35(1), 112–118.

Lillard, L. A., and Tan, H. W. (1986). *Private Sector Training: Who Gets It and What Are Its Effects?* Washington, DC: U.S. Department of Labor.

Mintz, F. (1986). "Retraining: The Graying of the Training Room." *Personnel* 63(10), 69–71.

Moody, H. R. (1976). "Philosophical Presuppositions of Education for Old Age." *Educational Gerontology: An International Quarterly* 1, 1–16.

Moody, H. R. (1993). "Overview: What Is Critical Gerontology and Why Is It Important?" In T. R. Cole, W. A. Achenbaum, P. L. Jakobi, and R. Kastenbaum (eds.), *Voices and Visions of Aging: Toward a Critical Gerontology.* New York: Springer Publishing Co.

Nuventures Consultants. (1990). *America's Changing Workforce.* La Jolla, CA: Nuventures Consultants.

Okun, M. A. (1977). "Implications of Geropsychological Research for the Instruction of Older Adults." *Adult Education* 27(3), 139–155.

Parnes, H. S. (1984). *People Power: Elements of Human Resource Policy.* Beverly Hills, CA: Sage Publications.

Perrault, G., and Raiford, G. L. (1983). "Employment Problems and Prospects of Older Blacks and Puerto Ricans." In R. L. McNeely and J. L. Colen (eds.), *Aging in Minority Groups.* Beverly Hills, CA: Sage Publications.

Plett, P. C., and Lester, B. T. (1991). *Training for Older People: A Handbook.* Geneva: International Labour Office.

Pursell, D. E., and Torrence, W. D. (1980). "The Older Woman and Her Search for Employment." *Aging and Work* 3, 121–128.

Quinn, J. F., and Burkhauser, R. V. (1993). "Labor Market Obstacles to Aging Productively." In S. A. Bass, F. G. Caro, and Y. P. Chen (eds.), *Achieving a Productive Aging Society*, 43–59. Westport, CT: Auburn House.

Rhine, S. H. (1984). *Managing Older Workers: Company Policies and Attitudes.* New York: The Conference Board.

Rix, S. E. (1990). *Older Workers—Choices and Challenges: An Older Adult Reference Series.* Santa Barbara, CA: ABC-CLIO.

Rix, S. E. (1998). "Employers Weigh Age in an Aging America." *Global Aging Report* 3(3), 2.

Rocco, T. S., and West, G. W. (1998). "Deconstructing Privilege: An Examination of Privilege in Adult Education." *Adult Education Quarterly* 48(3), 171–184.

Rosow, J. M. (1990). "Extending Working Life." In I. Bluestone, R.J.V. Montgomery, and J. D. Owen (eds.), *The Aging of the American Work Force: Problems, Programs, Policies*, 399–418. Detroit, MI: Wayne State University Press.

Rothstein, F. R., and Ratte, D. J. (1990). *Training and Older Workers: Implications for U.S. Competitiveness.* East Lansing, MI: National Center for Research on Teacher Learning. ERIC Document Reproduction Service No. ED 336 608.

Salmon, M.A.P. (1994). *Double Jeopardy: Resources and Minority Elders.* New York: Garland Publishing Co.

Sheppard, H. L., and Rix, S. E. (1989). *Training of Older Workers in the United States.* East Lansing, MI: National Center for Research on Teacher Learning. ERIC Document Reproduction Service No. ED 308 304.

Sterns, H. L., and Doverspike, D. (1988). "Training and Developing the Older Worker: Implications for Human Resource Management." In H. Dennis (ed.), *Fourteen Steps in Managing an Aging Work Force*, 97–110. Lexington, MA: Lexington Books.

Sterns, A. A., and Sterns, H. L. (1997). "Should There Be an Affirmative Action Policy for Hiring Older Persons? Yes." In A. E. Scharlach and L. W. Kaye (eds.), *Controversial Issues in Aging*, 34–39. Boston: Allyn & Bacon.

U.S. Bureau of the Census. (1987). *Statistical Abstract of the United States*. Washington, DC: U.S. Department of Commerce.

Watkins, K. E. (1989). "Five Metaphors: Alternative Theories for Human Resource Development." In D. B. Gradous (ed.), *Systems Theory Applied to Human Resource Development*. St. Paul: University of Minnesota, ASTD Research Committee.

Watkins, K. E., and Marsick, V. J. (1993). *Sculpting the Learning Organization: Lessons in the Art and Science of Systemic Change*. San Francisco: Jossey-Bass.

Withnall, A., and Percy, K. (1994). *Good Practice in the Education and Training of Older Adults*. Brookfield, VT: Ashgate Publishing Co., 11–26.

Part III

Classrooms and Communities: Contexts, Questions, and Critiques

Part III of *Making Space* takes us into the world of learners and teachers living in Appalachia and the prisons of Pennsylvania. We then are asked to examine whether or not one arm of the field is prepared or "equipped" to handle what lays ahead, and finally, we are told that we must understand that what we do as "teachers/educators" is political. As these chapters unfold, we find ourselves having to not only examine the ways in which the contexts affect us, but we are also told to examine the ways in which these contexts ultimately affect our content and our culture.

One's lived experiences evolve out of one's race, class, gender, language, and sexual orientation, and in this section it is even where one is situated in a given geographic location. As Wade Nobles[1] so adequately articulates, in order for us to appreciate the ways in which our lived experiences affect each one of us, we must begin to explore the ways in which the context shapes or influences who we are (culture) and what we say (content).

As we make our way through each context, we find ourselves in an Appalachian community, where Bingman and White, along with Kirby, explore the ways that programs can unfold when you rely upon the content that is provided by those whose lives we seek to serve. In Chapter 11, they describe their roles as facilitators of a program aimed at serving Appalachian young women living in poverty. They explore how language is used to create meaning and explain one's historical and socioeconomic base, as well as how class and gender influence the ways in which people think about needs and program development. To that end they state that their description of community-based organizations or programs is determined by how one's roots in a particular community are connected to the "locus of control and initiative" they exert in participating and changing what and how their communities operate. In using the term "hillbilly" as a way to describe one's self, we also begin to see how language affects how we see ourselves. Moreover, the use of this term embodies and gives meaning to what they describe as "where they live, the way they talk, and the way we feel," which is interconnected with what they do and how they do it. So, to that end they explore how they developed a program for poor young women on welfare. Through their work, these women in poverty were not only "empowered," but the authors found a shared, interconnected reality with these women. This is most evident in their concluding remarks: "Our experiences in facilitating a process has taught us both the value of participatory approaches, and the importance of explicitly addressing in our work the issues of race, class, gender, and sexual orientation" (Chapter 11, this volume).

Upon leaving this Appalachian community we find ourselves in the confines of those women's lives who no longer have any visible control over their contexts, yet still have their cultures and the content of their experiences to rely upon as they make their way through the prison system. Baird explores the ways in which education, incarceration, and the marginalization of women (Chapter 12) can be influenced by helping these women use the content of literature and poetry as a way to express their culture. It is through this understanding that they not only begin to take control of their lives while in captivity, but they are then able to determine their own destinies. Baird opens by providing us with information about how the prison system not only makes the needs of the women invisible, but also further negates who they are by silencing them. Ironically, these women's lives were negated and silenced long before they entered these "prison walls." Most significantly, the prison walls then become a living metaphor for how they live. Not only do the prison walls encase them in a world that makes them invisible to those on the outside, but they also serve to further marginalize them through the debasement of their gender and their race, so that, Baird argues, their voices are silenced. So, the first step toward creating new meaning and shattering the silence for these women is to help them find their voices. Using literature and poetry, Baird then offers them an opportunity to find their voices. In so doing they "were able to capture their world in words," and rediscover who they were. As for adult educators and adult learners in general, the shattering of these women's "prison wall" experiences can help us understand the significance of giving voice to one's race, gender, class, and sexual orientation. As we become more actively entrenched within institutions of higher learning and other institutional or community agencies, we must remember that our context is interconnected to our content and how we view our culture.

While the use of prison walls as a metaphor signifies that marginality is both internal and external, it is those policies constructed by those in positions of power, and unknowingly sanctioned by those of us in academia, that perpetuate hegemony and marginalization. Even though policies provide us with civil rules and procedures concerning how we "ought to" operate with one another, they often end up confining us or delimiting what we do. In Chapter 13, Amstutz explores the ways in which policies intended to provide direction for adult basic education oftentimes limits or prevents adult basic educators from engaging and educating people about their context, content, and their culture. Strapped by policies focused on morality and responsibility, educators find themselves engaged in literacy efforts aimed at teaching people how to read and write. While no one would argue that these skills are necessary, to singularly focus on them as a way to gain self-sufficiency or work can be not only harmful to the learners, but to the educational process. Amstutz contends that in order for educational policies to work effectively, appropriate resources must be allocated, as well as attention given to the learners' lived experiences, by both policy makers and adult educators. She concludes that the underfunding of programs will only serve to perpetuate the gender, social, and economic status quo. While change is clearly needed, she goes on to say that change in and of itself is not enough. She strongly argues that "Adult educators must understand that both adult learners and we are knowledge makers and culture makers." We live in a context that is fraught with outdated policies focused only on "employment goals and welfare reduction" as being the primary purpose of literacy programs. To this, she then vociferously argues that policy makers as well as teachers must not only confront these issues, but they must address issues of poverty, discrimination, and inequality. To do any less would, in her words, "be to abandon the very people we wish to serve," or teach.

As we begin to gain a greater understanding about the context, content, and culture, we can see that our role as teachers is intricately interwoven into where we come from, how we view ourselves, and ultimately what we are able to do given the resources we are provided. Moreover, we begin to see that the context in which we operate is political. In Chapter 14, Bounous argues that relationships between teachers and learners are marked by inequitable social arrangements. Moreover, this relationship is tempered and supported within a social structure that not only supports hegemonic relationships, but is used as a way to determine what culture and whose content will be used in a given context. So, rather than developing critically reflective practitioners and learners in our schools, we end up developing individuals who become accustomed to being limited and powerless. Thus, those who have been disenfranchised because of their race, class, gender, ability, sexual orientation, or other markers of "otherness" find that education tends to not only further remove them from the source of power, but tells them that they are not entitled to it as well. Bounous then suggests a way for those practitioners interested in creating critically reflective learners to develop environments in which they learn to shift and share in the construction of knowledge, learning, and ultimately relationships, as defined by the traditional, hierarchical teacher–student arrangements. She concludes that through collaborative teacher–student relationships, we can begin to not only change what occurs between teacher/learner and learner/teacher, but we can begin to more visibly see how these new arrangements influence how we operate within the larger context of society. So, in order to change these socially contrived arrangements, teachers/learners must engage in counterhegemonic activities. As Bounous suggests, if those teachers/learners interested in changing the teacher/learner relationship want to create change, they must first recognize that teaching is political. To be a counterhegemonic force means that we not only acknowledge but act on this position. We must understand that this practice is interconnected with the way we view the learning environment and use language; and with the conceptions we hold about the "other," the ways we articulate class differences, and the cultural context within which we operate as both teachers and learners.

As these authors articulate through their involvement in communities and classrooms, change can only occur at the macro or micro levels of our social and educational systems when we fully understand the interconnected and interwoven polyrhythmic realities of learners/teachers operating within a political context.

NOTE

1. Conversation with Nobles (April 2000), in which he described an analysis of African-American-centered perspective in terms of the intersection of culture, context, and content. Culture could then be described by one's race, class, and gender; whereas context is viewed as the place or situation one found oneself historically; and content is the outgrowth of how one interprets one's culture and context.

Chapter 11

Communities in the Classroom: Critical Reflections on Adult Education in an Appalachian Community

Mary Beth Bingman and Connie White
with Amelia R. B. Kirby

The Community in the Classroom project worked to build community literacy programs with ten Appalachian community organizations. The authors served as facilitators of this project. In this chapter we describe the project, the processes that supported building community literacy, and the factors that made it difficult, including issues surrounding race, gender, and sexual orientation. Throughout this chapter we will move in and out of our voice of personal reflection and the voice as authors. We have chosen to italicize our voice as a way to highlight our thoughts and understandings about what occurred throughout this community engagement project.

COMMUNITY LITERACY

Adult education and adult literacy are often seen as ways to build individual skills or to empower individuals. We use the term "community literacy" to mean the literacy practices that members of a community use to build, maintain, and change the community. We see literacy not as a have-it-or-not skill, but as a collection of practices used in a wide variety of social settings. Street calls this an ideological perspective on literacy, seeing literacy as implicated in power relations and embedded in specific cultural meanings and practices (Street 1995).

We are also interested in adult education as a way to build communities. Therefore, community literacy practices might include: taking notes at meetings, reading the newspaper with a critical eye, writing about issues that affect people in their everyday lives, or reading about the experiences of other communities on the Internet. More importantly, after obtaining the knowledge/information, they then take what they have learned and make it more accessible in order to strengthen their organizations. It more than often includes looking critically at uses of literacy and at how others' use words. So, when we think about *community literacy* it is in the context of a self-conscious community that works together, usually in an organization.

COMMUNITY-BASED LITERACY PROGRAMS

The organizations we write about in this chapter can be described as community-based organizations, because we believe that *the locus of control and initiative of the organizations are rooted in and come from particular communities*. The organizations in this chapter were founded locally, are independent, and exist to meet community needs and address community issues. While some of them operate literacy programs, they were not required to do so. For us, community-based as applied to literacy programs is used in a variety of ways:

1. It may mean programs that operate *in* a community setting (a church, community center, storefront) but are not necessarily controlled by the community.
2. It may mean programs that are *controlled by* the community but are not necessarily using community teachers or curricula. Even though these programs are in the community, and controlled by the community, they may not look that different from programs operated by school systems or outside volunteer organizations. They offer learning opportunities for individual change.
3. The third way is to have a program that comes *from* the community with the organizational purpose of strengthening the community.

While these programs might help participants develop their individual literacies, the primary goal of the program is to build and establish community, as well as develop the literacy skills of those participating in the program(s) as needed.

WHO WE ARE AND WHERE WE'RE FROM

Who are you? and Where are you from? are defining questions in the Appalachian region, placing people by family and community. We are middle-aged White women, one from a working-class and one from a middle-class family. Both of us grew up, studied, and taught public school in rural Appalachian communities. Both of us have been members and staff of regional organizations working for change in the mountains. Our current work is at the Center for Literacy Studies in Tennessee. We came to literacy out of community organizations, and see literacy as building the efficacy of people in the community and of communities themselves.

Space: Place, Culture, Class

The space that we work in is structured by the history and culture of the central Appalachian region and is surrounded by the coal counties of eastern

Tennessee, southwest Virginia, eastern Kentucky, and southern West Virginia. Hence, factors like class, gender, and ethnicity in Appalachia are confounded by the location, history, geography, and culture of the people. We are hillbillies, and this means that where we live, the way we talk, and the way we feel are highly interconnected. We live in a region where much of the wealth is controlled or owned outright by people who live elsewhere. We know that the way we talk may be judged funny or ignorant. We feel a strong attachment to a place that is beautiful, that is *home*. We know that when we leave—because unemployment hovers at 20 percent, and we do leave—*we always plan on being back, next weekend, next year*.

In order to understand where we are coming from, you must understand where we live; the Central Appalachian is a region of many contrasts. The cities of the region may be a part of the national economic boom, but the more isolated coal counties are losing population and services. In eastern Kentucky, southwest Virginia, and southern West Virginia unemployment has been between 10 and 20 percent for several years. Welfare reform is exacerbating the problem. For many people access to health care involves an hour's drive. There is little public transportation. Consolidated schools mean children spend an hour or two every day traveling mountain roads in a school bus; and as schools close, communities are often left without a focus for community life.

But while communities are facing hardships, people have not given up. Communities have worked both to fight specific attacks on their *homeplaces* and to meet community needs for day care, food and clothing, improved housing, and recreation. Many communities also offer some kind of adult education.

COMMUNITY IN THE CLASSROOM

Beginning in 1991, staff members and volunteers from ten Appalachian organizations came together to teach and learn from each other about how to develop better community-based literacy programs, through collaboration. Some of the organizations were primarily educational organizations. Most addressed a broad range of community issues including economic development, polluted water, ways to provide for basic needs, housing rehabilitation, and children's programs. All were tenuously funded and depended on volunteers. They established the Community in the Classroom, with the help of the Center for Literacy Studies.

The groups came together in order to gain and share information, to think about and practice different ways of looking at education, and to support each other's adult education programs. As a group, we wanted to develop educational programs that would lead to more than a ticket out of the community for a few individuals. We wanted to develop programs that would give people a ticket in. By using those skills and knowledge to rebuild their communities they would no longer have to leave, because they would have access to those skills required to secure their place in the community. Reading and writing, as well as critical analysis, teamwork, problem solving, and leadership were essential to their development.[1]

The participants planned, hosted, and facilitated a series of six workshops over a year and a half. The workshop topics, chosen by the participants, focused on the issues they encountered in community-based literacy work and included curriculum, leadership development, and materials production. In addition to taking part in the workshops, participants worked in their own organizations on projects related to the goals of Community in the Classroom. Goals focused on how to:

- build community within their classrooms, a community of learners and teachers who share decision making about what is important to learn and how to go about learning it,
- bring community issues into their classes to create programs that connect with people's real lives and the issues they care about,
- bring classroom into the community by involving students in community work and organizations, and
- build a community of programs among the participants.

An Example: The Water Workshop—Developing Curriculum from Community Issues

These Community in the Classroom workshops were developed jointly with community participants and Center for Literacy Studies staff. The water workshop, developed with a team from a community experiencing severe water problems, is an example of the way participating organizations shared in the effort to learn how to integrate basic academic skills instruction into issues that organizations were addressing in their communities. We planned in this workshop to demonstrate, using a theme-based approach to instruction in basic academic skills. In this workshop, instead of just *talking* about community-based teaching, the planning team decided to really do it, using ourselves and our own experiences as a model. We began by asking, *Where do you get your water?* Answers (wells, reservoirs, town systems, etc.) were recorded on newsprint.

After brainstorming with the participants, we then asked, *What problems have you had with water?* People related a host of problems they had encountered, such as: surface run-off into springs, mercury spills into water, chemicals from coal run-off, raw sewage in drinking water, not having any water, poor management of water systems. We also recorded these statements on the newsprint sheets.

Next we asked, *What have you tried to do about water problems?* The actions tried were varied, including: organizing people in the community to help think about solutions, taking the owner of the water system to court; individual solutions such as digging a well, using filters, or buying water; filing a complaint with the Pubic Service Commission, setting up a community-owned service district. Again we recorded answers on newsprint.

Afterwards, we broke into groups and asked this question: *If you had just had this discussion with your students, how could you use it to build curriculum, develop activities?* The suggestions that evolved from these question included:

- use a water bill to teach math,
- set up a vocabulary glossary on water terminology,
- do a class project on what class has learned—do a role play—have a community meeting to show what they have learned,
- do graphs and charts to represent the number of class members who have wells versus the number who have city water,
- use the issue to stimulate research projects in different subject areas: What's in our water? What are health concerns relating to water? How do other communities address pollution problems?

As you might surmise, at this workshop it became clear that the issues that people were concerned about as community members could also be a source of content for adult basic education classes. The next step for us then was to determine to move from studying issues in classes to acting on them in community. This was a more difficult process, but one that some of these programs were able to accomplish on occasion.

MOVING OUT OF THE CLASSROOM INTO THE COMMUNITY

The organizations participating in Community in the Classroom structured learning activities using several formats. They included formal educational programs, such as literacy tutoring; classes to prepare for a commercial driver's license; and GED preparation classes. Clearly, the activities associated with these programs were aimed at building basic academic skills—skills that often led to a credential. There were less-structured activities that included general education and information, such as observances of Black History month, a panel on the Gulf War, as well as speakers who talked about water quality. Organizers of these activities did not necessarily consider building basic skills as a part of the reason for their efforts.

These organizations provided many informal learning opportunities, such as participation in a food project, and service on boards and committees. The skills participants developed through these activities, like compiling orders, taking minutes, and reading financial statements, were primarily valued as necessary in getting a task done and pushing forward the work of the organization. Although some mention was made about the learning involved, it was secondary. In a few instances, programs made a conscious effort to develop basic skills in the context of community work. This integration of basic skills-building with community-building activities was central to the goals of the Community in the Classroom project. An example of that integration was the organization of a teen center by an adult basic education class in an eastern Kentucky community organization.

The Teen Center

In late 1992, the staff of a community-based education center in eastern Kentucky started discussing the possibility of opening a Teen Center to provide positive activities for community youth. Adult education students, many of them with teenagers of their own, were involved right from the start. These students were a part of the Job Opportunity and Basic Skills (JOBS) class, a 20-hour-per-week class for women receiving welfare benefits. The organization of the Center was integrated into their classroom work. A Teen Center Committee of 12 adult education students (around half the class) was formed. An adult education student described the involvement of her class in the Teen Center:

When we first started talking about the Teen Center, it was really exciting, because everybody wanted something for the kids to do. They wasn't nothing. They closed the parking lot down and they couldn't go there. They run them off. They just wasn't no where . . . And some of us just got to talking about opening a teen center and couldn't figure out where to start to even go about one. And I don't know who brought it up that they had this teen center in McEvers County. So one day a bunch of us students loaded up and we went down there and checked it out.

And then we come back and we just started talking about it and [the Center director] said how are you going to manage without any money? And she asked us if somebody wanted to go to city hall.

We went to city hall and there was 52 of us, I think, women and kids that all piled in over there [to a meeting]. They got the law on us out there and everything. I don't know what they thought we was trying to do! . . . We told them that we was asking for money to start the Teen Center. And we was just asking for, I can't remember, anyway we got double for what we was asking.

Students used a portion of their school time to work on the many tasks needed to open the Teen Center. For example, one of the early efforts included visiting other similar Centers. A typical way the adult education students approached this was to develop a *to-do* list together. Adult students volunteered to complete the tasks, which included planning the trip, getting and writing directions to the place, getting input from participants, and writing the list of questions out that they needed to ask.

The Teen Center Committee meetings continued over the next four months. Students worked on issues like:

- How to assure that field trips were orderly and safe.
- Was it all right to discipline children and teens if their parents weren't present?
- What rules were necessary?
- Who could participate?
- Was there a way to have kids regularly involved in making decisions about the Center?

They had a recurring interest in making sure that children and teens were treated fairly, that it was a place where all could feel comfortable, *not just the kids from families with money*, the adult students warned. Of course, there were differences of opinion on several issues. Teachers helped resolve these conflicts. "We have to learn to solve problems together. We have to learn it's ok not to agree with everybody all the time. We need to speak up and say what we think, but not get mad just because there's disagreement. We can work things out."

Over the next year, the Teen Center opened and operated mainly with adult education students as leaders. Children came to play video games, watch TV and movies, and visit with friends. Adult students developed skills and confidence in addressing their community's need as they planned and supervised the activities, got others involved, kept financial records, and reported on their work to the organization. Participants developed leadership skills, and built a network of people to turn to for support. They increased their confidence in the skills they had learned and in the possibility of learning from others. They took ownership of their adult education experience and gained power through their willingness to learn and effect change.

SUCCESSFUL PRACTICES: WHAT WE LEARNED

Through an evaluation of our work with Community in the Classroom we identified the processes that had helped build ownership and leadership by project participants. We saw these same processes carried out in several of the community organizations. Planning was participatory and evolved with each project. At the first workshop the group set goals and parameters (such as no experts; show us, don't just talk; have co-planners for each workshop) and chose topics for subsequent workshops. The participants did major planning for later workshops. This led to involvement in long-range planning and to proposing and developing new work.

We spent a lot of time and effort in documentation. We created a notebook of what we had done for each participant. Several groups worked to document their own histories. We held a workshop to develop and share documentation techniques. For example, some used wall newspaper and a mural to collect memories and comments and used a grab bag of objects to elicit metaphors. For instance, *My classroom is like this* . . . There was a consciousness of supporting the *next step* for people whether that was welcoming the group to the center or testifying in national hearings. The way the workshops were planned and conducted by teams and held in different organizations, along with being facilitated by the participants provided many different opportunities.

The opportunity to visit other organizations and communities broadened our understanding of the problems we all faced. The curriculum we developed focused on *shared problems like bad water, unemployment, and community tensions.* Supportive personal relationships were established through discussions about personal as well as work issues. By providing time to talk informally, and having activities that got people to work together, we were also able to create and make space for all. From the beginning, the group insisted that this project be fun. The workshops modeled and demonstrated a wide variety of teaching/learning techniques and provided a process that people could take back to their own classes. Most importantly, ongoing sharing of techniques and materials became an integral part of what the community engaged in internally, as well as with other agencies.

CONFRONTING THE CHALLENGES OF BUILDING COMMUNITY IN THE CLASSROOM

We came a long way in the Community in the Classroom project. We made steps, saw examples, and gained a better understanding *of the difficulty of applying this approach.* But, we discovered that *our vision of programs where adult education and community development and activism are integrated is still a vision.* We understood some of the challenges to this work at the time, and we have recognized others since then.

We understand that the *legacies of poverty* pervade this work. Changing adult literacy education is not easy, even in an environment in which resources are sufficient. But in these communities where there is never enough to go around, every resource allotment becomes a major issue. Teachers may feel they have to compete for the resources to buy materials for a project. Students become upset when one or two get the opportunity to earn money by providing services to the organization and others don't. Small things become big issues; habits of competition or manipulation to gain resources damage relationships within organizations. All these factors serve to keep very standard, unimaginative activities in place in adult education programs.

We recognize that the *limited resources,* not only of organization, but of individual students and staff lead to a host of problems. Many have unmet health care needs that leave them unable to actively or consistently participate. Students may not have transportation or cannot afford the gas to go to community meetings. People are spread out and roads are bad. Making or changing arrangements is difficult when people do not have phones.

We learned that the literacy programs and the organizations that provide them are entwined and reflective of each other. If the organization struggles to meet its payroll every month, the literacy program will have high staff turnover and high levels of stress. It is hard to organize an innovative program without an office. Funding, even in older organizations, is marginal.

If relationships within an organization are hierarchical and authoritarian, it is difficult for classes to reflect egalitarian values that the organization does not. If there is prejudice or mistrust toward difference (race, gender, sexual orientation) in the organization, it is likely to be reflected in literacy classes. The ability of the literacy programs to critically reflect and re-create themselves is tied to the parent organization's ability to do the same. Community-based literacy programs need to work on all fronts at once. It is not enough to just look at processes within the classroom; we must look at them in the context of the communities that they are affecting.

As Community in the Classroom participant teams worked to make changes in their organizations and their own practice, they encountered the unexamined (the hegemonic) notions of what education is about, of what schools are for. To many students, working on community issues or a group project was not school. Working individually from books and workbooks and listening to the teacher is what school is about. Teachers fervently hoped to create classrooms that were accepting of their adult students, recognizing students' interests and contributions. Yet at the same time they often seemed to want their classes to look like the classes in the school system, with teacher as expert, commercial textbooks and workbooks, and students quietly working in the classroom on their own individual skill-based goals.

Even when teachers were able to question ingrained ideas about what education should be, it was difficult to take a new road. To plan curriculum from scratch takes time and energy. Participatory planning involves skills and knowledge about things that teachers have had few opportunities to develop. It takes a lot of time and effort to make little changes. It means work within ourselves about doing things in a different way, work with co-workers about why a change is needed, work with students who may resist. Community-based approaches to literacy are not generic. There is no cookbook. The whole idea of valuing local knowledge, responding to local needs, of bringing the community into the classroom is not the way it is usually done.

THE CHALLENGES WE AVOIDED

Looking back over our experiences with Community in the Classroom, we now see a number of effective approaches, but we also see some disturbing omissions. *In our effort to build cohesive organizations committed to both adult education and to community change, we overlooked, and in some cases looked away from, important issues of class, gender, race, and sexual orientation.*

Because the majority of the group members were struggling with poverty in their daily lives, class was a frequent topic of discussion. People's understanding of their own class positionalities, their attitudes and beliefs about the class system itself, and numerous other class-related issues were addressed formally and informally, *but the underlying structures of class oppression remained unnamed.*

Most teachers and most students in the Community in the Classroom programs were women. Traditional roles for women in Appalachia are changing as more and more women work outside the home (Maggard 1994), but for many women, to attend classes or a community meeting is a major step. While most community organizations can be sites of empowerment for women, community organizations are not women's organizations per se (Bingman 1996). In fact, most of the active members in these organizations are women. One student expressed this quite well, when she said, "Well I've never sat in on a board meeting before, but now I do. I used to just sit back and wouldn't say a word. But now I will speak up for what I believe in, and that's really good. But this participation is not without cost." Family responsibilities fall heavily on women, often going beyond children to include grandchildren, parents, in-laws, and other family members. For example, one of the most active students in the Teen Center program dropped out of adult education classes to care for an ill parent. Additionally, the men in their lives are often opposed to women's participation in these programs. As one woman said: "It's made a lot of guys mad. Women are seeing that they can do things." While many women were and are able to overcome the barriers created as a result of our gender, often they do so with the support of other women; others could not. Even though gender was an integral part of the group's dynamic, it was not frequently included in formal topics of discussion. Instead, *implicit understandings of each other's experiences took the place of the formal, directed conversation.*

Even though class and gender were dealt with, at least on some level, *race and sexual orientation were essentially ignored, even avoided.* In the group-building process, for instance, the issues defined as critical—participation, developmental building of leadership, bringing people together to make connections, group cohesion—were thought of as the point of the project, and other issues, particularly race and sexuality, were seen as stumbling blocks to those goals. While there was no conscious decision to avoid those topics, we did not take, or perhaps even understand, the explicit opportunities we had to address the issues. We see now that it is precisely because these issues do stand in the way that they must be addressed. Understanding how these factors can disrupt the communities we are trying to build and sustain, we regret not having faced them head-on in the program.

We recall one example in particular in which we could have provided some foresight about these issues. A White adult education student, working on the Teen Center, was quoted in a newspaper article about the adult education program in the Center. In her quote, she talked about how difficult it was for most people to accept her marriage to a Black man. The tension in the class after the article was published moved like an unseen current, but was not publicly acknowledged. It was as if participants thought it was too dangerous to confront. There was some indirect hostility expressed, even in this group that earlier talked about how important it was to create a place where all races and classes felt comfortable. *In this situation, without consciously deciding to, we simply let the issue slide, allowing our fear of conflict to overcome the clear need for a discussion on race.*

There were other instances in the Community in the Classroom project where addressing issues of race directly could have strengthened our group and the understanding and skills of participants about these issues. We also remember avoiding discussion of some participants' discomfort about being at a conference where lesbianism was openly discussed. *We realize now that our avoidance of conflict did not smooth anything over, nor did it strengthen the group, despite the surface peace it maintained. It is precisely in situations like these that it is most important for grassroots organizations to step forward and deal explicitly with the issues that emerge. To do otherwise is not only damaging on an immediate level, but contributes to broader systems of oppression.* We in the adult education community must not allow ourselves to reinforce in our classrooms practices that we oppose in other places.

CONCLUSION

We hope that the examples we shared about the organizations involved with the Community in the Classroom project can be a source of discussion about how we might involve our students, our communities, and teachers in the active engagement of change. We believe that listening skills, developing voice and agency, working together, reading, and writing for information to bring about change in issues are important to the learners and must be taken into account. *Our experiences in facilitating a process have taught us both the value of participatory approaches, and the importance of explicitly addressing in our work the issues of race, class, gender, and sexual orientation.*

NOTE

1. For this phrase and for our ongoing thinking about community literacy, we are indebted to Juliet Merrifield, who worked with us on this project.

REFERENCES

Bingman, M. B. (1996). "Women Learning in Appalachian Community Organizations." In S. Walters and L. Manicom (eds.), *Gender in Popular Education: Methods for Empowerment*, 167–180. London: Zed Books.

Maggard, S. W. (1994). *Gender and Schooling in Appalachia: Historical Lessons for an Era of Economic Restructuring*. Research Paper 9411. Morgantown, WV: Regional Research Institute.

Street, B. (1995). *Social Literacies: Critical Approaches to Literacy in Development, Ethnography and Education*. London and New York: Longman.

Chapter 12

Education, Incarceration, and the Marginalization of Women

Irene C. Baird

> We're only teaching them how to live within an institution. We're not re-
> habilitating them. They can learn to get through here to do easy time, but
> this may not necessarily help them on the outside.
> —Female prison guard (Watterson 1996)

INTRODUCTION

Adult education literature gives weak voice to the issues of women, people of color, and other ethnic groups (see Chapters 3, 5, and 7 in this volume). From that perspective, this chapter addresses the interlocking and marginalizing effects of sexism, racism, and classism within one particular group: incarcerated women. Until the emergence of feminist research within criminal justice, corrections studies centered primarily on men, who are the majority in the penal system and who commit the more serious crimes. Even though males represent a significant number of those who actually participate in adult basic education or continuing education activities, their educational needs receive little attention (see James, Witte, and Tal Mason 1996 as one exception). More disturbing, however, is the unequal treatment of female offenders, whose numbers continue to rise. The perception is that since they constitute only about 7 percent of the overall prison[1] population, it hardly seems worthwhile or practical to attend to their educational needs (Wolford 1989; Belknap 1996). Highlighted in this chapter, therefore, are some of the issues affecting these women and suggestions on how we, as adult educators, might learn to effectively respond to them.

WOMEN INCARCERATED: SILENCED AND INVISIBLE

While the literature on women's participation and involvement in adult education is weak, the dearth of research regarding women on the margins of mainstream society is even more evident. There is little adult education scholarship on single female heads of household on welfare, or on the homeless; for the incarcerated the silence is palpable. Sissel's (1993) review of the literature further highlights this limited scholarship on women in general. In analyzing a 22-year period between 1971 and 1993, she revealed that the preponderance of studies that had been done during that time focused on white, middle-class, educated women. The topics of this body of literature primarily addressed adult development, women's human resource development in the organizational setting, and their reentry concerns to higher education and continuing professional education. As a result of the research conducted by scholars such as Hugo, Flannery and Hayes, Sissel, Sheared, Colin III, Johnson-Bailey, and Peterson, however, there is now a slowly emerging body of work on women and minorities (see Chapters 3, 5, 6, 7, 15, and 16 in this volume). Despite this ever-growing knowledge base regarding race and ethnicity, as Belknap (1996) has argued and my own research supports (Baird 1995, 1999), the incarcerated and the paroled are "among the most neglected and oppressed groups in society" (Belknap 1996, 91).

Society has begun to address issues of gender, race, and poverty in our schools, in corporate America, and in other organizational systems; society prefers, however, to isolate itself from the incarcerated, to keep them locked behind bars. With the exception of criminal justice feminist research (Belknap 1996; Chesney-Lind 1997; Owen 1998; Watterson 1996 as notable examples), the experiences of those women living and learning in organized penal systems have largely been ignored. Having examined this group over the past five years, I have grown increasingly aware of the social, economic, psychological, and developmental factors affecting them and the ways in which adult education might better serve them. Because these women are typically perceived to be both dysfunctional and illiterate[2] (Baird 1995, 1999; Newman, Lewis, and Beverstock 1993), it is essential that we question our own assumptions and expectations about their potential for learning, and their possibilities for a life of dignity and hope. It is imperative, therefore, that we initially develop a grounded understanding of their lives. According to Belknap (1996), Chesney-Lind (1996), Owen (1998), and Watterson (1996), our continued failure in acknowledging the incarcerated and those factors affecting their survival both in and out of prison destines them for invisibility as well as silencing; it ensures their marginalization and limits their ability to successfully reenter society.

We must also recognize and remember that the same patriarchal structures, factors, and issues affecting women in general are intensified among this group because of its incarcerated status. Hill Collins asserts that the primary responsibility for defining one's own reality lies with the people who live that reality, who actually have those experiences (1997, 253).[3] So that we, as adult educators, might gain insights into how imprisoned women view themselves and their lives, I share with you their voices. Adding a face to a prison number personalizes and humanizes our literature on women and adult learning.

INCARCERATION OF WOMEN: AN ABERRATION

Colonial settlers brought with them a code of morality, a standard "befitting" women that blended into the puritanical ethos. As chattel, women's appropriate role was to be the good wife, mother, and helpmate. Behaviors outside of these normative roles were labeled aberrant, corrupt, and immoral. Thus, willfulness, the questioning of authority, or any other type of behavior in which women asserted themselves was deemed a crime. Those who committed such offenses were seen as not having the appropriate knowledge and skills required to perform their domestic duties. Considered failures in society by not living up to the prescribed codes of behavior that men had established for them, such women were often depicted as witches and prosecuted as such.

Sexual activity with men outside of marriage resulted in particularly harsh treatment. Men, perceiving themselves as "victims" of the seductive female, became unswerving in their judgments and condemnation of such behavior. Because of this perception, it was the women who were sentenced for prostitution and adultery.[4] Women who were condemned for such offenses were sometimes hung, often flogged, and typically confined to filthy dungeons and jails with their children. Upon leaving these prisons, they continued to suffer punishment. Their penance and penalties were prescribed by the church and state and were sanctioned by prominent forward thinkers of the time, such as Benjamin Franklin and Benjamin Rush.

Thus, the reasons given for women's incarceration were based on the fact that they lacked morality and feminine virtues: they were, in Watterson's (1996) words, "immoral women." The assumption was that if women were good mothers, daughters, and sisters, they would stay out of prison. Their problem was in not acting compliant, not being invisible, and not keeping silent; in other words, they were not acting like the proper female.

Beginning with the 1800s, Quaker activists and other reformers of means took up the issue of the incarcerated woman. The Quakers were determined that women should have separate housing and female personnel in order to correct the physical and sexual abuse occurring in integrated institutions (Belknap 1996; Watterson 1996). Mt. Pleasant represented a turning point in the imprisonment of women when it opened a separate wing for them at the Sing-Sing prison for men. In terms of treatment, the various reformers underscored the fact that since these women were not dangerous and had committed lesser crimes than men, such as prostitution or petty theft, then the goal of the prison system was to counteract these "wayward" tendencies. By providing such skills as homemaking, religious instruction as education, and work as therapy, it was thought that the prison system could help these women move back into society.

As a result of these humanitarian Quaker influences, the purpose of women's imprisonment shifted from punishment to rehabilitation (Owen 1998; Watterson 1996). Aimed at helping these women confront the errors of their ways, and to orient them toward acquiring and carrying out their appropriate gender roles, the domestic arts of cooking, cleaning, and sewing were emphasized. While successfully resisting and making change in one patriarchal system, the Religious Society of Friends (Quakers) nevertheless accommodated and reproduced other sexist aspects of society: the patriarchal practice of limiting the roles and normative expectations of women. It would take decades more and contemporary feminist thought to reveal this irony.

Indeed, this socially constructed role was so thoroughly entrenched within corrections that adult education activities (if any) provided in correctional facilities between the 1840s and 1940s mirrored society's view of women as domestics. In fact, up until the 1950s, female inmates in work-release programs were assigned as domestics to prison administrators (Owen 1998; Watterson, 1996).

A DIFFERENT VIEW: ROLE OF FEMINIST THOUGHT

According to Owen (1998), the purpose of feminist research is to examine women's realities in the various contexts within which they live and operate. In an attempt to gain a better understanding of how the criminal justice system affects women of all races and ethnicities, I utilized a feminist analytical framework. This enabled me to describe and interpret the realities of these women, the multitude of their experiences, and the ways in which race, class, and gender influence their lives.

In the same way that the field of adult education had largely ignored research on women until recently, early researchers in the criminal justice field also neglected the imprisoned ones. Prior to the 1970s, very few studies had been conducted on incarcerated women because they were often considered too insignificant as a category to be included in the research on criminality. They were viewed as an afterthought in corrections' reports, their status was primarily relegated to a footnote, and theorists stereotyped and stigmatized them by analyzing their experiences in prison from a male's perspective. Beginning in the 1970s, feminist scholars conducting research in this area began to have an impact on the way this group was viewed. Sometimes it, too, carried racist, sexist, and classist overtones. For example, during the 1970s, liberation/emancipation theorists hypothesized that promoting gender equity fostered crime by providing liberated women with more opportunities to commit "property" crimes (Belknap 1996; Chesney-Lind 1997; Owen 1998; National Women's Law Center 1994; Shaw 1994).

In the 1980s, the emphasis placed upon these women became even more critical as female incarceration rates rose 313 percent (Belknap 1996; Chesney-Lind 1997; Klein 1995; Leonard 1995; Price and Sokoloff 1995). These scholars began offering us an alternative way to critique and work with the incarcerated by placing the issues in context and by focusing on the roles and conditions these women encountered in correctional facilities. Most recently, through the works of Belknap (1996), Chesney-Lind (1997); Owen (1998), and Watterson

(1996), the voices of incarcerated women have begun to be heard, and their conditions within the penal system brought to light. We learn from these studies that there is a lack of programming and an almost complete lack of efforts that would help them make the transition from prison back to their communities. The institutions fail to acknowledge and respond to the fact that vocational training and job placement would help the women become self-sufficient.

The penal system also fails to acknowledge and respond to the deep-rooted gender and racial issues. In spite of the increase in the numbers of female inmates, the women are still being supervised and served by men. Furthermore, the treatment they receive continues to be grounded in patriarchal attitudes reminiscent of Puritan values regarding the proper roles and duties of women in society. The research conducted by Belknap (1996) reinforces this point as she concluded that there is a disparity that exists between the way women and men are treated by the criminal justice system. As one female inmate in my study stated: "he end up in the hospital and I end up in jail.

Chesney-Lind (1997) and Owen (1998) focused on risk factors—gender, race, poverty—that not only influence women's lives outside of prison but also affect how they are treated in the penal system. For girls and women of color, Chesney-Lind (1997) found that these factors further complicate problems for them once they are incarcerated. At an early age, many of them, due to impoverished situations, learn to deal with violence on the streets and in their homes. Regardless of their family situation or race, many young girls assume adult roles in which they become the protectors and nurturers of others. They are more likely to be overrepresented in low-paying jobs and often end up struggling or stealing to make ends meet in order to help their families survive.

Violence against women is often a significant mediating reason for a variety of crimes committed by them. Owen (1998) points out that when women exhibit violent behavior, it is often the result of previous "brutalizing conditions and relationships" they encountered earlier in their lives. In addition to the gender, race, and poverty factors, Chesney-Lind (1997) found that emotional stress, physical and sexual abuse and its resulting self-esteem factors, suicide attempts, and unwanted pregnancies all play a role in contributing to criminal activity.

These findings are consistent with my work with incarcerated women. It is not unusual for someone to admit to her feelings of nothingness, "of not being loved or understood"; nor is it uncommon for these women to reflect on their abuse and how they ended up in a hospital room or jail cell.

According to Harris (1997), feminist essentialism both questions and offers us a way to understand how race affects the sentencing of women of color. Often the imposition of mostly White, straight, financially stable women's traits becomes the template to judge all women. Harris cautions us against falling into this trap because it frequently has an adverse affect on how we address issues affecting poor Black women who have been incarcerated. We must recognize that although these women are viewed as a group, they come to this situation with their own individuality, histories, and realities. While there may be some overlapping similarities and issues, there is no one composite that can be used to explain all females in prison. Harris concludes that each female offender is the only one who can speak to who she is and fully understand that which has been taken away from her. In other words, "You are made that which is taken from you" Harris (1997, 12).

DIFFERENCES IN TREATMENT AND DOING TIME: GENDER, RACE, AND CLASS

A young woman in a correctional facility program shared the following barriers she faced as a Black woman in jail:

From birth I was considered inferior, less able to accomplish what a white person can. . . . My people all known for being ruled . . . yet and still this country is built for the white man to succeed off of what my people built, but yet built for me to fail. . . . Our neighborhoods are filled with drugs, liquor stores on every corner and jails to take the results of what this atmosphere makes our people out to be. Wow! It's so great to be black.

Being a women is even harder . . . if your always in pants or sweatshirts . . . your either a dike or not considered attractive to men or society. If you always in little skirts or fitting dresses your a hoe and considered a one night stand to men or society. Wow! It's so great to be a woman.

Being incarcerated makes me feel like an animal locked in a cage. Now I know what my dog feels like. . . . They expect you not to be bitter or want to fight. If you do fight your really an animal. That's what this place makes you. . . . The worst about it all is after you did your time for the crime . . . you are still considered that same animal because you now have a record. . . . You can't get a job . . . that pay enough for the bills . . . your still doing time just not in jail. Wow! It's great to be a black woman in jail.

This woman's experience supports the notion that women of color are often victimized (Belknap 1996; Chesney-Lind 1997; Owen 1998; Watterson 1996) while in prison as well as outside of prison. They are often stereotyped and not taken seriously by the penal system.

In reality, the situation regarding women's criminality continues to be negatively biased against poor women and women of color. Several research studies conducted between 1994 and 1997 (Belknap 1996; Chesney-Lind 1997; Mann 1995; Owen 1998; Watterson 1996; National Women's Law Center 1994) found that the prisons have been and continue to be populated by African-American women (46%) and Latinas (14%). African-American women, for example, are seven times more likely to be incarcerated than a White woman who commits the same crime.

In general, women prisoners are extremely poor and, of those incarcerated, 53 percent were unemployed prior to being sent to prison and 74 percent were unemployed prior to any jail sentence being given. Furthermore, being on welfare had a detrimental impact on the type of sentence women received. Those likely to return to prison are often poor women who have been victims of neglect, violence, abuse, and most likely committed crimes in relation to trying to provide some economic means for themselves and their children. Watterson (1996) found that drugs had a significant impact upon the rate of incarceration among certain groups of women. According to her research, men had most often introduced drugs to those women who were incarcerated for drug usage or sales. The women often used the drugs as "medication" or sold them for economic survival. Additionally, depending upon her economic standing, a woman will either be incarcerated or given treatment as a way to address her problem. Poor and Black women tend to be sent to jail, whereas women with the financial means go to the Betty Ford Clinic for rehabilitation (Watterson 1996).

There is not only a disparity in the treatment that females of different races and classes receive within the criminal justice system; there continues to be disparity in the treatment that female and male prisoners receive. Getting tough on crime for women means that they will be incarcerated for petty offenses or parole violations or inability to pay their fines. Women are most often placed in overcrowded prisons for longer periods of time to ensure they will learn their proper gender role. Ironically, it is there where sexual abuse and prolonged strip searches exist. Watterson's (1996, 297) succinct summation of the current system is that "if you are black, poor or a woman in 20th century America the dice are loaded against you."

SHATTERING THE SILENCE: THE INCARCERATED WOMAN

In 1992, I began a humanities-based, problem-solving program for a group of homeless women. The project was developed as an eight-week pilot, funded by the Pennsylvania Humanities Council, and housed at a YWCA. The intent of this project was to provide women in crisis with a program whereby they could collaboratively learn how to recognize and develop solutions to some of their most pressing issues and dilemmas.

Through the writings of established female authors who had written about similar experiences or who were similar to these women by virtue of their race or economic standing, these women engaged in a learning process that included critical thinking, dialogue, reflection, and, finally, creative self-expression. By reading or listening to the reading of an author's work, the women were encouraged to reflect on themes or experiences comparable to their own. Group discussion then provided for sharing different interpretations and perspectives which stimulated further reflection. The final step in the process was to engage in creative self-expression on a theme or thought generated by the reading, reflection, dialogue process. Those who could not or chose not to write dictated their thoughts. Each week the writing was converted to print form to be included in a publication of the women's naming and for their personal keeping. Although similar to journaling, this Freirian/humanities–oriented model provided a non-threatening medium that helped the women understand that they were not alone and that even successful authors shared similar experiences. This process resulted in self-awareness/self-definition. The women's newly acquired voice in print enhanced self-esteem and promoted self-empowerment. Above all, it shattered what Freire (1993) described as the culture of silence of the oppressed.

Based on the success of the pilot project, the Humanities Council granted additional funding with the express purpose of reaching audiences that did not fit into the traditional White, middle-class classroom profile. In 1994, the corrections administration approved the request to facilitate the pilot model in a jail site. Since that time, an ongoing program which incorporates women from various racial and ethnic groups has taken place. The majority of those who actively participate are African American; the remainder are Anglo-American, Native American, and Latina—all ranging in age from 15 to early forties. Four times annually, approximately 15 women participate in a program that extends over a period of 10 weeks. They represent one-tenth of those incarcerated and housed in a male-dominated and -operated facility. Because of the popularity of the program, there is currently a waiting list.

The Evolution of Voice

At each meeting within the jail, we assemble around a large table in the facility's only multipurpose room, separated from the guard's station by a wall of glass. Most of the women who volunteer for the program learn of its purpose and process by word of mouth; however, at each opening session this is reviewed by one of the participants as materials are distributed for reading and reflection. Some examples of the authors they have read include: Maya Angelou, Sandra Cisneros, bell hooks, and Nikki Giovanni. The process is identical to that of the pilot project.[5] The women take turns volunteering to read aloud, especially if we are using poetry. The personal reflection and group discussions generate ideas which the women explore in their writing. They learn that the better they understand how the story lines intersect with their lives, the better they will understand themselves and their lives. As an example, some of the themes that emerged during one 10-week session included identity, relationships, addiction, "doing time" (serving a sentence), and a change in perspective.

Regardless of the group's (or individual's) racial or ethnic composition, it has been Maya Angelou's work, by far, that seems to resonate with the life experiences of many of these women. In *Gather Together in My Name*, Angelou (1974) introduces them to her life as it unfolded at the age of 17. During this period she was a single mother and did not have any resources, other than her own will to survive and make something out of her life. At the end of this two-year journey, Angelou recounts that she had worked as a cook, waitress, madam, dancer, prostitute, restaurant manager, as well as model. She spoke about her distrust of Whites, about finding herself, and as being "a [volatile] mixture of arrogance and insecurity" (p. 15) whenever she was rejected by someone because of her skin color.

This revelation had an immediate effect on how the participants saw themselves and their own lives. In response, one woman wrote this:

> The feeling of nothing . . .
> (that) tells you you are worthless
> not one of a kind . . .
> tells you you are no good
> You're not loved
> not understood

Another woman made a connection with the various jobs Angelou took, not by choice but as a survival mechanism for herself and her infant son. This woman recounted:

My addiction is first of all, I like nice things for my children . . . I had a job but I need more money because when I pay the bills that's was all the money . . . I sell drug for money so that I can take care of my children . . .

Like Angelou, who acknowledged: "Love was what I was looking for" (p. 18), in many instances these women found themselves searching for love, only to find themselves incarcerated. The following verse focuses on the all-too-familiar destructive relationships that these women find themselves in:

> Abusive man I was with he said he love me,
> but I couldn't see it in no kind of way
> he end up in the hospital
> and I end up in jail.

Above all, Angelou's writings served as an inspiration to these incarcerated women. For instance, her 1980 work, *And Still I Rise*, helps these women by instilling in them a sense of pride as well as by offering them a positive outlook. In this excerpt, this woman was able to identify with Angelou's strength:

> I'm a beautiful black woman standing tall and strong
> Your the person that wants to see me fall
> like a broken song . . .
> You think your doing something
> by keeping me in a cell
> but you should know this is my heaven not my hell . . .
> I'm a strong black woman still alive
> just like Maya still I rise.

In these texts, and through their discussions, it became apparent that these women were able to capture their world in words, thereby illustrating that they were not illiterate. Also apparent was the power and efficacy of using this technique with a group of women who have been typically dismissed as not being capable of literary analysis and critical thought. In addition, this project establishes that self-exploration can be used effectively by adult educators inside and outside of the prison setting to promote identity, visibility, and to shatter the silence that pervades the lived experiences of women who have been marginalized by sexist, racist, and classist social systems.

INJUSTICE REFRAMED: AN ADULT EDUCATOR'S VIEW

In 1982, Rafter and Stanko called attention to the fact that women in prison were often viewed as being unworthy or incapable of being educated. Furthermore, educational programs were usually poor in quality, quantity, and variety, and continued to be framed in traditional, gendered views of what women were suited for in society; notably, for example, for low-paying domestic or service roles. While these jobs could lead them to having some form of employment upon leaving prison, they did not provide the women with what they needed in order to achieve a level of self-sufficiency (Edin 1995).[6]

Classes that increase the inmates' literacy skills are now more commonplace as a result of a 1982 federal mandate.[7] Currently, 25 states and the United States Bureau of Prisons are in compliance with this federal mandate. Lack of total compliance may be due to inadequate funding, placing education second to security.[8] Fiscal constraints notwithstanding, literacy classes are now being offered; however, they do not go far enough in terms of addressing female inmates' problems. Even though these classes stress basic reading and writing skills, these skills are approached merely in a technical way. Given that these women's lives and the reality of their imprisonment are interconnected with who they are in terms of their race, class, and gender, it is imperative that adult education classes reflect this reality.

The extensive Newman, Lewis, and Beverstock (1993) study on prison literacy looks at literacy from a different perspective, one that addresses the concerns about current curriculum and instruction. They contend that if literacy is a way out of criminality, then the education paradigm (their term) must include the humanities, an approach that is associated with cognitive learning about one's self, one's heritage, tradition, and community. It is about acquiring a sense of self-worth and self-preservation, a sense of being part of society, not an outsider. Although Newman, Lewis, and Beverstock recommend this as part of the right kind of education, it is not a cure-all. It is, however, a nonthreatening medium for initiating dialogue and providing women with an opportunity to see themselves through a different lens.[9]

This recommendation resonates with the experiences that I have had with the women I have met in prison. Through the validation of their experiences and the recognition that they can be and are in control of what happens to them, they can begin to take charge of their lives while in prison, as well as once they leave the system. It is quite clear that, in spite of perceived illiteracy on the basis of their incarceration, these women are capable of learning. All that it takes is for someone to offer them another way of viewing the world, not in a dispassionate and nonempathetic manner, but in a way that moves them to change. Once this occurs, it is quite evident that they are not only capable of learning but that they exhibit reading, reasoning, and writing skills that can be useful in exercising agency as they negotiate their way within "the system."

Finally, we must ask ourselves as educators, as well as ask our students, what does it feel like to be educated in a prison or jail? Through my work, I have concluded that adult educators must begin to examine programs systemically and structurally from a critical standpoint if we want to ensure that change does take place for these women. We must facilitate their self-exploration process; above all, we must stop making prejudgments about them. In spite of their uniforms and the prison I.D.s, we must recognize that these women are human beings who appreciate being taken seriously and being heard; to treat them otherwise is to exacerbate their marginalization.

Since the publication of *Women's Ways of Knowing* (Belenky, Clinchy, Gold-berger, and Tarule 1986), scholarship on women has been especially attentive to both "the why" of how women are silenced and "the how" they can gain voice and claim power over themselves and in their relationships with others. For women in prison, the silencing has been societally and structurally induced (Chesney-Lind 1997; Watterson 1996); once incarcerated, society forgets about them. They are, therefore, made invisible. Helping them to gain a voice is a first step in not only making them visible, but in making visible the oppressive structures that precipitated their criminal actions.

CONCLUSION

Women adult educators in particular, but all in general, should begin to question the silencing and the invisibility of incarcerated women; we must also learn more about the criminal justice system. If we are concerned about educating women in prison, we must begin to understand how gender, race, and poverty "shape and eliminate choices for females in a country that offers the [*sic*] promise of equality" (Watterson 1996, 180). For those engaged in social justice education, we must begin to recognize, as Watterson (1996, 91) suggests, that "prisons on the outside [and the inside] are made up of neglect and [believing] that no one cares. It is a prison of no limits, so everything's limiting." In a country ranking second to Russia in numbers of prisoners, we must be aware of those policies that inappropriately sentence and silence women who often engage in crimes as a means to survive, and not as a means to inflict violence, yet are punished as though they were. We must recognize that "Prisons have little to do with stopping crime and achieving justice" (Watterson 1996, 356).

We need, therefore, to look at alternative methods that will help these women achieve both self-identity and self-sufficiency.

The future is now; silenced, invisible women must become part of adult education theoretical scholarship. As we reflect on what types of programs and what kinds of curriculum models should be put in place for those who are incarcerated, we must consider factors such as race, gender, class, and the historicity and evolution of the criminal justice system in America. In so doing, adult educators seeking social justice can begin to make systemic changes at all levels of society.

NOTES

1. As in common usage, the terms "jail" and "prison" are used interchangeably in this chapter as a reference to being incarcerated. Specifically, jails are operated by local enforcement agencies and are intended for presentencing and short-term confinement, 77 days being average. Prisons are operated and funded by the individual states and the federal government. Prisoners do time for longer periods, even life time, for having committed serious crimes. Unlike in most jails, prisoners have access to programming.

2. Data on women are difficult to assess. The 75 percent illiteracy rate associated with prison inmates implies the inclusion of women. Age, race, and ethnicity seem to be more significant than gender in most studies. More frequently, reference is made to females as being undereducated with underdeveloped work and other functional skills. The National Adult Literacy survey states in its summary that no difference in proficiencies was apparent in their survey; however, they add that because of the small number of women in prison (approximately 7 percent of the total population), only a small number of women were represented in their sample.

3. Although Hill Collins speaks here specifically to African-American women, the admonition is relevant to all women.

4. This phenomenon continues today as female prostitutes are targeted by law enforcement while the johns (customers paying for sex) go largely ignored (Watterson 1996). In fact, even as recently as 1950, according to Massachusetts law, women who had sex outside of marriage were prosecuted (Belknap 1996).

5. A detailed description of this humanities model is available in my monograph, *Unlocking the Cell: A Humanities Model for Marginalized Women* (1997).

6. Women Work! The Washington, DC–based National Network for Women's Employment issued a report intended for legislators and membership on December 8, 1998, advocating for more training and educational programs for displaced homemakers and single parents who have been left behind economically. The report details, by state, selected characteristics and changes since 1992.

7. ERIC Digest No. 159 (Kerka 1995) presents a comprehensive overview of prison literacy programs. Unfortunately, it focuses on male inmates.

8. The Newman, Lewis, Beverstock (1993) perspective on noncompliance is that cutbacks, conservative forces in Congress, as well as local politics all have control over how money is spent on prison education; in other words, the focus is on custody and control rather than the self-actualizaton aspects of education.

9. Not to be downplayed are the educational by-products: demystifying literature as a learning tool and promoting creative writing.

REFERENCES

Angelou, M. (1974). *Gather Together in My Name*. New York: Bantam Books.

Angelou, M. (1978). *And Still I Rise*. New York: Random House.

Baird, I. C. (1994a). "The Humanities for Homeless Women: A Paradox in Learning." *Adult Learning* 5(3), 13, 15.

Baird, I. C. (1994b). "Learning to Earn 'the Right Way': Single Welfare Mothers in Mandated Education." Unpublished Doctoral Dissertation, Pennsylvania State University.

Baird, I. C. (1995). "Promoting a 'Culture of Learning' through Creative Self-Expression." In T. R. Ferro and G. J. Dean (eds.), *Pennsylvania Adult and Continuing Education Research Conference Proceedings*, 13–17 (ED No. 386 589).

Baird, I. C. (1997). *Unlocking the Cell: A Humanities Model for Marginalized Women*. Washington, DC: AAACE Publications.

Baird, I. C. (1999). "The Examined Life (II): A Study of Identity Formation, Agency, Self-Expression among Imprisoned Women." In *Proceedings from the 40th Annual Adult Education Conference* (ed. Amy Rose), DeKalb, IL.

Belenky, M. F., Clinchy, B. M., Goldberger, N. R., and Tarule, J. M. (1986). *Women's Ways of Knowing*. New York: Basic Books.

Belknap, J. (1996). *The Invisible Woman: Gender, Crime and Justice*. Belmont, CA: Wadsworth Publishing Co.

Chesney-Lind, M. (1995). "Rethinking Women's Imprisonment: A Critical Examination of Trends in Incarceration." In B. Price and N. Sokoloff (eds.), *The Criminal Justice System and Women*, 2nd ed. New York: McGraw-Hill.

Chesney-Lind, M. (1997). *The Female Offender: Girls, Women, and Crime*. Thousand Oaks, CA: Sage Publications.

Edin, K. (1995). "The Myths of Dependence and Self-Sufficiency: Women, Welfare and Low-Wage Work." *Focus* (University of Wisconsin–Madison, Institute for Research on Poverty) 17(2), 1–20.

Freire, P. (1993). *Pedagogy of the Oppressed*, rev. ed. New York: Continuum.

Giroux, H. (1983). *Theory and Resistance in Education*. South Hadley, MA: Bergin & Garvey.

Haigler, K., Harlow, C., O'Connor, P., and Campbell, A. (1994). *Literacy behind Bars*. Washington, DC: National Center for Education Statistics, U.S. Department of Education.

Hannah-Moffat, K. (1994). "Unintended Consequences of Feminism and Prison Reform." http://www.csc-scc.gc.ca/text/pblct/forum/e06/e061b.shtml (March 27, 1998).

Harris, A. P. (1997). "Race and Essentialism in Feminist Legal Theory." In A. K. Wing (ed.), *Critical Race Feminism*. New York: New York University Press.

Hill Collins, P. (1997). "Defining Black Feminist Thought." In L. Nicholson (ed.), *The Second Wave: A Reader in Feminist Theory*, 241–259. New York: Routledge.

hooks, b. (1981). *Ain't I a Woman*. Boston: South End Press.

Jackson, P. (1971). "Life in Classrooms—An Excerpt." In M. Silberman (ed.), *The Experience of Schooling*. New York: Holt, Rinehart and Winston.

James, W., Witte, J., and Tal Mason, D. (1996). "Prisons as Communities: Needs and Challenges." In P. Sissel (ed.), *A Community-Based Approach to Literacy Programs: Taking Learners' Needs into Account*. San Francisco: Jossey-Bass.

Kerka, S. (1995). *Prison Literacy Programs*. Digest No. 159. Columbus, OH: ERIC Clearninghouse on Adult Career and Vocational Education.

Klein, D. (1995). "The Etiology of Female Crime." In B. Price and N. Sokoloff (eds.), *The Criminal Justice System and Women*, 2nd ed. New York: McGraw-Hill.

Leonard, E. (1995). "Theoretical Criminology and Gender." In B. Price and N. Sokoloff (eds.), *The Criminal Justice System and Women*, 2nd ed. New York: McGraw-Hill.

Mann, C. R. (1995). "Women of Color and the Criminal Justice System." In B. Price and N. Sokoloff (eds.), *The Criminal Justice System and Women*, 2nd ed. New York: McGraw-Hill.

National Women's Law Center, Washington, DC, and Chicago Legal Aid to Incarcerated Mothers. (1994). "Women in Prison." http://www-unix.oit.umass.edu/kastor/walkingsteel-95/ws-html.

Newman, W., Lewis, W, Beverstock, C. (1993). "Prison Literacy: Implications for Program and Assessment." Bloomington: Indiana University Technical Report, TR 93-01. Co-published with ERIC Clearinghouse on Reading and Communication Skills.

Owen, B. (1998). *In the Mix*. Albany: State University of New York Press.

Parisi, N. (1982). "Are Females Treated Differently?" In N. H. Rafter and E. A. Stanko (eds.), *Judge, Lawyer, Victim, Thief: Women, Gender, Race and Criminal Justice*. Boston: Northeastern University Press.

Price, B. R., and Sokoloff, N. (1995). *The Criminal Justice System and Women*, 2nd ed. New York: McGraw-Hill.

Rafter, N. H., and Stanko, E. A. (1982). *Judge, Lawyer, Victim, Thief: Women, Gender, Race and Criminal Justice*. Boston: Northeastern University Press.

Schweber, C. (1982). "The Government's Unique Experiment in Salvaging Women Criminals." In N. H. Rafter and E. A. Stanko (eds.), *Judge, Lawyer, Victim, Thief: Women, Gender, Race and Criminal Justice*. Boston: Northeastern University Press.

Shaw, M. (1994). "Women in Prison: A Literature Review." http://www.csc-scc.gc.ca/text/pblct/forum/e06/e061d.shtml (March 27, 1998).

Singer, M. I., Bussy, J., Song, L., and Lunghofer, L. (1995). "The Psychological Issues of Women Serving Time in Jail." *Journal of the National Association of Social Workers* 40(1), 103–113 (32f).

Sissel, P. (1993). "Educational Scholarship on Women: A Feminist Analysis of Two Decades of Adult Education Literature." In *Proceedings from the 34th Annual Adult Education Conference*, University Park, PA.

Vachon, M. M. (1994). "It's about Time: The Legal Context of Policy Changes for Female Offenders." http://www.csc-scc.gc.ca/text/pblct/forum/e06/e061a.shtml (March 27, 1998).

Watterson, K. (1996). *Women in Prison: Inside the Concrete Womb*, rev. ed. Boston: Northeastern University Press.

Wing, A. K. (1997). *Critical Race Feminism*. New York: New York University Press.

Wolford, B. (1989). "Correctional Facilities." In S. Merriam and P. Cunningham (eds.), *Handbook of Adult and Continuing Education*. San Francisco: Jossey-Bass.

Chapter 13

Adult Basic Education: Equipped for the Future or for Failure?

Donna Amstutz

INTRODUCTION

Adult literacy and basic education practitioners are asked to educate adults who were initially "failed by the school system."[1] Yet, rather than compensating for this failure and supporting adult learners, the system of adult basic education (ABE) programming in the United States can also be depicted as having failed these students as well. This chapter critically addresses the system of ABE in the United States, provides alternative explanations for its failure, and suggests initial steps toward change. The three issues I believe that have had the greatest impact include:

1. The effectiveness of current federal programs and goals;
2. Workplace literacy and welfare to work policies; and
3. The roles and challenges of literacy instructors, including cultural, instructional, training, and gender gaps.

While these factors are often examined in isolated contexts, the intent of this chapter will be to show how these factors are interrelated and contribute to the success or failure that many students continue to face, even when they return to the schooling process.

EFFECTIVENESS OF FEDERALLY FUNDED PROGRAMS AND GOALS

While some would argue that an ability to read and write is necessary in order to be successful in society, literacy is not an end in itself. Rather, I believe, it is a means to other ends, such as political, economic, or social development. I would further argue that an equally vital goal of these programs is to maintain the status quo, since, as Auerbach (1991) noted, ABE efforts have been marginalized primarily because of societal marginalization of its learners: people of color, lower socioeconomic workers, immigrants, and the unemployed. In spite of this reality, programs in the United States continue to operate under the assumption that the primary purpose of federally funded ABE programs is to increase employability. As we examine these issues we find that there is a domino effect. Inadequate funding leads to inadequate staffing arrangements; inadequate staffing leads to an inability to plan for the future; an inability to plan leads to an inability to evaluate either the successes or failures.

Moore and Savrianos (1995) and Young, Fleishman, Fitzgerald, and Morgan (1995), along with Stein (1997), provide us with ample evidence in studies they conducted concerning federal involvement as to how funding has affected personnel and ultimately the success of students in our programs. Within these reports the inadequacy of resources was addressed as a key reason for programs failing. These studies reported that programs receive roughly $258 per year per adult student, compared to an average of $5,721 per year per K–12 student. With these funding levels, it is no wonder that many programs continue to fail. This gross underfunding has meant that programs have to operate without a corps of full-time, professional educators. Sixty percent of programs have no full-time instructors. Eighty percent of instructors are part-time, often with little or no training in adult education.

Limited funding often means that there will be limited resources available to pay teachers for preparation time—in fact, most ABE teachers are not paid for this critical work. In spite of this, they are expected to help adults make significant learning gains in an average of four hours of instruction per week. The lowest-achieving students, often those with learning difficulties, end up being served by well-intentioned but relatively ineffective volunteers. Moreover, programs tend to end up operating without a consistent vision of what is important to teach. Most emphasize school-based subject matter, using a remedial approach.

The literature of adult education calls repeatedly for programs to be learner-based, but only a small percentage of literacy programs display characteristics that reflect learners' realities and interests. In a recent study of 271 adult literacy programs, 73 percent were described as "using activities and materials that are not related to their students' lives and as teacher directed and controlled rather than collaborative" (Purcell-Gates, Degener, and Jacobson 1998, 2). These programs tended to be decontextualized and did not involve learners in decision making.

Yet, despite recommendations to utilize the context of learners' lives as a focus of learning activity,[2] many literacy practitioners actively resist learner-centered curricula in favor of normative goals. Demetrion (1997) and Dill (1997) typify this top-down philosophy and approach. In his article "Pedagogy of the

Depressed," Dill (1997) argues for literacy teachers as experts: "If you make yourself the center of attraction then they will listen to you and learn from you" (p. 118). Like Dill, many literacy programs thus continue to promote teacher-centered, school-based instruction, in effect continuing assimilation and accommodation to Western thought and values.

The outcomes of such an inadequate system are not surprising. Students do not stay in programs long enough to make significant progress, and therefore they and the programs appear to have failed. Native English speakers with the lowest skill levels average only 35 hours before dropping out and the median retention is less than 60 hours. According to the U.S Department of Education (1995), the dropout rate approaches 80 percent as students quickly assess the uselessness of the system.

LITERACY POLICY AND THE WORKPLACE

In 1998, the Adult Education Act was replaced by Title II of the Workforce Investment Act. This law consolidates over 50 employment, training, and literacy programs into three grants to states: one for adult education and family literacy, one for disadvantaged youth, and one for adult employment and training. Under this law there are three goals that specifically relate to adult education and literacy. These goals specify that programs must assist:

1. Adults in becoming literate and obtaining the knowledge and skills necessary for employment and self-sufficiency;
2. Adults who are parents in obtaining the educational skills necessary to become full partners in the educational development of their children; and
3. Adults in completing high school or the equivalent.

Under the new law, funding appropriated to the states changed as a result of the funding formula used by the federal government, and it further solidified its economic impact on states and local communities. The old formula was based on the number of adults aged 16 and older without a high school diploma. The new law changes the funding formula so that literacy programs now serve adults between ages 16 and 61. States that have a large percentage of older adults (i.e., Florida) may receive a significantly smaller percentage of federal funding (although in the first year of authorized legislation states must receive at least 90 percent of the amount received in the previous year).

The most logical inference for the change is that people over the age of 61 are not expected to contribute to the economy in any meaningful way. The government, which is supposed to serve as a watchdog for discrimination based on age and other factors, appears to be guilty itself of age discrimination. Another group who cannot directly participate in the economy—prisoners—are also factored out of the new law by limiting the amount of funds that go to prisoner education. In a mean-spirited fashion, adult literacy federal policy has begun to reflect a corporate philosophy that investment is only for those who have a potential payoff for corporate owners.

The resultant impact of these factors is that workplace literacy tends to serve those who are already employed while neglecting those who are most in need— unemployed, low-literate adults. Hull (1997) noted, "The popular discourse of workplace literacy tends to underestimate and devalue human potential and to mischaracterize literacy as a curative for problems that literacy alone cannot solve" (p. 11).

LITERACY AND WELFARE

This contemporary connection between employment and federal support for ABE is particularly apparent in the recent welfare-to-work discourse. According to D'Amico (1997), 75 percent of jobs require high school diplomas, 70 percent require general work experience, and 50 percent of employers offering entry-level jobs required paper-and-pencil tests. Many of those affected by jointly offered welfare-to-work and literacy programs have been women. They often have not had any work experience, and although it is illegal to require the use of literacy tests as screening devices unless the literacy skills measured reflect actual job demands, these tests are routinely used to eliminate otherwise qualified job seekers (Castellano 1997).

From one-third to one-half of welfare recipients perform at the lowest level of literacy, while another third performs at the second to lowest level. Furthermore, 63 percent of women who receive welfare for five years or more lack a high school diploma. Even though welfare recipients with low literacy skills might obtain short-term employment, their income will not keep them out of poverty, because many end up in contingency jobs; and, perhaps more importantly, none of these job opportunities offer promising prospects for a sufficient income or long-term advancement. Newman (1995) found that after looking for a full year, 73 percent of applicants for entry-level jobs are still unemployed.

TANF

The federal welfare program, Temporary Assistance for Needy Families (TANF) of the Personal Responsibility and Work Opportunities Reconciliation Act of 1996, which replaced Aid to Families with Dependent Children as the federal government's primary public assistance program, has viewed literacy skill development as secondary to its mission. TANF emphasizes work and job placement with little explicit mention of skill development. For them the bottom line is clear: after five years of TANF assistance (and less in some states), welfare recipients will have to support themselves. As more recipients feel the effects of this law, increased literacy program enrollments are expected. However, the data on the lack of effectiveness of literacy programs, combined with the lack of entry-level jobs, presents a bleak future.

MYTH AND REALITY: LITERACY

Most literacy program personnel in the United States carry a firm belief that increased education leads to more employment opportunities. Recent studies, however (Friedlander and Burtless 1995; Pauly and DiMeo 1995; Grubb 1995), have seriously questioned the constancy of this relationship. In individual cases, success in literacy programs has resulted in employment. But the overall success of these programs in both short-term and long-term employment has not been achieved for the majority of literacy learners.

In a report issued by the National Institute for Literacy, eight exemplary programs containing welfare-to-work training and literacy services were identified and reviewed by Murphy and Johnson (1998). They recommended that adult education programs assist welfare recipients by developing shorter, more intensive classes that were more closely tied to work or training. While it is clear that they understood that, in order for these women to obtain and maintain jobs they needed adequate training, the funding differential between what they proposed and what is available in most programs is still great. The average cost per job placement was $3,169 in the programs they reviewed—a significantly higher investment than the $258 per year per student that the average adult literacy program receives from federal funding. Even in these exemplary programs, the job placement rate averaged only 50 percent (ranging from 21 percent to 88 percent).

ABE TEACHERS AND VOLUNTEERS AND THE CULTURAL GAP

ABE teachers and volunteers often make faulty assumptions about learners' job opportunities, access to health care, values, and culture (Sissel 1996). Some literacy teachers tend to discount the cultures of their students as less valuable than their own. Literacy learners may also idealize the cultures of their teachers as superior to their own (Foehr 1994). The relationships between primarily middle-class teachers and learners from working-class or underclass backgrounds are often strained due to a lack of actual experience in dealing with people from other socioeconomic cultures. More importantly, individuals may be blind to their own attitudes that permit or maintain oppression, both external and internal. In fact, one of the most damaging assumptions that literacy teachers make is that illiteracy is an individual problem, not a social problem derived from the economic and political structures of society. They may confuse lack of reading and writing skills with lack of knowledge or wisdom in general. This confusion often results in patronizing attitudes that affect learners as well as confirm policy makers' ideas about how best to solve the literacy "problem."

The demographics of literacy teachers, volunteers, and learners provide additional evidence of this cultural gap. A study by the Literacy Assistance Center, reported by D'Amico (1995), documented that in New York City, wide differences existed in the cultural/racial composition of the learner population (89 percent of whom were people of color) compared with program staff (37 percent of whom were people of color). A majority of both volunteer and paid staff were White and female. Over half of the paid staff were over 45 years old, while more than half of the students were under 45. The age difference was even more pronounced among volunteers, one-third of whom were over 60. While it is possible that many teachers who do not reflect the culture or community of their learners can be effective instructors, it is more likely that differences in culture and class are often substantial barriers to learner progress, if unacknowledged or explored.

The notion that literacy programs will have significant impact is specious if literacy programs continue to employ primarily White, middle-class teachers who have not acknowledged their own a priori assumptions about adults with low-level literacy skills. From my experience, the lack of understanding of learners' lives, in combination with volunteers and ABE teachers who adhere to the "pull yourself up by your bootstraps" mainstream philosophy, drives many adult learners away from literacy programs. Compounding this, teachers and tutors may lack an in-depth understanding of the reading acquisition process.

CRISIS IN THE CLASSROOM: INSTRUCTIONAL AND TRAINING GAPS

Literacy teachers and volunteers tend to be excellent readers who find significant meaning in their own reading. For most of them, reading comes naturally. It is difficult for them to analyze how they read, what factors are most important, or specific steps they take to make meaning. As a result, teachers tend to teach in the ways they were taught. This results in literacy practitioners emphasizing reading as a word-calling activity instead of a meaning-making process (Meyer and Keefe 1998). Students make very slow progress and become frustrated, often dropping out of the program. It is not only the students who experience this frustration. The extremely low retention rate of volunteer tutors (lower than for any other type of volunteer activity) may reflect their frustration as well (Ilsley 1990).

Volunteers and retired teachers can provide meaningful assistance to some adult learners. However, mainstream former elementary and secondary teachers often use methods that were inadequate during the literacy learner's first attempt at learning in schools. Teachers, for the most part, use analytic and impersonal models with tasks that are largely presented in a decontextualized method. Many African-American, Asian, Latino, and Native American authors have critiqued these approaches (for example, see Anner 1996; Cajete 1994; Castellano 1990; Colin 1989). Some feminists have also questioned the effectiveness of individualistic, linear forms of instruction for many women (see hooks 1994; Moraga and Anzaldua 1983).

However, most teachers and programs continue to make primary use of individualized study. Many literacy learners attend learning labs where isolated instruction is based on their "specific diagnosed needs." Most students then work individually to master the skills identified. Teachers must reexamine their methodology to include more interactions between and among students and staff. Lack of progress results from inappropriate instructional methods, and students voice their displeasure by leaving the programs that are supposedly designed for them; however, there does not seem to be very much interest by teachers in examining instructional methods that require a more holistic process. Instruction for ABE learners is generally not based on research on the reading acquisition process of adults, and the fact that most are not full-time, experienced instructional personnel creates a crisis for professional development.

Literacy teachers often receive little instructional assistance in pre-service or in-service training. Having worked with numerous literacy programs to design professional development for over 20 years, I am continually surprised to learn that pre-service training often consists of the viewing of one or two videotapes prior to beginning instruction in a classroom. Some teachers receive only a textbook and wishes for "good luck." Only a few programs have substantial preparation programs in which new teachers are involved, usually concurrently, with their first few months of instruction. Training that does occur is usually not offered on paid time and not related to increases in pay. Furthermore, training very seldom addresses the cultural gaps described previously. While this situation most likely comes from a philosophical viewpoint of knowledge as neutral, it adversely affects large numbers of literacy learners. Too many training solutions relate to helping the instructors "understand" the literacy population. Instead of trying to understand "the other," literacy practitioners need to begin their training with an examination of their own assumptions about themselves, about how learning occurs, and about the race, gender, and class contexts that shape their thinking about literacy.

Gender Gaps

Literacy workers have much to gain from feminist literature. Learning needs among women and program differences based on systems of privilege and oppression should be major considerations of literacy programs and instructors (Tisdell 1997). Much of feminist literature supports the notion that women tend to be connected learners and value relational and affective forms of knowing. However, most programs are content-based and are delivered individually. The field needs to recognize that individualized instruction may be counterproductive for many women.

Issues of gender consistently arise in the literature related to adult education. However, there are very few studies that discuss gender issues in literacy programs. In practice, the reality that females, both unpaid volunteers and underpaid part-time teachers, dominate literacy instructional programs is well documented. This is in stark contrast to the majority of administrators and policy makers who are primarily male. As noted by Quigley (1997), "virtually all feminist critiques support the observation that to publicly locate a social problem in a traditional female framework in this way is to immediately diminish its significance in power terms" (p. 27).

Through the ERIC Clearinghouse on Adult, Career and Vocational Education, Imel and Kerka (1996) published a guide to information and resources related to women and literacy and to assist the development of woman-positive programs. Tisdell (1997) suggested that discussions of work from explicitly feminist perspectives are purposefully avoided. Perhaps an aversion to "feminist" perspectives results from a legacy of "feminist" being interpreted as "radical." Most literacy teachers and volunteers are White, middle-class women who do not view themselves as part of intersecting systems of privilege and oppression that include gender and related systems of race, class, sexual orientation, sizism, and ableness. This may explain the tendency of teachers to ignore or remain unaware of the violence women may face as literacy learners. Rockhill (1987) described violence in a group of Mexican American women whose simple act of attending literacy programs was viewed as disloyalty to their men and resulted in battering and other forms of violence against women literacy learners.

Beginning Solutions

Facing overwhelming pressures by legislation and by traditional instructional practices, how do adult educators begin to provide meaningful literacy instruction? My first inclination is to insist that only through bypassing federally funded programs can literacy practitioners have any real effect on literacy students. One could argue that the only appropriate solution is to work in communities on literacy tasks as they arise. There are some outstanding examples of community-based programs and associations. The New England Literacy Resource Center/ World Education in Boston publishes The Change Agent, focusing on adult education for social justice as it relates to literacy learners. Focus issues have included crime and violence, health, workplace, and civic participation. The Change Agent is an excellent resource for alternative visions of literacy programs. The North American Popular Educators is an association of community workers and scholars who integrate literacy with other meaningful community projects. These adult educators, working outside the system in learners' communities, deserve our support and encouragement.

I am often frustrated, however, by well-meaning academics who critique the problems with literacy programs, but never "dirty" themselves by working with literacy students and personnel. As an idealist, and as a practitioner, I believe that we cannot abandon the well-intentioned people who both deliver and enroll in literacy programs. The following ideas are beginnings that could lead to improved literacy programs if adult basic educators are committed to working within the system for change.

Dialogue with Community. Literacy teachers can assist with the literacy attempts of their students by fostering dialogue about real issues in the students' communities. Becoming a member of that community is a first step. That means attending to the issues of structural oppression. Assisting community members to take control of their housing, their public schools, and other issues should be an integral part of literacy efforts. Dialogue is one way to engage with these issues. Foehr (1994) suggested that by creating open, reciprocal dialogues, teachers could play a role in providing better opportunities for understanding and learning. She believed that a "public policy that truly honors equality, liberty, human life and difference" (p. 50) can be developed to break down stereotypes and reduce the stigmas that separate cultures. These dialogues can help people value cultures that are different from their own. Education which is marked by open exchange and which promotes attitudes of working with people—not dominating or subjugating them—can liberate both teachers and learners (see Chapter 11 in this volume).

Review Successful Programs. By looking at the history of literacy programs, there are models of effective literacy learning and instruction. The citizenship schools of the 1960s avoided the cultural gap problem by having teachers from the learners' communities who reflected the heritage of the learners. Myles Horton, founder of the Highlander Center, was convinced that teachers had to come from the culture of learners. These community members would value others and expect them to achieve their goals. Most people who became teachers in the citizenship schools were not formally trained as teachers, and had not been indoctrinated in the philosophies and traditional instructional methods that university-trained public school teachers generally acquire. They provided dialogue and a common purpose that had powerful effects. Together they learned, both to learn and to teach.

In addition, both teachers and students had a common goal: increasing the number of Black adults who could vote by passing the literacy test that was required at that time for them to exercise their democratic rights. The assumption that the illiterate students had little knowledge was not given credibility. Rather, the teachers believed that the students had an enormous store of knowledge that would inform their voting behavior. This affirmation of the students' knowledge provided a powerful participatory method. Quigley (1997) noted, "the field will never engage more low literate adults in traditional programs as long as the time and effort learners put into such programs do not produce a truly relevant end. In most instances, this would mean the chance to clarify and resolve a personal or community problem arising, for example, from gender, race, or economic issues" (p. 121). Perhaps by studying the operation of citizenship schools, current literacy teachers could find useful alternative ways of viewing literacy instruction.

Revise Our Notions of Professionalism. Professionalization in the traditional sense is not what the literacy field or our students need. To professionalize often means to attain credentials, and promotes the possibility that we will move further away from the communities in which learners live. In her review of professionalization of adult education personnel, Auerbach (1991) was quite clear:

The best way for us to become professionals may be to act unprofessionally (according to traditional definitions of professionalism): this means to work collectively, to challenge the norms of the academy, to ally ourselves with students, and to resist the kind of stratification that professionalism often implies. It means linking politics, pedagogy and professionalism as different aspects of the same process. (p. 8)

Instead of viewing adult literacy students as deficient in intellectual skills or functional skills, literacy teachers should begin instruction with a spirit of community being foremost, becoming student advocates in all realms, not just literacy.

Appropriate activities for literacy practitioners include a new vision of the types of information literacy practitioners need. Revising training must begin with an examination of the assumptions that many literacy teachers have about learners and instruction. They need to be helped to understand their role in blaming the victim (Ryan 1976), and to take on a new view that students are not deficient. Torres (1994) coherently argued,

The conventional negative vision that stresses disabilities, has to be substituted with a positive vision which stresses strengths and abilities; for ideological reasons, because literacy is fundamentally an equity and a human rights issue; for pedagogical reasons, because starting from what learners know and are capable of—and not from what they do not know and are incapable of—is an elementary principle of education. (p. 52)

This is a fundamental change that will not occur quickly. Changing how one views the world is a long-term process, both for teachers and students. But unless we begin to provide light for those involved in literacy activities, their methods will never change.

Provide Protected Spaces for Women

Women in literacy programs could be encouraged to find their "voices" by the provision of a place to discuss, write, and read about their own power as women. This process opens the possibility that there are many truths, and that the truths women with low literacy skills have are as valid as other forms of "truth." Literacy programs that provide for mutual support among women through group work may have a more potent impact on women's literacy skills than individualized, academically based programs. Literacy teachers must first believe that every woman has something valuable to say (Mace 1992).

CONCLUSION

ABE programs are clearly designed to justify poverty and place blame on the adult illiterate. Programs ensure the failure of these adults by providing an appearance that assistance is being given to those "most in need." The reality belies this description. Programs are underfunded and perpetuate the gender, social, and economic status quo. It should be evident that doing more of the same— in terms of program and instructional provision—will not have a significant impact on literacy for most learners in ABE programs. Failure, frustration, and wasted monies are the logical result of continuing old frameworks and practices (Torres 1994).

Change does not mean making minor, irrelevant adjustments; it requires doing things perhaps radically differently from the current form. Adult educators must understand that both adult learners and we are knowledge makers and culture makers. We live in educational worlds that are fraught with practices established in the past, many of which may no longer be relevant. We need to construct a multitude of programs and instructional strategies that make sense for learners, not just literacy practitioners.

Too many politicians focus only on employment goals and welfare reduction as the primary purpose for literacy education. Too many adult literacy educators focus only on academic skills, neglecting the importance of addressing the related issues of poverty, discrimination, and inequality. Without addressing these issues concurrently, adults will wisely continue to reject federally funded literacy programs. Multiple strategies must be devised on both the legislative and academic levels. To ignore the three million adults currently in literacy programs is to sacrifice them. Adult educators can no longer just talk about critical theory—we must begin the messy process of change. To do less would be to abandon the very people we wish to serve.

NOTES

1. Adult basic education refers to those programs that serve learners who have not completed high school or who have limited English-speaking skills.

2. Most recently, the National Institute for Literacy (see Stein 1997, 25) recommended programming based on a customer-driven vision and the development of performance standards along contexts such as role of worker, citizen, and parent. This effort, however, is equally problematic due to the middle-class normative expectations of its designers.

REFERENCES

Anner, J. (ed.). (1996). *Beyond Identity Politics: Emerging Social Justice Movements in Communities of Color*. Boston: South End Press.

Auerbach, E. (1991). "Politics, Pedagogy and Professionalism: Challenging Marginalization in ESL." *College ESL* 1(1), 1–9.

Cajete, G. (1994). *To the Mountain: An Ecology of Indigenous Education*. Skyland, NC: Kivaki Press.

Castellano, M. (1997). "It's Not Your Skills, It's the Test": Gatekeepers for Women in the Skilled Trades." In G. Hull (ed.), *Changing Work, Changing Workers*, 189–213. Albany: State University of New York Press.

Castellano, O. (1990). "Canto, locura y poesia." *Women's Review of Books* 7(5) (February).

Coles, G. (1989). *The Learning Mystique: A Critical Look at "Learning Disabilities."* New York: Fawcett Columbine.

Colin, S.A.J. III. (1989). "Cultural Literacy: Ethnocentrism versus Self-ethnic Reflectors." *Thresholds in Education* 15(4) (November), 16–20.

Collins, M. (1991). *Adult Education as Vocation: A Critical Role for the Adult Educator*. New York: Routledge.

D'Amico, D. (1995). *Staffing Patterns in New York City Adult Literacy Initiative Programs: Data and Directions*. New York: Literacy Assistance Center.

D'Amico, D. (1997). "Adult Education and Welfare to Work Initiatives: A Review of Research, Practice and Policy." *Literacy Leader Fellowship Program Reports* 3(1) (August). Washington, DC: National Institute for Literacy.

Demetrion, G. (1997). "Student Goals and Public Outcomes: The Contribution of Adult Literacy Education to the Public Good." *Adult Basic Education* 7(3) (Fall), 145–164.

Dill, L. (1997). "Pedagogy of the Depressed." *Adult Basic Education* 7(2) (Summer), 104–118.

Ehringhaus, C. (1992). "Review of the Book *The Learning Mystique: A Critical Look at Learning Disabilities.*" *Adult Basic Education* 2(1) (Fall), 62–66.

Fingeret, A. (1983). "Social Network: A New Perspective on Independence and Illiterate Adults." *Adult Education Quarterly* 3(3), 133–145.

Foehr, R. P. (1994). "If You Don't Like Me Because I'm Black, I'll Understand: The Pain of Multicultural Illiteracy in the Schools." *Literacy Networks: A Journal of Literacy Providers* 1(1) (October), 43–50.

Friedlander, D., and Burtless, B. (1995). *Five Years After: The Long Term Effects of Welfare to Work Programs*. New York: Russell Sage.

Grubb, N. W. (1995). *The Returns to Education and Training in the Sub-baccalaureate Labor Market: Evidence from the Survey of Income and Program Participation, 1984–1990*. Berkeley, CA: National Center for Research on Vocational Education, University of California at Berkeley.

hooks, b. (1994). *Teaching to Transgress: Education as the Practice of Freedom*. New York: Routledge.

Hull, G. (1997). "Introduction." In G. Hull (ed.), *Changing Work, Changing Workers: Critical Perspectives on Language, Literacy and Skills*, 3–39. Albany: State University of New York Press.

Ilsley, P. J. (1990). *Enhancing the Volunteer Experience*. San Francisco: Jossey-Bass.

Imel, S., and Kerka, S. (1996). *Women and Literacy: Guide to the Literature and Issues for Woman-Positive Programs, Information Series No. 367*. Columbus, OH: ERIC Clearinghouse on Adult, Career, and Vocational Education.

Mace, J. (1992). *Talking about Literacy: Principles and Practices of Adult Literacy Education*. London: Routledge.

Meyer, V., and Keefe, D. (1998). "Supporting Volunteer Tutors: Five Strategies." *Adult Basic Education* 8(2) (Summer), 59–67.

Moore, M., and Savrianos, M. (1995). *Review of Adult Education Programs and Their Effectiveness: A Background Paper for Reauthorization of the Adult Education Act.* Washington, DC: U.S. Department of Education.

Moraga, C., and Anzaldua, G. (eds.). (1983). *This Bridge Called My Back: Radical Writings by Women of Color.* New York: Kitchen Table Press.

Murphy, G., and Johnson, A. (1998). *What Works: Integrating Basic Skills Training into Welfare-to-Work.* Washington, DC: National Institute for Literacy.

Newman, K. S. (1995). "What Inner-city Jobs for Welfare Moms?" *New York Times*, May 20, 23.

Pauly, E., and DiMeo, C. (1995). *The JOBS Evaluation: Adult Education for People on AFDC: A Synthesis of Research.* Washington, DC: U.S. Department of Education and U.S. Department of Health and Human Services.

Purcell-Gates, V., Degener, S., and Jacobson, E. (1998). *U.S. Adult Literacy Program Practice: A Typology across Dimensions of Life-Contextualized/Decontextualized and Dialogic/Monologic.* Cambridge, MA: National Center for the Study of Adult Learning and Literacy.

Quigley, B. A. (1997). *Rethinking Literacy Education: The Critical Need for Practice-Based Change.* San Francisco: Jossey-Bass.

Riemer, F. (1997). "From Welfare to Working Poor: Prioritizing Practice in Research on Employment Training Programs for the Poor." *Anthropology and Education Quarterly* 28(1), 85–100.

Rockhill, K. (1987). "Literacy as Threat/Desire: Longing to Be Somebody." In J. Gaskel and P. McLaren (eds.), *Women and Education: A Canadian Perspective*, 315–333. Calgary, Alberta: Detselig Enterprises.

Ryan, W. (1976). *Blaming the Victim.* New York: Random House.

Sissel, P. (1996). "Reflection as Vision: Prospects for Literacy Programming." In P. Sissel (ed.), *A Community-Based Approach to Literacy Programs: Taking Learners' Lives into Account.* San Francisco: Jossey-Bass.

Stein, S. G. (1997). *Equipped for the Future: A Reform Agenda for Adult Literacy and Lifelong Learning.* Washington, DC: National Institute for Literacy.

Stuckey, J. E. (1991). *The Violence of Literacy.* Portsmouth, NH: Boynton/Cook.

Tisdell, E. J. (1997). "Review of Information Series, No. 367, Women and Literacy: Guide to the Literature and Issues for Woman-Positive Programs." *Adult Basic Education* 7(3) (Fall), 189–191.

Torres, R. M. (1994). "Literacy for All: Twelve Paths to Move Ahead." *Convergence* 27(4), 50–72.

U.S. Department of Education, Division of Adult Education and Literacy. (1995). *Adult Education Program Statistics for Fiscal Year 1994.* Washington, DC: Author.

Young, M., Fleishman, H., Fitzgerald, N., and Morgan, M. (1995). *National Evaluation of Adult Education Programs.* Arlington, VA: Development Associates.

Chapter 14

Teaching as Political Practice

Ruth Bounous

INTRODUCTION

Elementary, secondary, and postsecondary educational systems as well as adult
basic education programs in the United States reflect the unequal positions that
people with particular identities hold in our society (Flannery 1994). Women,
African Americans, Latinos, gay, lesbian, poor, elderly, mentally ill, and physically disabled people experience numerous barriers to educational opportunities.
Education, as a social institution, reproduces the power inequalities of the larger
society and reinforces the way in which power is created and maintained through
its function of socializing students to acceptable values and ideologies (Freire
1970).

In this chapter, I examine ways in which the relationship between teacher and
student accommodates and is structured to reproduce the inequities of the
broader society. Within the education system, students are at the bottom of a
hierarchy of privilege and power. While the ostensible focus of all education is
on students, in fact, the position of students is often not a valued one. Those in
traditional adult basic education programs and those enrolled in universities normally have little, if any, say in the process or content of their educational experience.

At first glance, the situations of adult basic education students and higher
education students appear very different. However, even though one clearly
appears more disadvantaged than the other, when both enter into a formal classroom their knowledge and experiences are often not valued or considered meaningful in the learning environment. My experience as a social work educator
and an Adult Basic Education Director validates this view and has led me to
believe that these adult students in two different educational contexts share im-

portant characteristics. For example, the experiences and knowledge they bring to the educational situation are often not recognized or valued. As a consequence, the student frequently feels disempowered in the classroom.

The disempowerment of students, especially as reflected in the traditional teacher–student relationship, is problematic on several counts. First, one of the major goals of education is human growth and development, and an essential element in growth is becoming empowered and gaining control over one's life (Pinderhughes 1989). It is paradoxical to attempt to help people grow within an educational system that disempowers students and thus erects barriers to such growth. Second, the K–12 experiences of most students may have led to their disempowerment, which ultimately impacts negatively their decision to enroll in adult basic education programs. These disempowering experiences have often been linked to the types of relationships that exist between teachers and students—a critical factor affecting the high attrition rates for these students. Furthermore, for students who are disenfranchised because of their race, class, gender, ability, sexual orientation, or other markers of otherness, the result is an intensification of this disempowerment.

While some educators doubt the potential of schools to systematically promote counterhegemonic practices (Freire 1985), *other* educators have explored the ways in which students in the educational system resist the dominant ideology (Willis 1977; Giroux and McLaren 1987; McLaren 1989), and the ways in which educators can engage in liberatory practices in the classroom (Illich 1976; Shor 1992; Freire 1985). Therefore, it is important that we continue to work with students to explore these dynamics and collaborate around strategies of resistance. To do this, I believe we must radically alter the way in which we approach teaching.

Like many contemporary adult educators (Bagnall 1989; Giroux and McLaren 1987; McLaren 1989; Sissel 1997; Tisdell 1993), I am convinced that teaching is inherently political, in contrast to "the traditional view of classroom instruction and learning as a neutral process antiseptically removed from the concepts of power, politics, history, and context" (McLaren 1989, 160). To assert that teaching is political practice is to accept the perspective that the world we live in is constructed symbolically by the mind through social interaction with others and is heavily dependent on culture, context, custom, and historical specificity" (McLaren 1989, 169).

In using the term "political" I refer to the way the educational system is structured. This includes the language used, the methods employed, and the content and subject matter. Through these mechanisms, teachers create power arrangements that result in greater or lesser access to educational resources and, ultimately, influence students' ability to gain economic and social privileges in society. Teachers are the primary actors in this political arena. Even though teachers may see themselves primarily as dispensers of knowledge, in fact they are more than dispensers. As primary actors in this political arena, teachers are, in fact, cultural agents who accommodate or resist racism, sexism, or classism in the classroom. I believe that teachers who commit to understanding these social inequities and work to develop a critically reflective practice have the potential to engage in counterhegemonic practice through the development of collaborative relationships with students. To do this, they must begin to change the way in which they and their students perceive their relationship, and how they operate with one another in the learning environment. In so doing, they— and the students—become empowered.

MERGING THEORY TO PRACTICE

For many years I have been involved in teaching, designing, and directing an adult basic education program and, simultaneously, teaching undergraduate and graduate students at the postsecondary level who are also adult learners. As the framework of this book suggests, we must not only merge theory to our practice, but conversely, we must construct theory from our practice. In so doing, I would like to suggest some of the ways that this can be done. As an educator who is critically reflecting upon issues of power and empowerment, I have begun to pose for myself the following questions:

1. What does empowerment mean? How can it be defined? How is it manifested? How can it be evaluated?
2. What kind of relationship between teacher and students leads to empowerment for both teacher and students?
3. How can I foster a collaboration with the students in the courses I teach that takes into account the unique identities of the students and the resources that they bring?
4. How can I structure my relationships with students so as to resist and redefine, rather than reflect, the inequities toward people of differing classes, races, ethnicities, genders, and ages which permeate educational institutions and broader social structures?

My questions are similar to those posed by Elizabeth Ellsworth in her article "Why Doesn't This Feel Empowering? Working Through the Repressive Myths of Critical Pedagogy" (1989). As with Ellsworth, these concerns emerge out of my day-to-day practice as an adult educator. To place collaborative teacher– student relationships in context, there follows a brief analysis of various approaches to adult education and the philosophical assumptions that have influenced my practice.

Types of Teacher–Student Relationships

As a means of reflecting on these questions, I began looking at some of the philosophical perspectives that are the basis of widely used educational methods, and the ideological frameworks that undergird them. Upon closer examination under a political lens, and not merely an instrumental one, the ideological nature of dominant approaches to education become apparent, as does the way in which power and resources function in one's practice.

For instance, liberalism, the predominant philosophical basis for formal education in the Western world, focuses on the transmission of expert knowledge. The teacher, as the expert, exercises power over the learner, who is the recipient of knowledge. Similarly, the philosophical traditions of materialism and empiricism influenced the development of behaviorist adult education in which the relationship of teacher and student is that of master to apprentice. The teacher has ultimate power in the relationship and functions as a manager in predicting and directing learning outcomes. Although power is not expressly discussed in the philosophy of progressivism, as represented by John Dewey (1938), it is an inherent factor that constructs the teacher/learner relationship. The conception of power as control is the common denominator in these two philosophies. The one who makes the decisions about what is taught in the classroom is the teacher, who is, therefore, invested with the power.

In contrast, both humanism and radical adult education philosophies provide a basis for the establishment of collaborative models within the learning environment. While these two philosophical frameworks have markedly different perspectives on the notion of collaboration and power, they do have one overriding similarity: they see both teacher and student as facilitator and learner, simultaneously.

Freire: Radical Educator

While others have written on the subject, much of my practice has been influenced by Paulo Freire's work (1970, 1973, 1983, 1985, 1992), because he conceptualized a radically new potential in the student–teacher relationship. In *Pedagogy of the Oppressed* (1970), Freire challenged two basic assumptions in traditional adult education: (1) the presumed neutrality of educational practices and (2) the assumed difference in status of the teacher and student. He referred to this traditional teacher–student relationship as the "banking method" of education. In this framework, the teacher is a depositor of knowledge, and the student is the receptacle.

As Freire saw it, knowledge is a major way to obtain power. The classroom, then, as a place of both knowledge dissemination and construction, is a site where unequal power relationships are either accommodated or resisted. If we are to revisit the development of unequal relationships within that setting, we need to strive to understand the reality of the other and to promote mutual growth—in ourselves as well as in them. It is through praxis that these relationships are established and challenged. Freire went on to say, "it is through dialogue [that] the teacher-of-the students and the students-of-the-teacher cease to exist and a new term emerges: teacher-student with students-teachers" (1990, 61). In order to create these new arrangements, instructional methods must include dialogue, problem posing, and discussion groups. Furthermore, educational experiences must be based in the learner's reality in order for them to gain meaning, and use it to create change in their everyday lives.

One major limitation of Freire's work is his singular attention to socioeconomic class as the primary human characteristic upon which oppression has been based. He focused solely on the way in which poor people are disenfranchised in society, without distinguishing the role of race, gender, or other ways of being. Nonetheless, Freire is the one adult educator that many refer to when they discuss systemic inequities in the philosophy or theory of education.

Contemporary feminist educators, such as Hart (1990), Weiler (1988), Collins (1991), and hooks (1994), have been critical of Freire for overlooking the way in which race and gender differences have been used to prevent women and people of color from having equal access to education and other resources. Since the initial feminist critique of Freire's work, it has become clear that many other characteristics in addition to gender, including race, ethnicity, age, and sexual orientation, are used to disempower some groups and shore up the power of others (see, for example, Flannery 1994; Sheared 1994; Hayes and Colin III 1994).

A NEW CONCEPTION OF PRACTICE

As I have indicated, much of my practice has been influenced by Freire. In this section, I will address the ways in which I have applied this theory to my practice. As Freire postulated, key to the concept of teacher and student as collaborative learning partners is the recognition of the power dynamics inherent in the teacher–student relationship. The student is recognized as an indispensable, valuable partner in the learning experience, and power between teacher and student must be shared.

Kreisberg (1992), building on postpositivist perspectives as well as Freirean and feminist theories, described the difference between "power over," the dominant paradigm of power, and an alternative paradigm: that of "power with." He traced the first appearance of this alternate idea of power to the writings of Mary Parker Follett (1918, 1924, 1942) who, in her studies of industrial organization and administrative management, defined power as individual capacity developed through interaction with other people. She maintained that "Coercive power is the curse of the universe; co-active power, the enrichment and advancement of every human soul" (1924, xii). "Power over" was seen as coercive power and she spoke of "power with" as co-active power.

Underlying "power with" are assumptions derived from systems theory that our world is constituted of open, interdependent, and mutually influencing systems. Causality is multidimensional and synergistic. Within this synergistic paradigm, one can conceive of valued resources which are accessible, expanding, and renewable rather than scarce (Kreisberg 1992, 74–86). In contrast, the notion of "power over" is built on a paradigm of scarcity, and this is the dominant paradigm for power in the Western world. Power is seen as a scarce commodity; one person's power implies another person's loss of power. This paradigm, rooted in mechanistic conceptions of causality, leads to an understanding of power as domination (Kreisberg 1992, 74–86). Such an understanding of power aptly describes the traditional student–teacher relationship.

The alternate paradigm of "power with," as implied by Freire and others and explicated by Kreisberg, establishes the context for arguing that teaching is a political act. To avoid reproducing the hegemony of the broader society, adult educators must seek alternate ways of structuring their relationships with adult learners; they must engage in counterhegemonic practice.

COLLABORATIVE PRACTICE

In structuring a collaborative teacher–student relationship, the focus of attention should be on the relationship between the teacher and student. The focus needs to be on changing the relationship from the traditional "power over" relationship between teacher and student to a "power with" relationship (Sissel 1997). I use the term "collaborative" to describe this alternate relationship.

My teaching has been shaped by my efforts to create a collaborative relationship with students. For example, as a new teacher in a university classroom, I struggled with the tremendous burden of being the expert. Since my teaching was in the field of social work, which has an emerging and frequently nebulous knowledge base, the identity of expert was both uncomfortable and dishonest. Furthermore, I was teaching adults from ages 20 to 60 who had diverse life experiences from which they had learned much. There was no way they could passively receive information from me unless they separated classroom learning from the rest of their lives. This, however, was not an option, because the focus in social work education is on assisting students with the integration of their experiences with concepts learned in the classroom. I found that the teacher-as-expert identity was at odds with the needs of the students I was expected to teach, and with the goals of professional social work education.

From this realization I began a search for better ways to teach adult students. I became more flexible in my approach to the material and attempted to relate the concepts I wanted to teach to the individual needs and interests of students. I learned to tell students "I don't know." While I was more comfortable in my teaching role, the students I taught continued to separate what they learned in the classroom from the rest of their lives and from their practice as social workers. They continued to expect me to be the expert and, when I refused to act as such, they evaluated me as a poor teacher.

When this first occurred, I realized that refusing to act as a traditional teacher did not, by itself, succeed in changing the culture of the classroom, because the students resisted the change. They had learned the traditional roles of teacher and student well. They knew that they, as students, were supposed to absorb information from their teacher—me—who was the expert. If, at the end of a class period, they did not have at least a page or two of notes, they were not, in their opinion, being taught effectively. After further experimentation and frustration, I realized that both the students and I needed to make changes. In thinking that I could, by my actions alone, change the relationship, I was acting from the "power over" paradigm. The students and I together needed to create a collaborative relationship (Ellsworth 1989).

The major challenge that I had as a teacher in developing a collaborative relationship with these students was finding a way to begin to operate from a paradigm of "power with" rather than "power over." I found, and continue to find, that sharing power is difficult because it requires me, the educator, to give up the myth of total control over the learning experience. But it is difficult for students too, because they need to learn how to share control over what is to be learned (the content) and how the learning is to occur (the process). When students share control, the teacher and students become interdependent in that they need one another to create a successful learning experience.

I knew that if this relationship was going to change, there had to be trust established between the teacher and student. Such trust is a precondition for interdependence. How does one then develop trusting relationships, particularly given the different identities among students and between teachers and students in regard to race, ethnicity, age, gender, sexual orientation, socioeconomic status, and mental and physical ability?

I was given the opportunity to further explore this question when I received funding from the U.S. Department of Education to design and implement an adult literacy program at Cornell University. The funder's requirement was that undergraduate college students needed to serve as tutors to persons in need of basic skills.

The needs assessment that I conducted in a small city in upstate New York revealed that the most underserved group were employees at the university where I taught. Upon further examination, I learned that university employees who most needed literacy services held positions as janitors, cooks, and house-keepers; their average age was 40, and most earned a minimum wage and lived in isolated rural areas because of the high cost of housing near the university. In contrast, the students, who were to be tutors in the literacy program, were middle to upper class with an average age of 21. Most came from large cities. How could I expect 21-year-olds to teach 40-year-olds? In what ways would class differences affect the relationships between students and tutors?

EDUCATION AS A DISINCENTIVE

Society's power imbalances in relation to race, ethnicity, class, and age are encoded in the language used within the adult basic educational system, includ-ing the relationship between teacher and student, and such language further discourages adult learners from pursuing and completing basic skills curricula. Little attention has been directed to an examination of the ways in which the very design of adult basic education programs and classes can become a dis-incentive to adult learners (see Chapter 13 in this volume). In fact, many adult basic education classrooms reconstruct the traditional hierarchical teacher–student relationship found in formal classrooms. The problem for many students is that the design of these classes often resembles formal classrooms that many dropped out of or were unsuccessful in when they were younger. Many adult learners in the literacy program I directed said that they viewed themselves as failures, drop-outs, and dummies in the formal education system. Many of these negative labels were an outcome of disempowering transactions between teachers and students. These were identities that they actively sought to avoid.

I realized that as long as I thought of the relationship between employee and student in the literacy program in terms of the traditional "power over" paradigm, I would, in designing the program, recreate the hegemony of the broader educational system. Instead, I decided to create a program structurally designed for collaborative learning and to provide students who wanted to tutor university employees with a classroom setting where we could dialogue about how to create a collaborative teaching-learning environment. As the director of the program and instructor of the college students, I hoped to engage the students in an alternatively structured educational relationship within which we could explore the potential of collaborative teaching-learning relationships for ourselves and for students' relationships with university employees. I recognized that program planning is political (Rees, Cervero, Moshi, and Wilson 1994). Because I did not want to exercise "power over" in the way the program was designed and implemented, I invited employees, students, university administrators, and representatives of the employees' union to serve as an advisory and policy-making group for the program.

The Environment

We deliberately avoided structuring the learning environment for college students and employees like a traditional classroom. Instead, university students met with employees on a one-to-one basis wherever it was convenient and comfortable for employees to engage in dialogue. There was no standardized curriculum or textbook. Instead, each pair developed a learning plan based on the needs of that particular employee. Simultaneously, university students participated in a course in which I was the designated teacher. The course offered the students opportunities to reflect upon and dialogue about their experiences with employees. Class assignments required the university students to engage in discussions with employees about their similarities to, and differences from, one another. As a result, employee and student were interdependent in that neither could reach their learning goals without the assistance of the other.

The Language We Use

A different language of teaching and learning also had to be used, if the students and employees were going to be able to authentically communicate with each other. This notion is based on the premise that language is a tool that not only reflects perceptions of reality but can be used to create alternative perceptions. As Rees et al. (1997) point out, "Praxis through language use . . . is key to both the egalitarian exercise of power and ethical discourse" (p. 75). In this case, the college students identified themselves to employees as "learning partners" and employees were addressed as "learners."

The new terminology was quickly adopted by both college students and employees. But the naming process did not stop there, and learning pairs began to address each other in more familiar and connected ways. Some described their relationships as mother-daughter, sister-sister, or brother-brother; others described their relationships as friendships. For instance, in one exchange, an employee said this about the student who taught him: "She's like a very good friend. This means I like her and I trust her. If I had a bag of money and gave it to her to put in the bank, I would trust her completely to do that. . . . Even more, I would trust her with my life." In another exchange, a university student said this about her employee-partner: "We formed a close relationship, closer than a friend. I could tell him anything and he would try to help me. He didn't judge me. We really listened to each other." And finally, this student said: "I look up to him as a big brother since I never had one. I ask him about personal things and he gives me advice. I have advisers and professors but I go to (employee) for other things. With professors an authority figure is there, but with (employee) I feel on an equal level." These are just some of the examples of how students and employees negotiated new relationships with each other.

Changing Conceptions of the Other

As I reflected on this program, I asked myself: Why did student/employee dyads rename the relationship the way they did? In response, I must say that the primary reason was that the students simply did not see themselves as traditional teachers, and the employees did not respond as traditional students. This indicates that interventions which employ a critically reflective model in teacher preparation can lead to the establishment of nonhierarchical, collaborative relationships between student and teacher!

A second major reason was that while many employees had harsh and bitter experiences in the K–12 system with their teachers, they were still responsive when given an opportunity to rename the process. In fact, many of them told me that the last thing they wanted was to reproduce a traditional teacher/student relationship. Through the renaming process, employees began to engage in learning activities that reduced their anxieties. By assigning different names to their partners, both university students and employees redefined the power dimension in their relationships in which the teacher had "power over," to one in which teacher and student negotiated power with each other.

Recognition of Class Differences

In order to achieve a collaborative learning environment among these two economically disparate groups, the issue of class differences had to be addressed. While students were given an opportunity to address class issues in their academic course, a focus group for employees was also convened so they could discuss how they viewed the class differences between them. Several of the employees explained that the stereotypical image they had of people from a higher socioeconomic class did not represent their partners. Consequently, employees who initially felt inferior to their partners on the basis of class differences no longer felt that way. One person explained: "She (the partner) came from a well-to-do home, but she was such a down-to-earth person. I mean, she wasn't snooty . . . because like before, I'm thinkin' 'oh yeah, they're well-to-do, you know you ain't. They (will) look down on me' . . . but that's not true." Employees/students consistently expressed a change in attitude toward each other. Employees reported reduced feelings of inferiority in relation to the university students.

Significance of Cultural Context

In nonformal adult education programs where the structure and curriculum is collaborative, adult learners are able to develop a collaborative relationship relatively quickly, whereas in the university classroom—a formal venue—it takes more time. As I have worked and learned with the students in my university courses, I have come to appreciate the complexity of developing a collaborative classroom in the context of a traditional postsecondary institution. I surmise that one reason for the complexity is that the cultural practices in the traditional university system tend to support the hierarchical relationship between teacher and students. For example, the physical arrangement of most classrooms accommodates the traditional power dynamics. Students sit in rows of chairs—the teacher stands behind a table or podium. These seats are arranged to enhance the dominant social arrangements between teacher and student.

Seeking to restructure the relationship I have with graduate and undergraduate students, I rearrange my classroom so that there is a circle of chairs, including one for me. After I conducted several classes in this manner, the dean of my school contacted me, and cautioned me that several faculty members were complaining. My rearrangement of chairs was an inconvenience for them, because when their class followed my class, they had to take time to put the chairs back in rows. I was told that if I chose to rearrange the chairs from the way they were "supposed to be," they needed to be put back in the "right" order at the end of my class. Thus, it was made apparent to me that the act of teaching itself was political, and that by changing social arrangements in the classroom I engaged in an act of resistance that challenged the status quo.

CHALLENGES TO COLLABORATIVE PRACTICE

The challenge for the collaborative educator is that we must ultimately find a way to share control with students. In traditional postsecondary institutions, the educator holds a position of ultimate power over students. It is the instructor who is authorized by the system to give students' grades. Therefore, students and instructor must acknowledge that this power differential exists. In addition, the effects of this unequal power situation need to be explored by the students and instructor so that the sharing of power can occur in an authentic way.

For students, the invitation to develop a collaborative classroom also presents challenges (Shor 1992). Chances are great that their other classes use the traditional banking method of education. When students move between collaborative and traditional learning environments, it can be stressful. In addition, teachers must realize that there are risks to students inherent in the free-flowing dialogue and critical analysis of a collaborative classroom. The risks can appear to be especially high to students who identify with one or more marginalized groups. The risks may also be perceived as higher when the invitation for collaboration comes from a middle-aged, middle-class, White female (some of my identities). Nonetheless, students and teachers must be encouraged to take the risks because it is no longer tenable, in my opinion, to continue the flawed methods we, as adult educators, have traditionally used.

CONCLUSIONS AND RECOMMENDATIONS

In this chapter, I have explored the assumptions about power that underlie the differing approaches to adult education, including the collaborative approach. I have also posed questions that I hope are helpful for those interested in developing collaborative learning environments. Finally, I believe that the best way to address these issues is to create a counterhegemonic educational experience for both teachers and students. If the learning experience is to be empowering for students, we need to share power with, rather than over, our students.

In conclusion, we in adult education must recognize that many of the problems we attribute to our participants are ones that we have constructed. Problems such as retention and motivation of adult learners, which have been the subject of much research in adult education, are problems that adult educators have themselves created. These problems are created because educators have reproduced the hegemony of the larger society by establishing relationships of domination with adult learners.

REFERENCES

Bagnall, R. (1989). "Researching Participation in Adult Education: A Case of Qualified Distortion." *International Journal of Lifelong Education* 8(3), 251–260.

Collins, P. (1991). *Black Feminist Thought: Knowledge, Consciousness, and the Politics of Empowerment.* New York: Routledge.

Dewey, J. (1938). *Experience and Education.* London: Collier-Macmillan.

Ellsworth, E. (1989). "Why Doesn't This Feel Empowering? Working through the Repressive Myths of Critical Pedagogy." *Harvard Educational Review* 59(3), 297–324.

Flannery, D. (1994). "Changing Dominant Understandings of Adults as Learners" In E. Hayes and S.A.J. Colin III (eds.), *Confronting Racism and Sexism,* 17–26. San Francisco: Jossey-Bass.

Follett, M. P. (1918). *The New State: Group Organization the Solution of Popular Government.* New York: Longman's, Green.

Follett, M. P. (1924). *Creative Experience.* New York: Longman's, Green.

Follett, M. P. (1942). *Dynamic Administration.* New York: Harper.

Freire, P. (1970). "Cultural Action for Freedom." *Harvard Education Review,* Monograph #1. Cambridge, MA.

Freire, P. (1973). *Education for Critical Consciousness.* New York: Seabury.

Freire, P. (1983). *Pedagogy in Process: Letters from Guinea Bisseau.* New York: Continuum.

Freire, P. (1985). *The Politics of Education.* South Hadley, MA: Bergin & Garvey.

Freire, P. (1992). *Pedagogy of Hope.* New York: Continuum.

Freire, P. (1993). *Pedagogy of the Oppressed,* rev. ed. New York: Continuum.

Giroux, H. (1983). "Theories of Reproduction and Resistance in the New Sociology of Education: A Critical Analysis." *Harvard Educational Review* 53, 257–293.

Giroux H., and McLaren, P. (1987). "Teacher Education as a Counterpublic Sphere: Radical Pedagogy as a Form of Cultural Politics." *Philosophy and Social Criticism* 12(1), 51–69.

Hart, M. (1990). "Critical Theory and Beyond: Further Perspectives on Emancipatory Education." *Adult Education Quarterly* 4, 125–138.

Hayes, E., and Colin, S.A.J. III (eds.). (1994). *Confronting Racism and Sexism.* San Francisco: Jossey-Bass.

hooks, b. (1994). *Teaching to Transgress: Education as the Practice of Freedom.* New York: Routledge.

Illich, I. (1976). *Deschooling Society.* Harmondsworth: Penguin Books.

Kreisberg, S. (1992). *Transforming Power: Domination, Empowerment, and Education.* Albany: State University of New York Press.

McLaren, P. (1989). *Life in Schools.* New York: Longman.

Pinderhughes, E. (1989). *Understanding Race, Ethnicity and Power: The Key to Efficacy in Clinical Practice.* New York: Free Press.

Rees, E., Cervero, R., Moshi, L., and Wilson, A. (1997). "Language, Power, and the Construction of Adult Education Programs." *Adult Education Quarterly* 47(2), 63–77.

Sheared, V. (1994). "Giving Voice: An Inclusive Model of Instruction—A Womanist Perspective. In E. Hayes and S.A.J. Colin III (eds.), *Confronting Racism and Sexism.* San Francisco: Jossey-Bass.

Shor, I. (1992). *Empowering Education: Critical Teaching for Social Change.* Chicago: University of Chicago Press.

Sissel, P. (1997). "Participation and Learning in Head Start: A Sociopolitical Analysis." *Adult Education Quarterly* 47(3/4), 123–137.

Tisdell, E. (1993). "Interlocking Systems of Power, Privilege, and Oppression in Adult Higher Education Classes." *Adult Education Quarterly* 43(4), 203–226.

Weiler, K. (1988). *Women Teaching for Change: Gender, Class & Power*. New York: Bergin & Garvey.

Willis, P. (1977). *Learning to Labor*. Lexington, MA: D.C. Heath.

Part IV

Cultural Infusion: Reflections on Identity and Practice

Just who are we, and how does this knowledge of self affect or influence what we do? Through a very thoughtful exploration of themselves and their "life-work," the authors in Part IV of *Making Space* provide us with a glimpse of the ways in which their racial/ethnic, language, gender, and sexual orientation have helped shape their identities. Not only do they offer their life stories, but they share with us the ways in which their individual identities have challenged and shaped their thinking about their practice and lifework. For these authors, it appears that their lifework is an interweaving of who they are, what they call themselves, and what they do, or, as Bingman and White suggest in Chapter 11: "where we live, the way we talk, and the way we feel are highly interconnected," and interwoven with how one operates within one's local and global community—that is, within one's personal life and across borders. Moreover, they challenge us to think about staying in the margins as a way to not only challenge those in the center, but as a way to obtain and maintain power and authority over one's story, socioeconomics, politics, and culture.

This section begins with an examination by Brown of life stories and lifework of African-American women teachers in Chapter 15. Through the use of an Africentric feminist analysis, Brown explores the life stories of two African-American women teachers, as well as her own life story as a teacher. In spite of the adversities in these women's lives, and being treated differently by their students as a result of their race, gender, and class, these women have overcome the difficulties and have been able to impart to their students a spirit and desire for learning. By giving voice to the life histories and lived experiences of these women, Brown hopes to "challenge the myths and untruths established about African Americans and African American women," teachers and learners in particular. Through her voice, as well as that of Septima Clark and bell hooks, we begin to see the ways in which one's identity and understanding of it helps shape or influence one's practice. In the case of African-American women, the "uplift of the race" becomes a metaphor for not only one's purpose in life, but a way of thinking about who one is and how one must think about the self in relation to the collective. She concludes by asking us to reflect on and think about the ways in which our lifework is influenced by our life story and our lived experiences.

How one sees one's self and one's work is often colored and shaped not only by one's skin, but by the language one uses both in and outside of the academy. In Chapter 16, Marcano, a Latina scholar, offers us an understanding of the ways in which language and gender intersect both within and outside of one's *home culture*. As a Latina in a professional world she learns to cross borders both among and with those who look and sound like her as well as those who do not look like her, or sound like her. She shares with us the Latinas' lived experience in relation to *machisimo* and the patriarchical American society. Through her voice, we can see the intermingling of not only race and gender, but of language and culture as well. Her experiences in obtaining tenure within higher education, and her previous work in the community provide us with a view of what it means to have to negotiate between and across borders. One learns that while one needs to have *resiliency* as one moves between borders, one must remember to make space for others like oneself as they cross borders. She challenges those in positions of power and authority to not become complacent because they have managed to bring each other across borders, for it is the system that must be changed, and individual efforts alone are not enough if they want to change the facial/racial and language landscapes in the professions.

Harper, along with "Mira," then takes us both literally and figuratively across borders in Chapter 17. It is the story of an Arab-Lebanese refugee's experience as lived and seen by Mira and narrated by Harper. Relying upon life history, Harper identifies historical fact, and helps us to "understand the personal meanings" that both Mira and Harper have come to not only understand, but live. Harper, an Arab woman, shares both in and through Mira's story her own story, as well as the story of others in the Lebanese community in Canada. She weaves a tapestry of understanding about how one learns to both accommodate and resist one's former and new culture in a new land. As we come to the end of Mira's story we learn that one can choose to "live in the margins" of society, for by living there, even though one has a deep need to belong, one learns that there are advantages to remaining in the periphery. The advantage for Mira and perhaps others like her, who choose to remain in the margins, is that they can maintain power and authority over their stories and their cultures, thereby retaining their identity while others all around them are losing theirs. If one chooses to remain in the margins, however, one must realize that one can no longer remain silent, for the struggle for change and the need for it continues to live on through the work one chooses.

Border-crossing requires reclaiming and renaming one's reality and the contexts within which one operates. In Chapter 18, Grace not only reclaims a term, but reclaims identity and challenges us to rethink who we are and what we do.

So, language, culture, gendered realities, and work are interwoven and used to reexamine the very theoretical foundation of what it means "to be educated." Grace challenges us to leave the comforts of our present spaces and transgress into one that asks us to reexamine culture and the meaning-making structures that have influenced our thinking and learning. Who and what we are is embedded in heterosexist language that entangles us in a series of meaning- and symbol-making that leads to stereotypes and homophobic thinking. By challenging this language, it is argued, one then is able to develop an oppositional worldview and knowledge base.

Finally, Tisdell (Chapter 19) takes us across borders into what it means to be feminist and what being a feminist means to one's lifework. Given the ever-changing racial/ethnic, gendered and cross-gendered, language, and socioeconomic landscape, we in education must not only understand our own positionality (that is, gender, race, and class consciousness), but we must be prepared to address it in relationship to how we engage in teaching and learning. Tisdell argues that we just need to look at our theories and practices as they relate to women in adult education in order to see that there is a serious void in perspectives. As others in this section have shown through the use of narratives and stories, and reclaiming of identity, Tisdell asks us to engage in the development of narratives. Through the sharing of stories about both our individual and collective selves, we can begin to not only shift our understanding about what it means to be the other; we can begin to make space for the multiple and varied perspectives that shape our world.

As we move in and through these ever-shifting terrains of identity, we begin to see that it is through the reclaiming and renaming of one's self that one begins to shift one's understanding of what it means to be in the center, and more importantly, one learns about what it means to be in the margins. For, as hooks has suggested and these authors have articulated, to be in the margins provides one with a way to claim and rename one's position of power and authority over one's story, culture, history and economic base.

Chapter 15

African-American Women of Inspiration

Angela Humphrey Brown

After years of teaching mathematics, I have come to believe that my culture, race, and gender—I am an African-American woman—have provided me with experiences in the classroom that are different from most of my colleagues' experiences. Most of my colleagues are either White and/or male, and for the most part have had very different life experiences. While I had come to an understanding about the differences that my colleagues and I had, I was convinced that there must be others that had experiences like mine. So, I began my quest. Given that I was engaged in the teaching of adults, and had been taught to believe that adult education was an area in which those who were marginalized were represented, I began to examine the literature to see how others like me were represented. To my disappointment, I found little if any of my experiences represented in the adult education literature. Ironically, this literature base tended to treat adult educators as a monolithic group, and it failed to acknowledge in any depth that African Americans, let alone African-American women adult educators, enter into and are treated quite differently because of their race, culture, or gender. While no malice was intended, the lack of attention to groups or people of color has tended to render them invisible, not only in the literature, but more importantly, in the classroom. Most importantly, I discovered through this journey that the reason I felt alone and invisible was not an illusion. I felt invisible because for years the voices of those who looked like me were not represented in the literature, nor in the academy.

This chapter attempts to give voice to the silent. It is a journey into the lives of women like me, women who went before me and laid the groundwork for others to enter into the academy and engage in the discourse and dissemination of knowledge. So, I began talking to other African-American women educators about this and discovered that there were many similarities in our stories. This led me to an interest in the narration of African-American women educators. My quest began with those women who had served as teachers from the early 1900s on into the present. To my wonderment, I learned that these African-American women had a teaching style that reflected a unique way of viewing the world. They had a way of disseminating knowledge that was grounded in their culture, and this then had a significant impact on their roles as teachers (Brown 1997).

The engagement of narratives and the voicing of any group's life stories is not always welcome. All too often, when people attempt to tell these stories, they are told that they must look at the larger picture and compare it with others' experiences in order for their stories to be validated. They fail to recognize that if the intent is to give voice to the silent, then their stories must not be clouded by inclusion of everyone's agenda. To do so would tend to not only silence their voices, but render them invisible. For African-American women, this has all too often been the case; therefore, I deliberately focused on their life stories, for they seemed more like mine. In doing so, they would no longer be the invisible group. As Etter-Lewis (1993) concludes, and I concur, "The notion that African American women are an invisible group on the sidelines and that they can be easily combined with other groups is a convenient fiction that conceals their power and importance" (p. xvii). Moreover, the limited research on African-American women in higher education has "suffered from scholarly disinterest and been filtered through perspectives that are androcentric and/or ethnocentric" (Howard-Vital 1989, 191). Finally, as I began this examination, I began to realize, through the work of Collins (1991), that any literature base that includes the life stories of African-American women should and must be constructed by African-American women. This does not mean that others cannot or will not be able to tell the story; it just means that there is a sense of authenticity that goes with telling the stories of others like you.

Consequently, this chapter attempts to offer the stories of these women as a way to not only make the invisible visible—it also hopes to add to the development of a body of literature in the field of adult education. This work is aimed at adding to the knowldege base that is being constructed by and about African Americans and African-American women (Johnson-Bailey 1994; Peterson 1996; Sheared 1994). I believe that we must do this if we intend to challenge the myths and untruths established about African Americans and African-American women educators' contributions to the field of education in general (James and Farmer 1993).

Accordingly, this chapter is an attempt to bring a missing perspective to our literature base. I believe that my cultural perspective offers an accounting of the experiences of three African-American women adult educators. Because of my personal stake in this endeavor as an African-American woman educator, I am aware of the fact that our struggle for visibility occurs on many different levels. It is from this perception of invisibility that I write this chapter. My aim is to examine the hegemonic forces that have operated in the field of education, which have ultimately led to the concealment of the pedagogical practices used by African-American women in general. Additionally, I hope to create a space for African-American women adult educators that will, as James and Farmer (1993) propose, "shape a reality and make a space for African American women to creatively share our stories" (p. 3).

MULTIPLE REALITIES: RACE, GENDER, AND CLASS

There are multiple factors that contribute to the ways in which African-American women scholars have analyzed African-American women and their contributions to African-American and American life. Most of these scholars have used race, gender, and class as the unit of analysis to frame their world and their worldview. According to King (1995), "The relative significance of race, sex, or class in determining the conditions of Black women's lives is neither fixed nor absolute but, rather, is dependent on the socio-historical context and the social phenomenon under consideration" (p. 298). African-American scholars as well as some Euro-American scholars have suggested that White women have benefited greatly from their position. McIntosh (1995) concluded that even though White women have been oppressed, they have also had privileges that come with being White in America. Conversely, as a result of their positionality, African-American women have not had the same opportunities as their White female counterparts. Moreover, while African-American men have suffered greatly, the unit analysis around race, generally speaking, includes their voice, while often silencing or omitting the voices of African-American women. Hence, some Euro-American feminists and many African-American scholars have suggested that African-American women live with the double-jeopardy of racial and gender oppression. The double-jeopardy African-American women encounter in terms of race and sex is viewed by some Black feminists as a reason for conducting research specifically on Black women and their role and contributions to American society.

As a Black feminist scholar, I am writing this chapter as a way to help other educators gain an understanding of the "theoretical interpretations of Black women's reality by those who live it" (Collins 1991, 22). Collins' research presupposes that historical and material conditions have informed the unique perspective on African-American women and that the everyday lives of African-American women are shaped by a connection between these two realities. Brewer (1993) further advocates that the theories derived from our understanding of this reality are crucial to not only acknowledging, but understanding the multiple realities of African-American women. Consequently, by using race, gender, and class as a unit of analysis we should be able to capture the meanings and understandings of African-American women through their eyes (Collins 1991).

The use of autobiographies and biographies of African-American women as data for interpreting women's lives builds on the principles inherent in Black feminist theory in that this data is generated from African-American women and responds to their lives (Etter-Lewis and Foster 1996). Merriam (1988) supports the use of personal literature such as biographies and autobiographies as a means of collecting viable information on a person's perspectives of the world. Using the autobiographical and biographical literature of African-American women is a powerfully fertile source of data (Etter-Lewis and Foster 1996). Therefore, I deemed it important to use biographical and autobiographical literature in this chapter, as I wanted to give voice to those who had been silent.

CONTEXTUAL FACTORS IN ACADEME: PERCEPTIONS AND STEREOTYPES

There is sure to be trouble when an African-American female educator enters the classroom; she will not be perceived as competent, because the universal teacher is one who is White and male, not African American and female (Rakow 1991). In essence, "an African American woman is viewed through lenses colored by gender and racial biases; therefore, ideas, instructions, and feedback from her may be received hostilely, in a patronizing manner, or sometimes blatantly ignored, with impunity" (Farmer 1993, 206). An African-American female professor accurately summed up how problematic teaching is for African-American women by saying, "racism and sexism can affect many areas such as perceived credibility; her [African-American women educators'] perceived competence as a professor and researcher; her teaching experiences, assignments, and evaluations; her perceived interpersonal skills; and her perceived decision-making skills" (Phelps 1995, 260). In order for an African-American woman educator to gain the respect and authority that is automatically granted to White male teachers, she must engage in mental battles and sometimes even verbal battles with her students and colleagues (Brown 1997; Rakow 1991).

Another dilemma faced by some African-American women faculty members is that African-American learners may expect special treatment from them (Moses 1989), just as White learners expect care taking. Due to views of African-American women teachers as mothers or nurturers, students may expect a type of sympathy from them (Ruzich 1995). These expectations can have a negative influence on the teaching-learning environment. Moreover, Williams (1992) summarized that because most students have not had the opportunity to experience formalized instruction from an African-American woman professor, they distrust her knowledge base and certainly feel a need to challenge her authority.

All of these problems have not only been present in the classes in which I teach adults, but also in the classes that bell hooks teaches (Brown 1997; hooks 1994). This literature seems to highlight the contextual factors which I and other African-American women adult educators face when we enter our classrooms. Because of society's views concerning our race and gender, I feel that we

African-American women educators are on the front lines when we enter our classrooms.

AFRICAN-AMERICAN WOMEN EDUCATORS: ON THE FRONT LINE

As a way to help us understand the significance of African-American women scholars' contributions in the academy, I conducted an analysis of three African-American women educators who have written stories about their own teaching experiences. Two of these women are Septima Poinsette Clark and bell hooks. The third person is myself, for I have also included my own phenomenological writing, using my own lived experience and my reflections about that experience as an additional reference. I believe that our stories are representative of what many African Americans and women in general have experienced as they have negotiated their way into the academy. We adult educators felt that there was something about our teaching experiences that needed to be documented and shared with others (Brown 1997; Clark and Blythe 1962; Clark and Brown 1986; hooks 1994). This story then is told through our voices, with the hope that through our lives one can begin to see how race, gender, and class for the most part have been overlooked in praxis and do in fact contribute to whose voices are heard and believed in the academy.

It should be noted that neither Septima Clark nor bell hooks referred to themselves as adult educators. Nevertheless, by Courtney's (1989) definition of adult educator—one who is skilled in teaching adults and one who uses these skills to make a change in competence or knowledge of another adult—they are indeed adult educators. For my part, however, I *have* made a conscious choice to call myself an adult educator. I teach mathematics to adults. Often times mathematics educators are not explicitly represented in the adult education literature, although they may fit the definition of adult educator. I feel that the title of adult educator gives me access to the field of adult education and thus makes my story all the more important to fill in the missing pieces of the adult education literature base. I also feel that I have made a deliberate attempt to utilize the teaching strategies advocated by many of the mainstream adult education writers (Brown 1997). When reviewing the lives of Septima Clark and bell hooks, I felt they too exemplified the endorsed adult education teaching strategies. Furthermore, Septima Clark was the founder of a major adult education institution and hooks' situation mirrors many of the teaching situations of African-American female adult educators in today's colleges and universities. Unlike the life stories of Clark and hooks, my story seemed insignificant until I decided to report on my own experiences as an adult educator in the mathematics classroom. My story is representative of many of the African-American women adult educators who are in the field on the front lines, but invisible in the adult education literature base.

EDUCATORS IN THE MAKING: SEPTIMA CLARK, BELL HOOKS, AND ANGELA HUMPHREY BROWN

While much could be said about our lives, this is not an autobiography, but it is a review of our lives in the making as teachers/educators in our communities. I offer these stories because they are three ways of representing what I believe is the untold story of African-American women adult educators. Septima Poinsette Clark was born in 1898 in Charleston, South Carolina, and died there in 1987. She was the daughter of a freed Black male slave and a free-born Black woman. Her parents had little formal education, and they worked as cooks, or custodial workers, or in the case of her mother, as a laundress. They instilled in Clark the importance of education. After completing elementary school, Clark attended Avery Institute where she completed the twelfth grade. She went on to obtain her B.A. from Benedict College and M.A. from Hampton Institute in 1942 and 1945, respectively. Clark stated, "from my early childhood I wanted to be a school teacher. That desire grew and strengthened throughout the years. And I believe it was born and nourished out of both my heredity and my environment" (Clark and Blythe 1962, 13). She wanted to be remembered as "a worker who loves her fellow man . . . and who strove with her energy, working in the true spirit of fellowship to lift him to a higher level of attainment and appreciation and enjoyment of life" (Clark and Blythe 1962, 132). Clark believed that to teach was an honor and a privilege. As such she strove to be the best teacher she could be. She said, "It has been my observation during almost half a century of teaching . . . that a good teacher is always learning herself" (Clark and Blythe 1962, 152).

Clark was involved in many different types of educational activities. She taught in integrated, segregated, formal, and informal settings and was very instrumental in the establishment of the Highlander Folk School. It was here that she started her work at Highlander Folk School. The goal of Highlander's citizenship schools was literacy training and democratic empowerment. She also worked with the National Association for the Advancement of Colored People (NAACP) on the Charleston School Board for NAACP membership from 1947 until 1956. She helped the NAACP prepare a 1945 court case that helped get equal salaries for teachers, regardless of race, in Columbia Public Schools. Clark started serving as the Director of Education and teaching in the Southern Christian Leadership Conference (SCLC) in 1961. In her work with adults, Clark helped to hone the skills of many natural leaders who were among those she worked with to change the status of those poorly educated.

The National Education Association (NEA) honored her with two awards: the Race Relations Award in 1976 and the Living Legend Award in 1978. In 1970, the SCLC honored her with the Martin Luther King, Jr. Award. After her death she was noted as the Queen of the Civil Rights Movement. Clark's role as an educator and teacher was fraught with much historical and political upheaval, while bell hooks' life begins at the start of a major change in the way African

Americans were not only viewed in education, but how they were treated in the U.S. educational system.

bell hooks was born in 1952 in Hopkinsville, Kentucky, which by her own admission was a small, segregated town with relatively few Whites. Her given name is Gloria Jean Watkins. She changed her name to bell hooks (her grandmother's name) to symbolize a way of celebrating female legacies. hooks felt this name embodied her charge in life, even though they grew up during different times. Like Clark, her parents did not have much formal education; her mother worked as a maid in order to provide for their family. Unlike Clark, hooks attended segregated schools prior to entering an integrated high school. In 1973 she received a B.A. in English from Stanford University and an M.A. from the University of Wisconsin. She earned her doctorate in 1983 from U.C. Santa Cruz. Her primary teaching experience has been at the collegiate level and she has never taught in segregated schools, or at the K–12 level. Her teaching was done in California, Wisconsin, and in the northeastern United States including Yale University and Oberlin College. She currently teaches at the City College of New York.

In her reflections about why she became a teacher, hooks notes that she had some fears about it. In one of her reflections, she states, "Aware of myself as a subject in history, a member of a marginalized and oppressed group, victimized by institutionalized racism, sexism, and class elitism, I had tremendous fear that I would teach in a manner that would reinforce those hierarchies" (1994, 142). So, in some cases she struggled with what her role as teacher should be because she felt she was torn between doing that and being a writer. hooks (1994) notes, "it was always assumed by everyone that I would become a teacher. In the South, Black girls from working-class backgrounds had three career choices— marry, become a maid, or teach. . . . From grade school on I was destined to become a teacher" (p. 2). Unlike Clark, hooks did not want to become a teacher, but became one because of what society dictated, and familial backing of choosing teaching over the other two choices (Perkins 1989). In part she became a teacher because she had trouble getting her first book published. In addition to this, she chose teaching because she felt that she could serve those who did not know about important principles and did not have the knowledge she deemed important for one to have (hooks 1994). Ultimately, she came to see teaching as the most important role she could play, in spite of her great love of writing. She felt that teaching would allow her to pursue her goals of writing and respond to the need to help those on the margins like herself (hooks 1994).

Unlike Clark and hook, my work is not widely documented in sources outside of my own dissertation on African-American women postsecondary mathematics teachers. I was born in 1966 in Greensboro, Georgia, which at the time was a small rural town with only two red lights. My mother was a high school dropout who worked at various jobs ranging from maid to teacher's aid. My father was a high school graduate who pursued a career in the army; he died when I was four, leaving me to become a child of a single-parent home.

All of my educational experiences as a learner and as a teacher have been in integrated settings. In 1988, I received a B.S.Ed. in Mathematics Education from the University of Georgia, and eventually, in 1997, earned my doctorate in Adult Education there as well. I became an educator because I felt I had a gift for teaching. I have taught mathematics at both the high school level and at a postsecondary technical institute. It is in my work at the postsecondary technical school that the data from my adult education teaching experiences are reported. I currently teach in a Teacher's Education Program at Piedmont College in Athens, Georgia.

THE ROLE OF TEACHER: UPLIFTING THE RACE

Historically, the burden of racial uplift has been placed on the shoulders of all educated African-Americans. Still, the primary uplifters of the race were African-American women, and so much so that the term "racial uplift" was synonymous with African-American women (Perkins 1989). African-American women were seen as the nurturers of the race and to that end they have been responsible for helping others in their families and communities achieve and appreciate their lots in life and in history. Clark and hooks' stories reflect women as nurturers as they have taken on the role of educating students so that there will be people in the community to help sustain and increase its longevity. Clark states, "The course I dreamed of taking was that of teaching and particularly teaching the poor and underprivileged of my own underprivileged race. In teaching them and thereby helping them raise themselves to a better status in life. . . . I am convinced that in lifting the lowly we lift likewise the entire citizenship" (Clark and Blythe 1962, 52). Furthermore, through her teaching she strove to work in a spirit of fellowship with her students and to lift them up so that they could serve their communities and learn to enjoy and appreciate their histories and cultures (Clark and Blythe 1962). While Clark was interested in helping her students gain an appreciation for life, hooks has taken a more political position, and states, "For black folks teaching-educating was fundamentally political because it was rooted in antiracist struggle" (hooks 1994, 2).

Similarly, because of my experience as a marginalized learner in the mathematics classroom, I sought equity in my mathematics classroom by engaging the entire class in the learning process and not just those society labeled as mathematically elite (Brown 1997). I felt that I was more than a mathematics teacher—that it was also my job to empower my students for the future by helping them to develop skills that would make them lifelong learners (Brown 1997). My philosophy of teaching is one in which all learners, regardless of sex, gender, age, class, or, educational background, were invited to partake of mathematics in sundry ways. I go on to report that I felt that I was the "instrument that bridged students to lifelong learning . . . and the person who reached those who are normally marginalized [in the mathematics classroom] and brought them to the center alongside those who are traditionally privileged in the mathematics classroom" (p. 173). In my role of uplifting the race I have written about counseling my students, getting them to value themselves, and building self-esteem among my learners (Brown 1997). Like hooks and Clark, I felt I needed to nurture my students. Although I did not discriminate against any student, I felt that my attitude, efforts, and support ultimately helped those students of my race who are stereotypically viewed as mathematically challenged. In doing so I helped them to excel in the mathematics classroom.

RACIAL UPLIFT IS A TWO-WAY VENTURE: ROLE OF THE STUDENT

Clark noted that one way to measure your achievement is through the end results or grades that students achieve in your classes. These things can be measured in terms of how articulate and knowledgeable they are about critical and current or contemporary issues that affect their communities (Clark and Blythe 1962). In other words, measuring their achievement should include looking at how involved your students become in making not only themselves better but also in making their communities better.

While teaching is and has been viewed as an honorable profession for African-American women in the African-American community, this has not transferred into equal pay or equal standing in society. This has led to a significant decrease in the numbers of African-American women as well as others choosing this profession. In spite of these decreasing numbers, for those who choose this profession, they do so by continuing to focus on the positives rather than the negatives.

Despite the lack of support, inferior materials, and close scrutiny of their teaching practices, African-American women teachers like Clark, hooks, and myself continue to surface. We continue to set lofty goals and to work diligently to achieve them because we see the profession of education as a means to uplift our race. These women went the extra mile to do more than impart mere subject matter. Not only did we teach our students to read, write, do mathematics, and understand literary works—we taught them the value of learning and thinking and how to use them so that they could make a difference in their communities. As educators we felt that if we were able to get our students to see how they could improve not only their lives but others' as well, ultimately, the student would become a better person. Our concern with the whole individual as well as society was transferred onto our students, who themselves would be an uplift for the community. I felt that I was not only teaching the principles of mathematics, but was also teaching my students to be proficient learners so that they could become adept beyond the classroom (Brown 1997).

PEDAGOGY IS A POLITICAL ACT

To be an African-American woman educator for us meant that we understood our roles in society as well as in the African-American community. We understood that we played both roles and have therefore "operated both within the power structure and without it in terms of race, gender, and class" identities (Ladson-Billings and Henry 1990, 75). As previously mentioned, African-American women have served as nurturers within their race and have often been responsible for holding up their race. Irvine (1989) noted that when one's pedagogy is influenced by one's culture it tends to have an impact on one's "perceptions of authority, instructional delivery" as well as on how one sees oneself as a teacher (p. 51).

Teaching then becomes a political act that will either reinforce or transcend social norms. African-American women are often subconsciously viewed by White students as having less authority, and, as Henry (1993) has suggested, Black women educators' role then often becomes a political act. Henry, who is a Black woman, has said that the students in her classes not only question her credentials but also her actions more than they have questioned her White and male colleagues. Teaching is not a neutral act, and, as hooks states concerning her own experiences in the classroom:

Since my formative education took place in racially segregated schools, I spoke about the experience of learning when one's experience is recognized as central and significant and then how that changed with desegregation, when Black children were forced to attend schools where we were regarded as objects and not subjects. Many of the professors present at the first meeting were disturbed by our overt discussion of political standpoints. Again and again, it was necessary to remind everyone that no education is politically neutral. Emphasizing that a White male professor in an English department who teaches only work by "great white men" is making a political decision, we had to work consistently against and through the overwhelming will on the part of folks to deny the politics of racism, sexism, heterosexism, and so forth that inform how and what we teach. (1994, 37)

Consequently, whether one acknowledges the fact that one's pedagogy is a political act or not, the very selection of materials or resources by an educator is indeed a political act. For instance, I felt that I made a tremendous effort to make mathematics accessible to all, through the diverse methods of instruction I used. I contrasted this with what I refer to as the "male norm of teaching mathematics"—lecture only. By choosing not to just lecture I was engaging in a political act to liberate those traditionally marginalized by the method in which mathematics is usually transmitted (Brown 1997).

RACE, CLASS, AND GENDER FACTORS

African-American women educators have had to face many interesting challenges in the classroom because of their race and gender, as well as their class standing. As a result of this, they often have felt alone and isolated from others. Describing her experiences with White women professors in the Women's Studies Department at the University of Wisconsin in Madison, and at the University of Southern California in Los Angeles, hooks noted that her work was not accepted by White women feminists. She believed that they did not accept her work because it challenged their privileged way of thinking (1994). hooks further highlights her challenges with her colleagues as well as her students:

Students at various academic institutions often complain that they cannot include my work on required reading lists for degree-oriented qualifying exams because their professors do not see it as scholarly enough. Any of us who create feminist theory and feminist writing in academic settings in which we are continually evaluated know that work deemed "not scholarly" or "not theoretical" can result in one not receiving deserved recognition and reward. (1994, 71)

In addition to the lack of acceptance of African-American women professors, colleagues sometimes exhibited a fear of them. hooks related the following incident: "I talked about writing this essay with a group of white female colleagues—all of them English professors—and they emphasized the fear many privileged white women have of black women" (p. 107). hooks talks about the fear of exposure; that is, that some White women feel that African-American women have the power "to see through their disguises to see the parts of themselves they want no one to see" (p. 107). Moreover, she told of the general ignorance certain professors and students held about African-American women. She was disturbed by the fact that White female professors and students were so ignorant of gender differences among African Americans. hooks reported that they used the term "women" inclusive of only White women. As she tried to enlighten these White colleagues and students as to knowledge about African-American gender relationships and about the status of the identity of African-American women being different from that of White women, she was ignored (1994). I explain that because mathematics was perceived to be a White male domain and I, as an African-American woman, had to actively go about establishing credibility in the classroom. In my narrative I told of many instances of confrontations from students, especially those that where male, White, or both (Brown 1997).

Educators like hooks, Clark, and myself often draw upon our own experiences to construct their teaching philosophy and methodologies (Brown 1997; hooks 1994; Clark and Blythe 1962). hooks expressed this by saying, "As a teacher, I recognize that students from marginalized groups enter classrooms within institutions where their voices have been neither heard nor welcomed, whether these students discuss facts—those which any of us might know or personally experience. My pedagogy has been shaped to respond to this reality" (1994, 83). Although hooks has taught only in integrated settings, she drew from her schooling, which included both segregated and integrated settings. From this perspective, she conveyed the following phenomenon:

The majority of my students who enter our classrooms have never been taught by black women professors. My pedagogy is informed by this knowledge, because I know from experience that this unfamiliarity can overdetermine what takes place in the classroom. Also, knowing from personal experience as a student in predominantly white institutions how easy it is to feel shut out or closed down, I am particularly eager to help create a learning process in the classroom that engages everyone. (p. 86)

Similar ideas were expressed in my narrative. I said, "Many of the students had not had an African American woman teacher and as a result they devalued the experience or actively resisted the experience" (Brown 1997, 293). I was committed to eliminating psychological barriers to the study of mathematics—barriers that were built on students' experiences. Therefore, I had to develop a climate conducive to learning (Brown 1997). Like hooks, I was acutely aware of my role in the classroom, the effect it had on my students, and the importance of establishing the welcoming classroom climate, despite students' stereotypical notions of what a postsecondary mathematics teacher should look like.

IMPORT FOR ADULT EDUCATION

We African-American women adult educators used many of the suggested teaching strategies for effective adult education. For instance, we encouraged active learning; demonstrated competency in our subject areas; balanced presentation with learner involvement; created a conducive physical climate for learning; recognized and understood the diversity of our learners; and combined support with challenges for our learners. Nevertheless, our positionality affects how these strategies are employed in the classroom and how our students and colleagues receive us. This chapter has used examples of three African-American women educators—Septima Clark, bell hooks, and myself—as a way to highlight the importance of one's race, class, and gender in teaching and learning practices. Our narratives are filled with many examples that I can not share because of space limits. Like Dilworth (1990), I believe that the way one teaches is influenced by culture and a sense of personal agency. I encourage all adult educators to study the autobiographical and biographical literature of African-American women adult educators, because their pedagogies are rich with insight into a group underrepresented in our literature.

The stories of us as African-American women educators raise issues about the effect culture can have on teaching. hooks proposes that "no matter what one's class, race, gender, or social standings . . . that without the ability to think critically about our selves and our lives, none of us would be able to move forward, to change, to grow" (1994, 202). I hope that this chapter will urge adult educators to recognize and address the impact their culture has on the teaching-learning environment. Just as Septima Clark's, bell hooks', and my culture had an impact on our classroom, so does the culture of any adult educator, regardless of what that culture might be.

REFERENCES

Brewer, R. M. (1993). "Theorizing Race, Class, and Gender: The New Scholarship of Black Feminist Intellectuals and Black Women's Labor." In S. M. James and A.P.A. Busia (eds.), *Theorizing Black Feminisms: The Visionary Pragmatism of Black Women*, 13–30. New York: Routledge.

Brown, A. H. (1997). "Making the Invisible Visible by Challenging the Myth of the Universal Teacher: African American Women Post-secondary Mathematics Teachers." Doctoral Dissertation, University of Georgia. *Dissertation Abstracts International* 58-06A, 2023.

Clark, S. P., and Blythe, L. (1962). *Echo in My Soul.* New York: E. P. Dutton.

Clark, S. P., and Brown, C. S. (1986). *Ready from Within.* Navarro, CA: Wild Trees Press.

Collins, P. H. (1991). *Black Feminist Thought: Knowledge, Consciousness, and the Politics of Empowerment.* New York: Routledge.

Courtney, S. (1989). "Defining Adult and Continuing Education." In S. B. Merriam and P. M. Cunningham (eds.), *Handbook of Adult and Continuing Education*, 15–25. San Francisco: Jossey-Bass.

Dilworth, M. E. (1990). *Reading between the Lines: Teachers and Their Racial/Ethnic Cultures.* Washington, DC: ERIC Clearinghouse on Teacher Education.

Etter-Lewis, G. (1993). *My Soul Is My Own: Oral Narratives of African American Women in the Professions.* New York: Routledge.

Etter-Lewis, G., and Foster, M. (eds.). (1996). *Unrelated Kin: Race and Gender in Women's Personal Narratives.* New York: Routledge

Farmer, R. (1993). "Place but Not Importance: The Race for Inclusion in Academe." In J. James and R. Farmer (eds.), *Spirit, Space, and Survival: African American Women in (White) Academe*, 196–217. New York: Routledge.

Fultz, M. (1995). "African American Teachers in the South, 1890–1940: Growth, Feminization, and Salary Discrimination." *Teachers College Record* 96(3), 544–568.

Henry, A. (1993). "There Are No Safe Places: Pedagogy as Powerful and Dangerous Terrain." *Action in Teacher Education* 15(4), 1–4.

hooks, b. (1994). *Teaching to Transgress: Education as the Practice of Freedom.* New York: Routledge.

Howard-Vital, M. R. (1989). "African American Women in Higher Education: Struggling to Gain Identity." *Journal of Black Studies* 20(2), 180–191.

Irvine, J. J. (1989). "Beyond Role Models: An Examination of Cultural Influences on the Pedagogical Perspectives of Black Teachers." *Peabody Journal of Education* 66(4), 51–63.

James, J., and Farmer, R. (eds.). (1993). *Spirit, Space and Survival: African American Women in (White) Academe.* New York: Routledge.

Johnson-Bailey, J. (1994). "Making a Way Out of No Way: An Analysis of the Educational Narratives of Reentry Black Women with Emphasis on Issues of Race, Gender, Class, and Color." Doctoral Dissertation, University of Georgia. *Dissertation Abstracts International* 55, 2681.

King, D. K. (1995). "Multiple Jeopardy, Multiple Consciousness: The Context of a Black Feminist Ideology." In B. Guy-Sheftall (ed.), *Words of Fire: An Anthology of African American Feminist Thought*, 294–318. New York: The New Press.

Ladson-Billings, G., and Henry, A. (1990). "Blurring the Borders: Voices of African Liberatory Pedagogy in the United States and Canada." *Journal of Education* 172(2), 72–88.

McIntosh, P. (1995). "White Privilege and Male Privilege: A Personal Account of Coming to See Correspondences through Work in Women's Studies." In M. L. Anderson and P. H. Collins (eds.), *Race, Class, and Gender: An Anthology*, 76–86. Boston: Wadsworth Publishing Co.

Merriam, S. (1988). *Case Study Research in Education: A Qualitative Approach*. San Francisco: Jossey-Bass.

Moses, Y. T. (1989). *Black Women in Academe: Issues and Strategies*. Report No. He-022-909. Washington, DC: Project on the Status and Education of Women, Association of American Colleges (ERIC Document Reproduction Service No. ED 311 817).

Perkins, L. (1989). "The History of Blacks in Teaching: Growth and Decline." In D. Warren (ed.), *American Teachers: Histories of a Profession at Work*, 344–367. New York: Macmillan.

Peterson, E. A. (ed.). (1996). *Freedom Road: Adult Education of African Americans*. Malabar, FL: Kreiger Publishing Co.

Phelps, R. (1995). "What's in a Number? Implications for African American Female Faculty at Predominantly White Colleges and Universities." *Initiatives* 19(4), 255–268.

Rakow, L. F. (1991). "Gender and Race in the Classroom: Teaching Way Out of Line." *Feminist Teacher* 6(1), 10–13.

Ruzich, C. M. (1995). *Are You My Mother? Students' Expectations of Teachers and Teaching as Related to Faculty Gender*. Report No. CS-215-044. Washington, DC: Paper presented at the Annual Meeting of the Conference on College Composition and Communication (ERIC Document Reproduction Service No. ED 386 739).

Sheared, V. (1994). "Giving Voice: An Inclusive Model of Instruction—A Womanist Perspective." In E. B. Hayes and S.A.J. Colin III (eds.), *Confronting Racism and Sexism*, 27–37. San Francisco: Jossey-Bass.

Williams, M. A. (1992). "The Ultimate Negotiation: Communication Challenges for African American Women in Higher Education." In L. B. Welch (ed.), *Perspectives on Minority Women in Higher Education*, 41–59. New York: Praeger.

Chapter 16

Through the Eyes of a Latina: Professional Women in Adult Education

Rosita Lopez Marcano

INTRODUCTION

Throughout history, leadership research and studies of leadership have been conducted by men and have focused primarily on male leaders (Edson, 1987; Hansot and Tyack 1981), and the interpretive frameworks derived from these studies have been used as a way to describe all human behavior. Moreover, the interpretive frameworks that were derived from the study of these men's lives have been found to be inadequate when applied to women (Marshall 1993). Furthermore, while new studies on women have begun to include minorities, there continues to be little literature and research on Hispanic[1] women leaders. Professional women of color have historically encountered the discriminatory double bind of racism and sexism once they arrive at the workplace (Comas-Diaz and Greene 1995).

Not much has changed. Women continue to be misunderstood and often mistreated in the workplace; and Latinas, in particular, because of a constellation of cultural expectations and societal biases, have had many hurdles to face as they move into leadership roles.

CHANGING AND DEFINING ROLES FOR LATINAS

Hispanic women share a history of discrimination and oppression with other marginalized groups in America as a result of their culture, class, and color differences. In addition to this, language differences can also be a factor that impacts their lives and their leadership aspirations. This in part may be due to the fact they have multiple experiences that intersect with one another. For instance, many have their cultural and historical roots in Spain; they speak the

Spanish language; Catholicism is their religion; many have Indian traits and heritage, and others have their roots in Africa. These factors have meshed together to create the Hispanic woman of today. Moreover, traditional gender roles within the Spanish culture have caused Hispanic women to be torn between their desire to acculturate and be accepted by the new culture while simultaneously remaining true to their familial expectations, even when such narrow gender roles have sometimes kept them from achieving success. Machisimo is another prevailing force for many of these women as they aspire to take on leadership roles. For many of them, machismo or male chauvinism, which is still very prevalent in their families, has placed them in a dual bind.

As they attempt to negotiate and integrate both the workplace and home, their expected roles of being the submissive, self-effacing, self-sacrificing female are often in conflict with their roles as leaders. This then leads to their being overwhelmed with stress, conflict, and guilt as they attempt to live and work in an American culture that promotes independence, self-fulfillment, and assertiveness, which are characteristics that may be viewed as culturally inappropriate. According to Gil and Vazquez (1996), this *marianismo*[2] paradox stifles Latina women, limits their dreams, and ultimately must be addressed and overcome for the good of the entire Hispanic community. Since traditionally and culturally, Hispanic women have placed great value on the whole family, and their approach to success has been one in which both the man and family are included in their struggle for achievement, we must begin to examine this issue.

In coming decades, Hispanics will make up the largest segment of the U.S. minority population, with an estimated 64.2 million by the year 2040 (Wagonner 1992). Approximately half of this growth is due to foreign immigration and half is due to births in the United States (Chapa and Valencia 1993). Unfortunately, census information, surveys, and other statistics rarely provide breakdowns of information within Hispanic groups, but it is important to note that a large percentage of Hispanics are low income, regardless of generational status in the United States (Padilla, Salgado de Snyder, Cervantes, and Baezconde-Garbanati 1987). Furthermore, educational attainment within this group has not come about easily, nor has there been great support, financially or emotionally. Many Hispanics are first-generation college students and are the first to obtain college degrees in their families, as my own story shows.

In this chapter, I offer my own story of learning and leadership development. In it, the reader will get a glimpse of the complex experiences shared by many Latinas in the educational and workplace arenas. For women, and especially for Hispanic females, the complexity becomes even more tangled, because in the traditional sense, they are still the outsiders.

LEARNING MY PLACE

As a Puerto Rican female growing up in Chicago, my experiences with schools, with teachers, and with the system left me wondering about whether I should even try to belong in a world dominated by English speakers—and by Euro-American whiteness. I remember that I was very excited about going to school on the first day. I could read and write in English, but the school did not know that I could do the same in Spanish. They placed me in the first grade because I was too old for kindergarten, even though it was my beginning year. My mother had fixed my long black hair into a beautiful set of braids, tied with strips of colorful cloth at the ends, and dressed me in her "native Puerto Rican" handmade dress.

She went to great lengths to make sure I was clean and well dressed. I could tell she was very proud of me and had great hopes for my future. I tried not to let her down, but my tears flowed as she left the classroom. Strange sounds and faces surrounded me. Small eyes stared at my clothes, my hair, and my face. I had an inner strength of my own that stared them back to their seats. If they stared at me I would stare back at them until they stopped. At the tender age of 6, I was desperately trying to preserve my dignity. I looked and felt like an immigrant in a strange land. When I wasn't sure about something I learned to stay quiet, observe, and study it until I figured it out. *I spent many days being quiet.*

My mother had already taught me most of what they were teaching in school. Subsequently, I was on the honor roll regularly. In the meantime, I began to learn about other things, among them the cruelty shown to others who are different. One day, my class was standing in line waiting to enter the bathroom. A couple of teachers began walking around the line sniffing our heads. This behavior puzzled me. They continued their "sniffing" research and every so often would comment to each other, confirming their hypothesis. Then, one of them approached me and picked up the tip of my braid and then abruptly let it fall as if to be careful as not to make too much contact. *I remember feeling insignificant and dirty. I was "sniffed," commented on (I think I passed the experiment), and they continued down the line.* That was many years ago, but I will never forget it. It was only one of many other similar incidents I would experience while being in school.

As years passed, I began to feel indifferent, no longer the daughter who could read and write in two languages and of whom my parents were so proud. I was beginning to lose a part of me to something that I was not. *I began to feel ashamed of my parents, of being a Puerto Rican, and of the way I looked.* Many days I wished I had blonde hair and blue eyes or at least a different last name. I wanted my mother to smell like Chanel No. 5 like my teacher, not like cilantro (a fragrant, parsley-like herb used in Puerto Rican and Mexican cooking). I felt ashamed about feeling this way, but I also began to feel ashamed of belonging to a community that was not well liked by the dominant society. *The messages were clear: assimilate and give up "those" traditions or be shunned.*

For instance, when I was in the fifth grade, the teacher asked the class to write a composition about what we wanted to be when we grew up. I ran home to write my composition, mainly because it was my chance to write about my possible future. You see, I had the talent of healing. I would find dying frozen cats and other animals and nurse them back to health. Then I would let them go. I also had a knack for helping people get better. I wrote with passion and hope.

I remember reading my first line to the class nervously: "When I grow up I want to be a doctor." The teacher stopped me and, slowly and clearly, said, "Rosita, this was not a make believe assignment. This was about what you really want to be when you grow up." The students laughed. I was so embarrassed. I sat down and promised myself never to dare to dream too big again. I rewrote the composition, and until this day I do not remember what I wrote the second time because it did not matter. I rarely wrote from the heart again. I remember the incident so clearly I can still remember my teacher's face, how she smelled, and the kids in the classroom with bolted-down wooden desks all in a row. That day, I learned that my people had a place in society, such as being the "Marias" as maids in affluent families' homes, or the "Juans" as gardeners in those same families' yards. Media, especially television, constantly affirmed those perceptions for society, so I believed it must be true.

Something was happening to me in school that I did not like. School reversed the support and strength given to me at home. I was in a rigid environment where education seemed to be the last thing on the educators' minds. Cultural assimilation and social conformity had first priority. Nothing about my family or me could succeed in such a place. How could this be?

SELF-DETERMINATION: A DREAM REALIZED

I was determined to be educated in spite of my teachers. I realized that most of the actual education I had received came from my home, church, and community. I felt that someone had lied to me but I was not sure who that was. Was it my family and church? Was it the school or society in general? I was surrendering those things that made me unique—my language, culture, and personal identity. I was learning to become ashamed of them. It seemed ludicrous to me, even then, that a school would be the last place to be academically challenging and enlightening. Had it not been for the support and patience of my family and church, I would have lost my faith and spirituality and slowly faded away.

High school was the least supportive educational environment I had yet to encounter. It was a place of misery, with little respect for the acquisition of knowledge. I began finding excuses for not going to school, anywhere from a "bad hair day" to "cramps." I actually began to feel sick, and thought that maybe I had started to believe my made-up excuses. However, numerous visits to hospitals and specialists confirmed that I had Rheumatoid Arthritis. I was in my sophomore year of high school. My parents quickly arranged a trip to Puerto Rico, before the doctors performed the surgery that would leave me in the hospital for three months.

After the surgery it was hard to get back into the routine of school. I missed more days due to physical therapy treatments. It was a year before I could walk without crutches. Physicians predicted a lifetime of limited mobility and career choices. I now understood what it felt like to be handicapped. I was sure this was the end of the road for me. I felt certain that now that I was damaged and scarred, there would be little future for someone like me.

During my junior year in high school, riots erupted. School became an unsafe place. The riots were all over the news. There were different expectations for Whites and minorities. The students were fed up and angry. They rebelled violently against the racism and inequities exhibited by the administration. I understood the anger, but one day I was walking to school and a large brick flew over my head, missed my hair, and made a dent in the building's exterior wall. That could have been my brain! I decided never to go back.

After that incident I began to sleep late and lacked the energy to set goals or to do anything constructive. I decided to take some time off and go to the mountains of Puerto Rico where my grandparents lived. I took time to reflect, refresh, and replenish my spirit, but I missed my family and soon returned home, still having no clear goals.

I was ashamed of not having graduated with my class. My friends would ask if I was at the graduation and my response was always, "Sure, I saw you there, you just never saw me, but I was there." I never went to the prom. No one asked me, anyway. I never joined clubs. Looking back, I must have dropped out of school long before I physically left.

I met and began dating Enrique Marcano, a student at Northeastern University, who convinced me to take my GED. They were only offering the test in Spanish at the time. He accompanied me downtown and waited while I took the test. I passed my GED, gaining the equivalent of a high school diploma. I was grateful for his encouragement.

Experiential Learning: St. Elizabeth's Hospital

Shortly thereafter, I found a job at St. Elizabeth's Hospital as a nursing assistant. I discovered more about life in my experiences at the hospital than I ever had in any school. I learned about compassion, suffering, death, hope, and about diversity in our world. Medical terms and techniques became a normal part of life. First, I worked on the geriatric unit where I learned about the elderly, some of whom had so much wisdom to offer but had no one to listen to them. Others had emotionally expired a long time ago and were just waiting for their bodies to catch up. I became mentally exhausted from taking bodies of people who had been left to die in a hospital, often alone and rarely visited, to the morgue. I tried to make those last days meaningful for some of them. I listened to their stories, often feeling their pain and loneliness. My natural abilities to heal emerged once again, except this healing only dealt with their spirits, because so many were too old and tired to be helped in any other way. Sometimes

I was there, holding their hands, during those last few moments before they passed on to eternity. As I held their hands, I often thought about the children they once cared for or the lives they may have touched. My mother always said that when she looked at a person's wrinkled and tired hand, that is what she always thought about.

It was in giving of myself that I was able to liberate my spirit and begin my path toward growth. I felt that I was back on track, but to what? I had no idea, but was glad to be part of something meaningful again. What an education I was receiving! I could possibly have chosen to be satisfied with my life as it was, but I hungered for more. There was no turning back. I lived a few blocks from the hospital and they always called me in for overtime during blizzards and storms. I always said yes.

During my years at St. Elizabeth's Hospital, I was able to work in pediatrics, the intensive care unit, the cardiac care unit, orthopedics, and finally in the laboratory. I learned and experienced everything I could. Every day was different. I became popular with the nurses and doctors because I learned quickly and could speak two languages fluently. The pathologist in charge of the laboratory helped me to become a phlebotomist, which meant I drew blood from patients. I learned to read and analyze blood, urine samples, and identify cells and bacteria. The laboratory became another world of wonder for me. I accepted all the overtime offered.

Continuing Professional Development: The University Experience

Realizing that I had an aptitude for this type of work, I enrolled in the University of Illinois. This was the most difficult part of my formal education. First of all, I was not sure they would accept my GED for admission. I was surprised when they said yes. I was not sure I could handle the assignments, especially the math classes.

Everything had changed so much since I had been in school. Initially, I began to fail in algebra, and found that I was struggling through everything else. I needed tutors for algebra, because although I loved numbers, the techniques for arriving at the answers were alien to me.

My algebra teacher, Dr. David Page, was concerned and offered help. He could never remember his students' names but was a brilliant teacher who had written the textbook for the class. His solution was to take everyone's picture and put our names next to each picture. He never had to remember our names because he just had to look at his organizational chart. After a few weeks of tutoring, Dr. Page looked at me thoughtfully and said I had a gift for mathematics. It had been a long time since a teacher had said something positive to me. I really started to enjoy going to algebra. It was all I needed to gain a little self-confidence and not give up. It was during these years that I decided to become a teacher.

As I taught, I felt I should learn more about education and new methods of teaching. I enrolled in a master's program at National College of Education (now National-Louis University) in Evanston. The program was based on a cohort approach with a small group of students who stayed together throughout the program, mostly with the same professor. I invited my sister-in-law to join me. At first, she felt uncomfortable and questioned herself in terms of studying with others who might be of higher intelligence than she. According to Chance and Imes (1978), this is termed the "impostor syndrome."

Although men often share feelings of imposterism, this is a debilitating syndrome that blocks women's ability to realize their full potential with greater frequency. For Hispanic women, talking about one's self or realizing one's potential would be considered bragging. They therefore are discouraged from engaging in such activities. So, I encouraged her, even though inside I felt the same fears and questioned whether I could make it. She accompanied me and enrolled in the program, even though she had a newborn baby and had just undergone surgery two weeks earlier. She was excited and worked hard. We motivated each other, arranged babysitting, and helped each other through the tough times that lay ahead. To her amazement she made straight As. I was not one bit surprised, but I understood her lack of confidence at first because I felt the same way.

This program opened ideas in my mind I had never imagined before. I brought new methods and strategies into the classroom. Some things worked, while others did not. I shared ideas with teachers, to see if they had a better response. I found myself reading and researching new ideas all the time, as I tried to figure out ways to make methods applicable to my own students. There were few materials available to meet my students' language needs, since the bilingual materials at that time were of poor quality and dull. I learned to translate books from English to Spanish so that my students could also enjoy them. I even made my own pop-up books.

After graduation I heard about a doctoral program at Northern Illinois University (NIU) that was similar to the master's cohort at National College. The only difference was that we would have different instructors for each class. I decided to explore the possibilities, but it seemed like such a faraway dream. After several informational sessions I was convinced that I could do this. I gathered together some colleagues who were also interested, gave them the information, and off we went for the first day of a long and intense journey into higher education.

We were challenged, enlightened, and empowered. It was here that I met Dr. L. Glenn Smith. He was a leader in every sense of the word. We were motivated to face challenges and find solutions. I learned to work in small groups as well as alone. The projects were ours to create and own. We aimed at excellence. I worked harder than I had ever worked in my life. I must admit that there were days when I cursed the program and Dr. Smith, because I was so exhausted from all the work and requirements. A friend asked me, "why do you need a doctorate? Won't you be overly qualified for jobs?" A family member said, "haven't you taken enough time away from your family? Where are you going with this?"

The truth was that I had no concrete plans about what to do with the doctorate. That I was too qualified, or not, was not the issue. I just knew I had to finish. The reality was that my outer shell was being broken so that my inner self could emerge, and it was a painful process. I had to step out of my comfort zone and blow away old paradigms about how a Hispanic female should behave. Staying out late sometimes because of long study hours, while my husband stayed home with the children, or striving to excel via education, was not typical for Puerto Rican females, as viewed through the eyes of older Puerto Ricans. I had to discipline myself, and not be so sensitive to criticism. *In the end, I recovered what I had been denied for so many years: the opportunity to be formally educated.*

I was offered a position to coordinate desegregation programs for the Department of Equal Educational Opportunity Programs on Chicago's far northwest side. It was a difficult task, but I accepted. The communities I worked with were predominantly White and feared integrating their schools, even though they were in danger of having their schools closed because of low enrollments and segregated conditions. The only recourse was to bus minority children into their schools. Some communities were adamant about keeping the status quo. One school principal told me the people from the neighborhood often walked their dogs in the area where the children would dismount from the busses. The children stepped in the dog droppings and were humiliated. Other tactics included leaving roofing nails in the street where the busses parked. It never failed: there were at least two or three flat tires per week. Parents became nervous and stopped sending their children to this school. One parent told me she was more afraid of the internal wounds she could not see, than those which were visible, and I understood what she meant. I continued to seek solutions to the many problems involving desegregation. The hours were long and it seemed as if all the work involved was just a drop in the bucket.

Meanwhile, my family had quietly watched and hoped for my return. The years spent studying and missing social activities because I had classes seemed to last forever. They had temporarily lost me and were not sure I was ever coming back to them. And, finally, I graduated. *Would I be too educated to want to be with them? Would we still have anything in common that we could share?* Yet, while they questioned me, and sometimes criticized me, their faith in me, and the strength they gave me, never foundered; and, at last, that humiliated fifth grader was now gone, and a woman of passion and great spirit had emerged. I felt as though I had conquered something of great value. It felt good to be able to accomplish a difficult task against the odds.

I was home again. Once again I recognized the sense of pride toward my family, language, and heritage that I had questioned during my early years in school. I have learned to reject the rejection I once accepted. The respect and love for my family could never again be compromised.

After a few years of working for the Chicago Public Schools as an administrator, I applied for a tenure track assistant professor position in the College of Education. It was not easy, but I got the job. I knew that some faculty members were not thrilled about having a Hispanic female as part of their faculty, but I was hoping they'd eventually get over it. I heard comments from "you'd better thank God for affirmative action or you would not be here" to "don't get too comfortable, you're not going to be here for too long." I wanted to quit because I knew I would never belong here. I thought about something my mother says often: "you swim so far to drown at the shore." I felt like I was drowning at the shore after finally arriving at my destination. I started writing and publishing as much as I could and connecting with other professors around the country via conferences and the Internet—because the support system I needed at my university was missing. As a result, I begin to realize that it is imperative that educational institutions begin to identify and acknowledge the realities of gender bias and racism in the workplace and strive to create organizations where equality for all individuals is recognized and welcomed.

Within two years I became faculty chair in Educational Administration and School of Business. It has not been easy, but it has been worth the struggle. The nicest compliment I received from a colleague when I announced I would be stepping down to devote more time to writing was, "please don't step down now, we're actually moving ahead for the first time in years." It felt good to be appreciated.

Many wonderful opportunities have emerged. I have had the good fortune of meeting inspiring leaders and now understand that success is a journey that never rests. I am committed to being a lifelong learner. I also have come to realize that it is only with the wisdom and grace of God that I have been able to muster up the courage to push harder and carve out a new path. Although I now live about four miles north of my old neighborhood in Humboldt Park, my place of worship remains located in the heart of Humboldt Park. I speak to youth groups, parents, and teachers about the struggles our inner city youth face and strategies we need in order to avoid getting sucked into the abyss of large cities. The challenge is incredible, but I feel I am ready. Everyone needs to dream, and not all dreams will be fulfilled, but we need to dream them anyway. We all need to have dreams, even if some of us dream them in different languages and colors.

LEARNING, THE PRICE OF LEADERSHIP, AND BEING FIRST

The struggle I experienced in obtaining tenure almost convinced me that finding another job would be a better option. However, after discovering that other marginalized members of the academy had had similar incidents to mine, I decided to remain in the system in order to change it. Gaining membership into this much-sought-after exclusive group, which is so prized by faculty members on campuses around the world, is more like a hazing ritual rather than anything else. Even though White males experience this abuse, the abuse and torture sustained by many women and faculty members of color is even worse.

It is a system that can easily open the gates for some, while deterring others unnecessarily, as the deciding committees determine who gets in and who remains at the door. Too many of these committees are currently made up of tenured and promoted White males who are now feeling the pressure of change that is evolving around them. White males have been privileged within institutions of higher education, and the tenure process, albeit difficult at times, works better for them than for newly emerging ethnically, linguistically, and culturally marginalized groups. Many of these White males are often unaware of their privilege, and when it is brought to their attention they deny that it exists (McIntosh 1988). As Peggy McIntosh has pointed out,

Obliviousness about white advantage, like obliviousness about male advantage, is kept strongly inculturated in the United States so as to maintain the myth of meritocracy, the myth that democratic choice is equally available to all. Keeping most people unaware that freedom of confident action is there for just a small number of people props up those in power and serves to keep power in the hands of the same groups that have most of it already.

As I went through my own tenure process, as a Hispanic female I expected difficulties. The decision to hire me at all was a divided issue within the faculty to begin with. I worked twice as hard in comparison to others that went for tenure with me. In fact, the work I saw that the others had completed was one-fourth of what I had produced. They were not questioned, yet everything I had turned in was closely looked at and inspected for problems. It seems to me that they took great lengths and made extra effort to screen me out. This did not appear to be the case for those who looked liked the mainstream. In fact, one of them went forward with only one publication. The faculty did not unanimously support the decision for tenure and promotion in my case, yet the others were not questioned. Eventually, I got tenure, but despite my success I remain convinced that the system is clearly biased against those who are not White males.

Bronstein's research (in Ruffins 1997) in this area supports this claim. Her qualitative study on the lives and careers of 30 scholars who focused their research on feminist and multicultural issues concludes that tenure committees often treat ethnic and women's studies as ghetto disciplines, and that ethnically oriented journals are often viewed as inferior publication outlets. It appears that differences may add up against you, she says. It looks like the more people differ from the mainstream model, the more difficulties they have in their institutions, particularly on a personal level. Others also buttressed this view. The Latina or Hispanic female is underrepresented in administrative positions in schools (AASA 1991; Phelps and Taber 1996), and Latinas in higher education are even more underrepresented in tenure track positions.

The Latina experience in the academy has been one of perceived tokenism. They hire a token Hispanic as the only or first one and expect her to be representative of all Hispanic women as well. The irony is that if a Hispanic woman is too Hispanic, she may have difficulty succeeding in academia. If her Hispanic peers consider her too Anglo, she may lose their support. Hispanic women in this position walk a very fine line and tend to be isolated on both sides. For some women this creates immense stress and consumes a large amount of energy, which could and should otherwise be used toward the development of their research and professional growth. For other women, ignoring this has been the way that they have dealt with it, even though they admit they are fed up with it. Moreover, the relatively small number of Hispanic persons of either sex, faculty members or administrators, who can serve as role models, mentors, colleagues, and peers compounds the isolation for Hispanic women. The journey of Latinas into top positions in education is not an easy one, but these women have shown that in spite of the difficulties, *si se puede*, it can be done!

RECOMMENDATIONS FOR PRACTICE

I believe that having a deep sense of self is important to the Latina. This will help her to begin discerning when she should speak out as well as help her develop resiliency. Universities can be instrumental in assisting Hispanic women to succeed on campus by improving the academic climate and developing programs and services aimed at helping women, and Latinas in particular, present and promote their contributions to the knowledge base.

We may not always be cognizant of what we do, but our behavior is observed and critiqued by others. Therefore, I believe that professors must be accountable to their colleagues locally and globally. Latina professors, as well as other marginalized groups, must celebrate their victories with others and should not view their success as merely a moment of good fortune, but rather, as the result of excellent work. In order to sustain this effort, universities must increase the visibility of Latinas on campus, not only by hiring them but also by using their expertise and publicizing their activities. In their roles as faculty members they then can serve as role models for Hispanic women students on campus and in the community, as well as for other students who may not be accustomed to seeing Hispanic women in academia.

As educators, we must assume responsibility for educating others about what they do not know, when the opportunity arises. After all as leaders, it is our responsibility to mentor and to listen to those we serve. This applies to all leaders. There is a time to confront and a time to educate. No longer is ignorance about others an excuse for not giving them the respect they deserve. We can no longer accept excuses or pleas of ignorance concerning a lack of cultural sensitivity. We must encourage and teach others about ways in which they can gain an understanding about things that they do not know about others. As Maya Angelou (1969) so eloquently affirms, "Without willing it, I had gone from being ignorant of being ignorant to being aware of being aware."

As a marginalized group this does not mean that we should engage in self-defeating and debasing discourses. This means we should not create excuses for ourselves or blame others for our state. As women of color in the academic profession, Latinas must not solely engage in pity parties. However, when we must have one we should be encouraged to do so in the counsel of women whose wisdom and intuition we trust and value.

In looking at successful women role models, we find that they have achieved their goals by observing those successful people around them. Latinas can do no less when they join the academy. In order to do this, however, their presence must be realized through university hiring practices. As we know, role models and mentors provide valuable standards of achievement, inspire career choices, and lay out avenues for upward mobility. Weisfeld (1987) has emphasized that role models and mentors often help compensate for the isolation that minorities encounter in academic and professional settings in which they are greatly underrepresented. While the mentor does not necessarily have to be Hispanic, this person should be someone who is willing to listen to, and spend time with the novice Latina professional or academician, as well as teach her strategies for success.

As organizations continue to meet the educational needs of the increasing numbers of minority students from all cultures, more emphasis should be placed on hiring professional women of color in key positions that better reflect the ethnicity, language, and cultural identities of the student population. Professional women, and professional Latinas in particular, do not want to be considered "outsiders" by their colleagues. Even though they seek acceptance and entrance into the leadership domain and majority culture, they also recognize their continued connections to their communities, their cultures, their language, and their histories. Condescending attitudes and tokenism will not be tolerated, and once they are detected, should be addressed. As for the Hispanic woman, it is essential that she find her voice and use it. In working with other groups she will need to focus on the differences while at the same time acknowledge her similarities with those she finds herself working and operating with. Women around the world share camaraderie of strength in leadership skills and talents that are too often untapped. It therefore behooves organizations to examine this up front.

At the outset of this chapter, I noted that one of the major assumptions about Hispanic women is that they focus only on family and home. While this is true, we must also note that Hispanic women will allude to family, community, and culture as a source of strength as they seek out their goals. Successful Latinas in leadership positions have learned to celebrate their innate talents and abilities, instead of rejecting their Hispanic heritage and ethnicity.

While women in general will continue to play a significant role in organizations around the country, Latinas are now beginning to take their place as well.

This new group of women leaders must be given an opportunity to engage in dialogue with other administrators, including professional women of color, with differing cultures and languages. As institutions consider the small number of Latinas in top positions, they might well question the factors that keep their numbers low rather than simply assuming that there are not enough Hispanic women out there who are interested in such positions. No one wants to be treated like an outsider. We cannot continue to splinter the talents, gifts, resources, and ideas that Hispanic women bring to the workplace. This happens when people are not educated and skilled in managing and valuing differences. Differences must be treated with respect, dignity, fairness, and equality. This is fundamental if organizations around the country genuinely want to prepare all citizens for the challenges they will face in the twenty-first century.

Universities must address racism and prejudice as a phenomenon that limits opportunities and promotes injustice. The dismal numbers of females and faculty of color on campuses who are in decision-making positions and who comprise the committees who make major decisions on tenure and promotion and policies is a clear signal that something is wrong. I hope that through my life story and others like mine, we will continue to engage in dialogues that will help not only gain an appreciation for our differences, but will also help us celebrate our similarities. Leaders come in all shapes, colors, and languages, so we must begin to encourage their inner strengths and develop their talents as we move into a more diverse and global society.

NOTES

1. The term "Latina" or "Hispanic" comprises a very diverse group of people. The U.S. government describes "Hispanics" as persons of Puerto Rican, Mexican or Mexican American, Cuban, South or Central American, or other Spanish-language ancestry. Many people from these backgrounds use "Latino" or their actual country of origin (Puerto Rican, Mexican, etc.) to describe themselves to others. For convenience, I use the terms "Latina" and "Hispanic" or "professional women of color" interchangeably, although I know that some colleagues take exception to the terms, labeling, and marginalizing that they represent.

2. *Machismo* has been defined by Victor de la Cancela, a Puerto Rican psychologist, as a socially learned and reinforced set of behaviors in Latino society which men are expected to follow. If *machismo* is the sum total of what a man should be, *marianismo* defines the ideal role of a woman. And what an ambitious role it is, taking as its model of perfection the Virgin Mary herself. *Marianismo* is about sacred duty, self-sacrifice, and chastity; about dispensing care and pleasure, not receiving them; about living in the shadows, literally and figuratively, of your men—father, boyfriend, husband, son—your kid's and your family (Comas-Diaz and Greene, 1995, 7).

REFERENCES

AASA. (1991). *Survey of Women and Racial Minorities in School Administration.* Arlington, VA: American Association of School Administrators.

Adler, P. S. (1975). "The Transitional Experience: An Alternative View of Culture Shock." *The Journal of Humanistic Psychology* 15(4), 13–23.

Angelou, M. (1969). *I Know Why the Caged Bird Sings*. New York: Bantam Books (Reissue 1993), 230.

Bell, L. A. (1990). "The Gifted Woman as Impostor." *Advanced Development: A Journal on Adult Giftedness* 2, 55–64.

Bickel, J. (1996). *Enhancing the Environment for Women in Academic Medicine: Resources and Pathways*. Washington, DC: Association of American Medical Colleges.

Brilles, J. (1995). *Gender Traps*. New York: McGraw-Hill.

Chance, P., and Imes, S. (1978). "The Imposter Phenomenon in High Achieving Women: Dynamics and Therapeutic Interventions." *Psychotherapy: Therapy, Research & Practice* 15(3), 241–246.

Chapa, J., and Valencia, R. R. (1993). "Latino Population Growth, Demographic Characteristics, and Educational Stagnation: An Examination of Recent Trends." *Hispanic Journal of Behavioral Sciences* 15, 165–187.

Comas-Diaz, L., and Greene, B. (1995). *Women of Color*. New York: Guilford Press.

Deitz, R. (1992). "Hispanics in Educational Policymaking Positions: Where Are They?" *The Hispanic Outlook in Higher Education* 2(12), 6–8.

Edson, S. (1987). "Voices from the Present: Tracking the Female Administrative Aspirants." *Journal of Educational Equity and Leadership* 7(4), 2261–2277.

Gil, M. R., and Vazquez, C. I. (1996). *The Maria Paradox: How Latinas Merge Old World Traditions with New World Self Esteem*. New York: G. P. Putnam's Sons.

Grogan, M. (1996). *Voices of Women Aspiring to the Superintendency*. Albany: State University of New York Press.

Hansot, E., and Tyack, D. (1981). "The Dream Deferred: A Golden Age for Women School Professors." Policy paper No. 81-C2. Stanford, CA: Stanford University, Institute for Research on Educational Finance and Government.

Harrigan, B. (1977). *Games Mother Never Taught You*. New York: Warner.

Marcano, R. L. (1997). "Gender, Culture, and Language in School Administration: Another Glass Ceiling for Hispanic Females." *Advancing Women in Leadership* 1(2).

Marcano, R. L., Hudson, J., and Wesson, L. (1998). "What Women of Color Bring to School Leadership." In B. Irby and G. Brown (eds.), *Women Leaders Structuring Success*, 43–49. Dubuque, IA: Kendall/Hunt.

Marshall, C. (1993). *The New Politics of Race and Gender: The 1992 Yearbook of the Politics of Education Association*. Washington, DC: Falmer Press.

McIntosh, P. (1988). "White Privilege, Male Privilege: A Personal Account of Coming to See Correspondences through Work in Women's Studies." Paper presented at the Virginia women's Studies Association conference, Richmond, April 1986.

Minorities in Higher Education. (1988). Washington, DC: American Council on Education.

Montalvo, F. F. (1987). *Skin Color and Latinos*. San Antonio, TX: Institute for Intercultural Studies and Worden School of Social Services.

Padilla, A. M., Salgado de Snyder, N., Cervantes, R. C., and Baezconde-Garbanati, L. (1987). "Self-regulating and Risk-taking Behavior: A Hispanic Perspective." In *Research Bulletin*, 1–5. Los Angeles: Spanish Speaking Mental Health Association.

Phelps, D. G., and Taber, L. S. (1996). "Affirmative Action as an Equal Opportunity Opportunity." *New Directions for Community Colleges* 24(2), 67–79.

Reyes, Maria De La Luz, and Halcon, J. John. (1988). "Racism in Academia: The Old Wolf Revisited." *Harvard Educational Review* 58, 305.

Ruffins, P. (1997). "The Shelter of Tenure is Eroding and for Faculty of Color Gaining Membership May Be Tougher than Ever." *Black Issues of Higher Education* 14(17).

Sanford, J. A. (1970). *The Kingdom Within.* New York and Ramsey, NJ: Paulist Press.

U.S. Department of Commerce. (1991). "Race and Hispanic Origin" (No. 2) (Bureau of the Census). Washington, DC: U.S. Government Printing Office.

Wagonner, D. (1992). "Dramatic Changes in U.S. Population. Numbers and Needs." *Ethnic and Linguistic Minorities in the United States* 2(6), 1–3.

Weisfeld, V. D. (ed.). (1987). "Networking and Mentoring: A Study of Cross-generational Experiences of Blacks in Graduate and Professional Schools." Special Report No. 1. Princeton, NJ: Robert Wood Johnson Foundation.

Chapter 17

By My Own Eyes: A Story
of Learning and Culture

Lynette Harper and "Mira"

The twentieth century has been called the century of the refugee because of the vast numbers of people uprooted by war and politics from their homes and their accustomed lives (Bateson 1990). While most immigrants choose to come to a new life, refugees are forced to flee, often for their lives. They face a double crisis. Like all immigrants, they need to survive: to find shelter and work; to learn to speak an unknown language; and to adjust to a drastically changed environment despite barriers of poverty, prejudice, minority status, pervasive uncertainty, and culture shock. In addition, the refugee must come to terms with what has been involuntarily lost from the past, including home, country, family, friends, work, social status, material possessions, and meaningful sources of identity.

Even the best prepared refugees experience distress, which is intensified by the complex and restrictive regulations imposed upon them in most host countries. Emminghaus (1987) concludes that as a result of these regulations and their exclusion from participation in their home country, refugees often begin to feel alienated from both their indigenous culture and from the society in which they now live. Attendance to these dual factors is a much overlooked area in programs for immigrants. While immigrant and refugee services and education programs are proliferating, most programs are designed to serve only a remedial function, focusing on communication skills, job skills, and activities of daily living. Programs rarely consider how migrants learn and adjust in new cultural environments. This chapter offers one woman's life history as a way to revisit and reframe our thinking about refugees.

I am the grandchild of refugees, and in an effort to honor their lives, I began to study refugee learning and transition and the implications of this knowledge as it relates to program design. I have always valued personal narratives told by family and friends, so I turned to life history as a research method. This chapter facilitates an understanding of refugee experiences by interweaving my perspectives with those of a Lebanese woman named Mira. Our stories contribute to the growing awareness of the relationships between individual, culture, and society within the context of the life history of a refugee. The life history genre is undergoing a political evolution. Life histories provide us with an opportunity to challenge how knowledge is constructed and used by those being studied. The primacy and authority shifts from the investigator and toward the narrator. It gives voice to the silent or oppressed, and can provide a critique of academic traditions and modern society.

Conventional research describes the way things are. The purpose of this life history is not to identify historical facts, but to understand the personal meanings that life experience represents. It is a particular selection and arrangement of memories, an encounter between what is remembered of the past and a current social reality. Through this process, the narrators may be building a theory of self. Mira's story provides an opportunity to explore the way she interprets her life experiences.

The collaborative nature of life history projects raises complex questions of voice and power. Issues of power, privilege, and intimacy frame every life history, whether or not they are explored and articulated by the participants. The power differences between the narrator of this life story and myself were lessened because I chose to work within my own Arab community.

THE CONTEXT OF A LIFE

The starting point for this life history is how one person, "Mira," makes sense of her world. According to Mira, a Lebanese refugee now living in Canada:

Half of the problems, or tension, or suffering, that the immigrant or refugee has, when they come not only to Canada, anywhere in the world, is this big question, "How can I become a European, or a Canadian?" And they feel, I am not. I am Middle Eastern. This is terrible; I want to go back. I can't fit here. They need somebody to tell them, you don't have to be Canadian. You have to understand Canada.

Although Arab women are a familiar part of my world, they have long represented a very exotic other for most Western researchers. Until the 1970s, Arab women were consistently portrayed as one-dimensional characters of limited significance. They were described and dismissed as completely subordinate to men, and treated as a homogeneous whole which ignored social, economic, religious, ethnic, regional, rural-urban, and individual differences (Eickelman 1989). The popular media continue to perpetuate the stereotype of passive, veiled female victims of oppression in the 1990s.

My own relationship to the *local* Arab community is not a simple one. As I was growing up, my family maintained a distance from the community, and I became involved only as an adult. I was raised in a middle-class family with two working parents. By the time I finished school, I had thoroughly internalized cultural assumptions that I have only recently come to realize are peculiarly Canadian. I felt comfortable with mainstream North American culture and the White, Anglo-Saxon Protestant neighborhood that I lived in. I looked like I belonged, with my fair skin, tall body, and my father's Scottish heritage. It wasn't until I visited the Middle East that I recognized that other aspects of my character may be more Lebanese than Canadian. I've come to realize that my personality and values have been strongly influenced by my mother's Lebanese immigrant family.

Abu-Lughod (1991) would call me a "halfie"—a person whose national or cultural identity is mixed by virtue of migration, overseas education, or parentage. While involved with this life history process, I have been subject to the politics and ethics of multiple communities: the academy, the Arab community, and the participants in this publication. But there have been advantages to my halfie status. My network of connections with local Arabs made it easy to meet potential narrators, and I found it easy to establish rapport with them. As an insider, I was already aware of Arab expectations of close relationships between women. Joseph (1988) has characterized these relationships as "merging." To merge means that one has obtained a strong identification with another person, and has a deep understanding of and is invested emotionally with them. I became familiar with this immersion into others' lives through my experiences and observations with the Lebanese women in my own family.

Experiences of closeness and embeddedness are not unique to Arab or Lebanese women. Young and Tardif (1992) shed some light on this process as they describe the mutual disclosure and self-discovery that can take place when women interview women over a period of time. But Joseph's experiences suggest that Lebanese women are more intensely relational, more deeply embedded within their families, and more ready to extend their merging with family to merging with friends. Although it was not originally Joseph's intention, she found that merging was a research tool which allowed her to figuratively get inside people, to experience and learn about the nature of interpersonal relationships and self from a specialized vantage point.

INTERACTIONS AND INTERPRETATIONS

To learn more about refugee transition through life history research, I wanted to find an Arab narrator who felt comfortable in Canada, and who had vivid memories of her migration and transition. In my community, Lebanese make up a small invisible minority of about 5,000 people. Most of them are Christians of various sects, though there is a small and growing Moslem population. Although Lebanese do not physically appear very different from the Europeans and their descendants who dominate Canadian culture and population statistics, their Arabic language and culture is substantively different (Abu-Laban 1980; Altorki 1988).

Mira and I felt that we had many things in common. We were both middle class, university-educated, and involved in the field of education, things which would prove to minimize the inequities of the research relationship. Although Mira had spent her time in Canada as a refugee and could not yet apply for Canadian citizenship, she was fluent in English, and employed full-time in her chosen profession.

Mira was enthusiastic about the idea of being involved in a life history research. She too prefers to learn by reading about people and their stories, so it made sense to her that my research would focus on her and her story. She also wanted to help me learn more about my Lebanese heritage, and to tell people about Lebanon, to counter popular misconceptions perpetuated by North American media, like the notion that all Arabs are terrorists.

Mira chose the topics which were most important to her, and only near the end of our sessions did I become more directive, pursuing specific topics that I felt needed expansion. We reviewed the transcripts together. They seemed awkward, and without accompanying facial gestures and body language they were also misleading. So with Mira's approval, I smoothed our words, so they could be read easily as text.

While privacy was an issue, Mira and I wanted the finished work to be publicly accessible. Mira also wanted to be sure that she could not be identified, and so together we have altered aspects of the story to that end.

MIRA'S STORY: A DIALOGUE

Mira began by telling about her childhood. She described it in this way:

I had a very, very happy childhood. We grew up in a small village in Lebanon. I thought the whole world was there in my hometown. Because I was not that anxious to go and learn about something else, or know about anything else.... When the civil war started ...At that time they started to slaughter people, just if you were either Moslem or Christian. That's how it started. It was very, very bad. So even though you were innocent, even though you are not affiliated or involved in any political organizations or anything, just because your last name is Christian or Moslem, they put an end to your life, and that's it.... Near where we lived, it was much worse than in Beirut. Because we had no shelters, nothing. We lost everything in our house, and the house was blasted ... I never quit university.... After graduation, I was working twelve hours a day, I was teaching in four different schools, four different contracts, it was part-time. It was like running away from something that is following you—you have this kind of race with something very bad and evil.... We were living in a country where everything was sick—the atmosphere, the mentality. I was trying to convince myself that I have to be more tolerant, and try to be patient. But you know thirteen years is enough for a young girl, more than enough ... I wanted a major change. So, I came here. But I never thought I was going to stay five years. I thought six months, maximum one year. Because I needed a good rest. At that time, I was so exhausted, hardly able to move my body. . . . Well, when I came here, I was not equipped. It was like being a soldier going to a big battle, no weapons, nothing. Just myself. And my belief in myself, and God. That's all that I brought with me. Everything was so discouraging. I didn't go to school here, my English was not very good. I didn't have confidence, I was tired, I didn't know whether I was going to make it or not. I was living with my cousins in a small apartment. And I was very happy the first six months. I'd rest, and I gained weight, six kilos. I wondered why do people get depressed here? It's peaceful, they can go everywhere they want. The government is like a family, to everybody. I never thought that they were going to reject my cousin's sponsorship of me at immigration. . . . So that's why I had to become a refugee. Because that was the only way to stay in the country. At that time, it was very bad, the situation in Lebanon, I couldn't go back anyway. I was very, very miserable and upset and depressed. I found it very very hard, after suffering 13 years in Lebanon, to come to Canada and claim refugee. The feeling that I got, it was something burning, as if I had all the mountains around here, on my shoulders. It was very hard, because I was in the air, I was not on a solid base.

In Lebanon I was upset, I was depressed, and everything, but I was on a solid base, with a family. The land. But here, I was like a feather in the air, the wind. You don't know where you are going to be. You are nothing here, nothing at all. You have to start from the very beginning.

As she told her story, I asked: "You were telling me about a girlfriend of yours who told you about how hard it would be here in Canada. Did you go back (to Lebanon) and talk to her?" Mira responded by saying:

She couldn't believe it. She thought that I changed. After four years, I thought that she was going to be more flexible, and more mature. And I found that she was still in the same place, where I left her. But she found that I have changed, I became stronger. Maybe she expected me to be very depressed, because of what happened. But I'm stronger, I am more flexible, and I have courage. . . . But I survived, I think. I'm not that great, but I'm OK. I'm working, teaching, which is good, because teaching for me is very important. I can't see myself doing anything else. And I learned also a lot, about myself, through dealing with other people. From different cultures, and different religions, and different mentality. I also got to appreciate a lot the things that I had in Lebanon that I didn't have here. And at the same time, I have stronger belief in throwing away the things that I wanted to throw away when I was a little girl.

The thing that is surprising me, is the harmony between the different stages [in my life]. I stayed myself. Sure, when . . . I was very depressed, but still, I was looking forward to the time when I'd start again, and put more smiles on the wounds. The little girl I was at the beginning is in every single part of my life. And she's so stubborn. So, now, if you want to know what's next, I myself, I don't know what. Maybe, I'm going now, with this new image, a relaxed face, smiling again to my people, with more energy, starting again. I wanted to be exactly as I am now, when I was a little girl. I did a few things that I didn't want to do, because but there was no chance to do anything else, so I did it.

I didn't want to leave my country, I love Lebanon. It's the beginning and end of all what I want, and my longing. But I had to.

As she spoke about her time in Canada, Mira divided it into three periods. In the first six months, she appreciated the peace and order of a new environment. This was followed by misery and anxiety. She had moved from a place of belonging to being marginal, like a feather in the air. For Mira, as for most refugees, migration represented estrangement and the loss of everything familiar. The impact on her relationships, roles, actions, and understandings was tremendous. In the third period, she established a kind of equilibrium, a harmony in which she felt comfortable and able to cope with her life.

SEEING THINGS FROM DIFFERENT CORNERS

Mira often spoke about the duality of her existence. In this exchange, she spoke about the impact this had on her life. "One of the things that I learned here, or one of the things that made me change in life, is to look into things from different corners, different perspectives. That's how I started to know about myself, what I really want, what I don't want. And I also started to review certain things I used to think about, as perfect, or the best. It was the best that I knew in Lebanon."

"What do you mean by looking at things from different corners?" I asked her. Mira thought a moment, and then responded.

Well . . . perspectives. Corners means like taking photos. In order to take different shots, you have to move. And each one, it has its own beauty. So, if you stay in the same place, you might think that this is the only shot you can take, or only picture you can take, which is wrong. You are still the same person, but you see yourself from different corners.

Before, whatever my mom told me, whatever my neighbors told me, whatever the old women in the neighborhood told me, that was it. It was absolute. I thought that there was nothing beyond that, there can never be anything better than what I learned from them. And when I came here and I started to see how people live here, how people deal with each other. How people here make their living, for example, how people go to school, how people socialize, and sometimes I compare it between here and there. It's not to see which one is better. I found that no, there's no "this is better than that," or "that is better than this."

But there are many interesting things in life. More than the one that I learned. And that's the beauty about the whole thing. . . . For example, one of the things that when I came here I used to say, Thank God I am Christian. Now, I don't say that. Thank God there is a chance to go and meet people from different religions, and learn about other religions. And thank God for learning that I'm not the best. But, if you live in one place, you think that the whole world, everything is there. You can't think of anything else, on the other side of the globe. You know what I mean? So it's not age, it's how much you learn.

The main change was when I started to accept people. Or start to accept the fact that people are different. And they conduct themselves in different ways. Before, that was very hard to accept everybody should be exactly like me.

I then asked her several questions about her history of interaction with those who were different from her. "Didn't you meet different kinds of people when you lived in Lebanon?" She noted, "If you don't intermingle with a people, and socialize with them, and live their problems, and they live your problems, you get to know about them, but very little."

"So how did that happen when you were here in Canada?" I asked. "When I started to work here. I don't know whether I told you, that the first job I got here, it was in a store. It was the first time in my life I did something different."

LEARNING THROUGH PARTICIPATION

Since coming to Canada, Mira has shifted from having an ethnocentric perspective to one defined by cultural relativism. In other words, her previous belief was that being Lebanese and Christian was the best and only way to be, and now she had developed an acceptance of differences. Moreover, she discovered that all of humanity has much in common, and that different cultures have developed different strategies and norms of conduct.

All the learning processes that Mira has described were socially situated. As a result of her friendship and interdependence with her co-workers at the store, she experienced profound changes. Mira did more than just listen to their stories, she empathized with them. Her ability to merge, to get inside people and effectively identify with their troubles and their patterns of belief, was the catalyst for her learning. By listening to people she cared about, she began to understand about abuse and loneliness: the dark side of Canadian family life. Mira respected her co-workers' stories and their interpretations of their lives, and she attempted to understand the different cultural-meaning systems that framed their beliefs and actions. Her observations and friendships subsequently informed her analysis, not only about the Canadian society she lived in, but also about her Lebanese identity and how the two might coexist. Through critical reflection during long solitary walks and discussions with co-workers and friends, Mira came to understand the duality of her existence; a crucial step toward understanding the self as it is socially situated.

BEYOND THE BEAUTIFUL UMBRELLA

As Mira continued to talk about her new life in Canada, and the experience of culture shock, I expected her to talk more about the prolonged period of depression and grief that occurred during her second year in Canada. However, Mira's interpretation of culture shock differed from the traditional view of what is typically defined as culture shock. My understanding was based on Furnham and Bochner's (1986) definition of a stress reaction to a new cultural environment which results in a person becoming anxious and confused, and having a lack of reference points which guide their own actions and understanding of others' behavior. But for Mira, culture shock was a series of minor episodes. She talked about them in this way:

> For any immigrant, you know, this is the main topic. Culture shock. When I was in Lebanon, it was not that difficult there. If I wanted a job, I don't have to apply, because they know my father, or my brothers. It's below my dignity to go and apply for a job. Now, when I came to Canada, and I started to look for a job . . . It was something very, very, very difficult for me. It was a big shock! There, you don't have to apply, because people, they know who you are.
>
> Something else, the family life here, it was really shocking. For example, where my sister was, there were many buildings . . . only for senior citizens. I said, why senior citizens? She said, because, you know, here in Canada, it's not like in our families, their children don't have to look after them. They get money from the government. It was a big shock to me. I said, what do you mean, because my grandpa was very important in the family, even though he was ninety-eight when he died, we used to look after him . . . I said, "What about if somebody is like my grandpa, and cannot help himself?" She said, "They send him to the hospital, or to a special place. And they go and visit him." I couldn't believe it! I couldn't believe it, even now, I couldn't.

Mira's experience in and with her family allowed her to develop a critical world-view. Each time she was confronted with a situation that didn't make any sense to her, and which contradicted her own meanings and expectations, she utilized a framework of analysis which was based upon her experiences in her own family.

Given that a critical aspect of Arab life is familism, a form of social structure in which the needs of the family as a group are more important than the needs of any individual family member (Eickelman 1989), Mira's emphasis on family is not a personal idiosyncrasy. Although the family is important in North America, this cultural norm coexists with a pervasive emphasis on individualism (Podeschi 1986). The challenge for Mira was to reconcile these two ideologies.

At the time I interviewed Mira, she was no longer shocked by the ideology of individualism in family life. But this doesn't mean that she unquestioningly accepts the Canadian interpretation of family. Instead, she found ways to understand and explain what she observed, based on her own expanding frame of reference. She explained this way:

> When people talk about animals here . . . they love animals, they respect animals, they care a lot for animals and pets, especially for pets . . . I sent a letter home, and I told them how nice it is here, and how lucky people are here, and how lucky the cats are here, and the dogs. Now I've got used to how people think, I know why they do that.
>
> I didn't know that the cat, or the dog, is very important in the life of a lonely person here. I didn't know that people were so lonely, and they need anything, even an animal. Really, it's very sad. I understand that, definitely, and it's a very important thing, thank God that there are animals, and pets like this.

When I asked her, "Was that a surprise for you, to discover that people could be lonely?" She went on to say: "It was very sad. I felt so sad. And now, sometimes, we are lonely here. I mean, we have friends, and everything, but we still feel that we are lonely."

From these and other episodes, Mira began to scrutinize her own assumptions relating to familism as she had come to understand it from her Lebanese upbringing. For her, being a part of a family was like being sheltered from the world by a beautiful umbrella. Mira went on to say that

In Lebanon, you are not by yourself. There's nothing called I. It's ours, or our, or us. Because you, it means your family—you can't separate yourself from your surroundings. So you feel that you are part of the world, and you don't care. Whatever will happen to you, will happen to everybody else. It's so secure.

Mira went on to talk about how her life had changed since she had come to Canada.

Nothing has changed at all, but now as I've told you I've become more aware of things, and more practical, and more flexible, and more experienced. . . . I was over-protected in Lebanon. I didn't have the chance to see, because I had this big umbrella, a beautiful parasol. It was very nice, but I couldn't see anything beyond it. So now, once the beautiful umbrella was removed, I was able to use my own eyes, and see the sky, and the clouds, and the rain, and the rainbow, and everything. By my own eyes.

PERSPECTIVE TRANSFORMATION AND CULTURE

As Mira and I discussed her story, I began to see how her changing understanding of family was a form of learning about culture which had been triggered by a series of culture shocks. This process corresponds to perspective transformation, as described by Mezirow. According to Mezirow (1991), this is a process in which we become critically aware of how and why our assumptions have come to constrain the way we perceive, understand, and feel about our world. "[By] changing these structures of habitual expectation, [makes] possible a more inclusive, discriminating, and integrative perspective" (p. 167). From this, Mezirow concludes that this allows individuals to make choices or act in different ways based upon these new understandings.

In theorizing about such shifts, Mezirow proposed that there are several phases that one must go through in order for perspective transformation to occur. "Perspective transformation involves a sequence of learning activities that begins with a disorienting dilemma and concludes with a changed self-concept" (Mezirow 1991, 193). Correspondingly, Mira's transformation began with a disorienting dilemma and culminated with reintegration and action. In each phase, Mira reflected on her assumptions about family, and questioned and revised her meaning schemes around areas of knowledge, beliefs, judgments, and those feelings that guided her actions. For instance, her new understandings about how pets were viewed in Canadian life is just one example of how particular information contributed to her transformation. It was through events like this that Mira began to reach a new understanding about the meaning of family in Canada. She had become aware of alternatives to her own meaning about the family and the beautiful umbrella of her previous assumptions.

While Mezirow's theory of perspective transformation stresses that understanding life events is key to transformation, it fails to adequately address the role that culture plays in one's identity. The rhetoric of transformative learning theory connects culture with conservatism, distortion, barriers to praxis, and contextual influences to be overcome (Mezirow 1996; Taylor 1997). Like many theories of adult education and learning, it narrowly conceptualizes culture as a constraint rather than as a nexus of learning (Mezirow 1996). Culture has been narrowly defined as norms, rules, and standards, which are learned and unconditionally accepted. As a result, theoretical discussions of adult learning have rarely taken culture into consideration, but instead have placed emphasis on the psychology of the individual (Rubenson 1982).

If this understanding of the influence of culture and context was the only one applied to Mira's story, and the analysis focused only on the psychological, it would fail to adequately address her lived experience. Mira didn't automatically internalize new cultural meanings—nor did she have to unlearn culture in order to change her perspective. Instead, she has developed a more critical awareness of her familism, and realized it is something that provides structure and meaning to Lebanese society and her life.

From Mira's life history, we learn how psychological and cultural aspects are intertwined. Just as the study of learning has shifted from external, observable behaviors to internal consciousness, cultural studies now emphasize the abstract values, beliefs, and perceptions which lie behind actions. Culture is visualized as a web or network of meanings both internal and external to the individual, a lifelong dialogue of action, interaction, and meaning (Spindler and Spindler 1989). Individuals are not passive receivers of culture. Our response to often-conflicting systems of power and knowledge can be interpreted through the concept of human agency, and our capacity to make our own meanings in interaction with others (Abu-Lughod 1991).

As Mira began to examine her life experiences in Canada, she began to develop strategies which would allow her to accommodate or resist her new cultural understandings.

SHIFTING STRATEGIES OF COMPLIANCE AND RESISTANCE

As long as she was living in Lebanon, Mira's critical reflections on gender relationships, and Lebanon's oppressive religious and political structures, remained theoretical and unexpressed. It was only after migration and her perspective transformation that she felt she had the strength and commitment to act on some of her decisions. Speaking about her struggles in Lebanon and Canada is now an important way for Mira to take action on her new commitments. She says, "I dare to talk about things, not like before." Mira's storytelling is a testimonial, a way of bearing witness to the suffering of the Lebanese people. She is enthusiastic and willing to speak to anyone in Canada about her beliefs, and her friends often refer people curious about Lebanon to Mira for that reason. Mira has been aware of patriarchal dominance and oppression throughout her life, particularly in Lebanon. There she felt the restrictions imposed on her gender, and felt dominated by men in her family and Lebanese society. She talked about those restrictions in this way:

One time I came back from university, and we were having dinner together, me and my dad, and I was talking about equality between men and women. I said society should do something about it, and we should start at home by sharing the responsibility for doing things. Why should I, for example, set the table, or clean the dishes? My brothers should help us. . . . He said "Yes, that's right, but this is the way we're brought up, and it will take time to erase this." So I said, "Do you agree with me?" He said, "Yes, I do agree with you." I said, "OK, fine, now you clean up, I'm going! Bye Bye!" See? It's fossilized. There are a few things that girls have to do, and there are other things that it's not nice for women to do, in Lebanon.

Mira's feelings about her duties and obligations as a daughter and sister were ambivalent. While she appreciated the absence of loneliness, and the positive feeling of always being loved and busy, she sometimes resented the lack of privacy. When she thought of objecting or resisting, she would feel guilty. Her every action reflected not just upon her as an individual, but upon her entire family.

Now that she is in Canada, Mira can openly act more freely as a woman. This new understanding of human agency has strengthened her desire to challenge patriarchal ideology and norms. Her resistance is tempered, however, by her desire to comply with the norms of both Lebanese society and Canadian society. This has allowed her to meet her desire for intimacy and belonging while living in Canada.

Balanced in the tension between dependence and resistance, Mira creatively constructs her own meanings in her relationships with others. Mira redefined herself through a transformative learning process, which was participatory and charged with emotion. Unlike her girlfriend, who stayed in Lebanon, she has become more practical and more flexible, with more options for coping with her environment. Her practicality is associated with an increasing competence in Canadian ways and a growing sense of autonomy. But it is more than that. It represents a developing sense of agency. Working in a store, for example, would have been beneath Mira's dignity in Lebanon, and a source of shame to her and her family. In Canada, her changing understandings of what was possible and acceptable gave the store job a different meaning. It became a viable way of earning a living while learning more about her new surroundings.

Mira feels empowered as she discovers existing cultural schemata and meanings that are shared among Canadians. For example, as her sense of agency developed, it motivated Mira to not only adapt to Canadian norms, but it gave her space to resist as well. She talks about one form of this resistance:

The way people socialize here, in general, is very different from the way it was in Lebanon. . . . I found that people here are not so—how can I say it, warm? For example, [when you walk in a room], they hardly stand up, they don't shake hands, they just say "hi," and that's it. I found it shocking. I arrived, and it was as if there was no one there. Well, in Lebanon, when you have guests, when you invite people over, you show them that they are welcome. This is one thing that I thought I would like to maintain. The way I got it.

IDENTITY AND CONTINUITY

Identity is a complex and dynamic web of perspectives, commitments, and dimensions. As Mira reflects critically, strategizes, and makes decisions, she creatively constructs her own identity and actions from a broadening repertoire of possibilities. Amid the discontinuities of her transition process, Mira's ethnic identity provided a sense of continuity and stability. She affirms and reaffirms its primacy by telling stories of herself and her homeland to others. Tied to her powerful cognitive and emotional needs for belonging, her Lebanese identity strengthens her autonomy and ability to make decisions to accept or resist aspects of the Canadian culture system.

Mira does not feel a sense of contradiction in her cultural identification. She lives in Canada, but is not becoming Canadian. Instead of having two selves, Mira feels she can simply have two homes:

I'm still Lebanese, because I am Lebanese. I was born in Lebanon, brought up in Lebanon, my parents are Lebanese. But, what's wrong in being Lebanese, and knowing about another country, like Canada, and having two homes? What's wrong in that?

MARGINAL BY CHOICE

In Lebanon before the civil war, Mira was a full member of mainstream Lebanese society, not an "I" but part of an "us." Although she was aware of the inequalities of her female status, she shared that position with other Lebanese girls and women. During the civil war, her status changed in frequent and confusing ways, and became a matter of life and death. Power shifts were manifested in violence between religious, regional, family, and political communities, and she felt powerless and voiceless.

When Mira arrived in Canada, after the initial relief from the uncertainty and danger of the war, she felt very much Lebanese, and very much on the periphery of life in Canada. As she described it: "You are nothing here, nothing at all." Refugee legislation imposed barriers to her full participation in society, while others urged her to conform to Canadian cultural and social practices. Although apparently contradictory, they all delivered the same message. As a refugee, Mira was still powerless and voiceless.

When Mira became familiar with Canadian society and culture, she identified herself as an agent in the Canadian social and cultural system. Returning to a teaching career affirmed a long-standing occupational identity, placing her within a particular professional community with Canadian colleagues. When she questioned the assumptions she had once uncritically shared with other Lebanese, she became different from friends and family in Lebanon. Without her beautiful umbrella, she had a more individualistic perspective on the world.

At the same time, Mira's Lebanese identity has distanced her from full participation within mainstream Canadian society. Her Lebanese affiliation is deeply and emotionally felt, fulfilling her needs while fueling her desire for family, belonging, and continuity. By deliberately choosing to maintain her ethnic identity, along with many cultural attitudes and behaviors, Mira has chosen life in the margins, and to operate from a position of resistance.

A PERSPECTIVE ON PRACTICE

Mira's story testifies to the resilience of the human spirit, and is a tribute to a woman who has maintained a lifelong commitment to personal growth despite the traumas of civil war and migration. Mira experienced social change throughout her life, as the very fabric of Lebanese society and culture has undergone dramatic changes in the last century, accelerated by modernization and war. Although raised in a small mountain village, Mira has become a middle-class professional, critical of certain aspects and sectors of her society.

Mira's story poses a critique of educational practices which define immigrants and refugees as deficient or inferior. It argues for a critical awareness of culture, agency, and identity in both research and practice. Mira's transformative learning process would have been enabled by an education system based on collaborative relationships, as advocated and documented by Cummins (1996). As I found in my experience with this study, educators who use storytelling and life history techniques can foster critical reflection, and construct new meaning along with their learners. In Canada, where classes in English as a second language dominate the immigrant education agenda, critical literacy practices should provide opportunities for immigrants to examine their life histories, the complexity of their current existence, and from that consider the possibilities for personal and social change. Mira's voice provides a testament to the power of this medium:

Canada is built by immigrants and refugees like me, and this is very healthy to have more people coming to this country. Right? Your ancestors were one. Maybe your grandmother grew up, and went through the same thing I went through. When you talk about cultures, and people, and adult education, it's nothing like when you say, I want to write a story, and at the end you put a full stop and that's the end. No. It's like art. There is no final stop. You always find something, you always learn about something, every time you learn about something you discover that there are so many things you still need to learn about.

CONCLUSION

Mira has chosen to live in the margins of Canadian society. Although she feels a deep need to belong, she has learned that there can be advantages to being a peripheral participant. Mira sees advantages, which justify and support her marginal position. It has given her new ways of knowing, flexibility, and strength; and it is a source of power, which gives her voice the authority to represent alternative perspectives, to criticize, and to educate. At her school she educates her fellow teachers about the Arabs and Lebanese, contradicting their stereotypes of Arabs as terrorists. When she returns to Lebanon as a visitor, she finds that she can express her criticisms of religious and political leaders.

As for me, as a result of doing this study with Mira, I found myself questioning my own Canadian identity. As Mira described her family relationships, I was shocked by the similarities in her life experience and mine. As I listened to her descriptions I confronted the long-standing contradictions in my life that existed between Canadian individualism and familistic expectations. By recognizing Lebanese dimensions in my identity, I have discovered new ways of coping with my own ambivalence about both Canadian and Arab communities. I have also become a more active advocate for minority rights.

REFERENCES

Abu-Laban, Baha. (1980). *An Olive Branch on the Family Tree: The Arabs in Canada.* Toronto: McClelland and Stewart.

Abu-Lughod, L. (1991). "Writing Against Culture." In R. G. Fox (ed.), *Recapturing Anthropology: Working in the Present.* Santa Fe, NM: School of American Research Press.

Altorki, S. (1988). "At Home in the Field." In S. Altorki and C. F. El-Solh (eds.), *Arab Women in the Field: Studying Your Own Society.* Syracuse, NY: Syracuse University Press.

Bateson, M. C. (1990). *Composing a Life.* New York: Plume.

Cummins, J. (1996). *Negotiating Identities: Education for Empowerment in a Diverse Society.* Ontario: California Association for Bilingual Education.

Eickelman, D. (1989). *The Middle East: An Anthropological Approach.* Englewood Cliffs, NJ: Prentice-Hall.

Emminghaus, W. B. (1987). "Refugee Adaptation: Basic Research Issues and Applications." In J. W. Berry and R. C. Annis (eds.), *Ethnic Psychology: Research and*

Practice with Immigrants, Refugees, Native Peoples, Ethnic Groups and Sojourners. Berwyn, PA: Swets North America.

Furnham, A., and Bochner, S. (1986). *Culture Shock: Psychological Reactions to Unfamiliar Environments.* New York: Methuen.

Jabbra, N. W., and Jabbra, J. G. (1984). *Voyageurs to a Rocky Shore: The Lebanese and Syrians of Nova Scotia.* Halifax: Dalhousie University.

Joseph, S. (1988). "Feminization, Familism, Self, and Politics: Research as a Mughtaribi." In S. Altorki and C. F. El-Solh (eds.), *Arab Women in the Field: Studying Your Own Society.* Syracuse, NY: Syracuse University Press.

Mezirow, Jack. (1991). *Transformative Dimensions of Adult Learning.* San Francisco: Jossey-Bass.

Mezirow, Jack. (1996). "Contemporary Paradigms of Learning." *Adult Education Quarterly* 3, 158–173.

Podeschi, R. L. (1986). "Philosophies, Practices and American Values." *Lifelong Learning* 9(4), 4–7, 27–28.

Rubenson, K. (1982). "Adult Education Research: In Quest of a Map of the Territory." *Adult Education* 32(2), 57–74.

Spindler, G., and Spindler, L. (1989). "Instrumental Competence, Self-efficacy, Linguistic Minorities, and Cultural Therapy: A Preliminary Attempt at Integration." *Anthropology and Education Quarterly* 20, 36–50.

Taylor, E. W. (1997). "Building upon the Theoretical Debate: A Critical Review of the Empirical Studies of Mezirow's Transformative Learning Theory." *Adult Education Quarterly* 48, 34–59.

Young, B., and Tardif, C. (1992). "Interviewing: Two Sides of the Story." *Qualitative Studies in Education* 5(2), 135–145.

Chapter 18

Using Queer Cultural Studies to Transgress Adult Educational Space

André P. Grace

TWO CHALLENGES

In this chapter I would like to challenge you in two particular ways. First, I invite you to explore possibilities for learning outside the hetero-normative box. By this I mean that I would like you to journey beyond familiar ways of knowing, seeing, thinking, and acting to explore queer cultural studies as a counter-cultural and political way of reading what Freire (1998) calls "the word and the world." In my work I use the word "queer" to name lesbians, gay men, bisexuals, the transgendered, and transsexuals. I also use it to represent how w/e[1] act in this world. For me, the word queer names and represents my identity and difference. Like many other queer persons, I take back the word from homo-phobes who use queer as a derogatory word to assault my integrity, and I use it to engage in linguistic jousting with them. This engagement interrogates hetero-sexist language and meaning, and it questions hetero-normative boundaries to being and acting. From this political perspective, some of us embrace queer as a powerful word. However, Others in our community refuse to use the word, and even feel that it excludes them. For them, queer neither names nor represents who they are or how they act in the everyday. The debate over such naming and representation is a vital and ongoing one in our loosely configured queer community. It is an important part of a politics of identity and community formation that is concerned with the intricacies of queer being and acting.

Of course, you will only get a capsular view of queer cultural studies and its possibilities for transgressing "mainstream" adult educational space within the limits of this essay. However, should you choose to journey further along this revealing culture-and-power terrain, a rich and substantial queer literature in cultural studies and other academic discourses can be found in inclusive libraries and bookstores. And you can supplement what you learn in these spaces with what you've learned, and continue to learn, from both stereotypical and more real representations in popular culture. Throughout the 1990s, popular culture has provided a space where queer culture has been increasingly explored while still being contested culturally and politically. Notably, television sitcoms (like *Spin City* and the now defunct *Ellen* and *Roseanne*), motion pictures (including *Priscilla, Queen of the Desert* and *The Object of My Affection*), and magazines (such as *Advocate* and *Out*) have provided a spectrum of courageously honest representations of queer Others. These cultural media remain primary sites for learning about queer persons and queer culture.

Second, if you resist theory and theorizing, then I would also like to challenge you to transgress that space. I invite you to explore the new language and ideas that I find useful and necessary to speak and write about the personal, political, and pedagogical in relation to queer cultural formations, questions, problems, and projects. For me, the questions and problems raised by queer cultural studies often necessitate new languages and new ways of theorizing to extend possibilities for finding answers and reaching solutions. The theory and language I use in this essay are part of a critical postmodern discourse[2] that helps me to theorize and name queer culture and its representations. For me, processes of making meaning and making sense are interwoven with the process of theorizing; that is, with "texturing"[3] knowledges and understandings. It is from this perspective that I work to shape pedagogical practice and other cultural practices as theory lived out in the everyday. Freire also takes this stance. For him, theory and practice are in dynamic equilibrium, mutually informing one another in the teaching-learning interaction. Thinking about practice means thinking about the theory inherent in it. Thinking about theory means thinking about how it emerges "soaked in well-carried-out practice" (Freire 1998, 21). With this understanding, let's continue to explore the theory and language of queer cultural studies and their possibilities for informing pedagogy in adult education.

In the first part of this chapter I provide insights into the theory and language that I use to describe queer culture as a formation and queer cultural studies as a project that takes up cultural questions and problems. I also give a status report on the queer cultural project in the United States. In the second part, I explore the value of queer cultural studies to adult education and I present a range of ideas for the reflection of readers concerned with inclusionary and transformative practice. I speak to possibilities and risks associated with an engagement with queer cultural studies. I consider how queer cultural studies as a way of knowing and understanding is able to contribute to a critical practice of adult education. I take up how this discourse provides ideas to inform transformative pedagogy in the face of a critical challenge to andragogy. I then specifically focus on political and cultural ideas from queer cultural studies that can be used to infuse education for citizenship.

SEEING, REMEMBERING, RESISTING, TRANSFORMING: UNDERSTANDING THE PROJECT OF QUEER CULTURAL STUDIES

Culture, in any of its many formations, is complex. It is woven from dispositional, relational, and contextual threads provided by the people who make it. Rosaldo (1989/1993, 20, 26) frames culture as a "porous array of intersections where distinct processes crisscross from within and beyond its borders. . . . Culture encompasses the everyday and the esoteric, the mundane and the elevated, the ridiculous and the sublime." To study culture, then, is to work from multiple perspectives and on multiple levels in a seemingly boundless space. Queer culture is one such space and the object of study and reflection in this chapter. Queer cultural studies, as a discourse attempting to make meaning and sense of the diversity of forms of queer being and acting, draws on themes, ideas, issues, and language that are historically produced and loosely brought together within permeable and unfixed queer cultural borders. It is an engagement with the many textures that shape hetero-sexist culture and the queer counterculture that variously contests and resists it.

Queer cultural studies problematizes cultural formations and takes up how resilient queer persons might resist oppression and transform their lives. Its project is to investigate (indeed, interrogate) and transform power relations and cultural conditions contributing to the social misery of those inhabiting the spectral community of queer Others. Queer cultural studies is embodied and embedded in a culture of communicative learning and expression concerned with being, expectation, self-preservation, resistance, becoming, and belonging. From this perspective, it is about how w/e and others perform in different cultural spaces. It is about transgressing cultural spaces; that is, it is about exposing and contesting cultural practices that dismiss or defile our identity in the effort to deny us agency. Moreover, it is about transforming practice to affirm queer integrity within a politics of hope and possibility.

The Meaning and Politics of Queer Cultural Identity-Difference

For me, cultural difference constitutes much of the sum that is cultural identity. Thus, I use the term "queer cultural identity-difference" in my work. It signifies a complex and fluid formation. In making sense of it, queer persons affirm "their own histories through the use of a language, a set of social relations, and body of knowledge that critically reconstructs and dignifies the cultural experiences that make up the tissue, texture, and history of their daily lives" (Giroux 1983, 37). In coming to terms with queer cultural identity-difference, queer persons challenge a hetero-sexist cultural politics that dishonors queer being and acting by allowing the unfreedoms and inequities that maintain the status quo. From this perspective, its politics are about courage, change, visibility, transformation, and the struggle for equity and mobility within and outside queer cultural borders. They are also about integrity, which Fromm (1968, 84) tells us "simply means a willingness not to violate one's identity in the many ways in which such violation is possible."

The politics of queer cultural identity-difference are kindled by how w/e see, remember, engage, and resist those who would keep queerness invisible. These politics oppose dominant cultural politics that have historically acted as points of power and privilege opposing the constitution of queer cultural identity-difference. This opposition is grounded in hetero-sexism, which Hill (1995) describes as the repressive social system of obligatory heterosexuality. Hill details that hetero-sexism is enshrined in the language, deliberations, and symbols of the dominant culture in matter-of-fact ways that insidiously neglect, omit, distort, and eradicate queer persons. He describes how hetero-sexism is taken up in hetero-centric discourse that envelopes gender identity, cultural behavior, social relationships, and issues of sexuality. This discourse embodies language, perceptions, meanings, assumptions, policies, beliefs, and values that discard queer Others and assault our integrity by dismissing queer identity, needs, desires, relationships, and values. Queer persons respond by producing what Hill calls "fugitive" knowledge. This oppositional knowledge of the queer counter-culture and community informs queer discourse and resistances in education and other social spaces. It infuses the struggle to live what Hill (1995, 153) calls "unambiguous, unapologetic lives."

A Status Report on the U.S. Queer Cultural Project

While the struggle is not over, queer persons in the United States continue to make progress, through their cultural and political work, toward enjoying the rights and privileges of full citizenship. Alan S. Yang's (1998) empirical research of public opinion on moves toward equality by lesbian and gay Americans indicates this. His results are summarized in a report[4] (*From Wrongs to RIGHTS*) released by the Policy Institute of the National Gay and Lesbian Task Force. They infer that the majority of Americans not only tolerate but also support lesbian and gay civil rights. The institute's director, Urvashi Vaid, believes this indicates that the post-Stonewall[5] strategies of coming out, public education, steady lobbying, direct action, and campaigns for legal equality have helped to shift public opinion. Significantly, Yang's results expose a myth that those on the political and religious right have traditionally taken for granted. This myth has suggested that "mainstream" U.S. culture and society oppose queer persons and their civil rights with respect to living, working, and associating in alternative constructions of family.

Yang's research, examining public opinion from the late 1970s to the present, indicates a real emerging social consensus supporting queer civil rights. It infers that the U.S. queer cultural project to achieve equity for queer citizens is increasingly successful. It counters myth with evidence that attests to progress in endeavors to achieve equal rights in employment, housing, military service, and access to social benefits and inheritance rights. It also indicates slowly growing support for equal protection of same-sex relationships and queer family formations. While these trends are encouraging, it is important to note that Yang's research also reveals a disturbing paradox: Clear support for particular and tangible kinds of queer civil equalities coexists with continuing disapproval of queer persons on moral grounds. This suggests that equality from a legal perspective does not guarantee cultural or political acceptance and social civility. Progress in the courts does not necessarily domino into progress in larger cultural and political arenas. In fact, forward moves by the legal system are often countered with backward moves by rightist elements in culture and politics. Thus, crucial work remains to be done. The contemporary melding of the moral and the political has meant that certain key civil rights related to living a full life are still not rights accorded to queer citizens. For example, civil rights with respect to same-sex marriage (as a symbolic protection of queer partners) remain a contested matter. Same-sex marriages are considered by many to be immoral and an affront to the "hetero-sacred" traditional family. Adoption by same-sex couples is also met with disdain. Furthermore, queer citizens have to be guarded in occupations where public opinion, shaped by hetero-sexist perceptions and beliefs, continues to link hetero-normative morality to the ability to perform jobs. Many queer teachers, doctors, and clergy still hide in order to work in public spaces. While this cultural state of affairs exists, the sorry consequence is that queer persons truly are not full citizens.

Throughout his research, Yang indicates the significant influence of political ideology in the refusal of civil rights for queer citizens. While liberals and moderates have grown more supportive of queer civil rights over time, conservatives have remained opposed. This is reflected in the antigay stance of socially conservative Republican leaders and party factions associated with the religious right's infiltration of the GOP. For more than a decade, rightist politico-religious groups have visibly penetrated the Republican Party to fight their moral battles on political ground. They continue to attack queer persons and queer culture as they uphold sexist and hetero-sexist traditions. Waving the banner of "tradition," they fuse the political and the moral into a politics of exclusion. These politics of fear are bent on thwarting queer persons as they struggle for social and cultural visibility. They feed a culture of resentment and violence that continues to see queer persons as pathological, and queer cultural identity-difference as deviant.

This tendency to meld the moral with the political in U.S. politics is historically constructed. The trend has taken on a vexing significance at least since the 1950s, when a new cultural alloy melding politics and morality reconfigured the cultural landscape in the United States (Bell 1960). Reflecting on this cultural phenomenon, Daniel Bell remarked that the political temper in the McCarthy era was altered by the large-scale infusion of moral issues into political debate.

He concluded that McCarthy was the catalyst in changing the historical U.S. predilection for compromise in politics and extremism in morality. In a period of frantic fear of Otherness, the moral became the political. The contemporary politico-religious ploy to beatify traditional social and cultural values is a recasting of this cultural alloy. It reminds us that the struggle for queer civil rights takes place in the intersection of culture, politics, and history.

QUEER CULTURAL STUDIES AND ITS VALUE TO ADULT EDUCATION

Using queer cultural studies to transgress adult educational space is an act that places educator work in the risky and political realm of work for cultural change. In a broad sense, this work is concerned with education for citizenship that replaces the prejudicial melting-pot paradigm with transformative thinking and action centered on equity for different citizens across relations of power. It is attentive to human diversity and integrity issues and to possibilities for using border-crossing education to build cultural democracy. In other words, this work situates a critical practice of adult education within an ecology of learning that is sensitive to responsible individualism, honored Otherness, and the politics of building democratic communities of difference in living, learning, and work spaces.

Teaching Queer Cultural Studies to Transgress Adult Educational Space—Possibilities and Risks

Of course, an ecology of learning, especially one that speaks to the civil rights of queer persons as learners, workers, and citizens, is not easily embraced. As Browning (1993/1994, 9) argues, queer persons are "the most 'other' of all 'others,' historically excluded as unnatural even by *other* [his italics] excluded peoples." Thus, queer educators and learners, working in the intersection of queer cultural studies and adult education, should not proceed without considering the consequences. W/e must always be mindful of the risks and repercussions of exposing our queer selves and how w/e act in the everyday. W/e can be violated in many ways in classrooms and other institutional spaces just as easily as w/e can be violated walking down main streets in our hometowns. There are many risks associated with border-crossing education. They are connected to dangerous knowledge, target groups, communication, dialogue, and the learning environment. It is not for the faint of heart to talk a queer talk and walk a queer walk. It takes courage, strength, and resilience to be border-crossers who move our queerness beyond rightist pathologizing as w/e continue the struggle to be full citizens.

Informing a Critical Practice of Adult Education

Collins (1991, 120) believes that a critical practice of adult education is attentive to issues of freedom and justice when it seeks to work directly with popular constituencies, and when it creates occasions for developing and engaging alternative democratic discourses. He concludes, "Ultimately, a vocation of adult education seeks to realize, as critical practice, a just state of affairs where education is determined through the practical interests of free men and women." A critical approach to adult education, informed by ways of knowing from queer cultural studies, helps to situate adult education as a vocation. An engagement with queer cultural studies augments ongoing feminist and multicultural initiatives to transgress adult educational space.[6] It provides further opportunity for the field to investigate its own social and cultural boundaries and the extent to which they may be oppressive. It becomes a way to theorize and problematize the social and cultural formation of the field in order to recast adult educational space as a truly democratic border zone where equity issues are kept front and center. For example, one way that adult educators can invigorate modern practice as an inclusionary cultural practice is by critical analysis of the stories[7] of resilient queer persons who trespass upon hetero-sexist terrain in their desire to alter its sociocultural landscape.

Hill (1996) investigates ways that queer persons historically have been border-crossers, transgressing oppressive boundaries socially and culturally fixed by tradition into accepted and acceptable designs. He locates fugitive knowledge, described above as knowledge produced outside the domain of dominant discourse, as the keystone for adult transgression. For Hill, fugitive knowledge is crucial to building learning communities where we come to terms with what is right, fair, moral, legitimate, desirable, and valuable. Fugitive knowledge production involves indigenous interpretations whereby what it means to be queer is determined by the subjects themselves. It also involves unlearning hegemonic knowledge that defines the acceptable and accepted in hetero-normative terms only. This unlearning in the name of inclusion is crucial to transform understandings of culture and citizenship in education and the broader culture.

MEETING THE CRITICAL CHALLENGE TO KNOWLESIAN ANDRAGOGY

Andragogy, defined by Malcolm Knowles (1970) as a theory of how adults learn, ascended to prominence in mainstream U.S. adult education after the publication of his seminal text, *The Modern Practice of Adult Education: Pedagogy versus Andragogy*.[8] In contemporary adult educational culture, fugitive knowledge from queer cultural space can inform new pedagogical possibilities as a response to a critical challenge to Knowlesian andragogy. Critical deliberations over the meaning and value of Knowlesian andragogy, which have taken place in earnest since the 1980s, have effectively served to dismantle this notion as a theory of how adults learn (Grace 1996). Indeed, andragogy continues to lose its punch in the 1990s, as emphases on human and cultural diversity and inclusion education expose Knowles' idea as one caught up in a politics of exclusion. Andragogy has tended to contract self-directed learning to concerns with the individual and technical, sidelining concerns with the social and cultural. Knowles' conceptually muddled understanding of andragogy situates adult learning as a depoliticized and decontextualized process. In his work, Knowles reduced adult learning to matters of technique and self-direction. He appeared more concerned with individualistic learning and survival, with maintenance and conformity, than with resistance and transformation in social and cultural spaces. He failed to see adult learning spaces as sites to build social vision or resist the status quo in the way that Lindeman (1926/1961) had in *The Meaning of Adult Education*. He also failed to focus on learning in community as a social engagement where history, culture, and politics matter in processes of making meaning and planning action as reflective, informed activities.

The legacy of Knowles' limited development of andragogy is a modern practice that has forgotten many citizens still hanging onto the lower rungs of the U.S. social ladder.[9] Indeed, in turning to andragogy, mainstream adult education has been complicit in maintaining a dominant social hierarchy designed to fix social positions in oppressive ways that benefit those perched on the rungs above. In this light, how might a turn to queer cultural studies inform transformative pedagogy that challenges normative field discourse? Moreover, how might this in turn expand possibilities for change in adult learning culture and the broader culture and society? Answers to these questions begin with a recognition that queer cultural studies offers ways of knowing and understanding that animate possibilities for communication and sociocultural inclusion. More than four decades ago, John Walker Powell (1956, 232, 234) spoke to the connection between communicative learning and inclusion in *Learning Comes of Age*. Powell believed that communication starts with and is shaped by the people in our lives, our "circles of intimate response." He located communication as the absolute requisite for democratic culture and society. By this he meant revealing particular knowledges, purposes, beliefs, dispositions, and actions, and problematizing the ways they affect citizenship and possibilities for building cultural democracy. For Powell, anything that worked against communication— barriers like lying, prejudice, ignorance, anger, fear, and partiality—subverted culture and society and opposed education. Hetero-sexist discourse provides an example of this subversion and opposition. Barriers to communication shape this discourse in malevolent ways that deny or demean queer being and action in relation to life, learning, and work issues. Powell called these barriers " 'faults' across the terrain of our society." Adult education can turn to queer cultural studies to explore this terrain and the barriers that attempt to make it uninhabitable for queer citizens. The knowledge gained can help the field to live out its responsibility to contribute to cultural democracy by expanding its circle of intimate response and creating inclusive learning spaces where adult learners may "know accurately, live joyously, think freely, [and] act thoughtfully."

QUEER CULTURAL STUDIES INFORMS EDUCATION FOR CITIZENSHIP

Usher, Bryant, and Johnston (1997) speak to the fact that a growing recognition and affirmation of cultural diversity accents the need to question further identity, difference, and pluralism as cultural dimensions of citizenship. In making a case for exploring linkages between adult education and cultural studies, they see this questioning as a key factor helping to recast education for citizenship in today's learning milieu. Queer cultural studies can add important insights to this reformulation. It brings new knowledges to adult education as the voices of the spectral community of queer Others speak to remaining civil rights issues, some of which are noted above in the summary of Yang's research. It offers perspectives important to the creation of a discursive space, enabling dialogue to redescribe citizenship in terms of contemporary understandings of culture and the dimensions of cultural democracy. This dialogue of difference is needed so adult education can grow as a field truly recognizing, respecting, and fostering Otherness.

To date, however, mainstream adult education has essentially mirrored the dominant culture and done little to assist the emancipation of queer persons. Modern practice, especially in its professionalized form, has been distant from the struggle of queer persons to secure the rights and privileges of full citizenship accorded the majority of persons whose sexual orientation is unquestioned. In fact, as Hill's (1995, 153) research indicates, "mainstream adult education has been the guardian and caretaker of heterocentric discourse, continuing the processes of disenfranchisement that begin in preparatory schooling." In fulfilling this role, modern practice reduces possibilities for social and cultural education. When queer persons are treated as censurable objects, w/e are stifled in our attempts to grow individually and socially as visible and integral subjects. These politics of disenfranchisement work to deny us individual expressive spaces and they exclude us from participation in debate and decision making in education and society. Usher, Bryant, and Johnston (1997, 30), speaking to the relationship between education and citizenship, argue that limits are placed on participation and visibility in mainstream educational space. They conclude, "Any educational endeavour implies a certain type of citizen and a certain type of citizenship through the curriculum it constructs and the values it espouses."

Queer persons know this. W/e are often not represented in real or meaningful ways in curricula and instruction in exclusionary mainstream learning circles. Moreover, our attempts to be vocal and visible in various educational spaces have been misinterpreted by some, notoriously those on the political and religious right, as threats to the maintenance of these spaces. This hetero-sexist and homophobic response is an attack aimed at outlawing any queer presence in education. Critical exploration of these exclusionary tactics is instructive to adult educators who wish to question and problematize the social and cultural purposes of modern practice. It is also informative to new forms of community adult education based on the desire to build communities of difference. Usher, Bryant, and Johnston advance community adult education as a way to address structure and agency in an encompassing approach to education for citizenship. As they see it, community adult education places value on local knowledge and experience. It emphasizes participatory education as it explores dialectical private/public and personal/political relationships. With its emphases on fugitive knowledge production, contexts, identity, inclusivity, agency, and cultural democracy, queer cultural studies is a rich source of local knowledge and experience and a rich resource for dynamic and inclusive forms of community adult education. It contributes to critical probing of the meaning and dimensions of citizenship. It helps adult education to develop further as a sociocultural enterprise giving primacy to human diversity and equity issues.

Queer cultural studies also provides adult education with ideas and examples to shape adult learning spaces as sites to begin building cultural democracy. Fraser (1994) recounts that members of subordinated social groups, including queer persons, have formed what she calls "subaltern counterpublics" time and again. By this she means that they have formed parallel discursive arenas beyond mainstream culture where they communicate desires, needs, objectives, and strategies in expressive, productive spaces. These countercultural spaces are, in a real sense, alternative learning spaces where the disenfranchised produce and distribute counterdiscourses (fugitive knowledge) that inform the construction of identities synchronized with living oppositional lives. This countercultural learning serves two key purposes instructive to transformative adult education. First, this cultural work builds queer community and a sense of belonging within a community of difference. It helps queer persons to know their circle of intimate response. This circle is a site for communicative learning and a power base. Second, this secure space can be used as a clearinghouse for fugitive knowledge; that is, it can provide a site for knowledge exchange and distribution involving the wider public. This sharing of knowledge and understanding is crucial in nurturing a politics of visibility and possibility. As Yang's research suggests, simply knowing a queer person is associated with increased tolerance toward queer citizens and support for their civil rights. Thus, it is important that queer persons continue to inform and educate the public. W/e must continue to speak to and with other citizens about queer civil rights as part of a communicative learning process where every adult learns. The success of this process is evidenced in the United States, for example, by the special case of gays in the military. While queer citizens are still banned from military service, President Clinton's "Don't Ask, Don't Tell, Don't Pursue" policy in 1993 has led to controversial debate and communicative learning about lesbian and gay issues. Yang's (1998, 5) research indicates that it has actually led to greater support for lesbians and gay men to serve in the military. He concludes:

[Voices from] a vital and vocal lesbian and gay community . . . have added more information and new perceptions to old debates and mythologies. . . . [They have] moved the discussion of homosexuality from the realm of "not acceptable for polite society" into a public, contentious discourse around the role of lesbians and gays in contemporary American society.

Of course, in doing this cultural work w/e must never forget that education for transformation is a complex and dangerous undertaking. Dominant cultural violence is always a threat. Thus, engaging in a politics of visibility and possibility also means counteracting a politics of negation that attempts to create more barriers to full citizenship as queer persons become more culturally visible. Rightist cultural terrorists employ a politics of negation to perpetuate myths and stereotypes that assault queer integrity. Browning (1993/1994, x) gauges the results of increased cultural visibility in the United States:

The gay bashers, the military, even the epidemic [AIDS/HIV]: these . . . are the forces that have worked to codify and strengthen the social phenomenon that has come to be called American gay culture. Tragedy and hostility are, for the short term at least, the ramparts of cultural identity. They intensify our sense of solidarity and inform the quality of memory.

CONCLUSION

In this chapter, I argue that mainstream adult education mimics the dominant culture in its commitment to the hetero-normative status quo. Browning (1993/1994, 18) purports that in U.S. culture, "gay people are admitted only to the degree that they sequester their difference and conduct a sexless public life that offers no model, no quarter, no inspiration to others—child or adult—who would explore all that is queer about themselves." As a complicitous social and cultural formation, mainstream adult education abides by these parameters to participation. However, as Collins (1991) argues, we can do without a modern practice that fails to question hegemonic arrangements; that is, we can do without a practice of adult education that fails to question dominant ways of knowing, seeing, thinking, and acting. He believes that, as vocation, adult education works with human and cultural diversity, and makes space for alternative democratic visions and discourses. Since various Others continue to struggle for space in its mainstream practice, I believe that the field has yet to truly live out adult education as vocation. However, I also believe that the field is making strides in that direction, fortified by contributions from queer cultural studies, along with feminist, multicultural, and other counterdiscourses. Each way of knowing contributes to an inclusive and transformative practice of adult education.

In conclusion, by speaking to issues of citizenship and cultural democracy, queer cultural studies provides a challenge to adult education as a mainstream cultural practice. That challenge is to invigorate contemporary practice by building communities of identity-difference committed to creating a society where *all* disenfranchised persons experience freedom, justice, and the rights and privileges of full citizenship. This redescription of mainstream practice as inclusion education revitalizes adult education as social and cultural education. Powell (1956, 235) suggests, "The *principles* [his italics] by which adult education selects its goals and its methods are derived by direct implication from the function which it undertakes to perform for society. Its *energy* derives from the love of people, its courage from faith in them." Today this energy must come from the love of *all* people, every Other person. It is this energy that will continue to shape adult education as vocation.

NOTES

1. W/e, thus represented in this chapter, is a w/e that recognizes queer diversity as it informs and places value on the notion of at least a loosely configured unity in queer identity-difference. This representation recognizes that lesbians, gay men, bisexuals, transgendered persons, and transsexuals are not located in some cohesive community that blurs identity-difference within some generic understanding of queerness. Instead, "w/e" situates diverse queer persons within a spectral community of queer Others.

2. To understand further ideas from critical postmodern theory and language presented in this piece, it is worthwhile to explore the work of theorists including Ben Agger (1992), Henry A. Giroux (1992), Peter McLaren (1998), and William G. Tierney (1993). For a description of critical postmodernism that is more specific to adult education, see my essay, Grace (1997a). In it I elucidate what critical postmodernism is, building on Giroux's typology. Set out in *Border Crossings*, it incorporates (a) modernism's emphases on ethical, historical, and political contexts; (b) postmodernism/poststructuralism's concerns with exploring identity and difference, contesting totalizing forms of knowledge, and creating new languages; (c) feminism's theorizing of the notion of partial closure and its aim to ground vision in a political project; and (d) postcolonialism's foci on privilege and exclusion.

3. For me, to "texture" knowledges and understandings is to develop descriptions, analyses, and interpretations that are attentive to disposition (attitudes and values), contexts (social, economic, historical, political, and cultural) and relations of power (race, ethnicity, gender, class, age, ability, and sexual orientation). This texturing is crucial to the investigation of social and cultural formations and the problems and projects arising from them. It involves a turn to theory and an exploration of the nature and meaning of language.

4. Alan Yang's empirical analysis of public opinion toward queer equity is a project of the New York–based Policy Institute of the National Gay and Lesbian Task Force (NGLTF). The task force describes itself as "a think tank dedicated to research, policy analysis and strategic projects to advance greater understanding and the equality of lesbian, gay, bisexual and transgender people" (Yang 1998, 29). Yang's analysis of publicly available data is substantial and revealing because he draws only on public-opinion research (conducted between 1973 and 1997) that used systematic and representative samples of the American adult population as a whole; that is, empirical research where the

universe was all American adults. He is clear that his research only measures trends in public opinion toward lesbians and gay men because polling data on other members of the larger queer community, including bisexual and transgendered persons, do not exist in a way that would enable them to be indicative of trends.

5. D'Emilio (1992) relates that the gay liberation movement was given impetus in June 1969, when police in New York City raided a gay bar, the Stonewall Inn. The police raid provoked three nights of rioting by enraged "homosexuals" no longer willing to succumb to forms of oppression that denied fundamental rights like freedom of assembly. After this decisive moment in gay history, radicalized queer persons formed the Gay Liberation Front. D'Emilio relates that the impulse quickly spread from New York throughout the United States and much of the industrialized West. Disenfranchised queer persons were choosing visible means to confront hegemonic structures that denied them basic human rights.

6. The work of Ross-Gordon, Martin, and Briscoe (1990), Taylor and Marienau (1995), and Tisdell (1995) exemplify important feminist and multicultural initiatives to transgress adult educational space.

7. For an overview of aspects of this work, see the proceedings of the symposium conducted by Edwards, Henson, Henson, Hill, and Taylor at the 1998 Adult Education Research Conference.

8. Collins (1998) relates that andragogy was first mentioned by Knowles in an article published in the April 1968 edition of *Adult Leadership*. Andragogy represented more than a name for how adults learn. It was a term and an approach tied to new directions in adult education that emerged in the post–World War II period. These developments were caught up in professionalization moves and the field's desire to be a recognized discipline separate from education for children.

9. While U.S. modern practice is the focus of this chapter, a similar story can be told about the emergence of modern practice in Canada, especially since World War II. My historical research (Grace 1997b) indicates that the Canadian field has also been deeply affected by what I call the "Ization Syndrome": individualization, institutionalization, professionalization, and techno-scientization. I contend that decontextualized Knowlesian andragogy represents the most pervasive expression of the effects of this syndrome. This is signified by shifts away from the social and cultural and toward the individual and instrumental in modern practice above and below the 49th parallel.

REFERENCES

Agger, Ben. (1992). *Cultural Studies as Critical Theory*. London: The Falmer Press.

Bell, Daniel. (1960). *The End of Ideology*. Glencoe, IL: The Free Press.

Browning, Frank. (1993/1994). *The Culture of Desire*. New York: Vintage Books.

Collins, Michael. (1991). *Adult Education as Vocation: A Critical Role for the Adult Educator*. New York: Routledge.

Collins, Michael. (1998). "From Andragogy to Lifelong Education." In S. M. Scott, B. Spencer, and A. Thomas (eds.), *Learning for Life: Canadian Readings in Adult Education*, 46–58. Toronto: Thompson Educational Publishing.

D'Emilio, John. (1992). *Making Trouble*. New York: Routledge.

Edwards, Kathleen, Grace, A. P., Henson, B., Henson, W., Hill, R. J., and Taylor, E. (1998). "Tabooed Terrain: Reflections on Conducting Adult Education Research in Lesbian/Gay/Queer Arenas" (Symposium). *Proceedings of the 39th Annual Adult Education Research Conference.* University of the Incarnate Word and Texas A&M, San Antonio, TX, 317–324.

Fraser, Nancy. (1994). "Rethinking the Public Sphere: A Contribution to the Critique of Actually Existing Democracy." In H. A. Giroux and P. McLaren (eds.), *Between Borders: Pedagogy and the Politics of Cultural Studies,* 74–98. New York: Routledge.

Freire, Paulo. (1998). *Teachers as Cultural Workers: Letters to Those Who Dare Teach* (D. Macedo, D. Koike, and A. Oliveira, trans.). Boulder, CO: Westview Press.

Fromm, Erich. (1968). *The Revolution of Hope.* New York: Harper and Row.

Giroux, Henry A. (1983). *Theory and Resistance in Education.* South Hadley, MA: Bergin & Garvey.

Giroux, Henry A. (1992). *Border Crossings.* New York: Routledge.

Grace, André P. (1996). "Striking a Critical Pose: Andragogy—Missing Links, Missing Values." *International Journal of Lifelong Education* 15(5), 382–392.

Grace, André P. (1997a). "Where Critical Postmodern Theory Meets Practice: Working in the Intersection of Instrumental, Social, and Cultural Education." *Studies in Continuing Education* 19(1), 51–70.

Grace, André P. (1997b). "Identity Quest: The Emergence of North American Adult Education (1945–70)." Unpublished Doctoral Dissertation, Dalhousie University, Halifax, Nova Scotia.

Hill, Robert J. (1995). "Gay Discourse in Adult Education: A Critical Review." *Adult Education Quarterly* 45(3), 142–158.

Hill, Robert J. (1996). "Learning to Transgress: A Sociohistorical Conspectus of the American Gay Lifeworld as a Site of Struggle and Resistance." *Studies in the Education of Adults* 28(2), 253–279.

Knowles, Malcolm S. (1970). *The Modern Practice of Adult Education: Andragogy versus Pedagogy.* New York: Association Press.

Lindeman, Eduard C. (1926/1961). *The Meaning of Adult Education.* Montreal: Harvest House.

McLaren, Peter. (1998). *Life in Schools: An Introduction to Critical Pedagogy in the Foundations of Education,* 3rd ed. New York: Longman.

Powell, John W. (1956). *Learning Comes of Age.* New York: Association Press.

Rosaldo, Renato. (1989/1993). *Culture and Truth.* Boston: Beacon Press.

Ross-Gordon, Jovita M., Martin, L. G., and Briscoe, D. Buck (eds.). (1990). *Serving Culturally Diverse Populations.* San Francisco: Jossey-Bass.

Taylor, Kathleen, and Marienau, C. (eds.). (1995). *Learning Environments for Women's Adult Development: Bridges toward Change.* San Francisco: Jossey-Bass.

Tierney, William G. (1993). *Building Communities of Difference.* Toronto: OISE Press.

Tisdell, Elizabeth J. (1995). *Creating Inclusive Adult Learning Environments: Insights from Multicultural Education and Feminist Pedagogy.* Information Series No. 361. Washington, DC: ERIC Clearinghouse.

Usher, Robin, Bryant, I., and Johnston, R. (1997). *Adult Education and the Postmodern Challenge: Learning Beyond the Limits.* New York: Routledge.

Yang, Alan. S. (1998). *From Wrongs to RIGHTS: Public Opinion on Gay and Lesbian Americans Moves toward Equality.* Washington, DC: NGLTF (National Gay and Lesbian Task Force) Policy Institute.

Chapter 19

Feminist Perspectives on Adult Education: Constantly Shifting Identities in Constantly Changing Times

Elizabeth J. Tisdell

For most of my adult life, I have defined myself as a feminist. Perhaps it was my ten years (from 1979 to 1989) of working for the Catholic Church as a campus minister that helped me define myself as such. The obvious patriarchy of the Catholic Church made me think about sexism. But I know my journey toward this self-definition was a growing one, and that in my early young-adult years, I believed in women's equality, but I didn't see myself as a "feminist." The image I had of feminists then was the one portrayed by the media—man-hating angry militants, who in their own unhappiness and anger, set fire to their underwear. But sometime in my later twenties, I began to understand that feminism is really about creating a society that not only gives women access to the pie that men have always had access to, but also about transforming societal structures. It is about transforming those structures that have created inequitable gender arrangements (and race and class arrangements) which have been counterproductive to both women and men. It is about examining how gender socialization messages affect us on the psychological level in conscious but mostly unconscious ways, and examining how this is manifested on a structural level and then taking action for change. Over the years, I had come to understand that feminism was far more complex and empowering than the media's portrayal of it—that feminism was about social action and social justice for women. Ideally, feminism was for all women, not just White, middle-class, heterosexual women. So I returned to school to pursue a doctoral degree in fall 1989, in order to study the intersections of feminism and adult education in a pluralistic and multicultural society.

In many ways, my personal odyssey and shifting identity around feminist and multicultural issues parallels the relationship the field of adult education also has with these issues. This is due, in part, to the fact that the field, and my own consciousness, are very much affected by what is going on in society, in academia, and in adult education practice with regard to these issues. As we examine how we are affected by our interactions with others in regard to our gender, race, and class consciousness (our positionality), and examine how our positionality shapes our thinking and acting in the world, our way of seeing ourselves as individuals—our individual identity—begins to shift. The way this happens on an individual level is parallel to the way it also happens in a field of study. As the demographics of American society continue to change, people of color become the New Majority (as in California). Along with this, the presence of women and people of color both in the workforce and in educational institutions becomes more apparent; adult education as a field of study needs to be able to respond to these changes, and to (in part) continually shift its identity. As Heaney (1996) notes, it has certainly done this many times throughout the course of history in this country, and surely these identity shifts in response to changing times will continue. How has this happened in the past 10 years in regard to feminist perspectives on adult education, and what do such perspectives offer the world in educating and working for social change on behalf of women and people of color?

In an attempt to get at answers to these questions, the purpose of this chapter is twofold. First, I will begin by briefly examining feminist perspectives on adult education largely by explaining my own journey with the feminist adult education literature, from the time I returned to school for doctoral study in 1989 until now. I believe in the power of personal narrative in teaching and learning. I also believe that having an understanding of how positionality affects learning, behavior, and action for social change is important for emancipatory adult education as a field of practice. Thus, in the second part, as an example of this on a personal level, I will examine my understanding of how aspects of my own positionality have affected my work as an adult educator and as a learner, and how I believe understanding and claiming positionality is beginning to affect the field. I will discuss the possibilities and limitations of what dealing with feminist and multicultural perspectives around issues of positionality have in contributing to social change, by using examples from my own teaching in adult higher education classrooms.

FEMINISM AND ADULT EDUCATION: THE LAST 10 YEARS

In the fall of 1989 the literature connecting feminism and adult education was scant indeed. It was three years after the publication of *Women's Ways of Knowing* by Belenky, Clinchy, Goldberger, and Tarule (1986), and there was one book chapter, by Betty Hayes (1989), entitled "Insights from Women's Experience for Teaching and Learning." In this chapter she made the connections between Belenky et al.'s work and the adult education literature explicit. In a conference paper, Jane Hugo (1989) begged the question of why feminist perspectives on the field were so absent. The following year, in a book chapter, Mechthild Hart (1990) explicitly discussed women's consciousness-raising groups as adult education. Other than these three publications in the U.S. adult education literature, in 1990, I could not find any literature specifically connecting feminist perspectives to adult education.

This was surprising. I was attracted to the field of adult education because I saw it as dealing specifically with social justice concerns. I knew the work of Paulo Freire from my own work in ministry and familiarity with the liberation theology movement in Latin America, and with Freire's *Pedagogy of the Oppressed* (1971). To me the connection between adult education and social justice for women was as obvious as that of adult education and social justice around class issues, as in Freire's work. Further, as a doctoral student in the late 1980s and early 1990s, I heard much discussion about the role of critical theory and critical pedagogy (almost exclusively by male authors) in contributing to an emancipatory adult learning theory. Many of these discussions were focused on whether or not Mezirow's theory of perspective transformation was also a theory of social transformation (Collard and Law 1989). The relationship of the individual to social structures, and issues of power relations between dominant and oppressed groups were key to these discussions, although the focus was still primarily on class. Serious consideration of power relations based on gender *as a social structure* was generally missing, but began to change soon thereafter.

The next few years yielded a number of new publications that dealt with feminist perspectives on adult education and/or adult education as it relates to women's learning. As I have discussed elsewhere (Tisdell 1993, 1998), there are three primary strands. The first two, evident in the early to mid-1990s, dealt with women's learning from an individual psychological perspective, and with structural power relations based on gender and its intersections with race, class, affectional/sexual orientation, and ableness. A third strand based on feminist poststructuralism, developed a bit later (and is continuing to develop) in the 1990s, and is an outgrowth of the two earlier strands.

Psychological Feminist Influences

Adult education discussions that dealt with women's learning from an individual psychological perspective were heavily influenced by Belenky et al.'s *Women's Ways of Knowing*. They tended to focus on women's individual empowerment and on helping women see themselves as constructors of knowledge, by emphasizing the importance of relationship and the significance of affectivity and shared story in learning. By 1991 or 1992, the book was used as a text in many adult education programs. From a personal perspective, it was from reading and experiencing this book that I began to see myself as a constructor of knowledge—as someone who could potentially contribute to the knowledge base in the field. Nearly everyone in adult education who was familiar with this text was also affected by it, and the overall influence of this publication in thinking about women's learning was enormous. In fact, since about 1991, virtually all adult education writers who discuss any aspect of women's learning and/or feminist approaches to adult education cite this text (Caffarella 1992; Caffarella and Olson 1993; Collard and Stalker 1991; Taylor and Marineau 1995). As much as this book contributed to my own thinking and individual "empowerment" as a writer, it has its limitations. Given that it focuses more on psychological "empowerment" with little consideration to the social structures of race, class, affectional/sexual orientation, and their intersections with gender, the focus inadvertently tends to be on the learning needs of White, middle-class women.

Structural Feminist Influences

There is virtually no connection between discussions of women's learning that is based on Belenky et al.'s (1986) work and the critical theory/critical pedagogy work that is based in the thinking of Paulo Freire. But there began to be a body of feminist work in adult education that examined gender and its intersecting structural systems of privilege and oppression such as race, class, and affectional/sexual orientation. By the early to mid-1990s, some new feminist scholars in the field (myself included) began to be more heavily influenced, not only by Freire and other writers in critical pedagogy, but the writings of women of color, such as Audre Lorde (1984), bell hooks (1989, 1994), Patricia Hill Collins (1991), and Gloria Anzaldua (1990). There were also more feminists and people of color in the adult education professoriate, who began to write more about structural issues of race, and class, as well as gender. This began to cause a bit of a shift in the field with regard to attention being given to the intersecting structural systems of privilege and oppression.

It is important to note that due to the unconscious emphasis on White women in much of the feminist movement and literature (including Belenky et al. 1986), some women of color are hesitant to be associated with feminism per se. In fact, some Black women writers specifically use the term "womanism," coined by Alice Walker, where Black women are the central subjects, rather than the so-called generic "women" of some versions of feminist thought, who are implicitly White. Vanessa Sheared (1994) specifically discusses what womanism contributes to an inclusive model of instruction in adult education. Further, by the mid-1990s there were a number of adult education publications that examined gender and/or race and their intersections with other social structures (Cunningham 1992; Hart 1992; Hayes and Colin 1994; Johnson-Bailey and Cervero 1996; Tisdell 1993, 1995). There were also discussions of the necessity of creating more multicultural curricula, and a more pluralistic historical understanding of the field (Hugo 1990; Peterson 1996; Ross-Gordon 1991; Tisdell 1995), and a limited discussion of sexual orientation (Hill 1995). In addition, there is beginning to be more attention to globalization as it affects adult education, as well as more attention to the education needs of women worldwide. Walters and

Manicom (1996) made a wonderful and very practice-based contribution to the field in this regard, in the publication of their edited book *Gender in Popular Education*. The influence of such perspectives specifically within adult education is causing the field to shift, to respond to changing times. In addition, the implicit or explicit attention to race, gender, class, affectional/sexual orientation, ableness, and national origin in the wider U.S. culture—discussions of race relations, Rodney King, affirmative action, Welfare Reform, the Americans with Disabilities Act, women's reproductive rights, sexual harassment, gay pride, domestic partner benefits, immigrant rights, English-only initiatives, and so on—that are often in the news, demand that adult educators be able to respond to these issues of structural privilege and oppression.

Poststructural Feminist Influences

In being committed to emancipatory education models that challenge structural issues of power, privilege, and oppression, I have been strongly influenced by the work of those cited above. But another important, more recent influence on myself and many other adult educators are the discourses of postmodernism and poststructuralism, which emphasize the *connections between* mechanisms of structural systems of power and our identity. To be sure, the language of these discourses is fairly inaccessible to most readers; and because there is a strong emphasis on deconstruction of both language and of dichotomous categories (such as male/female, heterosexual/homosexual, Black/White), there are those who believe that these discourses are less than emancipatory. But there are feminist versions of poststructuralism that promote resistance and social change, and elsewhere I have discussed in some depth what poststructural feminist pedagogies (Tisdell 1998) offer to emancipatory adult learning theory. A brief discussion of some of the tenets of feminist poststructuralism is relevant to the remainder of this chapter.

First and foremost, feminist poststructuralism emphasizes the socially constructed nature of our identity around structural systems of power and privilege. Further, our identity is *constantly shifting*, particularly around our understanding of our "positionality"—our consciousness of our race, gender, class, and so on. In short, its emphasis is on making conscious the *connections between* one's individual (constantly shifting) identity and the social structures of race, gender, and class that inform that identity. The point here is, the more we are conscious of how structural systems of privilege and oppression inform our identity and behavior, the more we have capacity to act to change our behavior on behalf of ourselves or others, thus shifting our identity. It is perhaps easy to understand how our economic class could shift, or even how our affectional/sexual orientation might shift, and more difficult to understand how one's identity around race or gender might shift. But one's *understanding* of what it means to be White (as an example) constantly changes if one further reflects on how Whiteness (as a system of privilege) informs that identity. Some of what a poststructural feminist perspective offers to adult education is a strong emphasis on how issues of positionality—of instructors and participants, and their "constantly shifting identities" around their understanding of their positionality—affect and shape the learning environment. As I have discussed elsewhere (Tisdell 1998), these factors of positionality and shifting identity also interact with issues of authority, voice, and silence, as learners construct new knowledge and move to new action on their own behalf or that of others. But this generally doesn't happen through a strictly cognitive means. It happens because there is also a strong emotional component to the learning—something makes as angry, or sad, or happy, or inspired. In short, something touches our hearts that we relate to, and facilitates a new cognitive understanding. In my own experience as both a teacher and a learner, there is nothing more powerful in helping us to come to new insights than a shared story—better yet, a shared story that invites action. In the next section, I will discuss the power and limitations of narrative and shared story around issues of positionality to effect change in people's thinking, and its use in feminist adult education practice, that facilities a change in consciousness, and potentially a move to action.

PERSONAL NARRATIVES AND POSITIONALITY IN THE FEMINIST ADULT LEARNING ENVIRONMENT

Stories are powerful. Clearly, the field of adult education has long emphasized the importance of taking people's life experiences into account in adult learning activities. In so doing, it has advocated the use of personal stories and autobiographies (both of instructors and of learners) as one among many appropriate teaching tools to use in some adult learning situations. When is it appropriate to use it? What are its plusses and minuses? And in light of the current discussion, how does this relate to positionality and constantly shifting identity in considering its emancipatory possibility?

Stories can be used for many purposes—to help participants get to know each other, to facilitate group bonding, or perhaps to analyze one's life experience related to a particular theory of learning or human development. But for a story to have emancipatory potential, it has to raise consciousness and/or challenge structured power relations in society in some way—and have the potential to move people to action. As hooks (1994) notes, at times the use of a personal story can inadvertently serve to reinforce the power relations in society. This occurs when those people who easily share their stories or experiences—those with many forms of privilege and those who have had experience with speaking out in groups—become the ones to share all the time. It also occurs when someone makes faulty or essentialist assumptions about members of particular groups on the basis of one experience. In short, to be emancipatory, stories need to make issues of our positionality visible, and to suggest some possibility for action. To be sure, the positionality (race, gender, class, and so on) of participants in a learning environment—both instructors and students—and where they are in relationship to various aspects of their own shifting identity, are very significant to how classroom dynamics unfold. They are also significant to how participants construct knowledge, come to voice, develop their analytic skills, and deal with issues of authority. How is this manifested in relationship to the stories we tell in attempting to live differently? Perhaps some examples will make this apparent.

In 1998, when I began writing this chapter, I taught primarily master's level students at a university where the average student's age was 38. Only some of my classes were specifically about feminism, or diversity issues in adult education, but the curricula of all my classes included material about issues and by authors of a variety of gender, race, and class groups. I taught not only as a woman, but as a middle-class, White woman, with an impossible-to-categorize affectional/sexual orientation. These aspects (and others) of my own shifting identity affected what I saw, didn't see, constructed as knowledge, and so on. Like the adult learners I taught then, I was always in process with these issues, in my own intellectual pursuits, in my life experience, in my teaching, and in my own attempts to become more conscious of how those systems of privilege and oppression informed my own constantly shifting identity as I attempted to move to action.

I have benefited from a number of systems of privilege—being well educated, middle class, and White are a few of these. Specifically, I want to focus on the fact that I teach as a *White* woman. For years, I had no idea of the daily effects of White privilege (McIntosh 1988). I vividly remember the day in 1986 when an African-American woman student to whom I was quite close asked me what it meant to be White. I was a bit dumbfounded. I had no idea. I simply had never thought about it. But she could answer easily what it meant to be Black. It was then that I began to grapple with what White *privilege* can mean. I am still working on this, as privilege tends to be most invisible to those who have it. What awareness I do have has been from having relationships with people of color, from hearing their stories of negotiating being dark-skinned in a world that accords those of light skin more power and privilege. I have become especially aware of it when I have witnessed and have experienced differential treatment based on my fair skin in hotels or restaurants, when traveling with people of color. These experiences and my reflection on them continually contribute to my constantly shifting identity and understanding of what it means to be White.

There are also systems of privilege that I do not benefit from. I do not have male privilege, nor am I firmly heterosexual. I was *socialized* as heterosexual, and for 30 years I never really questioned it, for I had been in a long-term relationship with a man. Then I fell in love with a woman. It threw me for a loop! I have had two great loves in my life—very long-term relationships—one with a man, one with a woman. If I have other great loves, I'm not sure if they will be with men or women, for I fall in love with a person, not a gender. Because of our society's obsessions with binary categories, some might label me a lesbian. I am OK with this as a political category, for I have no desire to cling to heterosexual privilege. At the same time, such a label is too confining to my constantly shifting identity in regard to my affectional orientation, and doesn't account for the fact that I may in the future again have a primary partnership with a man.

In trying to teach for critical consciousness, how do these issues of "constantly shifting identity" come up in my own teaching? What is my responsibility, as an instructor who is trying to teach in an emancipatory way, in making systems of power and privilege visible, and when is the direct discussion of issues of positionality appropriate and relevant? There are no easy answers to these questions, and I can only discuss what I, as someone teaching in a specific context, have chosen to do in attempting to teach for social change. Clearly, all aspects of our positionality as instructors (and as students) affect the classroom dynamics that unfold in all classes, whether we openly discuss them or not. I teach many classes—the course content of some of them, such as "Leadership and Reform in Adult Education" or "Introduction to Research," is not specifically about issues of positionality, though there are readings in all of my classes that deal with gender, race, class, affectional/sexual orientation, and ableness related to the subject matter. Because positionality issues are not the *primary* course content, I tend not to directly discuss these aspects of my own shifting identity, although I may make a remark in passing about being White, or female, as an example to illustrate a point.

There are other classes I teach that focus more specifically on issues of positionality and on challenging systems of privilege and oppression—classes such as "Diversity and Equity in Education" or "Feminist Perspectives on Education." It is in these classes (which are usually team-taught) where my teaching partner and I directly problematize aspects of our own positionalities and shifting identities, as related to the course content. Typically, students will have had a writing assignment where they deal with some aspects of their own positionality in relationship to their cultural story or gender and education story (depending on the course) that they bring to the first class. In using aspects of our own stories as instructors around our own positionalities, we are attempting to model how our own consciousness is continually changing about these issues. I directly discuss what it means to me to be White, and to have White privilege. I also discuss my constantly shifting identity around affectional/sexual orientation issues in much the way I have discussed it here. It is never easy; I am always nervous about doing it, and wonder (as I do about writing this chapter!) if it will have bad effects, or if I will suffer a consequence. But I believe it has value for my students—not in sharing information about my so-called "personal life," but rather in examining power relations based on affectional/sexual orientation as a system of privilege, which are the themes of these courses. I also discuss my understanding of what it means to be female. In essence, in these classes, my teaching partner and I problematize our own positionalities, and how they affect our own teaching and learning.

So how does it work in those classes where we grapple with our own positionalities and constantly shifting identities? First, this is always related to the readings and the course content. We are primarily talking about the readings, and then relating it to our lives, and at times to our classroom process. One of the things that becomes evident early on in the "Diversity" class, where students need to write their cultural story, is that White folks have difficulty seeing that they have a culture. They don't see hot dogs and hamburgers, Pabst Blue Ribbon on a Saturday night, and some very specific ways of interrelating as part of culture. But this is one of the insidious ways that privilege works: when one is representative of the dominant culture, and one's culture is always represented in the media, it becomes difficult to see one's culture. This is also what makes White privilege so hard to get at—it is usually invisible to those who have it, much like water is invisible to fish. Writing the story at the beginning, having readings that address these issues, and re-addressing them in a paper at the end, relative to one's educational practice, invites students not only to think differently; it also invites action (or at least thinking about action) because relating it to one's practice *is* action.

One White woman in the feminist class speaks directly to her own thinking about dealing with positionality issues in light of the reading, and her own experience in life and in the course, and in a potential move to action. She writes:

Can I remember when I realized that I was white? My memory fails me. If I were black this memory would probably weigh heavily on my back. . . . I believe that ultimately it is the white person who needs to get rid of racism. I feel that my skin color and my gender obligates me to work for social change. (Purl 1998, 4)

In discussing the need to "act" in the class itself, another student discussed the issue of positionality in what he chose to reveal in class. He notes:

As a gay American Indian man, my positionality and identity were central. I made it that way when I decided to come out in class. My decision was based on the need to identify with and relate to the women in the class. As a gay man and a person of color, I know and understand the issues of subjugation and oppression. By bringing my perspective to this class I hoped it would be . . . useful in developing a better understanding of how the interlocking systems of oppression cut across gender, race, class and orientation lines. (Guerrero 1998, 3)

It is important in courses where issues of positionality are central to the course content, to attend to how power relations based on positionality are manifested in classroom dynamics. In these classes, as in any, those who benefit from more systems of privilege usually have an easier time speaking out; they are used to speaking, and to being heard. While we have readings about this phenomenon, it is often difficult to intervene in this while it is happening. One way of dealing with it is by establishing the "three-times guideline"—that is, a participant can only speak three times in a discussion about a given set of readings, and must wait to speak again until someone who has contributed nothing to the discussion speaks out. This is a way of preserving space for those who are more silent (and typically less privileged, often by race and class), and giving them an opportunity to speak. Not surprisingly, it is often the men in the class, and some of the more privileged women, who have to monitor themselves. Using such a guideline for class discussion has a way of making visible how systems of privilege and oppression are manifested in classrooms. This is not a magic solution, however; and even with the three-times guideline in effect, the agenda and perspectives of White students often tend to dominate the discussion, particularly if they far outnumber students of color. One Chicana student in the Feminist Perspectives class discusses her observation of how Whiteness is often manifested in dynamics. In referring to one class discussion where eating disorders came up, she writes:

As this discussion was occurring I wondered how I could insert a comment that would lead my classmates to rethink their perception that this was a problem that affected all women in some way. From the little bit that I know of eating disorders, I think it is more of an economic class issue, but again, I don't know enough about this to be sure . . . I don't know statistics . . . , but I know that many women of color (and poor White women) struggle everyday to get food on the table. (Aguilar 1998, 10)

She discusses her struggle with deciding when and when not to speak in class, particularly when Whiteness is the assumed norm, or when someone makes remarks based on stereotypic assumptions, in spite of readings that attempt to challenge these norms and assumptions. She says "sometimes as a woman of color, I get tired of having to explain, especially when I'm not sure the person is ready to hear. . . . The hardest times is when a person considers herself open and enlightened" (p. 11). Thus, while the three-times guideline might provide more space for more voices to be heard, it doesn't necessarily confront White norms in a predominantly White classroom. This is an example of one of the insidious ways White privilege works, and instructors (and students) need to be extremely proactive in attempting to raise consciousness about it in classroom dynamics, and to not assume that this will happen only through readings.

In order to facilitate emancipatory learning, it is necessary to activate more than just new cognitive understanding. Clearly, the development of cognitive thinking skills is a task of higher education that cannot be sacrificed. But emancipatory learning involves the cognitive, the affective/relational, and the behavioral, and their integration. One way to move from readings (cognitive mode), to story (affective/relational), to behavior (action mode), to synthesis (reflection and integration of these modes) is to create experiential learning activities. Through this you can begin to get at issues about positionality, and begin to incorporate and create *new* knowledge. It is not enough simply to tell a story, or conduct an experiential activity. The story or experience needs to be reflected on, unpacked, and some aspects of the positionality need to be made visible. It is important to do these around various categories of identity, so that all participants—not just members of a particular group—have to do the work of unpacking their own positionality. Given that the focus of this chapter is on feminist perspectives on adult education, I want to talk about one such experiential activity around gender positionality from my recent "Feminist Perspectives on Education" class.

Feminist Perspectives on Education: A Case

To be sure, we usually construct learning activities out of our own experience. One of the benefits of team teaching is that in planning activities, there is the teaching partner's expertise and experience to draw on. As a result of a reading assignment that dealt with educational issues for mothers in the 1990s, my teaching partner suggested we do a fish bowl. The activities required that we have the mothers in the class sit in the center of the circle and talk about their reactions to the reading and its relevance to their own lives. I never would have thought of doing such a thing—perhaps it is because I am not a mother. The fact that we would unpack the discussion and attempt to tie it back into the reading, and that participants would be expected to write about aspects of their synthesis in their final papers was a given. Indeed, this was one of the more powerful discussions in the class. The discussion of these mothers in the center of the circle made the double-edged nature of their positionality visible—as women, and as mothers. Particularly apparent were the many conflicting standards of the "good mother" that they feel judged by, standards that are not applied to their male partners. It also made issues visible not only for mothers, but also for women who are not mothers; as one young mother wrote in her final paper, "it is not okay to be a poor mother; it is not okay to be a working mother; it is not okay NOT to be a mother" (Santamaria 1998, 4). In reflecting on this in his final paper, a Native American man commented on his construction of knowledge in relationship to this experience. He notes:

This session was searing to my cognition because the vulnerability involved on the part of the mothers clearly demonstrated the cognitive dissonance this society operates under. We have all these over-glorified images, symbols and literary types of what we say motherhood is suppose to be. As a society, we promise to love, honor and cherish mother, and yet, the stories . . . were just the converse—we are shamed, saddened and made small by our hypocrisy. It would be an understatement to say that the mothers in the circle discussion was like a laser beam aimed at us and illuminating our hearts and souls. . . . I found myself thinking . . . that I wish more men could hear what I am hearing . . . to commit to changing a system. (Guerrero 1998, 6)

He goes on to discuss the ways in which the group constructed knowledge as we challenged each other to look at how our positionality affects our thinking, and to some extent our behavior. Further, he wrote a poem about why men should take feminist classes, and asked that it be included in the course catalogue the next time the course was offered or otherwise posted around campus.

In some respects, it is easy to see how the discussion led to new insights for participants, including myself. But is new insight around issues of positionality enough evidence of emancipatory learning? Does new insight lead to action, and what kind of action is evidence of the fact that emancipatory learning has taken place? These are not easy questions to answer. But there are other actions that came out of our class together. One 40-year-old White woman, pregnant for the second time, who is the mother of an 18-year-old, has decided to start a feminist group of new mothers, to attempt to deal with the conflicting images of the "good mother." Another multi-ethnic woman who writes about position-ality notes:

Positionality is a difficult issue for me personally because of my lifelong uncertainty in relation to my race, and my conflicting experiences with class. . . . I feel like my posi-tionality resides in a sort of no-man's land in which nothing can be claimed with any certainty. In this role I have felt myself to be highly sensitive to those in privileged positions and shut down in the face of their righteousness. (Romero 1998, 7)

She writes about how this feeling of being shut down has at times prevented her from claiming her voice in classes. She talked specifically about her efforts to claim her voice in this class, and writes, "Sure I felt inarticulate and dumb-founded, but I also recognize that coming to voice is an essential part of my learning that I am committed to no matter how fearful it is." She lived differently by claiming more space—by forcing herself to speak in spite of the fear.

One might wonder, are these actions—learning to speak in the public space of a classroom in spite of fear, writing a poem about why men should take feminist classes, starting a feminist mothers' group—are these evidence of emancipatory learning? Indeed, they provide some evidence of the power of shared story, and greater understanding of positionality; and they provide evi-dence of some ways of acting differently. I'm not sure if these examples are necessarily "social action." It probably depends on how one defines "social action." I typically think of "social action" as working together with others and taking a public stand about some issue of social justice, and working toward greater equity. Is taking a stand in the learning environment in adult higher education a public stand? Is this a "public space?" Perhaps it is, but there may be some limitations in higher education settings that may place limitations on the extent to which education in these settings can be emancipatory. Gore (1993) refers to these limitations as "institutionalized pedagogy as regulation" (p. 142), such as those that require instructors to be in an evaluative role, and require them to satisfy the demands of academic rigor which emphasizes rationality. But there are limitations and possibilities for emancipatory education in all adult education situations; and it does seem to me that by making use of some of the pedagogical strategies of poststructural feminist perspectives of education discussed here provides some of the seeds that potentially can lead to social action. The seed is not just a good story. It is the unpacking of the story around issues of positionality, and the critical reflection both on the story and on the story's unpacking that helps us understand our constantly shifting identity around systems of power, privilege, and oppression that inform our lives. It raises our consciousness, it changes our behavior, it does indeed, move us to action.

CONCLUDING THOUGHTS

Since I returned to school in 1989, my own feminist thinking has changed considerably, in light of both the adult education and the feminist literature I have read, and my experiences in the world and in the classroom. My own identity has shifted; my consciousness been raised around various categories of positionality in the past 10 years. In similar ways, the field of adult education has also shifted its consciousness and its identity in regard to women's adult learning needs, in order to meet the needs of changing times. As we have seen, adult education has been primarily influenced by psychological feminist perspectives, which are primarily based on Belenky et al.'s (1986) work, and somewhat on structural feminist perspectives. It is beginning to be influenced by poststructural feminist perspectives, but I do hope such feminist perspectives influence the field more widely, for they offer something a bit different than "generic" approaches to social justice education. First is the continued emphasis of gender as an important category of analysis, not just another one in the list of many things that can easily get lost. Second, and related, is the *gendered* nature of experience. Adult education and student-centered learning approaches have always emphasized the importance of experience in adult learning, but it is only feminist pedagogies that point to the *gendered* nature of human experience and its relationship to adult learning. Third, there is direct attention to the positionality (including the race, class, affectional/sexual orientation, ableness, age, as well the gender) of the instructor and the participants and how this affects the learning environment. While there has been discussion in some of the literature about how to deal with learners of a particular race, gender, or class background, much of the emancipatory education literature does not deal with these positional factors of instructors and how this affects learning. Fourth, there is also an emphasis on action, on doing something to live differently in order to challenge systems of privilege and oppression.

Clearly, some aspects of these ideas are implicitly assumed in adult education. The *direct* discussion of the shifting nature of identity, as well as the attention given to the "connections between" the individual and structural in the social construction of identity, foregrounds the fact that the identities of neither the learners nor the instructors remain static in the adult learning environment. This is highlighted in the poststructural feminist perspectives on adult education. These major insights from poststructural feminist pedagogies, particularly around the themes of positionality or difference; identity as shifting; the construction of knowledge, voice, and authority; are what distinguish it from other approaches to teaching and learning. But it is these insights that offer new possibilities for the continued development of a theory and practice of emancipatory adult education. It is these insights that will contribute to helping the field to constantly shift its identity to meet the needs of constantly changing times.

REFERENCES

Aguilar, Viviana. (1998). Unpublished manuscript.

Anzaldua, Gloria (ed.). (1990). *Making Face, Making Soul.* San Francisco: Aunt Lute.

Belenky, Mary, Clinchy, Blythe, Goldberger, Nancy, and Tarule, Jill (eds.). (1986). *Women's Ways of Knowing.* New York: Basic Books.

Caffarella, Rosemary. (1992). *Psychosocial Development of Women: Linkages to Teaching and Leadership in Adult Education.* Information Series No. 350. Columbus, OH: ERIC Clearinghouse on Adult, Career, and Vocational Education.

Caffarella, Rosemary, and Olson, Sandra. (1993). "Psychosocial Development of Women: A Critical Review of the Literature." *Adult Education Quarterly* 43(3), 125–151.

Collard, Susan, and Law, Michael. (1989). "The Limits of Perspective Transformation: A Critique of Mezirow's Theory." *Adult Education Quarterly* 39(2), 99–107.

Collard, Susan, and Stalker, Joyce. (1991). "Women's Trouble: Women, Gender and the Learning Environment." In Roger Hiemstra (ed.), *Creating Environments for Effective Adult Learning,* 71–82. San Francisco: Jossey-Bass.

Collins, Patricia Hill. (1991). *Black Feminist Thought.* New York: Routledge.

Cunningham, Phyllis. (1992). "From Freire to Feminism: The North American Experience with Critical Pedagogy." *Adult Education Quarterly* 42(3), 180–191.

Freire, P. (1971). *Pedagogy of the Oppressed.* New York: Herder & Herder.

Guerrero, Robert. (1998). Unpublished manuscript.

Hayes, Elisabeth. (1989). "Insights from Women's Experience for Teaching and Learning." In Elisabeth Hayes (ed.), *Effective Teaching Styles,* 55–65. San Francisco: Jossey-Bass.

Hayes, Elisabeth, and Colin, Scipio A. J. III (eds.). (1994). *Confronting Racism and Sexism.* San Francisco: Jossey-Bass.

Gore, Jennifer. (1993). *The Struggle for Pedagogies.* New York: Routledge.

Hart, Mechthild. (1990). "Liberation Through Consciousness-Raising." In Jack Mezirow (ed.), *Fostering Critical Reflection in Adulthood.* San Francsico: Jossey-Bass.

Hart, Mechthild. (1992). *Working and Educating for Life: Feminist and International Perspectives on Adult Education.* New York: Routledge.

Heaney, Tom. (1996). *Adult Education for Social Change: From Center Stage to the Wings and Back Again.* Information Series No. 365. Columbus, OH: ERIC Clearinghouse on Adult, Career, and Vocational Education.

Hill, Robert. (1995). "Gay Discourse in Adult Eduction: A Critical Review." *Adult Education Quarterly* 45(3), 142–158.

hooks, bell. (1989). *Talking Back: Thinking Feminist, Thinking Black.* Boston: South End Press.

hooks, bell. (1994). *Teaching to Transgress: Education as the Practice of Freedom*. New York: Routledge.

Hugo, Jane. (1989). "Adult Education and Feminist Theory." In Phyllis Cunningham and John Ohliger (eds.), *Radical Thinking in Adult Education*. Occasional Paper No. 1, 16–36. Battle Creek, MI: Kellogg Foundation.

Hugo, Jane. (1990). "Adult Education History and the Issue of Gender: Toward a Different History of Adult Education in America." *Adult Education Quarterly* 41, 1–16.

Johnson-Bailey, Juanita, and Cervero, Ronald. (1996). "An Analysis of the Educational Narratives of Reentry Black Women." *Adult Education Quarterly* 46(4), 142–158.

Lorde, Audre. (1984). *Sister Outsider*. Trumansburg, NY: Crossing Press.

McIntosh, Peggy. (1988). "White Privilege: Unpacking the Invisible Knapsack." *Peace and Freedom*, 10–12.

Peterson, Elizabeth (ed.). (1996). *Freedom Road: Adult Education of African Americans*. Malabar, FL: Kreiger Publishing Co.

Purl, Kamala. (1998). Unpublished manuscript.

Romero, Marcia. (1998). Unpublished manuscript.

Ross-Gordon, Jovita. (1991). "Needed: A Multicultural Perspective for Adult Education Research." *Adult Education Quarterly* 42(1), 1–16.

Santamaria, Jennifer. (1998). Unpublished manuscript.

Sheared, Vanessa. (1994). "Giving Voice: An Inclusive Model of Instruction—A Womanist Perspective." In Elisabeth Hayes and Scipio A. J. Colin III (eds.), *Confronting Racism and Sexism*, 63–76. San Francisco: Jossey-Bass.

Taylor, Katherine, and Marineau, C. (eds.). (1995). *Learning Environments for Women's Adult Development: Bridges Toward Change*. San Francisco: Jossey-Bass.

Tisdell, Elizabeth. (1993). "Feminism and Adult Learning: Power, Pedagogy, and Praxis." In Sharan Merriam (ed.), *An Update on Adult Learning*, 91–103. San Francisco: Jossey-Bass.

Tisdell, Elizabeth. (1995). *Creating Inclusive Learning Environments for Adults: Insights From Multicultural Education and Feminist Pedagogy*. Information Series No. 361. Columbus, OH: ERIC Clearinghouse on Adult, Career, and Vocational Education.

Tisdell, Elizabeth. (1998). "Poststructural Feminist Pedagogies: The Possibilities and Limitations of a Feminist Emancipatory Adult Learning Theory and Practice." *Adult Education Quarterly* 48(3), 139–156.

Walters, Shirley, and Manicom, Linzi (eds.). (1996). *Gender in Popular Education*. London: Zed Books.

Part V

Reconstructing the Field: Our Personal and Collective Identities

In this, the concluding part of *Making Space*, contributors present readers with alternative ways of thinking about our roles as adult educators and the way in which they intersect with, accommodate, and/or resist hegemonic structures that are present within the institutions with whom we work. As with other contributors in this text, the critical stance taken by these authors provides a compelling critique of how we both conceptualize and construct our work with learners, now and in the future.

In Chapter 20, Childs examines the Australian context of adult education and analyzes a decade of rapid change resulting from the intersection of class transition, shifting capitalism, globalization, and the movement of the marginalized toward the center, on a terrain of government social policy, organizational change, and vocational engineering. While Childs' discussion is context-specific, her analysis of the shifting terrains of adult education practice is useful to all who wish to critically reflect about the tension that exists between the roots of the field that promote social justice, grassroots activism, and participatory inclusive democracy, and the new realities of the role of adult education in a global economy.

In Chapter 21, Garrick and Solomon explore the relationship between the development of identities in and through experiences of postindustrial work. Analyzing how workplaces today shape and control not only worker knowledge, but also workers, in desired corporate ways, Garrick and Solomon call our attention to the complicit role of the trainer in the corporate agenda. By drawing on Foucault's theorizations of power, they provide a compelling assessment of the human resource development function and its power to co-opt and seduce both workers and trainers alike. In doing so, they argue for renewed reflection on adult educators' roles, and active resistance against the rhetoric of empowerment that is so prevalent in the workplace today.

In a similar way, Jeria also takes a systems approach in his critique of adult education practice in Chapter 22. Jeria discusses issues of globalization, internationalization, and regionalization of the world economy, and addresses the relationship of these structures with education from the point of view of human capital formation. In specifically examining the interrelatedness of these forces as they have been played out in Latin America, he explicates the way in which the increasing demands for adult education and the segmentation of labor are producing increasing disparities within education and social arenas. As a result, Jeria also envisions the further marginalization of certain communities of learners and argues that such progressive marginalization must be resisted.

Chapter 23 concludes this part, and the book. In it, we, the editors, urge adult educators to consider some fundamental questions that must be addressed if inclusive practices are to be developed, fostered, and maintained. We ask questions such as: How have we as adult educators participated in the marginalization of others? What should research and practice look like if our work is to be emancipatory and authentic? How can we engage others as well as our colleagues in dialogue that revolves around these issues, such that change will occur in our lifetime? Where should this dialogue occur? In doing so, we challenge each of us who self-identifies as an adult educator to embrace our own forms of marginalization as a way of rethinking our relationships with our colleagues, our communities, and the communities of learners whom we may previously have thought of as the Other. In this emphasis of both the individual and the collective, we maintain that we must build bridges with a wide range of communities, and cross borders that we may have previously avoided. Clearly, if we wish to make space for others, then the goal must include the widening of the circle.

Chapter 20

Between a Rock and a Hard Place: Confronting Who "We" Are

Merilyn Childs

I feel that over the past two decades I have seen some change in the expectation one puts into work. What I mean is that in the past my parents
sought security and now they seek challenge and are more career motivated.
. . . Now they encourage me to seek a career, rather than a nice job that
offers long term security with minimal change.

—Jane, adult educator, 1997

INTRODUCTION

The aims of this chapter are fourfold. First, it provides a broad overview of the
changes that have been taking place in the Australian educational system and
labor market. Second, it discusses one aspect of broad labor market change—
the social construction of the "new model worker" (Flecker and Hofbauer 1998,
113). Third, it explores some of the changes that have taken place through some
insights developed during a five-year qualitative research program about adult
education work in Australia. Finally, it uses these insights to question the assumed "we" of adult education theory.

Adult educators have given much attention to adult education theory and
practice and the contribution "we" can make toward the betterment of society.
Almost invisible in this discourse is a frank critique about adult educators as
workers. Perhaps this is because worker education and community development
programs were established either by enlightened volunteers with limited funding
or as a part-time activity, done out of self-interest. In Australia, from where I
am writing, this is no longer the case. Over the past decade, adult education has
become a billion-dollar "industry" and, as a result, adult education as a form of
work has become a core wage activity for many workers—albeit still in many
respects a part-time, consultative, market-driven activity.

An illustration of the changing landscape and the concomitant shifting adult educator identities can be found in four articles[1] that I have on my desk. Each of these publications says something about adult education in the 1990s (as does this book), yet each draws on different frames of reference. Only one of them— Phyllis Cunningham's—connects in some way to grassroots social activist formations of adult education theory.

Why are these items on my desk? These articles analyze the ways in which neo-capitalist ideologies in the media and government policy have influenced our work, and they hint at new discourses that are shaping adult education in Australia in the 1990s. They reflect my search for greater understanding of adult education in these times, for I can no longer rely on the development of postwar adult education concepts, grounded in what Sue Shore (Chapter 4 in this volume) refers to as liberal humanist values—values that Mezirow and others have supposed are at the center of "our" work.

[As] adult educators in a democracy we have no trouble understanding the importance of social action to our work, the importance of helping adults learn how to make their voices heard, to collaborate to bring pressure to influence the formation of public policy, to make public institutions more responsive to those they serve and places of employment more responsive to the needs of those who labor in them ... Adult education, as a field of practice within the context of Western democracy, has historically sought to empower the powerless in their role as public citizens. (Mezirow 1995, 1)

This sentiment assumes, then, that adult educators are committed to social justice, public institutions are valued, and adult education is about fighting for democracy and the empowerment of citizens. It also assumes a ubiquitous "we," as in "we are all the same," and "we are in this together." Who is this "we," so often an assumed voice in adult education texts? Who belongs to "we?" Where do "we" work? How does work shape what "we" can do and say? How do changing contexts, such as a historic, uneven shift from Fordist to post-Fordist economies, affect "us?" Is the effect the same for all of "us?"

In Australia, as we struggle to develop a hopeful pedagogy for the twenty-first century, questions about the changing face of the politics of educational work have become a central issue. A decade ago, I would never have written a paper that included words like "globalization," "state regulatory mechanisms," or "competition policy," as I am now doing, but now it is commonplace in adult education language (see Chapters 13, 21, and 22 in this volume). Policy and funding decisions, training packages, national regulations, changing practices, and the values and beliefs of the enterprise culture are now influenced by such ideology. These changes provide the context for the discussion in this chapter.

GLOBALIZATION AND LABOR MARKET OPPORTUNISM: RECONTEXTUALIZING ADULT EDUCATOR ROLES

The labor market in Australia can be taken as one broad context shaping adult education work. In the labor market more generally, there has been a decay of blue-collar work (for males) that was accompanied by rapid growth in casual and contract labor (often for females) in new service industries (Freedland 1997). Within this changing labor market two trends have emerged for education workers. First, adult education work (community education, vocational education, university education, and human resource management) has become the primary source of wages for many workers as the educational industry has grown. Second, the work itself has increasingly been unified and homogenized conceptually as "lifelong learning," and structurally through "learning pathways" and the Australian Qualification Framework. The impetus for the rapid 1990s rise of the adult educator came from the convergence of two succesive waves of government reforms.

The first was an injection of government funding following the 1989 *Working Nation* policy document by the Labor Government, led by Prime Minister Paul Keating. Enshrined in this document was the fantasy that Australia is a "clever country" surviving in the global economic stage. Millions of dollars have been poured into restructuring industry and the development of a national education and training system. This has led to an unprecedented amount of funding and employment of adult educators.

The second occurred following 1996, when the Labor Party lost power and the newly elected conservative Howard Liberal Government extended reforms by furthering privatization and competition policy[2] as the systemic basis of the Open Training Market. Free market economics, an ethos of family and individual responsibility, the defunding of public institutional "monopolies," and the centralization of accountability led to increasing changes being made in adult education and how it was viewed as work. As Geoffrey Shacklock commented, "(t)he reforms have been extensive and fast" (1998, 73).

The introduction of this competitive tendering amidst a political environment of public divestment resulted in the rapid growth of private training companies, the outsourcing of training and development, and a restructured landscape in which precarious, insecure work—the historic experience of many females— entered the heart of education work. At the same time, being an adult educator became an attractive white-collar career, and led to an increase in university-based adult education qualifications. The course I teach and co-coordinate commenced in 1994, during this heyday period.

DEFINING THE "NEW MODEL WORKER"

In Australia, changing labor market and organizational discourses shaped under the rubric of flexibility carried with them a new image of what it means to be a worker (see also Chapter 21 in this volume). Unlike the "old" worker, who was stereotypically male and securely employed, this "new model worker" is enterprising and self-sufficient, loyal to the company, yet independent and autonomous. Flecker and Hofbauer (1998) argue that this new model worker is shaped by a popularized vision of democracy and self, and is promoted in the guise of the pioneering spirit. The logic of this message is Darwinian—the future belongs to those specialists who can adapt to survive. Similarly, Freeman (1998) has further proposed that "white-collar workers should start to think of themselves as using [a] portfolio of skills or activities to generate income. Training and skill development are viewed as being really important, and as such people need to run themselves as a business" (Freeman 1998, 23).

The skills required by this new worker include "self-management, conceptualization, creative problem-solving, holistic thinking, self-directed learning, literacy, and fault diagnosis and rectification" (Field 1990, 7) and this new worker is valued by an "enterprise culture" (Heelas and Morris 1992; Wright 1997, 7–8). The commitments of the new model worker are quite different from the commitments expressed by Mezirow's vision of the ideal adult educator. The new model worker fits into corporate and capitalist structures—their fate is intertwined. The ideal "hero" adult educator critiques and resists the oppression caused by corporate and capitalist structures, empowers the oppressed, and mediates the disadvantage caused by class, gender, and ethnicity.

A CASE STUDY: CASUALIZATION AND PRECARIOUS WORK OF ADULT EDUCATION WORKERS

Over the past five years, we in the academy have faced the pain and disappointment of some of our students' labor market experiences. Dreams of full-time work have faded, and it has become increasingly difficult to sustain a critical educational paradigm, as new expectations have been placed on educational workers. We've watched the grand success of some students who have adjusted to new work patterns and practices, found new work after redundancies, and taken on new challenges.

We've struggled to find a pedagogy that is defensible, makes sense in rapidly changing times, and engages with the social realities of adult education work. Like Griff Foley (1996), we see the dominant tendency of current adult education work as "economistic, bureacratic and directive" (p. 141), and it has often come into sharp collision with our use of critical practices in our degree programs. This engagement attempts to challenge economic orthodoxy and instrumental approaches to teaching and learning, but it does not change the social reality of work or help our students develop new possibilities *as workers*.

During the period from 1994 to 1999, I conducted a qualitative research project that aimed to build knowledge and understanding of the adult education worker phenomenon. Specifically, I focused on the case of a population of adult educators living and working in the western suburbs of Sydney, and enrolled in the Bachelor of Adult Education degree. I wanted to understand local contexts and "little stories," and to ask "How have grand changes been shaped by grassroots adult educators?" Through this enquiry, I hoped to understand the contradictions caused by change, and thus to re-imagine the education of adult educators.

At the most basic level, I wanted to understand how educators respond when local employers like the one quoted below make statements such as the following:

I interview the casuals now and say to them, "I'm not recruiting anymore for full-time staff. You need to think about the way you approach work. Ask yourself, what research can I do? What curriculum writing projects can I be involved in? What about work for an Industry Training Advisory Board?" We talk about their careers in this way, so that they can see that there needs to be some different way of looking at their employment than just hoping for a full-time job.

This statement provides a clue that educators are simultaneously being asked to be inventive, take risks, and be creative, as well as engage in the routinization of adult education labor through national standards, competency-based training, and quality systems. At a local level, these contradictory demands have occurred amidst a climate of considerable organizational change. During the research, we identified over 40 structural and regulatory changes that had dramatically affected the ways in which our workplaces had changed over the past five years.

For the discussion in this chapter, these changes will be summarized under the following categories: (1) the rise in insecurity and individual opportunism; (2) changes in the locus of control of their practice; (3) the polarization of reward structures; and (4) the development of adaptive and survival behaviors.

RISE IN INSECURITY AND INDIVIDUAL OPPORTUNISM

In this market, in order to get the work, adult educators need to know about regulatory systems, demonstrate their knowledge of curriculum requirements and labor market reform, and be prepared to accept precarious forms of work. They are not employed as social activists, except in certain kinds of community education programs. Elite education workers (academics, policy makers) may be rewarded for idealism and experimentation, but grassroots educational workers are rewarded for opportunism, voluntary labor, and cooperation. This generalization does not mean that opportunistic behavior is always successful. Robert, who has been retrenched four times in the past three years and is currently unemployed, has lost his home and faces bankruptcy. Despite this, he continues to draw on the ideal of the new model worker when he talks about his future work. He notes: "The future as I see it is to look globally, and to sell knowledge. . . . I'm trying to use the internet as a training/learning resource to develop a fully transportable knowledge-based business to service the global market." Opportunism does not automatically protect employees from redundancy. By May 1998, the majority of 25 research participants had been affected in one way or another by redundancy: five were expecting to be made redundant in the next year, four had recently taken one, and a further six had close relatives (spouse, child) who had also been made redundant. Opportunism does, however, provide education workers with an invigorated access to the labor market, and with high levels of motivation and hope. For example, many females tell of enjoying the relative freedom of the classroom compared to other kinds of work, and the sense of pride and personal achievement they feel in helping students meet national standards.

Locus of Control

As workers, research participants expressed contradictory viewpoints about their experience of control. On the one hand, there was a strong sense of dissatisfaction about the value their respective employers placed on skills acquisition, their limited access to genuine decision making, and about the absence of reward for higher order functioning. As a body they perceived themselves to be voiceless in that they did not believe they had impact on the regulatory agents formulating government work policy. At the same time, within their classrooms they generally perceived high levels of control, despite regulatory mechanisms.

The contradictions were many. They existed between organizational rhetoric (learning organizations, teams) and poor management practices. They existed between low levels of systemic control and high levels of control in regulated environments; control as an employee, and control as an educator.

Polarized Rewards for Employment

After 10 years of economic reform in Australia the gap between high- and low-wage earners has continued to increase and reflects a hollowing out of the middle that polarizes wage earnings into high and low earners. In the case of adult educators, polarized rewards are endemic, ranging from elite salaries of Aust. $60,000 and above, to as little as Aust. $13 per hour for sessional workers. As in the United States (see Chapter 13 in this volume), Australia now typically employs adult educators either as part-time or sessional. These educators must provide their own resources, research, staff development, travel, and they work without sick leave, holiday pay, and other benefits that are given in more secure forms of work. As a result, the new adult education worker must engage in self-exploitation and offer employers volunteer, unpaid labor in order to obtain and/ or sustain paid employment. Their salaries are low because they are engaging in part-time activities and they often have to write project proposals or attend meetings in order to increase their chances of just gaining full-time work. Additionally, they must attend university courses at their own expense and on their own time in order to protect their jobs.

Wage polarization is a key aspect of change, and educational work is structured between those of us with full-time and secure employment on high wages and high levels of decision making and control (academics, policy activists, curriculum officers) and those with poor access to career pathways, and secure well-paid work. The extension and entrenchment of a class system in educational work between elite and grassroots educators is one outcome of this change.

Survivor Syndrome

Some educators, particularly those in full-time employment, experience what Littler (1998) describes as "survival syndrome." According to Littler's thesis, many employees experience decreased levels of job satisfaction and job security, lower levels of motivation, fewer expectations of promotional opportunities, and lower levels of staff commitment and staff morale following a restructure. In some instances, participants in this research had experienced multiple restructures, and all educators had experienced some form of organizational change. As Marion suggests in the following statement:

After three restructures, I am feeling like I should just keep my head down and "wait and see." Wait and see who takes the redundancy this time. Wait and see who stays, and what that will mean to me. Wait and see what opportunities there are. I can't see any point making waves now, or doing anything special or innovative. Who knows what will happen. Why should I stick my neck out?

On the other hand, some education workers had gained access to education work *as a result of restructures*. The creation of an Open Training Market, the growth of private companies, and the increase in education work meant that newcomers to education work were advantaged, even though precarious and exploited. Thus survivor syndrome stories were told about mistrust and feelings of insecurity, but these were juxtaposed by other stories about aspirations and opportunities for workers in precarious employment.

ADULT EDUCATORS, HOPE, AND LABOR MARKET CHANGE

The contradictory experience of the education worker phenomenon can be further understood by placing it within the context of adult educators' occupational biographies. The phenomenon of adult education work as it occurs in Australia in the 1990s is an invention of this decade. The rise of education work as a desirable white-collar occupation has occurred at the same time as the decay of blue-collar occupations and changing social expectations about the meaning and purpose of work. More females work outside the home than at any time in our history. More emphasis is being placed on learning throughout life, and on convincing generations of workers that the job for life enjoyed by males in the postwar boom is a thing of the past. The rapid rise in educational work during this decade has meant that educational work has become a hopeful career opportunity for mainly White workers. It carries the promise of status, the opportunity to engage in meaningful work, and the belief that education work has high levels of decision making and control when compared to other forms of labor.

The majority of our students have parents who had worked in blue-collar (unskilled, low-skilled, or trade-based) jobs in a postwar industrial era that placed value on full-time male breadwinners. Their mothers had stayed at home or had worked in marginal part-time unskilled and semi-skilled jobs. The defining characteristic of participants' occupational biographies was that they, too, had begun their careers in manual labor occupations, as tradesmen, shop assistants, hairdressers, nurses, cleaners, cooks, retail assistants, and so on. They were commonly the first in their family to gain a degree.

Educational work is aspirational. It promises access to new forms of white-collar labor that might reasonably be argued provided an entry point into a "non-class of post-industrial proletarians" that Gorz theorized in the 1980s (1980, 66). Female adult educators can aspire to a different life than their mothers. They seek occupational status, work flexibility (in order to maintain home duties), and financial independence. Male educators can aspire to new experiences of work patterns and practices, and for new kinds of reward and fulfillment.

The promise offered by educational work is that enterprise and resourcefulness will free people from the grind of work. For example, when I asked Tony what a stable career meant, he drew on his father's experiences, which he described as "dull, boring work all your life, doing what you hate." His preference was for "stimulating work, but I wouldn't mind some security," and employment that allowed him to participate more fully in his children's lives.

As Gorz (1980) predicted, the point for workers (in this case, adult educators) is to "free oneself *from* work by rejecting its [industrial] nature, content, necessity and modalities" (p. 67; emphasis in original). The phenomenon of education work creates a mythical space in which this might occur. Their parents' blue-collar work offers a backdrop to the staging of educators' own careers. Through their personal endeavor and individual enterprise, they become the first to attend the university, have high occupational status (even if poorly paid), and engage in challenging work. From this context, educators express the idea of *self-empowerment*, and in their own way imagine themselves to be defeating the gender and class limitations that affected their parents' lives.

Thus, they have potential access to what is now being called *gold-collar work*. This is classless white-collar work that rewards individual initiative, and encourages entrepreneurship—a form of career advancement unheard of in their (blue-collar) parents' generation.

In this new occupational location adult educators search for language and cultural knowledge that define them as professionals within the social realities of the labor market, and are consistent with the values and beliefs inherent within it. The image of the new model worker is seductive. It humanizes and makes hopeful the changing political order. This social and political reality redefines the relationship between adult education theory, adult educators, work and practice in Australia, and does not sit easily with the values and beliefs expressed by critical theorists or liberal humanists.

An adult educator who is managing a multi-job career will make decisions that are a working compromise between his or her needs for economic survival (gaining and maintaining work in an insecure work environment) and his or her needs for innovation and creativity in the "teaching" space. The boundaries around this relationship will be in direct relationship to the value (for example, intrinsic and extrinsic rewards) the employer places on it. If this relationship is perceived of as a contradictory spiral between viscous and virtuous aspects of change, the tensions will be resolved in multiple ways. However, such resolution will tend toward conservatism and the maintenance of the status quo, aimed at actions that secure future paid work opportunities and respond to the imperatives of perceived state regulation. The resolution of the spiral may have little or nothing to do with radical adult education orthodoxy, and destabilizes any simple notion that adult education is synonymous with risk-taking behaviors, resistance, transgression, social justice, and innovation.

CONFRONTING WHO "WE" ARE

In my discussions with others in the academy (adult and community educator colleagues) about these findings, they have hastened to argue that these students are not really adult educators or that they are a particular subset of adult educators involved in vocational training that isn't really adult education. Lying behind this rejection is the utopian view that the heroic commitments of the adult educator must lie above and beyond the pressure of the labor market. As an adult educator and educational researcher interested in hearing the multiple lived experiences of all, I can't accept these interpretations, as they deny the lived and spoken social realities of the adult educators I work with.

Here are voices that are often working class, female, disadvantaged, marginalized—the very subjects of adult education orthodoxy and activism. I ask myself and others engaged in so-called radical forms of adult education, "Do 'we' include these voices at the center only if they concur with (industrial era) adult education orthodoxy?" Or do we acknowledge new forms of educational work and find ways of engaging with and re-authoring practice with grassroots educators, working with the contradictions inherent in educational work?

The theories and practices that adult educators use and produce must now be interpreted within the changing context of postindustrial economies, and need to do much more than make moral judgments about such change. The challenge for academics as well as practitioners is to engage with this present, and to resist the temptation to fall backwards into a romanticized view of a heroic and radical past. The last five years have shown me that the adult educators I work with do not connect with the traditions on which the Bachelor of Adult Education is based in Australia. *Their* talk reflects the 1990s "alignment" between "education and the new capitalism" (Gee, Hull, and Lanksheare 1996, 49) and confronts who we imagine "we" are. *Our* talk sees the classroom "as a location of possibility"; a place where we "labor for freedom . . . (and) collectively imagine new ways to move beyond boundaries, and to transgress" (hooks 1994, 207).

Such transgression may be empty and theoretical if it remains detached from the lived realities of adult educators/workers and fails to engage in what can be described as the economic and social choices that a nation-state faces in a globalized world. These global policies and issues that are affecting our students also affects us—so, we need to recognize our connected realities. Our talk *connects* when "we" consider ourselves as workers struggling with changing imperatives and the need for new worker identities, and begin to see the relationship between our different occupational experiences (e.g., security, wage levels, status) and what is and what might be possible in terms of our practice.

In thinking about the changing labor market, I have come to more fully understand what is "at stake" when we fail to acknowledge issues like class and gender identities and their impact on labor market struggles. It gives me hope, as I am reminded of the long and rich traditions of capital–labor struggles in this country. The new model worker is a new formation of an old impulse, and is a point of continuity with old struggles.

By interrogating the new model worker and the values of enterprise culture with adult educators during the past year, we have been able to "make space" between theory and practice by engaging the rhetoric of change, and placing it within the context and contradictions of their lived realities as workers. This has become a new entry point for critical engagement with the image of the new model worker, and has created a new space in which we can develop changed conversations about (regulated) pedagogy.

NOTES

1. One is by Damon Anderson, called *Review of Research: Competition and Market Reform in the Australian VET Sector*. Another is by Phyllis Cunningham, called "Reconceptualizing Our Work in Socially Responsible Ways" (1996). John White's U.K. publication called *Education and the End of Work* (1998) is there, along with Tami Lohman's report called "High Performance Work Organisation. Improving Oregon's Competitiveness in the Global Economy" (1992).

2. The privatization and competition policy that developed meant that government funding could be released for competitive tendering between public and private institutions.

REFERENCES

Anderson, D. (1997). *Review of Research: Competition and Market Reform in the Australian VET Sector*. Leabrook, South Australia: NCVER.

Burchell, David. (1995). "Social Citizenship and Social Justice: An Unhappy Coupling." Paper delivered at the National Social Policy Conference, Social Policy Research Centre, University of New South Wales, July 7, 1–13.

Childs, M. (in progress). "Running as Fast as I Can: Adult Educators, Globalisation and Everyday Life." Doctoral Dissertation, University of Western Sydney, Nepean.

Cornwell, T. (1998). "Engage with the World." *Higher Education, The Australian*, November 11, p. 30.

Cunningham, P. (1996). "Reconceptualizing Our Work in Socially Responsible Ways." Paper presented at the International Adult and Continuing Education Conference, March 27–28.

Field, L. (1990). *Skilling Australia*. Melbourne: Longman Cheshire.

Foley, G. (1996). "The Debate We Have to Have in Australia." *AAACE News* (February), 141–145.

Flecker, J., and Hofbauer, J. (1998). "Capitalising on Subjectivity: The 'New Model Worker' and the Importance of Being Useful." In P. Thompson and C. Warhurst (eds.), *Workplaces of the Future*, 104–123. London: Macmillan.

Freedland, J. (1997). "The Anatomy of Vulnerability: The State of Unemployed Australia." In C. Sheil (ed.), *Turning Point. The State of Australia*, 15–38. St. Leonard's: Allen and Unwin.

Freeman, J. (1998). "The Great White Hope." *Sydney Morning Herald*, Employment Section, May 9, p. 23.

Gee J. P., Hull, G., and Lankshear, C. (1996). *The New Work Order: Behind the Language of the New Capitalism* St. Leonard's: Allen and Unwin.

Gibb, A. (1987). "Enterprise Culture—Its Meaning and Implications for Education and Training." *Journal of European Industrial Training* 11(2), 3–38.

Gorz, A. (1980). *Farewell to the Working Class: An Essay on Post-industrial Socialism.* London: Pluto Press.

Hart, M. (1996). "Education and Social Change." In "Social Action and Emancipatory Learning." Seminar, University of Technology, Sydney, School of Adult Education, September 18–20, 1–19.

Heelas, P., and Morris, P. (eds.). (1992). *The Values of the Enterprise Culture*. New York and London: Routledge.

hooks, b. (1994). *Teaching to Transgress: Education as the Practice of Freedom*. New York and London: Routledge.

Jackson, S. (1996). "The Way Forward—The Future of Work." Paper presented at the Making it Work Conference, a national summit on the Future of Work, Sydney, May 23–24, 1–25.

Lipsig-Mumme, C. (1997). "The Politics of the New Service Economy." In P. James, W. Veit, and S. Wright (eds.), *Work of the Future. Global Persepectives*, 109–125. St. Leonard's: Allen and Unwin.

Littler, C. R. (1998). *The Effects of Downsizing: Cross-Cultural Data from Three Countries*. Boston: Academy of Management Meeting, 1–28.

Lohman, T. (1992). "High Performance Work Organisation: Improving Oregon's Competitiveness in the Global Economy." A report to the Joint Legislative Committee on Trade and Economic Development, September 22, 2–40.

Macken, D. (1996). *The Australian Financial Review Magazine* (September), 21–23.

Maglan, L., and Hopkins, S. (1997). "VET and Productivity: Some Possible Lessons for Australia." Paper presented at the AVETRA Research Conference, Melbourne, February, 1–26.

Martin, H. P. and Schumann, H. (1997). *The Global Trap*. Sydney: Pluto Press.

Mezirow, J. (1995). "Emancipatory Learning and Social Action." In "Social Action and

Emancipatory Learning." Seminar, University of Technology, Sydney, School of Adult Education, September 18–20, 1–15.

Robertson, S., and Chadbourne, R. (1998). "Banning Voluntary Labour: A Study of Teacher's Work in the Context of Changing Industrial Relations Regimes." *Discourse: Studies in the Cultural Politics of Education* 19(1) (April), 19–40.

Sennett, R., and Cobb, R. (1993). *The Hidden Injuries of Class*. Toronto: Random House.

Shacklock, G. (1998). "Fast Capitalism Educational Change: Personally Resisting the Images of School Reform." *Discourse: Studies in the Cultural Politics of Education* 19(1) (April), 75–88.

Thompson, P., and Warhurst, C. (1998). "Hands, Hearts and Minds: Changing Work and Workers at the End of the Century." In P. Thompson and C. Warhurst (eds.), *Workplaces of the Future*. London: Macmillan.

White, J. (1998). *Education and the End of Work*. London: Cassell.

Wright, S. (1997). "Introduction: A Future that Works?" In P. James, W. F. Veit, and S. Wright (eds.), *Work of the Future*. St. Leonard's: Allen and Unwin.

Chapter 21

Technologies of Learning at Work: Disciplining the Self

John Garrick and Nicky Solomon

Throughout the nineteenth and twentieth centuries, adult education, and more recently, workplace learning and training, have been framed by political projects that promote inclusive representation of marginalized groups and/or seek to enhance the skills of learners so that they can be made more employable. People who have been disadvantaged or disenfranchised, historically, have been simultaneously "educated" in the interests of social justice and through the imperatives of labor market requirements. We contend that these dual interests have been shaped by beliefs about learner "autonomy," the importance of "self-direction," emancipation, and "empowerment." In this chapter we problematize the assumptions that accompany these beliefs by arguing that education processes in contemporary times need to be understood by their relations to disciplinary power and what Foucault refers to as "technologies of the self." Furthermore, by revealing these forms of control over workers and within workplace learning, we then suggest ways of resisting against these mechanisms.

FOUCAULT'S THEORIZATIONS OF POWER

To make our argument, we draw on two interrelated aspects of Foucault's work: theorizations of technologies of power and technologies of the self. The term "technology," as Foucault uses it, helps us make sense of the ways Foucault theorizes subjectivity. Foucault (1982) viewed the individual as constituted by power, and the relations of power cannot be established, consolidated, nor implemented without the production and functioning of a discourse. According to Hutton (1988, 135), the self that Foucault describes is "an abstract construction, continually being redesigned in an on-going discourse generated by the imperatives of the policing process." In this theory, the self is a kind of currency through which power over the mind is defined and extended. This is distinct from the Freudian view that has sought to explain how knowledge gives us power over the self. A key to understanding this distinction is that Foucault demonstrates how power shapes our "knowledge" of the self and technologies of power shape human conduct. The way he puts it is, "technologies of the self permit individuals to effect by their own means a certain number of operations on their own bodies and souls, thoughts, conduct and way of being" (Foucault 1988, 18).

Why are we using Foucault's theories at this particular point in history? Our concerns about the conditions of contemporary life—often referred to as "post-modern"—have led us to take Foucault's challenge about the interrelationships of discourse, power, and knowledge very seriously. We are concerned, for in-stance, that in postindustrial workplaces, learning techniques can be (and perhaps ought to be) theorized as being linked to intricate "technologies" that shape the organization and legitimation of knowledge.

TECHNOLOGIES, LANGUAGE, AND THE WORKPLACE

By using Foucault's framework, "training" in the workplace can be considered a "technology" and we argue that there are four complementary and interrelated corporate technologies that affect how individuals act upon themselves and oth-ers in the workplace. These technologies of the self contribute to the deliberate fashioning of employee identities through the following discourses, each of which will be discussed more in depth below. These are:

- the language of empowerment—the corporate promise of participation in decision-making processes with an accompanying sense of "ownership";
- the language of belonging—the construction of a sense of team work, community, and "corporate-family" bonds;
- the language of reward—the alignment of promotion and wages with skill levels, work titles, image, and status for increased "flexibility" and productivity;
- the language of difference—the promise of valuing diverse knowledges, skills, and experiences.

Integral to our argument is a particular view of language. Language is not a neutral medium that transmits information, nor is it simply reflective. Rather, language itself produces social realities. The focus is therefore not on the mean-ings constructed through a lexico-grammatical system of language, but on why and how meanings come to be organized and articulated. Language is always political and this understanding of language, and the discursive construction of identities, enables the educator to focus on the multiplicity of sites through which discourses operate.

Our interest here is in the discursive construction of employees as particular kinds of subjects shaped through the relationship between technologies of power (the desires of the organization to effect increased productivity, efficiency, and profitability) and technologies of self (the desires of individuals for personal self-recognition and self-worth). These technologies are constructed by and articulated through particular kinds of language. For example, du Gay (1996) theorizes workers as subjects whose lived experiences have been shaped by the discourse and politics of reform in the workplace.

When examining the following human technologies, it is important to keep in mind Foucault's (1982) argument that power is productive and "not merely repressive of culture" (in du Gay 1996, 63). There can be a temptation to view Foucauldian analyses as dis-empowering the individual, but they need not be viewed so bleakly. Structures of power and dominance are always contested and new alliances continually form to challenge existing ones. For instance, discourses of workplace reform and training do arise in specific political contexts and do not "simply" reflect those contexts as if they are pre-given. Discourses actively create new ways for people *to be* at work and in the practices of adult education. This is an argument extended by Whittington (1992, 695), who claims "all actors—workers and managers—participate in a dialectic of control that allows them at least the power of defiance." For us, a critical point here is that there is an active component to the human technologies and as such, this has direct application to the techniques of adult education, workplace learning, staff development, and HRD.

TECHNOLOGIES AND POSTMODERN CONTEXTS OF ADULT LEARNING AND THE WORKPLACE

Thus, in relation to adult education and workplace learning, some key questions arise: what are the benefits of deploying Foucault's theories to practice? Can these insights offer something beyond the current "normalizing" drive to up-skill and (falsely) "empower" employees so that they can be aligned with the performatory requirements of postindustrial workplaces? These questions illustrate some of the troubling aspects of the contexts of postmodern work and adult education practices, particularly when the "educative" effects of disciplinary power at work can be seen, not in the crushing or repression of individuals, but in creating "active" subjects who perform in efficient and productive ways. Disturbingly, even though this is termed multi-skilling, personalizing, humanizing, and empowering, we assert that these technologies are actually related to governing individuals. As such they tend to mask the regimentation, reductionism, and dehumanization that often underpin the practices of adult education and workplace learning. Rose (1989, 2) notes that the management of subjective experience in contemporary workplaces is related to this careful manipulation of group dynamics. "Thoughts, feelings and actions may appear as the fabric and constitution of the intimate self, but they are socially organised and managed in minute particulars [that is, governed]."

The performative requirements of contemporary work demand that the human technologies we are referring to are not repressive and indeed, it is their positive aspects which make them appear to be not only plausible but seductive. It is precisely the seductive power of these four technologies, conflated by their overlaps and interrelationships, that connects them to employee conceptions of themselves.

The effectiveness of these technologies is located within the contemporary interest of promoting workplace "cultures" as a management technique. This technique constructs relationships between the individual and the organization that play on the "productive subject," that is, the need for meaning and a sense of personal achievement among workers, and "managerial interest in organizational culture" (du Gay 1996, 41).

"Culture," in this context, is accorded a privileged position because it structures the way people think, feel, and act in organizations. The aim is to produce the sort of meanings that will enable people to make the right and necessary contribution to the success of the organization. In other words, the language of empowerment, belonging, reward, and difference are part of "that ensemble of norms and techniques of conduct that enables the self-actualizing capacities of individuals to become aligned with the goals and objectives of the organization for which they work" (du Gay 1996, 41).

Accessing new global markets, accumulating flexible capital, utilizing volatile labor markets, making quick switches from one product to another, creating niche marketing, and promoting ever greater levels of consumerism are central to these organizational cultures. The new patterns of management involve technologies designed to transform organizational and corporate cultures so that they can compete in the global market economy. Phrases like "organizational goals" and "knowledgeable selves" are increasingly used by employers then, as a way to encourage duplicitous compliance. In other words, today's "knowledge workers" are meant to examine not only objects of the world, but also one's own point of view—thus they are required to be disciplined, regulated subjects—*and self-disciplining and self-regulating*. The following four technologies, then, are mechanisms that reinforce a subjectivity that is subjugated to the organizational culture.

The Language of Empowerment

In order to fully utilize its flexible specialists, contemporary discourses have developed a language about "worker empowerment." Empowered, self-directed workers are required in flat/lateral work-hierarchies that characterize post-Fordist workplaces. They are a part of an economic/managerial formula that rests on the reconfiguration of human capital theory.

This reconfiguration is discursively constructed through the economic appropriation of humanist discourse and worker empowerment. The worker is *trained to be empowered* in the work situation. "Trainers" are thus temporary authors of an empowerment text and the vehicles through which one learns how to become empowered. They, in fact, direct a few moments in the corporate participation process and convey the corporation's ideals to the trainees. Trainers teach the trainees that they must have shared goals or work toward total quality for the good of the organization, as well as for themselves.

Many HRD practitioners have taken up the idea of worker empowerment following popular books on "The Learning Organization" and other HRD glossies that promise greater performance outcomes. Our concern about the language of worker empowerment is not so much that it is illusive. To the contrary, we are concerned about the various meanings that are given to it by those that use it. There is a belief among many new wave managers that empowerment offers greater worker freedom and a more rewarding/satisfying work environment. They have naively been seduced into believing that it also provides the workers with unprecedented opportunities for personal and professional advancement. Those who argue against this "logic" may be painted as being negative at best; and to deny one's negativity only serves to promote the need for this new form of liberation and empowerment among the workers.

Worker empowerment rests upon the logic of a positive human consciousness. For one to question it or deny the positive effects it has on the individual worker will only attract attention to one's self, resulting ultimately in corporate sanctions being levied. So, any questioning must be done in an appropriate manner. Pure positivity has become the corporate rule-game, with knowledge no longer possessing the "shadow-side," which always demands a cost. As Letiche (1990, 237) puts it, training becomes "a product of this epistemological shift in values . . . with the goal of training to convey purely positive knowledge."

Even though the corporate construction of "worker empowerment" is highly dubious, limited criticism has been levied against it. Some industry or workplace HRD managers and trainers might on occasion doubt the corporate message. However, when job markets are tight or training positions scarce (or being "devolved" to other workers such as line managers, peer coaches, and mentors), it makes it easier for them to fall into line and play along. Besides, the language is easy to play along with—it contains the humanistic qualities that they want their corporate trainers to promote. It also contains a language derived, ironically given its location in high capital, from socialism—about working more cooperatively in teams—becoming more a part of the corporate family.

The Language of Belonging

Team work and collective or group learning are now a familiar part of corporate social practices and a very powerful technology for many workers across a diverse range of industries. The lure of belonging to the organizational culture is a powerful one. It is through intersection between technologies, power arrangements, and the "self" that one is seduced into believing in the merged reality of self and the company. Workers now belong to the corporate family, and this is symbolically represented in the proliferation of logos and corporate images that are embedded in all written documentation and selective uses of democratic language such as "we," "our," and "shared." This helps to foster a sense of community with its accompanying, yet perhaps mythical, characteristics of belonging and security. Furthermore, giving workers an opportunity to participate in shared schemes not only motivates the linkage between the individual employee's work and productivity, but also reinforces the illusion of "our" company and "our" business. This notion is strengthened by the "public" display of company profits being offered in the work setting.

Reciprocity is essential to belonging to the corporate family and to the team. Employee commitment to the new partnering and team arrangements results in increased participation, energy, and output, and is rewarded by whatever the organization has to offer. In this case, it is a sense of autonomy, protection, responsibility, and financial rewards. However, such reciprocity has its limits. The problem is that it is difficult to offer protection and belonging when work is individuated. How can an organization protect its workers in an information technology environment that requires the monitoring of inputs and outputs on an individual basis? How can the workers be protected when their colleagues are assessing their competencies? And how can one be offered protection when large-scale downsizing or company reengineering takes place?

Even in competency-based approaches to training and assessment, workers learn more than the skills and competencies that are necessary to perform their jobs. They, too, experience the "normal" stresses of new corporate-partnering and team requirements. This, along with the reality that the "new corporate family" has an emotional effect on the lives of workers and on the broader community, is a reality typically glossed over in contemporary management and training literature.

There is a critical need for adult educators and human resource developers to be alert to the way these new partnerships (the family-style learning organizations), while offering a sense of belonging, can absorb more and more of the worker's self into the organization. The organization, after all, must, above all else, perform competitively at peak efficiency in order to make a profit.

The Language of Reward

Linked to the language of belonging, workplace reward systems seduce the workers into merging their values, attitudes, and abilities to that of the organization. Accepted as givens, these systems are often exempted from critical scrutiny due to powerful interests vested in them. We, however, suggest that the corporate reward systems set up the dialectic between submission and reward, which we think warrants the scrutiny of adult educators and others. To understand this dialectic, corporate reward systems need to be viewed as being tied to not only power, but also "technologies of sign systems" (Foucault 1988, 18). For corporate trainers this technology can be expressed through *processes* of training. *Who gets to do what counts?* Trainers as facilitators are supposed to engender trust. If training involves visible displays of power/reward systems in action, how can trainers be trusted? Contemporary (humanistic) corporations also stress the need for trust. It is a part of the "belonging" to which we have referred. However, in the end, what happens is that if workers trust the organization and learn to "fit in," they are rewarded, but if they don't, they are sanctioned.

Increasingly, but not conclusively, the new corporate culture's effort to establish team bonds and emotional commitments among team members is effective in obtaining this compliant fitting-in. As Lasch argues, "the team-family culture bolsters a fragile corporate self formed under the influence of traditional hierarchies and weakened by the cultural narcissism of advanced industrial society" (in Casey 1995, 150). The point is that *belonging* to a corporate family, complying with its processes such as feedback, recognition, and reward systems, provides a compensatory effect to the "acutely ambivalent and conflictual self" (Casey 1995, 150). That the employee feels valued and belongs to a major organization with the promise of career paths and salary packages helps eliminate resistance. The technologies of the reward system help maintain the corporatized self by promising future gratification and an enhanced self-image.

The processes of enhancing one's image at work often encompasses titles, money, the car (and where the car is parked), and status. These are powerful influences, even in the modern workplace. The promise of future gratification; the promise of *being someone* in the hierarchy continues to count.

Being someone in the corporate team is, however, a convenient cultural formation. It is the script used by the corporation to obtain the desired sensibilities from its employees. "Being someone" presupposes that *knowing* about the interplay of personalities, networks, formal and informal channels of communications will engender one to the organization and will enhance one's opportunities for upward mobile success. Without this knowledge, the corporate design is vulnerable because its team structures are orchestrated through communication patterns and artifacts representing images of the desired corporate employee. Teams are not based upon the spontaneous creation of groups of workers who wish to establish a community together. They are based on corporate work, and one's vulnerability is reflected in the reward and punishment systems established by corporations/organizations (see Garrick 1998).

The trainers' "performance" is increasingly being measured in monetary terms. Indeed, financially based instruments for assessing trainers' performance can readily take on the guise of an objective truth about the individual, but they will not necessarily reflect the elusive yet critical importance that teaching and helping others to learn has on corporate productivity or profits. From a Foucauldian standpoint, trainers are subjects of (and subjected to) the disciplinary regimes of corporations. As a result of this surveillance, individuals begin to discipline themselves in accordance with workplace norms. As Foucault explains, "normalisation occurs through comparison, ranking, judging, measurement, differentiation and setting the limits in relation to the 'Norm' " (Foucault 1977, 1988).

Other panoptic group norms[1] and organizational technologies for regulation are exemplified by fancy job titles, financially based performance reviews, participation in corporate profit-share schemes, and hyper-male cultures in which the message of valuing diversity becomes one of the technologies of compliance.

The Language of Difference

The need for valuing difference within workplace cultures has been heightened as a result of globalization and multinationalism. Globalization has led in some cases to the dismantling of national and trade borders and has often been accompanied by the growth of multinational companies and the migration and relocation of people for work. Globalization has also fueled a homogenization of values, organizational cultures, languages, and work practices that have produced unified and integrated common cultures. Paradoxically, globalization has strengthened the processes for establishing and maintaining local cultures and local differences. Featherstone (1995, 103), reflecting on this irony, notes that "it would seem that the processes of globalization and localization are inextricably bound together."

Despite the movement toward a global culture, local differences are becoming increasingly defined. As workplaces compete for market shares to meet the particular needs of niche consumer groups, boutique services are replacing mass production. Servicing this shift are employees' cultural and technological knowledge and skills—a relationship well appreciated by human capital theory. The intersection between production and intercultural marketing has increasingly led to the need for dialogue across national and local borders.

Such dialogues have focused on the co-existence of different cultural experiences and employee skills and the development of workplace cultures which are based on increasingly systematic/standardized training (and credentialing). Some critical questions concerning diversity, globilization, and multinationalism have also occurred. For instance, are the systematic and standardized training nomenclatures actually recognizing different "knowledges" and values? Or do they have the effect of homogenizing? Do management, work, and training practices support or conflict with the language of valuing difference? And to what extent is the corporate culture incorporated into the employees' personal identity?

As industry-driven vocational education and training systems increasingly frame workplace competencies, the training and credentialing of learning outcomes become part of the technologies for developing values around cultural differences, knowledges, experiences, and identities. Yet industry competency standards, a key technology for the construction of skilled workers, often only prescribe singular ways of performing. Such prescriptions, we suggest, do little more than provide templates for training that produce repetition and sameness.

They are not constructed to generate creativity. In the call for standardization and benchmarking, the strict boundaries around *units of work* and *units of learning* render invisible the overlapping and complex relationships that allow for different and competing workplace practices.

Recognition of prior learning, heralded as one of the key conceptual shifts that acknowledges and accreditates learning outside formal institutions, potentially provides the opportunity for giving space and reward for an individual's diverse knowledges, experiences, and skills. But when this meaning is recognized and assessed it has been framed within mono-cultural classifications of competence. In this way "each [person] can only be understood in terms of sameness and conformity" (Michelson 1996).

In terms of the workplace culture, recognition of the diverse experiences and knowledges of workers by employees shows promise. However, contemporary corporations promote "culture" as people sharing the same "visions," common goals, *doing* common tasks, and working toward predetermined workplace standards.

This is reinforced in a number of workplace practices. Increasingly, job seeking includes not only the application process, but personality tests, as well as family interviews, which reflect the continued blurring between the public and private domains. Accompanying these processes are recruitment practices and criteria that reflect very specific kinds of attitudes and values—those that match the imaging and reproduction requirements of the corporate culture. Applying Foucault's (1988) theory of technologies of power, these corporate practices are associated with a certain type of domination. Each practice implies "certain modes of training and *modification of individuals*, not only in the obvious sense of acquiring certain skills but also in the sense of acquiring certain attitudes" (1988, 18). The corporate sphere is penetrating more deeply into all aspects of employees' lives.

In addition, communication systems and practices, motivated by the need to improve information flow, are being standardized. While the standardization of modes and formats can assist in both the giving and receiving of information (by increasing reader predictability and by "scaffolding" writing tasks), it can also limit new meanings; for example, document templates ensure particular constructions of texts.

While written documentation increases, spoken information continues to be communicated through powerful informal networks. In team meetings, voices that use the "appropriate" language and communication strategies are listened to. Communication training thus tends to focus on individual language skills that empower, rather than examine the power relations within the organization that empower some while disempowering others. We would argue that training sessions that seek the narrow (highly instrumental) promotion of "cultural capital" resources can indeed contribute to the loss of dignity and sense of self-worth.

Furthermore, cultural knowledge is frequently utilized for productivity purposes. The incorporation of migrant employees' cultural knowledge by corporations, to shape and produce products (and services) for local or international niche markets and to communicate with multinational partners as well as the local community, is one example. However, if the value of the "human resource" doesn't have a direct relationship with the capital product or service being developed, the workers' realities have little or no place in the corporation's strategies. Subsequently, individual initiatives in meetings and other decision-making forums can be withdrawn. Additionally, overt or covert racism can silence employees who no longer feel willing or confident about what they can contribute—thus diverse contributions become invisible and/or inaudible.

Workplace practices, such as those described above, do suggest that language around difference is a technology for obtaining compliance with corporate objectives and production imperatives. Yet valuing diverse knowledges and skills needn't contradict the organizational culture in which pre-defined values, beliefs, attitudes, and behaviors (sameness) are rewarded. Perhaps one way of doing this is by utilizing the post-Fordist view of work as being a flexible specialization, team based, participatory, and collaborative work and decision making practices—all of which problematize the notion of norms or normality. If we view difference as the norm rather than simply the "exotic other" and difference as site of challenge, struggle, and contestation, then perhaps the arising tensions can be the point in which the seductions of the above four technologies can be problematized and critiqued.

POSSIBILITIES FOR "EMPOWERMENT"

Through the use of Foucault's theories, this chapter has raised a number of questions about mechanisms of control in the workplace, and adult education's role in supporting these systems. Now we suggest that this discussion leads to significant implications for action, particularly in relation to work participation schemes, changes in the construction of training, staff development, and learning more generally.

Our aim has been to disturb the meanings of "empowerment," "belonging," "reward," and "difference" by confronting the social practices that give them meaning. In other words, we have tried to surface the social and cultural reasons and show how the meanings that one gives to them are articulated in a particular way at a particular moment. By foregrounding the discursive construction of subjectivity, a Foucauldian analysis does suggest the emergence of possibilities of disruption and resistance. It provides a space for active subjects. We argue that by focusing on the language within these spaces, there exists the possibility for rewriting the texts of the workplace culture. In other words, we are arguing for new forms of resistance by deconstructing and reframing our understandings about the meanings we have attributed to our varied realities. Deconstruction is not, however, a strategy in a conventional sense. It is more an attitude—a way of working with that culture in order to influence its practices (Lemert 1997).

In the postindustrial scenario, we have argued that the contemporary fashioning of Western workers' learning is both systematic and associated with "technologies" of compliance. The technologies, as we have pointed out, do not only manufacture compliance, but actively create new images, cultural values, work and social expectations, and practices. Rose (1996, 130) suggests that workers can even come to "identify themselves and conceive of their interests in terms of the words and images that accompany the re-fashioning of the new learning workplaces." Du Gay (1996, 53) further argues that an effect of this identification "actively transforms meanings and realities of work," but with an effect that workers are increasingly bound into the required productive ways. Boje (1994) chillingly describes some of the implications of this so-called "humanization of work" for learning (and selves) as including:

a seamless web of instructional apparatus where we are taught to be "politically correct" bureaucrats. The learning occurs in the minute-by-minute interactions and the spaces along the hallways, lunchrooms and e-mail networks. The iron cage of the bureaucratic teaching machine is so ubiquitous and [seemingly] benign that the prisoners of modern learning no longer see the bars, the gears, or question the learning agenda. (1994, 447)

Boje's "bureaucratic teaching machine" can be readily linked with Foucault's ideas regarding the exercise of power. "It is not a naked fact, an institutional right, nor is it a structure which holds out to be smashed: it is elaborated, transformed, organised: it endows itself with processes which are more or less adjusted to the situation" (Foucault 1982, 224). The "situation" under scrutiny here is related to the human technologies that systematically (re)produce instrumental outcomes whereby "learning" no longer requires critical distance, dialogue, and critique. As we have argued, the hidden goals of "developing" or "training" staff can be related to obtaining compliance through the conveyance of a certain type of knowledge. Instrumental knowledge—that which is needed to "fit in" with the team and get the job done—is distinct from a questioning knowledge which may contain its own negation.

We ask, what can sustain those in staff development, training, and adult education roles in the face of such power? Some resistance can be located in problematizing "truths"—using deconstruction as a strategy for revealing contradictory messages and values that permeate training purposes and, increasingly, devolved learning strategies. We have argued that contemporary training practices do not currently address adequately issues of paradox, irony, or doubt, yet it appears to us that it is precisely these qualities that give substance to learning.

Our conclusions reflect this "lack." If conceptions of training are to be better, they will have to take seriously the contested status of knowing/knowledge and include the characteristics of self-reflexivity, self-criticism, irony, and doubt. This means that we must have a high degree of tolerance for unanswered questions, uncertainty, ambiguity, and difference. By definition, therefore, some problems will never be fully resolved, indicating new demands upon mental life. Further, more research and theoretical development is needed on the dialectical interaction between oneself and social formations; on the development of identities in and through experiences of work.

Some of our concerns about contemporary approaches to training stem from their location in a society of performability. The drive to align learning with enhanced production, more competitive outcomes, and greater efficiencies is very powerful. Human resources planners and managers will inevitably ask, "Will this get us anywhere?" "How does this relate to workplace 'realities'?" and so on. They are looking for techniques that will improve the quality and efficiency regimes of their organization. Indeed, Baudrillard (1993) asserts that a depth-level knowledge within contemporary organizations is impossible, and there is no choice but to become an apologist of performative reality.

By problematizing the disciplinary nature of training we have argued that training ought to be theorized to allow for different dialogues and different kinds of outcomes—within work and as a consequence of work. In part this can be achieved by surfacing and problematizing the disciplinary nature of workplace learning and training. This needs to include a recognition of the crisis in purpose which characterizes contemporary (postmodern) society and radical analyses of corporate work/life. This approach is not intended to deny instrumental learning in organizations, but it does require an unprecedented self-reflexivity of the "authors" of corporate training, staff development, and business learning.

NOTE

1. Central to Foucault's conceptualization of the workings of power is the "panopticon"—a technique of surveillance which sustains power relations *independent* of the personnel who exercise it. What is important about Foucault's panopticon for theories of learning is that the subject of surveillance disciplines his or her *self*. In the context of this chapter, group norms are posited as a form of panopticon in the sense that an organization's norms for team or group behavior (including electronic) do involve subtle techniques that impose codes of conduct, surveillance, and "self"-discipline.

REFERENCES

Baudrillard, J. (1993). *The Transparency of Evil: Essays on Extreme Phenomena* (J. Benedict, trans.). London: Verso.

Boje, D. M. (1994). "Organisational Storytelling: The Struggles of Pre-modern, Modern and Postmodern Organisational Learning Discourses." *Management Learning* 25(3), 433–462.

Brooks, A. K. (1994). "Power and the Production of Knowledge: Collective Team Learning in Work Organizations." *Human Resource Development Quarterly* 5(3), 213–233.

Casey, C. (1995). *Work, Self and Society after Industrialism*. London and New York: Routledge.

du Gay, P. (1996). *Consumption and Identity at Work.* London: Sage Publications.

Featherstone, M. (1995). *Undoing Culture Globalization, Postmodernism and Identity.* London: Sage Publications.

Foucault, M. (1977). *Discipline and Punish: The Birth of the Prison.* New York: Vintage.

Foucault, M. (1982). "The Subject and Power." In H. L. Dreyfuss and P. Rabinow (eds.), *Michel Foucault,* 208–226. London: Pathfinder Press.

Foucault, M. (1988). "Technologies of the Self." In L. H. Martin, H. Gutman, and P. H. Hutton (eds.), *Technologies of the Self: A Seminar with Michel Foucault,* 16–49. London: Tavistock.

Garrick, J. (1998). *Informal Learning in the Workplace: Unmasking Human Resource Development.* London and New York: Routledge.

Hutton, P. H. (1988). "Foucault, Freud and the Technologies of the Self." In L. H. Martin, H. Gutman, and P. H. Hutton (eds.), *Technologies of the Self,* 126–144. London: Tavistock.

Lemert, C. (1997). *Postmodernism Is Not What You Think.* Oxford: Blackwell.

Letiche, H. (1990). "Five Postmodern Aphorisms for Trainers." *MEAD* 21(3), 229–240.

Michelson, E. (1996). "Taxonomies of Sameness: The Recognition of Prior Learning as Anthropology." Paper presented at the International Conference on Experiential Learning, University of Capetown, South Africa, July.

Rose, N. (1989). *Governing the Soul: The Shaping of the Private Self.* London: Routledge.

Rose, N. (1996). "Identity, Geneology, History." In S. Hall and P. du Gay (eds.), *Questions of Cultural Identity.* London: Sage Publications.

Usher, R. (1997). "The Crucial Bind of Pleasure and Power." Unpublished public seminar at the Faculty of Education, University of Technology, Sydney, December 4.

Whittington, R. (1992). "Putting Giddens into Action: Social Systems and Managerial Agency." *Journal of Management Studies* 29(6), 693–711.

Chapter 22

The Political Economy of Adult Education: Implications for Practice

Jorge Jeria

There is little research in adult education exploring the relationship of the State to economic policy and political contexts and the implications and contradictions that exist within social structures. Those who have broached this topic (Torres 1990; Hart 1992; Collins 1991; Wangoola and Youngman 1996; Walters 1997) argue for a more comprehensive, critical view of adult education, and one that looks at social integration rather than economic homogenization.

This chapter explores some of the different ideas involved in the concepts of globalization, internationalization, and regionalization. In doing so, it offers a critical view of human capital formation—the driving force behind globalization—a discussion of the way in which changes in education are taking place as the globalization process expands, and at the same time it attempts to articulate some form of coherent educational response to this economic trend. In the first section of the chapter, I examine the use of the term "political economy" and its relationship to adult education, followed by a brief explanation of the historical patterns of economic globalization and regionalization. I then suggest a framework for developing strategies for adult education.

ADULT EDUCATION AND POLITICAL ECONOMY: A CONTEXT

The use of the concept "political economy" to explain what changes are occurring in the field of adult education and its relationship to economic development seems appropriate for a number of reasons. In employing this concept, several assumptions using the neo-classical economic theory of human capital are being made about this relationship. The first assumption is that there is a very close relationship between the basic skills of reading and writing, cognitive skills, and the ability to learn (McNabb, 1987, 159) how to do productive work. The second assumption is that the expansion of these skills will increase individual productivity. Following these suppositions, adult education, by its practical nature, is thus seen as an object of the educational process which is dedicated to this expansion of skills. Such skills, and the economic benefits derived from them, in turn determine social relations of class, race, and gender, and related issues of social justice. These assumptions are based on an understanding that the field of economics, and adult education by extension, will have to make some basic changes in how they view the market and decision making—two main functions of the State. This means that educators and economists must understand that their roles are interwoven. They must then come to terms with nonmarket decision making and its impact on knowledge production and economic power. This concept further assumes that as we come to understand how knowledge production and economics are interwoven, we will begin to understand how these factors in turn determine and shape class and gender social structures.

Education Leads to Modernization

In addition to examining these factors through the lens of the political economy, we must examine them through the lens of "modernization." As we begin to examine this relationship, it becomes clearer that literacy and basic education take on a new meaning and economic development cannot occur without them. In fact, the theory of modernization relies mainly on the skills associated with literacy, such as reading and writing, which is the primary focus of adult basic education practitioners (Torres 1990). However, adult basic education as part of an educational process "is not just literacy training or human capital formation, it is part and parcel of a political strategy" (Carnoy 1990).

Critical Departures

One of the criticisms that has been levied against the use of modernization as a means to explain the relationship between economic development and education has been that economic dependency, rather than political domination, is often used as a metaphor to describe what occurs in "peripheral countries." In setting up this scenario, it then plays into the hegemonic forces that serve the main economies of the world. For instance, during the 1960s, dependency theorists espoused the view that Third World countries' economies were subservient and dependent upon the main centers of capitalism—the industrialized countries of the North. Many of these countries had achieved political independence, setting up their own education systems and governments; however, it was argued that those countries who were on the margins—today the so-called "emergent economies," could not develop an economic infrastructure, or a domestic and social structure without support or leadership from their "center" countries. In other words, although these countries have become politically independent from their colonial masters, a new economic colonialism has emerged that keeps them from further developing their own economic infrastructures, and at the same time benefits the previous hegemony of imperialism (Frank 1969).

It is in acknowledging the interconnection between politics, economics, and education that we can challenge this so-called "dependent development." While this chapter is not specifically about Latin America, what occurred there serves as a starting point for our discussion. Furthermore, Latin America is illustrative of how the dependency model can be challenged.

For instance, in Latin America, monopoly capitalism was developed to satisfy the relations between a State bureaucracy, State managers, large corporations, and the elite. Their aim was to create "needed modernization in society." Yet, as Torres (1990) argued, modernization cannot be achieved if the educational system does not "promote societal progress by training its people and thereby raising productivity" (p. 36). As a result of the influence the educational system has had on the promotion of new technologies in changing production and diffusion of innovations, educational funding in the region was directed to enhance educational experiences at the university level. Because the purpose was to enhance the training of the more educated and qualified human resources, adult education that provided basic skills development was considered a consumption expenditure rather than an educational investment (Torres 1990). Using this argument, adult education is not considered a formative type of education, but rather a form of education that is used to augment skills or capacities of individuals. This view, then, accounts for the fact that there has been nominal interest or emphasis placed on adult education programming in Latin America by the State.

Ironically, the picture isn't that different in the United States. For example, Sassen (quoted in Cunningham 1996, 149) states that in the United States, mass education conceived as human capital development enhances economic mobility for the high-tech domestic employees while at the same time "foster(s) economic stagnation for a developing economic underclass" (Cunningham 1996). Given the conditions and prevalence of human capital theories that favor a form of education that is grounded in technical rationality and flexibility in order to allow businesses to compete globally, it will suggest that adult education is also considered a "consumption expenditure" in the United States. This may explain a strong—and growing—private business orientation for adult education, and the lack of support or intervention from the government even at policy level. If we take, for instance, investment in training in the United States, this accounts for only one-third of the total expenditure for general education (Woodhall 1987). At the same time, a social economic vacuum has developed as a result of this lack of government intervention and the privileging of free-market principals. Attempting to fill this void are a disorganized, underfunded array of local volunteers; and a few programs that work to counteract poverty, a prevailing lack of minority inclusion, and a gendered division of labor in society.

Education and Human Capital Theory: Market Effect

For the most part, the relation between education and human capital theory can be summarized in two ways. The first framework is taken from neo-classical human capital theory. This theory assumes that education can be used to aid in the expansion of economic development as we move into a globalized market. A central tenet of the neo-classical argument then, is that schools must adjust to the growing importance of knowledge in production. Most specifically, neo-classical thought is that that our economic decline can be blamed on schooling, and that if we make changes or reforms in our educational system, then and only then will economic revival occur within a postindustrial labor market (Davies and Guppy 1997).

The Economic Commission for Latin America and the Carribean: A Case in Point

In the case of Latin America, the Economic Commission for Latin America and the Caribbean (ECLAC) recently developed a proposal that had wide repercussions in the region. This proposal states that "ECLAC has embarked on a systematic effort to gain a more detailed knowledge for the interrelations between the educational system, training, research, and technological development within the context of the central elements of its proposal to change production patterns, create social equity, and develop political democratization" (ECLAC 1992, 2). While Stromquist (1996) does not support the findings in the ECLAC report, she does conclude that the report serves to identify gender bias as a major source of inequality, given that women must have four more years of education than men to earn the same salary. She goes on to say that even though the report discusses "decentralization, autonomy, privatization, better coordination with firms, and greater professionalism of teachers," it does so "without a single word on how these moves will translate into benefits for the subordinate groups of society" (1997, 45). Relatedly, Hart (1992) has concluded that "the internationalization of labor markets has created a housewifization of labor," and that behind all this economic change "lies a systematic utilization of the division of labor to cheapen both male and female labor" (p. 20)

There has been a trend toward relocating industries around the world through the use of infusion of "technological transformation." Rather than changing the hegemonic relationships between men and women that evolved under the old system, this infusion has instead served to promote greater inequality between them. This, then, has provoked even greater divisions of labor that are based on patriarchal social relations (Lim 1983).

Thus, societal modernization and adult education are very much interrelated. However, this interrelation carries contradictions that need to be explored and understood in light of societal structures and the political and historical nature of their relationship to economics.

THE GENERAL CONTEXT OF A GLOBAL ECONOMY, REGIONALIZATION, AND EDUCATION

In order to effectively discuss these issues, it is important to reach some kind of agreement in terms of concepts such as globalization, internationalization, and regionalization. So, for the purposes of our discussion, globalization will be defined as being a part of that increasing acceleration of global interdependence that we witness at different levels (Robertson 1992). While the term "globalization" in general is not new, given that it predates World War II, in which we saw an emergence of international institutions; its association to modernity is a recent development.

Regionalization, on the other hand, can be interpreted as "a set of policies that seek to regulate economic activity in a defined geographical area while at the same time reducing competition from outside competitors" (Michalak 1994). It is an outgrowth of the globalization. Regionalism has resulted in policies like the North American Free Trade Agreement (NAFTA) and the European Common Market (ECE) being established. These policies seek to open the markets up between countries connected by geographic boundaries, so that they can work together in order to fend off "so-called" external competition outside of their regional markets. In the case of NAFTA, the market is continental North and South America. Given the increasing competition from Asian and European markets, the North and South then are working together to fend off the "evil corrupters" from the Asian and European markets. While on the one hand the U.S. response to this role appears to be that it is becoming less hegemonic in its relations to its neighbors, this must be balanced out by the new U.S. view of its hemispheric role (Grinspun and Cameron 1993). Whereas regionalization is an outgrowth of globalization, internationalization is an extension of globalization. In some cases, internationalization refers to the realm of multinational enterprises, and in others it refers to nation-state policies. While the true extent of the internationalization of the economy has been widely recognized, it is also true that only highly industrialized economies are considered to have evolved or even been allowed to carry the banner of globalization (O'Hara-Devereaux and Johansen 1994). In more graphic terms, it has been stated that globalization is an "uneven process in which there is cleavage between skyscraper economies and shanty towns" (Korsgaard 1997). Thus, one of the most important economic trends during the 1970s and 1980s has been the acceleration of interdependence between the economies of highly industrialized countries (Gibbs and Michalak 1994; Wilson, 1992). To a large extent, the economists have debated what the difference is between internationalization and globalization. Much of this debate has focused on where one ends and the other begins.

Role of Adult Educators in the Marketplace

According to Ilon (1994), a new paradigm in education, focusing on the connections between education, economic growth, and the global economy, has arisen. This line of thinking supports and substantiates notions that human capital develops from educational attainment, contribution to productivity, personal incomes, and economic growth (Becker 1975), and that knowledge allocation is a source of competitive advantage and wealth (Drucker 1993). Moreover, economists like Schultz (1971) contend that the rate of return on investment in human capital has tended to exceed the rate on investment in physical capital. It is also thought the rate of return on investment in human capital is due in part to the same human competencies that account for productivity and effectiveness. In fact, today corporate managers talk more about strategic learning than strategic planning (see Chapter 9 in this volume). In doing so they place immediate needs at the core of their organization's mission, instead of focusing on its role in the future. Human competencies, then, are considered as being the most crucial of all resources required in order to achieve national economic development (Hornbeck 1991).

The need to understand the interconnection between economic, social, and political factors and educational institutions has, therefore, become the rhetoric used by those in educational circles, government, and private organizations to explain how countries can achieve economic development. Given the fact that human capital formation has become the anchor of the neo-liberal ideology, as adult educators we may need to interrogate ourselves about our roles and the role of adult education in preparing citizens for their roles in the new market or global economy. Whether we know it or not, those of us who have acceded to education have contributed to the direct reproduction of the capitalist system. We have done this through our writings and the reform policies we have supported, and through our very participation in the production of "knowledge." As a result of this, cultural capital has been assured a place in the exchange and consumption of knowledge and in all expenditures related to the global market economy. This is magnified by the fact that educational interventions have ultimately served to modify or amplify the existing economic forces.

ADULT EDUCATION: A FORCE FOR CHANGE IN A GLOBAL MARKET ECONOMY

It is important to recognize that an educational system or institution can be a place in which we begin to examine contradictions, engage in resistance, and move toward transformation. So, even though the picture appears bleak in that we are a part of the problem, the future is promising, because we are seeing more and more adult educators taking on the challenge of responding to economic internationalization and modernization. Many of these educators have, in fact, risked their lives as well as their families; they have not only issued the call and challenged others, they have begun to change the seemingly irreversible political and economic internationalism that has evolved in today's world (Duke 1994; Ilon 1994). This call has caused some to rethink the asymmetrical relationship that has developed between technology, society, and the economy of countries. While they recognize that economic modernization and globalization has produced important changes, they also recognize that these changes have produced further disparity, both socially and economically.

They recognize the effect globalization has had on their roles as educators and how they interpret and interpolate knowledge and its purpose in society. Global information and its images are therefore viewed critically, and issues such as training and improvements are placed in their true cultural space (McGinn 1996). Thus, the role of education, and adult education in particular, is viewed as being extremely important in helping others to recognize what the issues are and provide avenues for change.

Thus, while regionalization has been a topic of many recent debates, education should, by no means, be exempt from this discourse, because we are, in fact, a part of how the concepts of globalization, regionalization, and internationalization are transmitted and understood. In other words, as transmitters of knowledge, if we do not engage in critically reflective practice aimed at challenging these concepts, then when will equity and equality be achieved? As some researchers have noted, regionalization may further social inequality and, in fact, is a large part of a "global system of economic exchanges, albeit advantaging groups differentially." As Ilon (1994) suggests, given this, "the education response must be systemic" (p. 68). Gelpi argues further that the internationalization of the economy may be responsible for provoking selections, discriminations, or educational categorization, which will exclude some people and advantage others (Gelpi 1987).

Considering this economic realignment, the effect on adult education is an important one. Therefore, our response to globalization must move beyond making high-level policy decisions based solely on human capital theory, to decisions that are grounded in the local responses of a civil society.

Unmeasurable versus Measurable Impacts

From this point of view, then, societal modernization and globalization have direct links to those measurable attributes that we in society have come to use as a way to determine success or failure of individuals as well as society. In general, most societies, as well as individuals, tend to measure themselves by their achievements in education/literacy, occupation, and income/wealth. Rarely do we see culture, democracy, and other similar attributes being used to measure success/failure, except in those instances in which those in power have determined that it is their culture and their definition of democracy that we must all live by.

As a result of the former view, emphasis on economic development and modernization, and the rational allocation of resources (human capital theory) along with work, competition, and technology, are used to determine or validate the individual (Ilon 1994; U.S. Department of Education 1994; Ministry of Employment and Immigration 1984). The assumption is that education is a competitive sport and production is one way to measure one's success or failure within it. Therefore, a more educated population will, conceivably, lead to either a more literate workforce or an even better worker (Pines and Carnevale 1991).

This perspective also asserts that in order for any country to achieve its goals and rightful place in the global market economy, it is necessary to change and reform schools. They must be changed in order to keep them in line with the changing nature of the marketplace, establishing national education standards, raising educational attainment, and reducing drop-out rates. National policies of education that emanate from centralized ministries of education must transform local policies and schools in order to provide the necessary flexibility to supply the global market.

An example of policies that radically changed schooling from national policies to local-level policies and school decentralization and privatization is the case of Chile (Carnoy 1995) and, lately, Mexico (Calvo Ponton 1996). Although the results are not yet in, we are finding international agencies like UNESCO and UNICEF issuing calls for equity and equality, or "education for all." So even though we know the results are not complete, we can surmise that education has been provided unequally, and without economic resources its transformational intent continues to be unable to compete with those who support the system of human capital formation. As N. Telhaug (quoted in Korsgaard 1997) has so aptly stated in reference to school planning, "ideals about social justice and personal development are exchanged for concepts from management discourse such as competition, quality and productivity" (p. 18).

One of the unintended results of these policies for governments is that when they adjust their structures and their economies to a larger, global scale, their national boundaries become less demarcated. In the past, government-supported education systems were the main promoters of national identity. Now, however, education is no longer viewed as being the vehicle of an individual country; it is now viewed as a means to transmit knowledge within a global market, so that members within the society can compete to advance the needs of their country within the marketplace. If one is unable to compete in this global marketplace, he/she will have to remain in or return to his/her local community to use whatever available resources are there. However, for those who are globally employable, almost any country will open its doors in order for them to gain full access to all resources within it.

Another idea which has resulted from the globalization process is that education and learning are continuous and do not end with formal education. Therefore, adults will need to be engaged in this continuous learning process as long as they are employed or unemployed, in order to be effective members of the global marketplace. Organizations like the Organization for Economic Co-operation and Development have therefore argued that education has placed too much emphasis on young people or children. They have in turn called for life-long learning and the regeneration of human capital.

Lifelong Learning: A Vehicle for Equality

Lifelong education is seen as a prerequisite for the emerging knowledge-intensive economy in which initial education has been rendered obsolete as preparation for a lifetime career. Rather than constantly extending front-end education, proponents of this position argue that nations should focus more on adult learners and enterprise-based training. All these initiatives are being justified in the name of globalization. This perspective suggests that people will have to spread out their educational experiences according to the emerging needs in their working lives (Carnoy and Levin 1985) in order to make themselves useful to the market. Translated in economic terms, this means then that the individual must be flexible.

Thus, participation in formal education and training throughout life in order to maintain a job requires that the individual, as well as the company, be flexible. This position supports the notion that a more educated workforce will in turn result in higher productivity.

While this appears on the surface to support the ideals of equity and equality, upon closer inspection we find that it tends often to support the maintenance of the status quo. Studies that have been conducted on adult participation in recurrent, continuing education programs indicate that those taking advantage of these programs tend to be those who are highly educated and tend often to occupy higher occupational positions (Carnoy and Levin 1985; Cross 1981; Quigley 1990). Of course, this group is small, but in terms of influence over policy direction their actions are large.

As a result, a potentially ever-widening gap is created in terms of education and income, because those with more formal education tend to seek more, while those left behind continue to have a difficult time finding employment, thus creating further marginalization and in other cases, discrimination (Carnoy, Daley, and Hinojosa 1994; Rubenson 1987).

This neo-classical assumption is that adult continuing education and training is an essential ingredient in any country's attempt to maintain what is "considered a quality workforce" (Hornbeck 1991)—a workforce that will be able to compete for business and participate in international labor markets. However, while labor markets become competitive, flexible, and decentralized in an era of the new post-Fordism, the requirement of a continuous process of education and training builds social inequality.

CONCLUSION

In general, state government policies do not promote adult education and political participation of its clientele, since the citizenry may then become difficult to co-opt. Hence the role of non-governmental organizations is to channel legitimate people's participation through political bargaining, which in turn will create new forms of participative education. Anticipated results are stated in political mobilization and consciousness-raising, two characteristics of many nonformal adult education programs.

From the perspective of human capital formation, today's competitive advantages make access to raw materials and industrial production possible worldwide, while making economic gains minimal as competition globalizes. Highly skilled and channeled human resources, however, take long-term investment. The process requires careful planning and it needs to be of quality, as its function is to decrease the inequity that has existed between those in power and those that have been marginalized.

Perhaps the most daunting issue is, given that even though we, as educators, begin to challenge these inequities more in our classes, the fact is that we live in a society in which human capital prevails. So, we must recognize that even though we are engaged in critically reflective thought, the fruits of this labor may only benefit a few in the beginning. In fact, the globalization of the economy means that many people become even more marginal. Thus, this "education for all" may lead to the marginalization of many. This then is the real challenge, for in challenging the center and its notions, we, in fact, are shifting the margins and the center. This, as bell hooks suggests, requires the development of an "oppositional world view." It requires what Hill-Collins and Anderson refer to as a shifting of margins and centers. It requires an understanding that to be marginal means there is a change in the way those in the margins and center operate with one another.

The task for adult educators is of extreme importance. Critical analysis of current trends, on local and global scales, should provide us with a better understanding of how current trends will affect how we relate to one another in the future. Unmeasurable attributes like democratization, culture, and human rights must become an essential element in every educational context.

In summary, by addressing the political economy of adult education we are provided with a much larger view of education—one in which class, gender, and race intersect with the market and the State. Furthermore, when we incorporate an analysis of the political economy of education into analyses of our practice, we are able to more fully understand the rationalities and practices of adult education.

REFERENCES

Becker, G. (1975). *Human Captial: A Theoretical and Empirical Analysis, with Special Reference to Education*. New York: National Bureau of Economic Research.

Calvo Ponton, B. (1996). "Education Policy and the Mexican Project for Modernizing Basic Education." Paper presented at the Meeting of the Society for Comparative and International Education, Boston.

Carnoy, M. (1995). "Is School Privatization the Answer?" *Education Week* 14(40), 52–60.

Carnoy, M., Daley, H., and Hinojosa, O. R. (1994). "The Changing Economic Position of Latinos in the U.S. Labor Market since 1939." In R. Morales and F. Bonilla (eds.), *Latinos in a Changing U.S. Economy*. Newbury Park, CA: Sage Publications.

Carnoy, M., and Levin, H. M. (1985). *Schooling and Work in the Democratic State*. Stanford, CA: Stanford University Press.

Carnoy, M., and Samoff, S. (1990). *Education and Social Transitions in the Third World*. Princeton, NJ: Princeton University Press.

Collins, M. (1991). *Adult Education as a Vocation: A Critical Role for the Adult Educator*. London and New York: Routledge.

Cross, K. P. (1981). *Adults as Learners: Increasing Participation and Facilitating Learning*. San Francisco: Jossey-Bass.

Cunningham, P. (1996). "Race, Gender Class and the Practices of Adult Education in the United States." In P. Wangoola and F. Youngman (eds.), *Towards a Transformative Political Economy of Adult Education*. De Kalb, IL: LEPS Press.

Davies, S., and Guppy, N. (1997). "Globalization and Educational Reforms in Anglo-American Democracies." *Comparative and Educational Review* 14(4), 435–459.

Drucker, P. (1993). *Post-Capital Society*. New York: HarperBusiness.

Duke, C. (1994). "Trends in the Development of Adult Education as a Profession." *Adult Education and Development* (Institute for International Cooperation of the German Adult Education Association), no. 43, 305–337.

ECLAC-UNESCO. (1992). *Education and Knowledge: Basic Pillars of Changing Production Patterns with Social Equity*. Santiago, Chile: UNESCO.

Frank, A. G. (1969). *Capitalism and Underdevelopment in Latin America*. New York: Monthly Review Press.

Gelpi, E. (1987). "Education, Production, Development and Technological Innovation." In W. Leirman and J. Kulich (eds.), *Adult Education and the Challenges of the 1990s*. New York: Croom Helm.

Gibbs, R. (1994). "Regionalism in the World Economy." In R. Gibbs and W. Michalak (eds.), *Continental Trading Blocs: The Growth of Regionalism in the World Economy*. New York: John Wiley and Sons.

Gibbs, R., and Michalak, W. (eds.). (1994). *Continental Trading Blocs: The Growth of Regionalism in the World Economy*. New York: John Wiley and Sons.

Grinspun, R., and Cameron, M. (1993). "The Political Economy of North American Integration: Diverse Perspectives, Converging Criticism." In R. Grinspun and M. Cameron (eds.), *The Political Economy of North American Free Trade*. New York: St. Martin's Press.

Hart, M. (1992). *Working and Educating for Life*. New York: Routledge.

Hornbeck, D. (1991). "New Paradigms for Action." In D. Hornbeck and L. Salamon (eds.), *Human Capital and America's Future*. Baltimore and London: Johns Hopkins University Press.

Ilon, L. (1994). "Structural Adjustment and Education: Adapting to a Growing Global Market." *International Journal of Educational Development* 14(2), 95–107.

Korsgaard, O. (1997). "The Impact of Globalization on Adult Education." In S. Walters (ed.), *Globalization, Adult Education and Training*. London: Zed Books.

Lim, Y.C.L. (1983). "Capitalism, Imperialism, and Patriarchy: The Dilemma of Third-World Women Workers in Multinational Factories." In J. Nash and P. Fernandez-Kelly (eds.), *Women, Men, and the International Division of Labor*. Albany: State University of New York Press.

McGinn, N. F. (1996). "Education, Democratization, and Globalization: A Challenge for Comparative Education." *Comparative Educational Review* 40, 341–357.

McNabb, R. (1987). "Labour Market Theories and Education." In G. Pscharopoulos (ed.), *Economics of Education*. Oxford: Pergamon.

Michalak, W. (1994). "The Political Economy of Trading Blocks." In R. Gibbs and W. Michalak (eds.), *Continental Trading Blocs: The Growth of Regionalism in the World Economy*. New York: John Wiley and Sons.

Ministry of Employment and Immigration. (1984). *Consultation Paper: Training*. Ottawa: Department of Supply and Services.

O'Hara-Devereaux, M., and Johansen, R. (1994). *Globalwork*. San Francisco: Jossey-Bass.

Pines, M., and Carnevale, A. (1991). "Employment and Training." In D. Hornbeck and L. Salamon (eds.), *Human Capital and America's Future*. Baltimore and London: Johns Hopkins University Press.

Prebish, R. (1985). "The Latin American Periphery in the Global Crisis of Capitalism." *CEPAL Review* 26, 63–68.

Quigley, A. B. (1990). "Hidden Logic: Reproduction and Resistance in Adult Literacy and Adult Basic Education." *Adult Education Quarterly* 40(2), 103–115.

Reimers, F. (1991). "The Impact of Economic Stabilization and Adjustment on Education in Latin America." *Comparative Education Review* 35(2), 319–354.

Robertson, R. (1992). *Globalization, Social Theory and Global Culture*. London: Sage Publications.

Rubenson, K. (1987). "Adult Education: The Economic Context." In F. Cassidy and R. Faris (eds.), *Choosing Our Future*. Toronto: Ontario Institute for Studies in Education.

Schultz, T. W. (1971). *Investment in Human Capital*. New York: Free Press.

Stromquist, N. (1996). "Gender Delusions and Exclusions in the Democratization of Schooling in Latin America." *Comparative Educational Review* 40, 404–425.

Torres, C. (1990). *The Politics of Nonformal Education in Latin America*. New York: Praeger.

U.S. Department of Education. National Educational Goals Panel. (1994). *Building a Nation of Leaders*. Washington DC: National Educational Goals Department.

Walters, S. (ed.). (1997). *Globalization, Adult Education and Training*. London and New York: Zed Books.

Wangoola, P., and Youngman, F. (eds.). (1996). *Towards a Transformative Political Economy of Adult Education*. De Kalb, IL: LEPS Press.

Wilson, P. (1992). *Exports and Local Development: Mexico's New Maquiladoras*. Austin: University of Texas Press.

Woodhall, M. (1987). "Financing Vocational and Industrial Education." In G. Pscharopoulos (ed.), *Economics of Education*. Oxford: Pergamon.

Chapter 23

What Does Research, Resistance, and Inclusion Mean for Adult Education Practice? A Reflective Response

Vanessa Sheared and Peggy A. Sissel

Throughout this book the authors have told stories about our collective pasts and our present realities, as well as shared with us the implications of those realities for the future. More importantly, they have examined the ways in which our racial, sexual, and cultural identities, and the realities of economic conditions both locally and globally, have influenced and affected how our histories have either been unified or dichotomized in response to these factors. Thus, in this concluding chapter we'd like to summarize the key points offered by the contributors regarding these issues, and offer our reflections on the ways in which one's race, gender, class; one's sexual orientation, language, or experience have been negated or promoted within the field of adult education. In so doing, we will also address the following questions, which we hope will help the reader understand why we believe that these factors, as the authors have so ardently articulated throughout this book, are important to any discourse dealing with change. Given that we live in a racist, sexist, ageist, classist, and homophobic society, what significance will these issues have in adult education as we move into the twenty-first century? What should research and practice look like if one acts upon these understandings in a way that is emancipatory and authentic? How can we engage others as well as our colleagues in dialogues that revolve around these issues, such that change will occur in our lifetime? Where should this dialogue occur?

Clearly, an ongoing reflective response is not and should not be limited to our voices alone; nor do we pretend that we have all the answers to all the questions that have been raised by others in this text, or those that we pursue below. Due to the complexity of these issues, we believe that the only way that we can begin to make space for "others" as well as those of us in the academy, is to engage in critical, reflective dialogue. Some might argue that if you don't have the answers, then why raise the issues? We do so because we believe that the framing of the question is just as important as the answer we give.

We believe that the phenomenological act of questioning is elemental to understanding the individual self and the collective self. It is in the questioning and answering, or as Hill-Collins suggests, the call and response, that both the individual and the collective self begin to interact and participate fully in the determination of "our" shared and collective histories, and our social, economic, and political realities. It is through the active engagement of dialogue that we take responsibility, for not only what has happened in the past, but for what ultimately must occur if we are to begin to change and create a future in which all are recognized.

REFLECTIONS AND CONSIDERATIONS

As has been explicated in many different ways throughout the descriptions and analyses in this book, the ways in which race, class, gender, sexual orientation, age, geography, history, politics, and economics intersect with each other shape who we are and how we respond to each other. The evolution of the relationships that have emerged to form our present collective and individual realities has been influenced by unequal distributions of power and control, and the intersecting factors of racism, sexism, classism, and homophobia (just to name a few), which have served to negate our realities. Such factors have created caste-like situations whereby entire collective bodies become marginalized and isolated from those who maintain power and control. So ultimately, rather than celebrating diversity and difference, humankind has participated in a zero-sum game of winners and losers which is premised by racist, sexist, classist, and otherwise prejudicial rationales.

While we believe that changes need to be made in how we currently respond to each other, we believe that if we do not, as de Toqueville suggested, revisit our past, we will only repeat our mistakes as we move into the future. So, in our remaining pages we'd like to explore ways that marginalization and hegemony have and will continue to affect our individual and collective realities. We will also offer ways in which adult education can effect change, as well as be affected by change.

Adult Education: What's in a Name?

Shakespeare's words seem so appropriate here, for as we move into the twenty-first century, we in adult education must ask ourselves, what *indeed* is in a name? To be called by any other name would mean what to whom? Briefly, we'd like to say that much has been written about the importance of naming one's self and determining for one's self what it means to be called that name. We do not wish to engage in an elaborate discussion about what we call ourselves, or what we call others; we only wish to offer some things for us to consider as a field.

We believe that what we call ourselves is related to what Childs (Chapter 20 in this volume) addresses in her discussion about our changing roles, identities, and relationships with institutions, and is salient because it challenges us to rethink what it means for how we "live out" theory and practice. Therefore, we need to begin to engage in critically reflective dialogue about issues like race, class, gender, sexual orientation, age, and what it means to call ourselves adult educators. This should include discussions about what our relationships should look like in institutions of higher learning, K–12 systems, or community organizations. For example, adult basic education, which operates within a K–12 school-based system, needs to be examined in relationship to the policy-based rigidity it evolves from, which tends to negate the lived experiences of both teachers and learners, as well as determines and shapes hierarchical relationships that perpetuate hegemonic structures (see Chapters 9, 11, 12, 18, 19 in this volume).

Beyond this, however, as it now stands, the phrase "adult education" depicts a hybrid that has not yet borne the fruits of its promise. There have been many debates about why this might be so, including self-directed indictments in the journals of the field which accuse adult education of being about everything and nothing, and make inferences that adult education as a subject of study and a knowledge-base lacks depth. We would argue, however, that, rather than spending time debating whether adult education is a legitimate discipline, we perhaps ought to revel in the fact that it is marginal; and, more importantly, an alternative explanation for its marginalization in relation to the merging of these two words ought to be explored. Most people would say they know what an adult is or at what age one becomes an adult, and most could define what education is, but when you combine the terms, people tend to have difficulty discerning not only what adult education is but, who does it. Those of us in the "discipline" could probably agree that our work centers around helping adults understand who they are and where they have come from; how they learn; which practices and models work best for them; and that they can successfully participate in learning activities from the cradle to the grave. Despite how clear the scope of this activity is about what we do, it is not well understood by others, including our colleagues in colleges of education and other divisions within our universities, and those who live in our communities and represent us in government. Even our own families don't understand what it is we spend our lives doing! This lack of understanding contributes to our marginalization, and perpetuates the marginalization of many of the learners we serve.

Ironically, it is possible that we have contributed to the marginalization of not only our voices, but of those whom we hope to serve and liberate, as a result of the way we sought to become separate and legitimate within the academy. While we honor and understand the struggles that we went through as a discipline to be heard by others in the academy during the 1960s, 1970s, and

1980s, we believe that it led to the reliance on discourses of psychology, sociology, and political science. Although we recognize that it was necessary, on the one hand, as it helped academic adult educators isolate and distinguish themselves, we also understand how it has served to marginalize others. Sheared (1999) concludes that "The field of adult education is built on a foundation of theoretical paradigms that encompass psychology, sociology, philosophy, anthropology, history and education" (p. 35). While some would argue that the ability of adult educators to make these linkages served to legitimate the discipline of adult education, others might argue that it served to obfuscate or diffuse adult education as a whole.

The result of this borrowing process was the marginalization of our identities as adult educators with the broader academy. This dualistic way of being has also led to the perpetuation of the very hegemonic structures that, in fact, are fundamentally being challenged by many of us now entering the discipline. Thus, now is the time to ask ourselves: What role have we in the field of adult education played in the perpetuation of the marginalization of others? Hemphill, Shore, Amstutz, Smith and Colin III, Garrick and Solomon, as well as others in this book have offered some reasons as to how this marginalization of others has occurred at the hands of adult educators. They have suggested that our language, our policies, our views of ourselves, as well as the "other," have contributed to the serious omission of *others'* voices. Many believe that in spite of many of us in the field being conscientiously aware of our role in the perpetuation of these hegemonic practices, we continue to write for the *knowledge mill*—the academy, and persist in using language that marginalizes the *other*.

Ironically, it is a mill that we use to move ahead and ultimately achieve that which we believe and purport to be against—the creation of hegemonic relationships between those of us in the academy and those in the trenches. As Jeria (Chapter 22 in this volume) suggests, "Whether we know it or not, those of us who have acceded to education—have contributed to the direct reproduction of the capitalist system. We have done this through our writing and reform policies . . . and through our participation in the production of 'knowledge.' " So, we suggest that if things are going to change we must accept our role in the maintenance of hegemony, as well as challenge ourselves to shift our thinking and our actions in order to make space for others to join us (Cervero and Wilson 1994).

In our work as educators we can choose to accommodate and reproduce the structural and ideological frameworks of the institutions in which we work or we can engage in action that resists the institution or seeks to transform it (Aronowitz and Giroux 1985). Making choices about the stances and actions we take is often problematic, for as Michael Apple (1982) has observed, our:

ideologies [are] filled with contradictions. . . . Lived meanings, practices and social relations are often internally inconsistent. They have elements within themselves that see through to the heart of the unequal benefits of a society and at one and the same time tend to reproduce the ideological relations and meanings that maintain the hegemony of the dominant classes. (p. 15)

Kreisberg (1992) also observed that "while the mechanisms of hegemony are powerful, they are not all-encompassing, and they are always characterized by contradictions and conflict" (p. 16). Furthermore, even our acts of resistance may not be complete, or may be contradictory. Ball (1987) and Giroux (1983) have both noted that oppositional behaviors have differing levels of effectiveness for creating liberatory spaces. In fact, some forms of resistance are actually contradictory and lead to accommodation of oppressive structures and social relations (McRobbie, 1978; Willis 1981; Giroux 1983; Apple 1995; Sissel 2000), thereby perpetuating conditions of exploitation. This contradiction in terms is important because of the implications for our lack of recognition of the way we may be reproducing unequal and disempowering social relations situated in raced, classed, and gendered positions of power and privilege, powerlessness, or oppression.

As you may have observed throughout, the authors herein, as well as those they have represented, have been marginalized or felt isolated because of how those in the academy viewed their work, and deliberately or otherwise discounted their voices. Yet, we must ask ourselves: if the voices of those in the margins haven't been included, why is this? We contend that it isn't their responsibility, but ours as members of society, to seek their inclusion. This then means that we must go beyond the "academy walls" in order to hear the voices of the *other* and make space for those in the margins, as well as those in the center. It is this shifting of margins and centers that will allow for and create a new reality built on a foundation of inclusion of the multiple and varied realities of us all. While clearly, we believe that we as educators have played a role in the perpetuation of many being marginalized, we must not forget that many of us *have* struggled to make space for others. As Bounous articulates in Chapter 14:

Teachers are one of the primary actors in this political arena. Even though teachers may see themselves primarily as dispensers of knowledge, in fact they are more than dispensers. As primary actors in this political arena, teachers are in fact cultural agents who accommodate or resist racism, sexism, or classism in the classroom. I believe that teachers who commit to understanding these social inequities and work to develop a critically-reflective practice have the potential to engage in counter-hegemonic practice through the development of collaborative relationships with students.

She concludes by saying that teachers "must begin to change the way in which they and their students perceive of their relationship, and how they operate with one another in the learning environment. In so doing, they—and the students—become empowered."

We therefore would argue that reframing and renaming our histories, ourselves, and what we do, is just one step in what we believe can help us merge our margins and pivot our centers, so that the power and control can be shared by all in the process. This will require that we not only leave the comfort of our academies and go into communities of learners that we believe have been left out, but, as Hemphill suggests in Chapter 2, "as adult educators we must build theories and practices for our field that take us away from perpetuating universal myths."

In order to do this, we must review, rethink, and reframe the myths and historical inaccuracies that have undergirded our practice. Or, as Barbara Bush's popularization of the phrase "Each one teach one" suggests, and so many others have articulated, if we each "go back and reach one" we might see change occurring that not only promotes equity and equality, but assures it. This, however, will require, as Hemphill suggests, that we "devise approaches that help us to better understand and act in concert with the particular realities of diverse adult learners and complex adult learning contexts."

SEARCH FOR IDENTITY: THEORY AND PRACTICE

All too often the ways in which a discipline has been viewed and accepted or not is in direct correlation to the type of research and theory production that is conducted by those in it. Correspondingly, the research and theories developed from it are supposed to come through or form what is being practiced. Given this interconnection, one would think that there would be a natural symbiosis occurring among researchers/theoreticians and practitioners. However, more often than not these seemingly symbiotic entities have often engaged in concentric and hegemonic discursive dialogues. Generally, this has meant that those in the academy have gone out and gathered data from those engaged in practice, often interpreting the "practice" in ways that are divorced from the meanings attributed by those who created it. Conversely, those engaged in "practice" have often looked askance at those who engage in gathering data about their practices, resulting in their either not being willing or being sought out as active authors of official knowledge producers. So, even though the search for meanings and understandings that could lead to new and creative fertile educational opportunities is the aim, hegemonic relationships have become the reality.

The field of adult education is but one example of how hegemonic relationships have been forged and perpetuated, often leading to the marginalization, rather than the equalization, of those engaged in practice and those engaged in research. In an attempt to gain status or to change the ways in which adult education as a discipline is viewed in the academy, many have chosen to engage in research studies aimed at helping people. The content of this book and the chapters that emerged, we hope, have given us some examples of how attempts at legitimization by a discipline can often lead to the marginalization of some, even though the aim has been to equalize the playing field for all.

The Abstraction: The Perpetuation of Hegemony and Marginalization

Let's take a look, for example, at how we have abstracted the knowledge produced in the field of adult education through our research endeavors in the area of "who participates in adult education activities and why." A significant amount of research has been conducted on the participation rates of White, middle-class individuals pursuing education either at the community college level or beyond. However, more recently, studies have been conducted on those individuals attending adult literacy or English-as-a-Second-Language (ESL) programs. Much has been made of the barriers that have caused these individuals to not participate, while little attention has been given to why those who do participate do so (Sheared 1999).

Interestingly, the ways in which factors and conclusions are presented about the participation rates of adult students is indicative of how the marginalization of a group is perpetuated and hegemony of the other is maintained. In brief, if you are White middle-class or above, you participate because you want to continue or change your economic standing, whereas, if you are in a literacy or ESL program, you want to acquire basic skills in order to enter the workforce. However, more often than not, if you are in the latter group, you fail to participate because of the multiple barriers you have in your life that prevent you from "acquiring work." If you are in the former group, the discourse centers around ways to achieve your "career goals." In other words, one has goals and the other seeks a job.

Given this scenario, one could argue that the presentation of the data and findings in and of themselves is not the cause of either marginalization or hegemony, and that would be true. However, if one were to only look at what is, rather than looking at the more systemic and structural forces that led to why one group is entering whereas the other is moving on, or the reasons for participation or not, then one might ask another or different question(s). In so doing, we might begin to unfold that people are entering or moving on as a result of the power and control one group has over the other. In other words, we are not arguing that the questions and answers about who participates are the problem. We, are arguing, however, that unless we go beyond the simple explanation to the more systemic and structural factors (e.g., racism, sexism, classism, etc.) that contribute to this variance, we continue to perpetuate hegemony and marginalization of others.

To be sure, resisting the forces that have helped us achieve some level of status as a discipline in the academy is not easy. Moreover, we must remember that to resist does not mean that we throw out all that we have learned. However, unless we examine these forces in terms of how we have benefited and others have not, we will not only perpetuate their marginalization, but we will ultimately create a greater distance between those whom we serve and ourselves.

COUNTERHEGEMONY AND CHANGE

Sharing power and control over the resources, knowledge creation and production, and language will not occur unless we learn to dialogue with each other around issues of marginalization and hegemony. Those in the center must begin to grapple with understanding how they have benefited and been privileged as a result of being in the center as knowledge producers, researchers, and disseminators/dispensers, and determine what it means to them if they continue in their positions of power. Conversely, those in the margins must grapple with similar issues. The latter is in no way meant to suggest that those in the margins enjoy being there; for they may or may not even know they are in the so-called "margins" or that "hegemony" even exists. As Sheared (1994) contends, if one has been told that one belongs in the margins and is undeserving of power and privileges resultant from being in the center, then, one will eventually begin to believe it and act out on it. If one acts on this belief long enough, one develops an ontological view of one's self that is reflective of that belief. While those individuals/groups in the margins do not necessarily find enjoyment in being in the margin, that is, if they have been forced there, those in the center do find that they enjoy the privileges and rewards gained from being in the center. So, then, how can we change this and create a shared space?

First of all, we must acknowledge that for some of us, we are both in the center and in the margins, while for others we are either in the margins or the center. Recognition of this rather complex and multiple existence can only occur when we willingly engage in dialogue about what it means to be there. We recognize that this in itself sounds rather abstract, but when we place ourselves squarely in the midst of the problem, as being an actor in it, we can begin to work together to change the way the story is told and thereby affect the outcome of the story.

Some adult educators (Sheared, Freire, hooks, Bounous) have suggested that one way to change the ways in which we begin to share power and control with others is through the use of dialogue. Dialoguing around issues of power and control and the intersections between them and race, class, and gender will enable us to begin to recognize our differences as well as uncover our commonalities (Sheared 1994, 1999; Sheared, McCabe, and Umeki 2000). Given that we are living in an age in which information is moving at the rate of 115,000 baud (bits per second),[1] via the computer and Internet services, the types, forms, and substances of the dialogues in which we engage begin to take on new meanings.

As Garrick and Solomon (Chapter 21) and Jeria (Chapter 22) allude to, the advancement in technology adds new meanings to dialogues that occur both locally and globally. For too long, we have engaged in dialogues that centered on what McCarthy (1998) refers to as an "alienated representation of the other, that is the practice of defining one's identity through the negation of the other" (p. xi). Perhaps in this new era of technology, we must learn to embrace our marginalization, while gaining space and voice among those who previously controlled our political, economic, social, and historical realities. So, we must have our feet in both worlds, but must also be cognizant of the political, economical, social, and historical realities that shape our worlds and our understandings of them.

CONCLUSION

We believe that settings wherein learning and teaching are taking place are but one site in which contestation of events can occur. Given that we in the field of adult education have captive audiences, be it in adult literacy programs or continuing professional development programs, what better place, on the one hand, to engage in dialogue. However, on the other hand, it may be the worst place for us to pursue this activity. As McCarthy (1998) so aptly states about educational sites and issues in terms of race and culture:

A keenly contested site has been enjoined in schooling as socially embattled majority and minority groups competed with each other in the public sphere and in the domain of culture—the domain of signs. The world, all of a sudden, has become a very crowded place, and communities of minorities and postcolonial immigrants now populate metropolitan schools and suburban towns to an extent and in a manner that deeply unsettles racially homogenous groups. (p. xi)

The intersection of race, class, gender, language, as well other issues addressed in this book are not new; however, they are often overlooked when we engage in dialogue about change and our futures. Given that we live in an ever-changing, demographically and linguistically diverse society, unless we begin to incorporate these factors into our discourses in the classrooms as well as outside of them, we will continuously perpetuate the marginalization of some and maintain hegemony over others. However, we must not be naïve enough to think that dialogue alone will resolve this problem. We only want to suggest that it is a major first step. Giving voice to the multiple and intersecting realities or polyrhythmic realities of others is just one way to do this. Sheared suggests that the uncovering of one's polyrhythmic realities will lead to a greater understanding between ethnically and linguistically diverse groups. However, we agree with McCarthy (1998) and offer this caveat:

We are living in a time in which racial hysteria and racial anxiety ride the undersides of the public discourse on schooling and society as rapid demographic changes alter the racial and ethnic landscape of America. These developments have spawned what I wish to call the new essentialisms and have infected educational discourses on knowledge and culture. An increasingly rigid and constricted language has overtaken the discussion of curriculum reform in the Age of Difference. . . .

In all these matters race is never an absolute structuring force, but is instead one variable in an immensely rich and complex human environment. The struggle is always to understand racial dynamics in the light of other dynamic variables such as class, gender, nations, and sexual orientation. (p. xii)

We therefore offer this book as a step in helping us as a field to engage in dialogue. We do not purport or wish to suggest that this is the definitive word on the subject, for quite the opposite is true. We believe that this book should be used to create reflection and dialogue around past practices as they relate to how different cultural and linguistic groups view adult education, and assist us in gaining a better understanding about how current practices can inform future practices, as well as research. This book should assist both practitioners and academicians to engage in a dialogue around how their actions and philosophies influence research and practice. Then, where we go from here is up to us.

NOTE

1. According to the Mad Scientist (http://www.madsci.org, January 2000), "Very fast serial data transfer tops out at around 115,000 baud (bits per second). A modem is usually connected to the computer via the serial interface, and modems are typically much slower than the maximum available speed of the serial interface. Standard dual-channel ISDN can achieve data rates at 128 Kbps, IEEE 802.3 Ethernet can do 10 Mbps (megabits— roughly a million bits—per second), DSL can do ~ 1.5 Mbps (1.54 Mbps is also referred to as T-1 speed), and Fast Ethernet can do 100 Mbps (T-3 speed is 45 Mb/s)."

REFERENCES

Apple, M. (1982). *Education and Power*. Boston: Routledge and Kegan Paul.

Apple, M. (1995). *Education and Power*, 2nd ed. New York: Routledge.

Aronowitz, S., and Giroux, H. (1985). *Education under Siege: The Conservative, Liberal, and Radical Debate over Schooling*. South Hadley, MA: Bergin & Garvey.

Ball, S. (1987). *The Micropolitics of the School: Towards a Theory of School Organization*. London: Methuen.

Cervero, R., and Wilson, A. L. (1994). *Planning Responsibly for Adult Education: A Guide to Negotiating Power and Interests*. San Francisco: Jossey-Bass.

Giroux, H. (1983). *Theory and Resistance in Education: A Pedagogy for the Opposition*. South Hadley, MA: Bergin & Garvey.

hooks, b. (1984). *Feminist Theory: From Margin to Center*. Boston: South End Press.

Kreisberg, S. (1992). *Transforming Power: Domination, Empowerment, and Education*. Albany: State University of New York Press.

The Mad Scientist. (2000). http://www.madsci.org/posts/archives/jan2000/947014265. cs.r.html.

McCarthy, C. (1998). *The Uses of Culture: Education and the Limits of Ethnic Affiliation*. New York: Routledge.

McRobbie, A. (1978). "Working Class Girls and the Culture of Femininity." In *Women Take Issue*, edited by the Centre for Contemporary Cultural Studies. Boston and London: Routledge and Kegan Paul.

Sheared, V. (1992). "From Workfare to Edfare, African American Women and the Elusive Quest for Self-Determination: A Critical Analysis of the JOBS Plan." Unpublished Dissertation, Northern Illinois University.

Sheared, V. (1994). "Giving Voice: A Womanist Construction." In E. Hayes and S.A.J. Colin III (eds.), *Confronting Racism and Sexism*. San Francisco: Jossey-Bass.

Sheared, V. (1998). *Race, Gender and Welfare Reform*. New York: Garland Publishers.

Sheared, V. (1999). "Giving Voice: Inclusion of African American Students' Polyrhythmic Realities in Adult Basic Education." In T. C. Guy (ed.), *Culturally Relevant Adult Education*. San Francisco: Jossey-Bass.

Sheared. V., McCabe, J., and Umeki, D. (2000). "Adult Literacy and Welfare Reform: Marginalization, Voice and Control." In V. Sheared and D. A. Amstutz (eds.), "The Crisis in Urban Adult Basic Education." *Education and Urban Society* 32(2) (February).

Sissel, P. A. (2000). *Staff, Parents, and Politics in Head Start: A Case Study in Unequal Power, Knowledge, and Material Resources*. New York: Falmer Press.

Willis, P. (1981). *Learning to Labor*. New York: Columbia University Press.

Index

About the Contributors

DONNA AMSTUTZ is Associate Professor at the University of Wyoming and Director of the Wyoming Adult Literacy Center. Her major areas of interest are adult basic education, community colleges, and issues of race, class, size, and gender.

IRENE C. BAIRD, Affiliate Assistant Professor of Education, is Director of Pennsylvania State Harrisburg's Center City Women's Enrichment Center. She is the author of *Unlocking the Cell*, and her research interests focus on social justice issues, especially of incarcerated women.

MARY BETH BINGMAN lives in western Virginia and is Associate Director of the Center for Literacy Studies at the University of Tennessee, Knoxville, where she coordinates research and development projects in partnership with the National Center for the Study of Adult Learning and Literacy.

RUTH BOUNOUS is Associate Professor and Director of Practicum at the Worden School of Social Service, Our Lady of the Lake University, San Antonio, Texas. While at Cornell University she created an adult learning program for kitchen workers and custodians. This, along with her teaching experiences, serve as the context for her views on teaching and the teacher–student relationship.

ANGELA HUMPHREY BROWN is Assistant Professor and Secondary Education Coordinator at Piedmont College in Athens, Georgia. Her research interests include teacher training and issues related to African-American women as students and as teachers.

BERNADINE S. CHAPMAN is Assistant Professor in the Department of Human Development and Services at North Carolina Agricultural and Technical State University. Her research interests include education of the African-American adult, adult literacy in the Black diaspora, and philanthropy.

MERILYN CHILDS is Lecturer in Adult Education at the University of Western Sydney Nepean and Joint Director of the National Centre for Critical Social Pedagogy (NCCrisP). Her research interests include the changing nature of adult education work in Australia and the implications it has for the pursuit of courageous educational practices.

SCIPIO A. J. COLIN III is Associate Professor and Chair of Adult and Continuing Education at National-Louis University. Her research interests are in the areas of African-Ameripean adult education history and philosophy, and the impact of racism on theory and practice.

DANIELE D. FLANNERY is Assistant Professor of Adult Education at The Pennsylvania State University–Harrisburg. Her interests are in cognitive learning, the social construction of learning, and women's learning. She is co-author, with Elisabeth Hayes, of the recently published book *Women as Learners*.

JOHN GARRICK is a senior researcher and policy analyst at the Research Centre for Vocational Education and Training at the University of Technology, Sydney. He is author and co-editor of several international books on learning in work contexts, including *Informal Learning in the Workplace: Unmasking Human Resource Development*.

ANDRÉ P. GRACE is Assistant Professor in the Department of Educational Policy Studies, University of Alberta, Edmonton. His research interests include cultural studies, inclusive education, and the historical foundations of educational practice.

LYNETTE HARPER is a community educator, program planner, and museologist. She has specialized in collaborative and participatory research, evaluation, education, and exhibit projects in Canadian museums and at Malaspina University-College, British Columbia. Her collaboration with "Mira," who wishes to remain anonymous, was undertaken during graduate study at the University of British Columbia.

ELISABETH HAYES is Professor of Curriculum and Instruction and a faculty member in the graduate program in Continuing and Vocational Education at the University of Wisconsin–Madison. She is co-author, with Daniele D. Flannery, of the recently published book *Women as Learners*.

DAVID F. HEMPHILL is Associate Dean for Graduate Studies, Research, and Development in the College of Education at San Francisco State University. His research and teaching interests include cultural studies, literacy, critical theory, and sociolinguistics as applied to K–adult education.

JANE M. HUGO is a member of the national field service staff at Laubach Literacy Action in Syracuse, New York, and an adjunct instructor in adult education at Elmira College. Her research interests focus on women's history, adult education history, and women's informal education. Her groundbreaking 1990 article on women in adult education history in *Adult Education Quarterly* is credited with unmasking the silence that has surrounded women's contributions to the field.

JORGE JERIA is Associate Professor of Adult Education at Northern Illinois University. A native of Chile, prior to the coup d'état there he was Assistant Professor of Education at the Catholic University and was active in agrarian reform and literacy efforts. His current interests include international community development and adult education, especially concerning the U.S. Latino population and Latin America.

AMELIA R. B. KIRBY is an educator and writer. She lives and works in Tennessee.

SU-FEN LIU recently received her Doctorate of Adult Education from the University of Georgia. Her research interests include adult education participation, human resource development, older worker issues, research methods, and statistical analyses.

ROSITA LOPEZ MARCANO is Professor and former faculty chair of the Department of Educational Administration and School Business Management, Department of Leadership and Educational Policy Studies, at Northern Illinois University in DeKalb, Illinois. She is an associate with the firm of Souder, Betances, and Associates in Chicago. She has been recognized with full honor and distinction in the *International Who's Who of Professionals*.

FRANCES REES directs the adult education program for the University of Georgia's Department of Housing. She also works with the Department of Corrections and the Board of Pardons and Paroles. She conducts research in the area of deliberative group interaction.

FRED M. SCHIED is Associate Professor of Education at The Pennsylvania State University. His research interests include work and learning, the legitimization and delegitimization of knowledge, knowledge production, work, and resistance. He is the recipient of the 1994 Cyril O. Houle Award for Outstanding

Literature for his book *Learning in Social Context: Workers and Adult Education in Nineteenth Century Chicago.*

VANESSA SHEARED is Associate Professor of Adult Education and Associate Dean of the College of Education at San Francisco State University. She has served on the Board of Directors of the American Association of Adult and Continuing Education and as a steering committee member for the Adult Education Research Conference. She has also served on the editorial board of *Adult Education Quarterly*, the major journal in the field of adult education. Dr. Sheared teaches and writes in the areas of counseling, diversity, and Africentric womanist perspectives. The use of an Africentric feminist perspective has allowed her to examine the relationship between learning, knowledge, and power, the social organization of the adult school, and the political and economic factors underlying educational policy. She is the author of *Race, Gender, and Welfare Reform: The Elusive Quest for Self-Determination*, and she co-edited *The Crisis in Urban Adult Basic Education* with Donna Amstutz. She has also authored several articles, chapters, and journals on giving voice and issues of race, gender, class, literacy, welfare reform, and marginalization. In 1998, she was a recipient of the W. K. Kellogg Foundation's Cyril O. Houle Scholars in Adult and Continuing Education fellowship.

SUE SHORE lives in Adelaide and teaches courses in adult education and adult literacy at the University of South Australia. Her research interests include the social and cultural politics of education, investigating the effects of Whiteness on theory building in adult education, and feminist practice in everyday life.

PEGGY A. SISSEL is the former Director of the Center for Applied Studies in Education at the University of Arkansas at Little Rock (UALR), where she held the rank of Associate Professor. At present she is a full-time student at UALR's Bowen School of Law. In addition to *Making Space*, Dr. Sissel is the author of *Staff, Parents, and Politics in Head Start: A Case Study in Unequal Power, Knowledge, and Material Resources* and the editor of *A Community-Based Approach to Literacy Programs: Listening to Learners' Lives*. A fourth book, co-edited with Catherine Hansman, *Understanding and Negotiating the Political Landscape of Adult Education*, is forthcoming. Dr. Sissel has served on the editorial board of *Adult Education Quarterly* and has been a reviewer for *HRD Quarterly, NHSA Dialog: A Research-to-Practice Journal for the Early Intervention Field*, and *ERIC Digests*. She was the 1994 recipient of the Adult Education Research Conference's Graduate Student Research Award, and in 1998 was selected as a fellow in the W. K. Kellogg Foundation's Cyril O. Houle Scholars in Adult and Continuing Education program.

CHERYL A. SMITH is Assistant Professor in the Adult Baccalaureate College of Lesley College in Cambridge, Massachusetts. She was the 1998–1999

AAUW's Education Foundation American Dissertation Fellow. Her research interests are in nontraditional models of adult education entrepreneurship education, and reclaiming history.

SHERWOOD E. SMITH is Assistant Research Professor in the Department of Education at the University of Vermont. He is Director of the Center for Cultural Pluralism, teaches graduate and undergraduate courses for the Department of Education, and provides faculty and staff training.

NICKY SOLOMON is a senior academic in the Faculty of Education at the University of Technology, Sydney and is currently working as Program Director for Work-Based Learning across the University. Her writing and research interests focus on the increasing relationship between workplaces and universities and on the pedagogical and epistemological challenges these present to the academy.

ELIZABETH J. TISDELL is Associate Professor in the Department of Adult and Continuing Education at National-Louis University in Chicago. She is the author of numerous book chapters and journal articles focusing on feminist pedagogy, multicultural adult education, and the role of spirituality in emancipatory education efforts.

CONNIE WHITE is Associate Director at the Center for Literacy Studies, University of Tennessee, where she coordinates professional development for Tennessee adult basic education practitioners. Her interests include participatory and community-based education.